QUALITATIVE
INQUIRY
AND
RESEARCH
DESIGN

QUALITATIVE INQUIRY
AND
RESEARCH DESIGN
Choosing
Among
Five
Traditions

▼
▼
▼
▼
▼

JOHN W. CRESWELL

SAGE Publications
International Educational and Professional Publisher
Thousand Oaks London New Delhi

For information:

SAGE Publications, Inc.
2455 Teller Road
Thousand Oaks, California 91320
E-mail: order@sagepub.com

SAGE Publications Ltd.
6 Bonhill Street
London EC2A 4PU
United Kingdom

SAGE Publications India Pvt. Ltd.
M-32 Market
Greater Kailash I
New Delhi 110 048 India

Printed in the United States of America

Library of Congress Cataloging-in-Publication Data

Creswell, John W.
    Qualitative inquiry and research design: Choosing among five traditions / by John W. Creswell.
        p. cm.
    Incluces bibliographical references and index.
    ISBN 0-7619-0143-4 (cloth: acid-free paper). —
    ISBN 0-7619-0144-2 (pbk.: acid-free paper)
    1. Social sciences—Methodology. I. Title.
    H61.C73 1997
    300′.72—dc21   97-4820

This book is printed on acid-free paper.

98 99 00 01 02 03 10 9 8 7 6 5 4 3 2 1

Acquiring Editor:	C. Deborah Laughton
Editorial Assistant:	Eileen Carr
Production Editor:	Diana E. Axelsen
Production Assistant:	Denise Santoyo
Typesetter/Designer:	Janelle LeMaster
Cover Designer:	Ravi Balasuriya
Print Buyer:	Anna Chin

Contents

Analytic Table of Contents
by Tradition

Phenomenology

Grounded Theory

Ethnography

Case Study

Preface

▼ This book evolved over a period of 3½ years during which I developed and tested the material with talented qualitative researchers. To the many students in my "Seminar in Qualitative Research" at the University of Nebraska–Lincoln, I owe a huge debt. They offered suggestions, provided examples, and discussed the material in this book. Also, I benefited from capable scholars who helped to shape and form this book. Paul Turner, Ken Robson, Dana Miller, Diane Gillespie, Gregory Schraw, Sharon Hudson, Karen Eifler, Neilida Aguilar, and Harry Wolcott all provided thoughtful and constructive feedback as the manuscript developed. Ben Crabtree and Rich Hofmann helped shape the final text significantly and encouraged me to proceed, and they diligently and timely responded to Sage's request to be external reviewers. In addition, Keith Pezzoli, Kathy O'Byrne, Joanne Cooper, and Phyllis Langton served as reviewers for Sage and added insight into content and structure that I could not see because of my closeness to the material. As always, I am indebted to C. Deborah Laughton, who selected outstanding reviewers, offered insights into layout and production, and has been my advocate and supporter at Sage. Finally, to members of my family, who provided time to escape and become buried in this book, I thank you.

I dedicate this book to *Uncle Jim*
(James W. Marshall, M.D., 1915-1997)
who provided love, support, and inspiration.

———————

1

▼

Introduction

▼ As closely as I can determine, the genesis for this book evolved
  from discussions at a 1994 summer qualitative seminar in Vail,
Colorado, sponsored by the University of Denver under the able
guidance of Edith King of the College of Education. One morning, I
facilitated the discussion about qualitative data analysis. I began on a
personal note, introducing one of my recent qualitative studies—a
qualitative case study of a campus response to a student gun incident
(Asmussen & Creswell, 1995). I knew this case might provoke some
discussion and present complex analysis issues. It involved a midwestern university's reaction to a gunman who attempted to fire on
students in his undergraduate class. Standing before the group, I
chronicled the events of the case, the themes, and the lessons we
learned about a university reaction to a near tragic event. Then,
unplanned, Harry Wolcott, another resource person for our seminar,
raised his hand and asked for the podium. He explained how *he* would
approach the study as a cultural anthropologist. Before everyone, he

"turned" our case study into an ethnography. Now we were off on a grand adventure.

With the possibilities opened for our case study, Les Goodchild of Denver University next turned the gunman case into an intellectual history. This unforeseen set of events kindled an idea I had long harbored—that one designed a study differently depending on the type of qualitative research. I began to write this book, guided by a single, compelling question: How does the type or tradition of qualitative inquiry shape the design of a study?

PURPOSE

This book is my attempt to answer this question. My primary intent is to examine five different traditions of qualitative inquiry—biography, phenomenology, grounded theory, ethnography, and case studies—and compare them in six phases of research design. These six phases are philosophical or theoretical perspectives; the introduction to a study, including the formation of the purpose and research questions; data collection; data analysis; report writing; and standards of quality and verification. Early in the book, I sharpen the distinctions between traditions and research through the presentation of five short qualitative studies, each representing one of the traditions. Also, I provide tables in the chapters that summarize major differences among the traditions in research design. I end by turning a case study into a biography, a phenomenology, a grounded theory study, and an ethnography. Throughout the book, I hope that the reader will gain a better understanding of each tradition of inquiry and explore with me features common to qualitative research regardless of tradition.

By **tradition of inquiry** (see the glossary in Appendix A for definitions of terms in bold oblique type), I mean an approach to qualitative research that has a distinguished history in one of the disciplines and that has spawned books, journals, and distinct methodologies that characterize its approach. These traditions are known in other books as "strategies of inquiry" (Denzin & Lincoln, 1994) or "varieties" (Tesch, 1990). By a discussion of each tradition, the reader is guided to central elements, useful readings, and examples of studies. By **research design**, I refer to the entire process of research from conceptualizing a problem to writing the narrative, not simply the methods, such as data collection, analysis, and report writing (Bogdan & Taylor, 1975). Yin (1989) commented, "The design is the logical sequence that connects the empirical data to a study's initial research questions and, ultimately, to its conclusions" (p. 28). Hence, I include specific design features from the broad philosophical and theoretical perspectives to assessing the quality and verifying a study.

RATIONALE FOR THIS BOOK

After the Vail seminar, I began asking individuals who approached me with their qualitative studies, "What type are you doing?" From many, I was met with blank stares. From others, I might have heard "hermeneutics" or "participant observation." These were not the traditions I knew. Only a few years ago, some called all qualitative research "ethnographic" (Goetz & LeCompte, 1984) and considered it "monolithic" (Fetterman, 1987). But we know that the types of qualitative research come from diverse disciplinary perspectives. For example, ethnography originated in anthropology, grounded theory in sociology, and biography in history and sociology. We have a proliferation of journals and books given to specific types (e.g., Hammersley & Atkinson, 1995, on ethnography; Moustakas, 1994, on phenomenology; Strauss & Corbin, 1990, on grounded theory). These varieties subdivide into specialties such as critical ethnographies and transcendental phenomenology.

This leads to several reasons for this book. First, those conducting qualitative studies do not always understand the tradition they are using and its chief elements. I believe that qualitative research has reached the same point in its development as *quantitative* research had reached in 1964. In that year, Kerlinger authored his famous classical treatise on research designs, *Foundations of Behavior Research*. Kerlinger's (1964) book, used today after many editions, carved out, clarified, and distinguished among ex post facto, experimental, and survey designs. Earlier in the century, others had distinguished among quantitative types, such as the three forms of fieldwork reported by Chapin (1920) and the methods reported by Young (1939), but Kerlinger's work left an enduring stamp on our thinking about the types of quantitative designs. Drawing a parallel to Kerlinger now, I immodestly suggest that clarification and comparison are needed in *qualitative* inquiry as well.

Second, those conducting qualitative studies need to consider the differences among approaches to qualitative research. When comparisons and distinctions among qualitative approaches are made clear, researchers can design more rigorous and sophisticated studies. Researchers also can make informed choices about what qualitative approaches to use in their studies and why they are using them.

Third, no book currently addresses the relationship of tradition and research design. Current books assess the design within a single tradition (e.g., Moustakas, 1994, on phenomenology; Strauss and Corbin, 1990, on grounded theory), and others compare traditions, primarily in terms of historical and philosophical differences (e.g., Lancy, 1993; Tesch, 1990). But no books examine different traditions, side by side, and the phases of design of a study. I am reminded of the delightful little book by Redfield (1963), who explored the different anthropological and social views of a "village" by devoting a chapter to each view.

Finally, for individuals trained or socialized in a specific tradition, this comparative analysis can enlarge their scope of inquiry methods and encourage them to seek out alternative procedures.

SELECTION OF THE FIVE TRADITIONS

Those undertaking qualitative studies have a baffling number of choices of traditions. One can gain a sense for this diversity by examining several classifications or typologies. One of the more popular classifications is provided by Tesch (1990), who organized 28 approaches into four branches of a flowchart, sorting out these approaches based on the central interest of the investigator. Wolcott (1992) classified approaches in a "tree" diagram with branches of the tree designating strategies for data collection. Miller and Crabtree (1992) organized 18 "types" according to the "domain" of human life of primary concern to the researcher, such as a focus on the individual, the social world, or the culture. In the field of education, Jacob (1987) categorized all qualitative research into "traditions" such as ecological psychology, symbolic interactionism, and holistic ethnography. Finally, Lancy (1993) organized qualitative inquiry into discipline perspectives such as anthropology, sociology, biology, cognitive psychology, and history. Lancy's approach and those of other writers from the social sciences are shown in Table 1.1.

With many possibilities, how did I decide on the five presented in this book? My choice of the five traditions in this book resulted from personal interests, selecting different foci, and electing to choose representative discipline orientations. First, I have experienced the five either as an adviser counseling students or in my own research (in which I admittedly am partial to grounded theory, case studies, and biography). Second, I examined the qualitative studies being reported in scholarly journals. When writers refer to traditions, I find the five reported here to be popular and frequently used. Third, I espouse a rigorous, systematic approach to qualitative research; I prefer traditions with systematic procedures for inquiry. Undoubtedly, biography, and especially "interpretive" biography that introduces the view of the writer, barely falls within this parameter, whereas grounded theory exceeds it. Fourth, I wanted to use traditions that illustrate a representative picture of approaches in the disciplines. This criterion is met well, with biography originating from the humanities and social sciences; phenomenology from psychology and philosophy; grounded theory from sociology; ethnography from anthropology and sociology; and case studies from the human and social sciences and applied areas such as evaluation research.

Fifth, I found recent books and short chapters that illustrate the procedures for conducting research within each of the five traditions. I am pleased to have found a healthy spate of recent books such as Denzin (1989a) on biography, Moustakas (1994) on phenomenology, Strauss and Corbin (1990) on grounded theory, Hammersley and Atkinson (1995) on ethnography, and Stake (1995) on case study research. Taken as a group, these are the central works I rely on heavily as I construct my portrait of the five traditions and their approaches to conducting scholarly qualitative research.

Finally, I delimited my discussion to specific variants within each tradition, recognizing that several of these traditions have branched into numerous subfields. Briefly, my biographical stance is the interpretive approach by Denzin (1989a), acknowledging the postmodern concern about the role of the researcher in interpreting a study, rather

TABLE 1.1   Qualitative Traditions Mentioned by Authors

Author	Qualitative Traditions	Discipline/Field
Jacob (1987)	Ecological Psychology Holistic Ethnography Cognitive Anthropology Ethnography of Communication Symbolic Interactionism	Education
Munhall & Oiler (1986)	Phenomenology Grounded Theory Ethnography Historical Research	Nursing
Lancy (1993)	Anthropological Perspectives Sociological Perspectives Biological Perspectives Case Studies Personal Accounts Cognitive Studies Historical Inquiries	Education
Strauss & Corbin (1990)	Grounded Theory Ethnography Phenomenology Life Histories Conversational Analysis	Sociology, Nursing
Morse (1994)	Phenomenology Ethnography Ethnoscience Grounded Theory	Nursing
Moustakas (1994)	Ethnography Grounded Theory Hermeneutics Empirical Phenomenological Research Heuristic Research Transcendental Phenomenology	Psychology
Denzin & Lincoln (1994)	Case Studies Ethnography Phenomenology, Ethnomethodology, and Interpretative Practices Grounded Theory Biographical Historical Clinical Research	Social Sciences

Miles & Huberman (1994)	Approaches to Qualitative Data Analysis:
	    Interpretivism
	    Social Anthropology
	    Collaborative Social Research
		Social Sciences

Slife & Williams (1995)	Categories of Qualitative Methods:
	    Ethnography
	    Phenomenology
	    Studies of Artifacts
		Psychology

than the traditional, theory-oriented classical approach. In phenomenology, I advance the psychological approach represented in the works of psychologists (e.g., Giorgi, 1994; Moustakas, 1994) rather than sociologists. In grounded theory, I side with the more structured approach of Strauss and Corbin (1990) rather than the less structured Glaser, who has become an outspoken critic of Strauss in recent years (see Glaser, 1992). In ethnography, I appreciate and endorse the works of Wolcott (1994b) and Fetterman (1989), cultural anthropologists, as well as that of Hammersley and Atkinson (1995), two sociologists. For case studies, I recognize the many authors who write on case study research, but I am partial to Stake (1995), who speaks from an evaluation perspective and provides numerous helpful tables.

To enumerate further, the reader may appreciate a listing of the core books I used in developing this discussion of traditions of inquiry and research design.

Biography:

▼ Denzin, N. K. (1989a). *Interpretive biography*. Newbury Park, CA: Sage.
▼ Lomask, M. (1986). *The biographer's craft*. New York: Harper & Row.
▼ Plummer, K. (1983). *Documents of life: An introduction to the problems and literature of a humanistic method*. London: George Allen and Unwin.

Phenomenology:

▼ Giorgi, A. (Ed.). (1985). *Phenomenology and psychological research*. Pittsburgh, PA: Duquesne University Press.
▼ Moustakas, C. (1994). *Phenomenological research methods*. Thousand Oaks, CA: Sage.
▼ Polkinghorne, D. E. (1989). Phenomenological research methods. In R. S. Valle & S. Halling (Eds.), *Existential-phenomenological perspectives in psychology* (pp. 41-60). New York: Plenum.

Grounded Theory:

▼ Chenitz, W. C., & Swanson, J. M. (1986). *From practice to grounded theory: Qualitative research in nursing*. Menlo Park, CA: Addison-Wesley.

▼   Strauss, A., & Corbin, J. (1990). *Basics of qualitative research: Grounded theory procedures and techniques*. Newbury Park, CA: Sage.

Ethnography:

▼   Fetterman, D. M. (1989). *Ethnography: Step by step*. Newbury Park, CA: Sage.
▼   Hammersley, M., & Atkinson, P. (1995). *Ethnography: Principles in practice* (2nd ed.). New York: Routledge.
▼   Wolcott, H. F. (1994b). *Transforming qualitative data: Description, analysis, and interpretation*. Thousand Oaks, CA: Sage.

Case Study:

▼   Merriam, S. (1988). *Case study research in education: A qualitative approach*. San Francisco: Jossey-Bass.
▼   Stake, R. (1995). *The art of case study research*. Thousand Oaks, CA: Sage.

LIMITS AND SITUATEDNESS

My approach is to present the five traditions as pure approaches to research design when, in fact, authors may integrate them within a single study. But before individuals blend them, I find it as a useful heuristic to separate them out, to see them as distinct approaches and visit each one, individually, as a procedural guide for research. For beginning researchers, this perspective helps them to get started better; for experienced researchers, they will be reminded of procedures articulated within a single tradition of inquiry.

I limit the design discussion to specific components of the research design process. I leave for others additional aspects of research design such as defining terms, addressing the significance of the study, posing limitations and delimitations, and advancing the role of the researcher (Marshall & Rossman, 1995).

In a book of this scope, I cannot undertake an examination and comparison of all forms of qualitative inquiry. My focus on the five traditions is not to minimize attention to other worthy approaches.

But I include the five here because they represent different discipline traditions, have detailed procedures, and have been discussed recently in qualitative books. I work with a reasonable number of approaches that are popular in the human and social sciences, and I invite others into the dialogue about research. No best approach is suggested. As borne out by my Vail experience, there are simply different traditions of inquiry.

I situate this book within my thinking about qualitative research, and I hope to model **reflexivity**, or self-awareness, in this book. I advocate a rigorous approach to qualitative research using systematic procedures, well grounded in current texts within each of the five traditions. This is not to suggest that I am advocating the acceptance of qualitative research in a "quantitative" world (Ely, Anzul, Friedman, Garner, & Steinmetz, 1991). Qualitative inquiry represents a legitimate mode of social and human science exploration without apology or comparisons to quantitative research. Good models of qualitative inquiry demonstrate the rigor, difficulty, and time-consuming nature of this approach.

Unquestionably, too, my focus is on research designs or procedures, not on philosophical issues—issues that admittedly are inextricably linked to procedures. However, in my discussion, I position these issues in the background rather than the foreground, admitting openly that I am not a philosopher of education but rather a research methodologist, and my orientation in this book reflects this orientation. I also highlight my fascination with the writing process and how authors design the "architecture" of studies through overall and embedded structures. I place emphasis on the terms used by authors in each of the traditions and on the way in which they use **encoding** of significant passages with these terms to make the text a distinct illustration of a tradition. I highlight **foreshadowing** information early in a study to hint at topics or ideas to come later. Along this line, I concur with Agger (1991), who says that methodology can be read rhetorically and written in less technical ways, affording greater access to scholars and democraticizing science. Finally, my approach presents not a "lock-step" procedural guide but rather a general direction, presenting alternatives for the researcher and advancing my preferred stance. In many ways, I see this book as a "quest" (Edel, 1984) for materials and ideas to best display and convey design within the five traditions.

AUDIENCE

Although multiple audiences exist for any text (Fetterman, 1989), I direct this book toward academics and scholars affiliated with the social and human sciences. Examples throughout the book illustrate the diversity of disciplines and fields of study including sociology, psychology, education, the health sciences, urban studies, marketing, communication and journalism, educational psychology, family science and therapy, and other social and human science areas.

My aim is to provide a useful text for those who produce scholarly qualitative research in the form of journal articles, theses, or possibly dissertations. The focus on a single tradition is ideal for shorter forms of scholarly communication; longer works, such as books or monographs, may employ multiple traditions. The level of discussion should be suitable for upper division students and graduate students. For graduate students writing master's theses or dissertations, I compare and contrast the five traditions in hopes that such analysis helps in establishing a rationale for the choice of a tradition to use. For beginning qualitative researchers, I provide Chapter 2, an overview of the qualitative research design process, and I highly recommend introductory qualitative texts as supplemental reading—texts such as Bogdan and Biklen (1992), Glesne and Peshkin (1992), Marshall and Rossman (1995), Maxwell (1996), or the interdisciplinary handbook by Denzin and Lincoln (1994)—before proceeding on to other chapters. For both novices and more experienced researchers, I supply recommendations for further reading and sharpen some distinctions that have possibly lurked in the background. At the end of the book, turning the story from one tradition to another can be a creative exercise for beginning and seasoned researchers who seek to explore traditions beyond their specialized training and experience.

ORGANIZATION

The basic premise of this book is that different forms of qualitative traditions exist and that the design of research within each has distinctive features. Following this chapter, I introduce the general process of qualitative research design in Chapter 2. I review commonly accepted ideas about qualitative research and the central set of guiding assumptions about the design of a study. With these research design phases in mind, I follow in Chapter 3 with an introduction to five approaches to qualitative inquiry: biographies, phenomenologies, grounded theory studies, ethnographies, and case studies. This introduction is in the form of five published studies, each one illustrating one of the five traditions. I invite the reader to examine each article, and I briefly summarize the article and focus attention on major dimensions of the tradition of inquiry. In Chapter 4, I build a deeper understanding of each tradition by examining each one and exploring its definition, its history, its key elements, and its specific procedures.

These four chapters form an introduction to the five traditions and an overview of the process of research design. They set the stage for the remaining chapters that relate research design to each of the traditions of inquiry: using philosophical and theoretical frameworks (Chapter 5), writing introductions to studies (Chapter 6), collecting data (Chapter 7), analyzing data (Chapter 8), writing narratives (Chapter 9), and employing standards of quality and verifying results (Chapter 10). In all of these design chapters, I continually compare the five traditions of inquiry.

As a final experience to sharpen distinctions among the five traditions, I present Chapter 11, in which I return to the gunman case study (Asmussen & Creswell, 1995), first introduced in Chapter 3, and turn the story from a case study into a biography, a phenomenology, a grounded theory study, and an ethnography. This culminating chapter brings the reader full circle to examining the gunman case in several ways, an extension of my earlier Vail seminar experience.

Throughout the book, I provide several aids to help the reader. At the beginning of each chapter, I offer several conceptual questions that are addressed in the chapter. At the end of each chapter, I provide further readings and sample exercises. I advance more than one exercise at the end of each chapter. At least one of the exercises encourages the reader to design and conduct an entire qualitative study, with phases in this study identified progressively throughout the book. Also, in most of the chapters, I present comparison tables that show the differences among the five traditions of inquiry as well as figures to visualize distinctions and major design processes. For those individuals interested in following the "strand" of a single tradition, I present an Analytical Table of Contents at the beginning of this book. Thus, one might read this book either by following a single tradition of interest or by comparing the different traditions. Finally, each tradition of inquiry comes with distinct terms that may be unfamiliar to the reader. I provide a glossary of terms in Appendix A to facilitate the reading and understanding of the material in this book. I further set these terms in bold oblique type in the text when they are needed to provide key definitions.

2
▼

Designing a
Qualitative Study

I think metaphorically of qualitative research as an intricate fabric composed of minute threads, many colors, different textures, and various blends of material. This fabric is not explained easily or simply. Like the loom on which fabric is woven, general frameworks hold qualitative research together. To describe these frameworks, we use terms—constructivists, interpretivists, feminists, methodologists, postmodern thinkers, positivists "with a heart," naturalistic researchers. Broader yet are the traditions of inquiry that overlay the frameworks and the studies. We conduct an ethnography, we engage in developing a grounded theory, or we explore an unusual case. With the complexity of qualitative research, its terms, and its traditions, what common ground exists for qualitative research?

In this chapter, I suggest that there are some common elements that characterize qualitative research. I first look across several definitions of this form of research and establish core characteristics. These multiple characteristics make this form of research difficult, rigorous, and time-consuming. Rigor is a virtue, but it is only one among several reasons for undertaking a qualitative study. I explore these reasons. Having selected qualitative research, then, the investigator designs a study. In this chapter, I present the general approaches used to design each major phase of a study, followed by a typical format for organizing a qualitative study. I do not introduce the varieties or traditions of inquiry yet; they will emerge in subsequent chapters. It is essential at this point to see only the common features, the basic fabric of the material.

Questions for Discussion

▼ How is qualitative research defined?

▼ Why do we choose to conduct a qualitative study?

▼ What preliminary decisions need to be made?

▼ What type of questions are asked? Information collected? Analysis undertaken?

▼ How are the data and analysis represented in the narrative?

▼ How do we assess the quality of a study and check for its accuracy?

▼ What overall format is used to design a study?

DEFINING QUALITATIVE RESEARCH

Because a comparative approach will occupy our attention later in this book, I begin by comparing different perspectives about what constitutes qualitative research. As suggested in Table 2.1, the contours of qualitative research might be seen by looking across several perspectives shared by leading authors. Writers agree that one undertakes qualitative research in a natural setting where the researcher is an instrument of data collection who gathers words or pictures, analyzes them inductively, focuses on the meaning of participants, and describes a process that is expressive and persuasive in language.

These characteristics also are advanced in several textbook definitions available in the literature, and I provide two. First, Denzin and Lincoln (1994) define qualitative research:

Qualitative research is multimethod in focus, involving an interpretive, naturalistic approach to its subject matter. This means that qualitative researchers study things in their natural settings, attempting to make sense of or interpret phenomena in terms of the meanings people bring to them. Qualitative research involves the studied use and collection of a variety of empirical materials—case study, personal experience, introspective, life story, interview, observational, historical, interactional, and visual texts—that describe routine and problematic moments and meaning in individuals' lives. (p. 2)

This definition adds several elements not presented in Table 2.1. It suggests an a priori approach grounded in philosophical assumptions—the "interpretive, naturalistic approach"—to qualitative research and the multiple sources of information and narrative approaches available to the researcher.

My own definition of **qualitative research** relies less on sources of information, but it conveys similar ideas:

Qualitative research is an inquiry process of understanding based on distinct methodological traditions of inquiry that explore a social or human problem. The researcher builds a complex, holistic picture, analyzes words, reports detailed views of informants, and conducts the study in a natural setting.

Whereas my definition reiterates the characteristics mentioned earlier and expands on my earlier definition (Creswell, 1994), I emphasize a "complex, holistic picture," a reference to a complex narrative that takes the reader into the multiple dimensions of a problem or issue and displays it in all of its complexity. Today, writing about the traditions of inquiry, I add "based on distinct methodologies within traditions of inquiry." For purposes of this book, these traditions are the historian's biography, the psychologist's phenomenology, the sociologist's grounded theory, the anthropologist's ethnography, and the social, urban studies, and political scientist's case study.

Authors often define *qualitative* inquiry by comparing it to *quantitative* inquiry (e.g., Creswell, 1994). In general terms, I think that Ragin (1987) accurately characterizes a key difference when he mentions that quantitative researchers work with a few variables and many cases,

TABLE 2.1 Characteristics of Qualitative Research

Characteristics	Bogdan & Biklen (1992)	Eisner (1991)	Merriam (1988)
Natural setting (field focused) as source of data	Yes	Yes	Yes
Researcher as key instrument of data collection	Yes	Yes	—
Data collected as words or pictures	Yes	—	Yes
Outcome as process rather than product	Yes	—	Yes
Analysis of data inductively, attention to particulars	Yes	Yes	Yes
Focus on participants' perspectives, their meaning	Yes	Yes	Yes
Use of expressive language	—	Yes	—
Persuasion by reason	—	Yes	—

whereas qualitative researchers rely on a few cases and many variables. To see the differences, I recommend that an individual engage in a quantitative study prior to conducting a qualitative study. Then the broad versus the more focused view is learned firsthand. Also, I strongly recommend that one engage in a small pilot qualitative project to see whether he or she is at ease with the ambiguity and decision process involved in a study.

REASONS FOR CONDUCTING QUALITATIVE RESEARCH

Given these distinctions and definitions of a qualitative study, why does a person engage in such a rigorous design? To undertake qualitative research requires a strong commitment to study a problem and demands time and resources. Qualitative research shares good company with the most rigorous quantitative research, and it should not be viewed as an easy substitute for a "statistical" or quantitative study. Qualitative inquiry is for the researcher who is willing to do the following:

▼ *Commit to extensive time in the field.* The investigator spends many hours in the field, collects extensive data, and labors over field issues of trying to gain access, rapport, and an "insider" perspective.

▼ *Engage in the complex, time-consuming process of data analysis—the ambitious task of sorting through large amounts of data and reducing them to a few themes or categories.* For a multidisciplinary team of qualitative researchers, this task can be shared; for most researchers, it is a lonely, isolated time of struggling with the data. The task is challenging, especially because the database consists of complex texts and images.

▼ *Write long passages, because the evidence must substantiate claims and the writer needs to show multiple perspectives.* The incorporation of quotes to provide participants' perspectives also lengthens the study.

▼ *Participate in a form of social and human science research that does not have firm guidelines or specific procedures and is evolving and changing constantly.* This complicates telling others how one plans to conduct a study and how others might judge it when the study is done.

If an individual is willing to engage in qualitative inquiry, then the person needs to determine whether a strong rationale exists for choosing a qualitative approach, and I believe there are compelling reasons to undertake a qualitative study. First, select a qualitative study because of the nature of the research question. In a qualitative study, the research question often starts with a *how* or a *what* so that initial forays into the topic describe what is going on. This is in contrast to quantitative questions that ask *why* and look for a comparison of groups (e.g., Is Group 1 better at something than Group 2?) or a relationship between variables, with the intent of establishing an association, relationship, or cause and effect (e.g., Did Variable X explain what happened in Variable Y?). Second, choose a qualitative study because the topic needs to be *explored.* By this, I mean that variables cannot be easily identified, theories are not available to explain behavior of participants or their population of study, and theories need to be developed. Third, use a qualitative study because of the need to present a *detailed view* of the topic. The wide-angle lens or the distant panoramic shot will not suffice to present answers to the problem, or the close-up view does not exist. Fourth, choose a qualitative approach in order to study individuals in their *natural setting.* This involves going out to the setting or field of study, gaining access, and gathering material. If participants are removed from their setting, it leads to contrived findings that are out of context. Fifth, select a qualitative approach because of interest in *writing* in a literary style; the writer brings himself or herself into the study, the personal pronoun "I" is used, or perhaps the writer engages a storytelling form of narration. Sixth, employ a qualitative study because of *sufficient time and resources* to spend on extensive data collection in the field and detailed data analysis of "text" information. Seventh, select a qualitative approach because *audiences are receptive* to qualitative research. This audience might be a graduate adviser or committee, a discipline inclusive of multiple research methodologies, or publication outlets with editors receptive to qualitative approaches. Eighth, and finally, employ a qualitative approach to emphasize the researcher's role as an *active learner* who can tell the story from the participants' view rather than as an "expert" who passes judgment on participants.

PHASES IN THE DESIGN OF A STUDY

With a general understanding of the intent and rationale for conducting qualitative research, the investigator designs a study. In many ways, the format for the design of this study follows the traditional research approach of presenting a problem, asking a question, collecting data to answer the question, analyzing the data, and answering the question. But the qualitative approach to design contains several unique features. First, the researcher plans a *general approach* to a study; a detailed plan would not suffice given emerging issues that develop in a field study. Second, some issues are problematic for the qualitative researcher—such as how much literature should be included in the front of the study, how much theory should guide the study, and whether one needs to verify or report on the accuracy of his or her account. How one addresses these issues shapes the form of the qualitative narrative differently from traditional social and human science research. Third, the actual format for a qualitative study varies considerably from the traditional format of research. A qualitative dissertation, for example, may contain eight chapters rather than the standard five, and an author may write a journal article in a flexible style opening and closing with vignettes, as in qualitative case study research, rather than the traditional introduction, literature review, methods, results, and conclusions.

Given these phases in the design, one uses, either explicitly or implicitly, a set of philosophical assumptions that guide the study. These assumptions (discussed further in Chapter 5) speak to our understanding of knowledge: Knowledge is within the meanings people make of it; knowledge is gained through people talking about their meanings; knowledge is laced with personal biases and values; knowledge is written in a personal, up-close way; and knowledge evolves, emerges, and is inextricably tied to the context in which it is studied. Beyond these core assumptions, we may overlay a framework with a distinct ideological stance, such as the postmodern approach that situates a study within a particular context, historical framework, or social-political perspective and empowers participants in our study. We may overlay a tendentious perspective aimed at creating change and action, not the dispassionate form of research traditional in the social and human sciences.

With these preliminary considerations in mind, we begin by posing a problem, a research issue, to which we would like an answer. Problems in qualitative research span the topics in the social and human sciences, and a hallmark of qualitative research today is the deep involvement in issues of gender, culture, and marginalized groups. The topics about which we write are emotion laden, close to the people, and practical.

To study these topics, we ask open-ended research questions, wanting to listen to the participants we are studying and shaping the questions after we "explore," and we refrain from assuming the role of the expert researcher with the "best" questions. Our questions change during the process of research to reflect an increased understanding of the problem. Furthermore, we take these questions out to the field to collect either "words" or "images." I like to think in terms of four basic types of information: interviews, observations, documents, and audio-visual materials. Certainly, new forms emerge that challenge this traditional categorization. Where do we place sounds, e-mail messages, and computer software? Unquestionably, the backbone of qualitative research is extensive collection of data, typically from multiple sources of information. At this stage, too, we consciously consider ethical issues—seeking consent, avoiding the conundrum of deception, maintaining confidentiality, and protecting the anonymity of individuals with whom we speak.

After organizing and storing our data, we analyze them by carefully masking the names of respondents, and we engage in the perplexing (and "lonely" if we are the sole researcher) exercise of trying to make sense of the data. We examine the qualitative data working inductively from particulars to more general perspectives, whether these perspectives are called themes, dimensions, codes, or categories. Recognizing the highly interrelated set of activities of data collection, analysis, and report writing, we do not always know clearly which stage we are in. I remember working on our case study (Asmussen & Creswell, 1995) as interviewing, analyzing, and writing the case study—all intermingled processes, not distinct phases in the process. Also, we experiment with many forms of analysis—making metaphors, developing matrices and tables, and using visuals—to convey simultaneously breaking down the data and reconfiguring them into new forms. We (re)present our data, partly based on participants' perspectives and partly based on our own interpretation, never clearly escaping our own personal stamp on a study.

Throughout the slow process of collecting data and analyzing them, we shape our narrative—a narrative with many forms in qualitative research. We tell a story. We present the study following the traditional approach to scientific research (i.e., problem, question, method, findings). We talk about our experiences in conducting the study. We let the voices of our informants speak and carry the story through dialogue, perhaps dialogue presented in Spanish with English subtitles.

At some point we ask, "Did we get the story 'right'?" (Stake, 1995). Perhaps qualitative studies do not have endings, only questions (Wolcott, 1994b). Standards for assessing the quality of qualitative research are available (Howe & Eisenhardt, 1990; Lincoln, 1995; Marshall & Rossman, 1995). Here is my short list of *characteristics of a "good" qualitative study:*

■ We employ rigorous data collection procedures. This means that the researcher collects multiple forms of data, adequately summarizes—perhaps in tabled form—the forms of data and detail about them, and spends adequate time in the field. It is not unusual for qualitative studies to include information about the specific amount of time in the field.

- We frame the study within the assumptions and characteristics of the qualitative approach to research. This includes fundamental characteristics such as an evolving design, the presentation of multiple realities, the researcher as an instrument of data collection, and a focus on participants' views—in short, all of the characteristics mentioned in Table 2.1.

- We use a tradition of inquiry. This means that the researcher identifies, studies, and employs one or more traditions of inquiry. Certainly, this tradition need not be "pure," and one might mix procedures from several. But for the beginning student of qualitative research, I would recommend staying within one tradition, becoming comfortable with it, learning it, and keeping a study concise and straightforward. Later, especially in long and complex studies, features from several traditions may be useful.

- We begin with a single focus. The project starts with a single idea or problem that the researcher seeks to understand, not a causal relationship of variables or a comparison of groups. Although relationships might evolve or comparisons might be made, these emerge late in the study after we *describe* a single idea.

- The study includes detailed methods, a rigorous approach to data collection, data analysis, and report writing. This means, too, that the researcher verifies the accuracy of the account using one of the many procedures for verification.

- We write persuasively so that the reader experiences "being there." The concept of *"verisimilitude,"* a literary term, captures my thinking (Richardson, 1994, p. 521).

- We analyze data using multiple levels of abstraction. I like to see the active work of the researcher as he or she moves from particulars to general levels of abstractions. Often, writers present their studies in stages (e.g., the multiple themes that can be combined into larger themes or perspectives) or layer their analyses from the particular to the general.

- The writing is clear, engaging, and full of unexpected ideas. The story and findings become believable and realistic, accurately reflecting all the complexities that exist in real life. The best qualitative studies engage the reader.

FORMAT FOR PLANNING A STUDY

Look at the diversity of final written products for qualitative research. No set format exists. But several writers suggest general topics to be included in a written plan or *proposal* for a qualitative study. For example, Marshall and Rossman (1995) advance one format:

Example 2.1

Introduction
  Problem and Significance (in related literature)
  Focus and Research Questions
  Limitations of the Study
Research Design
  Overall Strategy and Rationale (and pilot study)
  Focusing on the Specific Setting, Population, and Phenomenon
  Sampling People, Behaviors, Events, and/or Processes
  Issues of Entry, Reciprocity, Personal Biography, and Ethics
Data Collection Methods
  Participation in the Setting
  Direct Observation
  In-Depth Interviewing
  Document Review
Recording, Managing, and Analyzing Data Resources for the Study
  Time Line
  Level of Data Collection
  Personnel Needed
  Resources Needed
The Value and Logic of Qualitative Research
  Criteria of Soundness

A second format is one that I use and advance in one of my earlier books (Creswell, 1994). It resembles Marshall and Rossman's (1995) format but departs slightly by focusing on more topics in the introductory section:

Example 2.2   Qualitative Format

Introduction
    Statement of the Problem
    Purpose of the Study
    The Grand Tour Question and Subquestions
    Definitions
    Delimitations and Limitations
    Significance of the Study

Procedure
    Assumptions and Rationale for a Qualitative Design
    The Type of Design Used
    The Role of the Researcher
    Data Collection Procedures
    Methods for Verification
    Outcome of the Study and Its Relation to Theory and
      Literature
Appendixes

Maxwell (1996) suggests a third format with fewer details:

Example 2.3

    Abstract
    Introduction
    Research Context
    Research Questions
    Research Methods
    Validity
    Preliminary Results
    Implications (or conclusions)
    References
    Appendixes

These three examples speak only to designing a plan or proposal for a qualitative study. The *complete* study contains data findings and a discussion as well as the problem or issue, research questions, methodology, and verification or validity. Because of the variety of compositional forms, it is best to view completed studies and explore their inner "architecture." I present this topic in the next chapter.

SUMMARY

Given the multiple perspectives on qualitative research, it is helpful to establish some common ground before proceeding to examine the varieties of qualitative traditions. Qualitative research is complex, involving fieldwork for prolonged periods of time, collecting words and pictures, analyzing this information inductively while focusing on participant views, and writing about the process using expressive and persuasive language. Moreover, researchers frame this approach within traditions of inquiry, and they engage in research to examine *how* or *what* types of questions, to explore a topic, to develop a detailed view, to take advantage of access to information, to write in expressive and persuasive language, to spend time in the field, and to reach audiences receptive to qualitative approaches. In designing a study, one works with broad philosophical assumptions; possible frameworks, problems, and questions; and data collection through techniques such as interviews, observations, documents, and audio-visual materials. Reducing the data into small categories or themes comes next, as does storing them and representing them for the reader in the narrative. The narrative assumes many forms—a theory, a description, a detailed view, an abstract model—and we know whether the narrative rings true using criteria about rigor, the philosophical assumptions of the design, detailed methods and approaches, and persuasive and engaging writing. The narrative will, in the end, reflect the creativity of the writer, although the plan for the study, the proposal, might follow several of the procedures being discussed in the literature. In the next chapter, we see how five authors shape these central elements of good qualitative research using a lens of a tradition of inquiry—the traditions of a biography, a phenomenology, a grounded theory study, an ethnography, and a case study.

▼ *ADDITIONAL READINGS*

Several books provide a good introduction to qualitative research. I recommend Marshall and Rossman (1995) and Maxwell (1996) as two recent excellent books. I highly recommend Maxwell's sample dissertation proposal at the end of his book as an example of a good qualitative case study proposal. Others' introductory texts are equally good, such as Glesne and Peshkin (1992), a basic introductory text for those new to qualitative research; Bogdan and Biklen (1992), a thoughtful introductory text often used in qualitative research classes, especially in education; Lincoln and Guba (1985), a classic and one of the early texts to discuss naturalistic inquiry; Eisner (1991), a book focusing on "educational connoisseurship" as an approach to qualitative research; Creswell (1994), a book that provides an introduction to the procedures of qualitative research and how they differ from quantitative approaches; Merriam (1988), an introduction to qualitative research but one cast within the case study approach; Meloy (1994), a short book about writing the qualitative dissertation; Crabtree and Miller (1992), an edited book of readings about qualitative research in the health care setting; LeCompte, Millroy, and Preissle (1992), the first extensive handbook on qualitative research, an edited book with a focus on ethnography; Denzin and Lincoln (1994), another edited, substantial handbook (644 pages) that covers all topics relevant to qualitative research and incorporates a strong interdisciplinary social science perspective. See the following:

Bogdan, R. C., & Biklen, S. K. (1992). *Qualitative research for education: An introduction to theory and methods.* Boston: Allyn & Bacon.

Crabtree, B. F., & Miller, W. L. (1992). *Doing qualitative research.* Newbury Park, CA: Sage.

Creswell, J. W. (1994). *Research design: Qualitative and quantitative approaches.* Thousand Oaks, CA: Sage.

Denzin, N., & Lincoln, Y. (Eds.). (1994). *Handbook of qualitative research.* Thousand Oaks, CA: Sage.

Eisner, E. W. (1991). *The enlightened eye: Qualitative inquiry and the enhancement of educational practice.* New York: Macmillan.

Glesne, C., & Peshkin, A. (1992). *Becoming qualitative researchers: An introduction.* White Plains, NY: Longman.

LeCompte, M. D., Millroy, W. L., & Preissle, J. (Eds.). (1992). *The handbook of qualitative research in education.* San Diego: Academic Press.

Lincoln, Y. S., & Guba, E. G. (1985). *Naturalistic inquiry*. Beverly Hills, CA: Sage.

Marshall, C., & Rossman, G. B. (1995). *Designing qualitative research* (2nd ed.). Thousand Oaks, CA: Sage.

Maxwell, J. (1996). *Qualitative research design: An interactive approach*. Thousand Oaks, CA: Sage.

Meloy, J. M. (1994). *Writing the qualitative dissertation: Understanding by doing*. Hillsdale, NJ: Lawrence Erlbaum.

Merriam, S. (1988). *Case study research in education: A qualitative approach*. San Francisco: Jossey-Bass.

EXERCISES

1. Organize a two-page overview of a study you would like to conduct. At this point, you need not be concerned about the specific tradition of inquiry unless you already have one selected. In your summary, include (a) the problem (or issue) you plan to study, (b) the major research question you plan to ask, (c) the data you wish to collect and analyze, (d) the significance of your study, and (e) your relationship to the topic and participants being studied. This preliminary plan will be modified later after you have chosen a tradition of inquiry.

2. For individuals new to qualitative research, examine one of the introductory texts I mentioned in the Additional Readings section and develop an outline of key ideas.

3
▼

Five Different
Qualitative Studies

The overview in Chapter 2 provided the basics for conducting a qualitative study. Beyond the overview, however, qualitative investigators overlay a tradition of inquiry—the methodology and methods of inquiry as advanced by writers in the disciplines of sociology, psychology, anthropology, and the humanities. I believe that the best studies have a strong inquiry procedure, and this procedure can be gained through engaging in field studies, by apprenticing with individuals with a strong tradition of inquiry focus, or by reading good examples.

This last approach is the crux of this chapter. I present several examples of qualitative research—examples that are reasonable models for a biography, a phenomenology, a grounded theory, an ethnography, and a case study. Each is of journal article length, and I would recommend at this early juncture that the reader examine each and then return to this chapter for my summary of the study and preliminary thoughts about how the article illustrates its tradition of inquiry. These articles are found in their entirety in Appendixes B, C, D, E, and F, respectively, and the reader may need to return to them often during the course of reading this book. To reinforce their applicability for understanding the five traditions, I will mention them occasionally in chapters to follow.

The first study, by Angrosino (1994), illustrates the broad genre of biographical research. It is the life history of Vonnie Lee Hargrett, a mentally retarded (or intellectually challenged) individual. The second article, a phenomenological study by Riemen (1986) from nursing research, presents a study of the interactions that exist between the nurses and the patients as told by the patients, who are adults in a university hospital in the southwestern United States. The third article, a grounded theory study by Morrow and Smith (1995), reports personal constructs of survival and coping by 11 women who survived childhood sexual abuse. The fourth article, an ethnography by Wolcott (1994a), discusses the process of selecting a public school principal by a Principal Selection Committee. The final article, a qualitative case study by Asmussen and Creswell (1995), details the response of a large midwestern university to a terrorist gun incident on campus.

I briefly summarize each of these articles, followed by the identification of key features that "mark" these studies within traditions of inquiry. At the conclusion of this chapter, I reflect on why one might choose one tradition over another for a qualitative study.

Questions for Discussion

▼ What is the focus of a biographical study?

▼ What experience is examined in a phenomenological study?

▼ What concept is the basis for a theory in a grounded theory study?

▼ What cultural group or people are being studied in an ethnographic study?

▼ What is the "case" being examined in a case study?

▼ How do the five traditions differ in their foci of study?

A BIOGRAPHICAL LIFE HISTORY
(Angrosino, 1994; see Appendix B)

This is the story of Vonnie Lee, a 29-year-old man whom the author meets at Opportunity House, an agency designed for the rehabilitation of adults with mental retardation and psychiatric disorders. Most of the people at the agency have criminal records. Vonnie Lee is no exception. He experiences a troubled childhood with an absent father and an alcoholic mother who takes up with countless physically abusive men. Vonnie Lee lives mostly on the streets in the company of an older man, Lucian, who makes a living by "loaning" Vonnie Lee to other men on the street. After Lucian is beaten to death, Vonnie Lee finds himself in and out of psychiatric facilities until he lands at Opportunity House. When the researcher enters the story, Vonnie Lee is in transition between Opportunity House and entering the community through "supervised independent living." A key step in preparing individuals for this transition is to teach them how to use the public transportation system.

The author finds Vonnie Lee open to talking about his life, but within narrow strictures. Whereas Vonnie Lee's stories are almost devoid of characters, they center on "a description of the bus route." As Angrosino says, "He was inclined only to offer what he seemed to feel were these deeply revelatory bus itineraries" (p. 18). Following this lead, the researcher takes a bus trip with Vonnie Lee to his place of work. This bus trip holds special meaning for Vonnie Lee as he travels for about an hour and a half to his destination with three bus transfers. Vonnie Lee has set ways; he tries to find a seat under the large red heart, the logo of the city's bus line. En route, he supplies the researcher with the details about people, places, and events of the journey. Arriving at his place of work, a plumbing supply warehouse, Vonnie Lee's supervisor comments, "It's the bus he loves, coming here on the bus" (p. 21). "Why do you like the bus so much?" asks the researcher. Vonnie Lee exclaims, "If I was a big shot, I'd be on the bus right now!" From this, the researcher deduces that the bus gives meaning to Vonnie Lee's life through both escape and empowerment on the bus, and that explains why he tells his life stories in the form of bus routes. Vonnie Lee's stable self-image—the bus trip—survives the vicissitudes of his life.

The study ends with the researcher reflecting on the use of the metaphor as a useful framework for analyzing stories of informants in life history projects. Furthermore, the study illustrates the benefits of the "in-depth autobiographical interview methodology" for establishing the human dimension of mentally disordered persons and for "contextualizing" the interview information within the ongoing life experiences of Vonnie Lee.

Biographical aspects. This article presents the life history approach to biography within the confines of a short journal article. Written by an anthropologist, it fits well within the cultural interpretations of anthropological life history research. Other forms of biographical research, to be explored later, may not raise such strong cultural issues of metaphors of self and self-images of cultural groups, such as those of the intellectually challenged. Still, this study contains many useful "markings" of the biographical genre of research:

- The author tells the story of a single individual, thus providing a central focus for the study.

- The data collection consists of "conversations" or stories, the reconstruction of life experiences as well as participant observations.

- The individual recalls a special event of his life, an "epiphany" (e.g., the bus ride).

- The author reports detailed information about the setting or historical context of the bus trip, thus situating the epiphany within a social context.

- The author is present in the study, reflecting on his own experiences and acknowledging that the study is his interpretation of the meaning of Vonnie Lee's life.

The outline of ideas in this article follows the following sequence:

1. The author first describes the individual (Vonnie Lee).

2. The author next talks about the relationship with this individual that leads to the research.

3. The author then focuses on one event (or epiphany) in the life of the individual.

4. The author interprets the meaning of this event (e.g., metaphor, empowerment).

5. The author relates the meaning to the larger literature.

6. The author discusses the lessons learned in conducting the study.

The elements of focusing on a single individual, constructing a study out of stories and epiphanies of special events, situating them within a broader context, and evoking the presence of the author in the study all reflect the interpretive biographical form of study discussed by Denzin (1989b), to be expanded in the next chapter.

A PHENOMENOLOGY
(Riemen, 1986; see Appendix C)

This study discusses the "caring interaction" between a nurse and his or her patient. The investigator explores the central issue of the essential structure of a caring nurse-client interaction and poses this question: "What is essential for the experience to be described by the client as being a caring interaction?"

The author begins this study with philosophical ideas, drawing on existential themes of Buber (1958) and Marcel (1971). These themes emphasize empathy, openness, life as a mystery (rather than a problem to be solved), and being present for others. This translates into an approach to studying the problem that includes entering the field of perception of participants; seeing how they experience, live, and display the phenomenon; and looking for the meaning of the participants' experiences. Moreover, the researcher says she needed to set aside her preconceptions to best understand the phenomenon as experienced by the participants.

The design includes studying 10 nonhospitalized adults who have prior interactions with a registered nurse and are able to communicate their feelings regarding these interactions. They are asked five questions, and their interviews are tape-recorded. The specific steps in data analysis used are as follows:

1. The researcher first reads all descriptions in their entirety.

2. The author then extracts significant statements from each description.

3. These statements are formulated into meanings, and these meanings are clustered into themes.

4. The researcher integrates these themes into a narrative description.

The analysis follows these steps resulting in significant statements, an analysis for males and females as well as for caring and noncaring interactions. Meanings are then advanced for caring and noncaring participants. Finally, these meanings are clustered into common themes from which the author provides two narrative descriptions of a caring and noncaring nurse-client interactions.

The article ends by the author returning to the philosophical base of the study, discussing how the results reinforce this base, and addressing implications for nursing education, practice, research and theory.

Phenomenological aspects. This study represents a psychological approach to a phenomenological study. Although it is a study on an interpersonal topic, the overall format of the article is highly structured, following many of the forms we typically associate with quantitative research (e.g., the literature review). I especially like the detailed attention to the philosophical perspective behind the study (i.e., existentialism, phenomenology) and the rigorous attention to procedures or steps in the process. The "treatment of the data," using Colaizzi's (1978) phenomenological data analysis (similar to that of Moustakas, 1994), is a useful procedure for analyzing phenomenological data.

This study illustrates several basic features of a phenomenological study:

■ The author suggests there is an "essential structure of a caring interaction."

- The study reports briefly the philosophical perspective of the phenomenological approach.

- The author studies a single phenomenon, the caring interaction.

- The researcher "brackets" preconceptions so as not to inject hypotheses, questions, or personal experiences into the study.

- The researcher advances specific phenomenological data analysis steps.

- The author returns to the philosophical base at the end of the study.

A GROUNDED THEORY STUDY
(Morrow & Smith, 1995; see Appendix D)

This is a grounded theory study about the survival and coping strategies of 11 women to childhood sexual abuse. The authors ask the following two open-ended questions. "Tell me, as much as you are comfortable sharing with me right now, what happened to you when you were sexually abused? What were the primary ways in which you survived?" Data are collected primarily through one-on-one interviews, focus group interviews, and participant observation by one of the researchers. The authors first form categories of information and then reassemble the data through systematically relating the categories in the form of a visual model. At the center of this model is the central phenomenon, the central category around which the theory is developed: threatening or dangerous feelings along with helplessness, powerlessness, and lack of control. Factors causing this phenomenon are cultural norms and different forms of sexual abuse. Individuals use strategies in two areas: avoiding being overwhelmed by feelings and managing their helplessness, powerlessness, and lack of control. These strategies are set within the context of perpetrator characteristics, sensations, and frequency as well as within larger conditions such as family dynamics, victims' ages, and rewards. The strategies are not without consequences. These women talk about consequences such as surviving, coping, healing, and hoping. The article ends by relating the theoretical model back to the literature on sexual abuse.

Grounded theory aspects. A distinguished qualitative researcher (Smith) and a counseling psychologist (Morrow) both bring their talents to this study. They present a visual model of their substantive theory, the theory that explains the women's actions in response to feelings of threat, danger, helplessness, powerlessness, and lack of control. The authors use rigorous procedures, such as collaboration and the search for disconfirming evidence, to verify their account. In this article, they also educate the reader about grounded theory by an extensive passage on coding data into categories of information and memoing their thoughts throughout the project. In terms of overall structure, it does not cover all facets of grounded theory procedures such as open coding, forming initial categories of information, developing propositions or hypotheses specifying relations among categories, and the conditional matrix (a diagram useful in conceptualizing the wide range of conditions and consequences related to the phenomenon under study). Perhaps space limits the presentation. However, the authors advance a study that models good grounded theory research:

- The authors mention at the beginning that their purpose is to generate a theory using a "construct-oriented" (or category) approach.

- The procedure is thoroughly discussed and systematic.

- The authors present a visual model, a coding diagram of the theory.

- The language and feel of the article are scientific and objective while, at the same time, addressing a sensitive topic effusively.

AN ETHNOGRAPHY
(Wolcott, 1994a; see Appendix E)

This study examines the interview process for choosing a new principal. The author uses the ethnographic approach, and the data collection consists of documents, participant observation, and interviewing. The study begins with details about the Principal Selection Committee's existence and clues about the formal context in which it works.

This discussion includes procedural issues such as whether the candidates are to be selected from within the district and the manner of conducting the interviews. Then the author provides a description of several candidates, beginning with "Mr. Seventh," not following the specific order of interviews but rather following the candidates' final ranking in the process except for the sixth candidate (i.e., seventh, fifth, fourth, third, second, first). Following the description of the interview process with each of these candidates, the author analyzes the proceedings and develops three themes: the lack of professional knowledge associated with the role, an esteem for personal feelings, and a proclivity toward "variety-reducing" behavior. This last theme takes on special meaning as Wolcott discusses its importance for "change" in the public schools.

Ethnographic aspects. Wolcott writes clearly and convincingly and takes the reader on interesting journeys. His overall intent is to see the culture of the school at work in the activities of the Principal Selection Committee. He creatively builds the narrative from the final candidate (Mr. Seventh) on to the winner selected in the process, thus adding suspense to the last scene of the story. I find this study to have many elements central to an ethnography:

- The author uses description and a high level of detail.

- The author tells this story informally, as a "storyteller" (Wolcott, 1994b, p. 109).

- The author explores cultural themes of roles and behavior of the committee.

- The author describes the "everyday life of persons" (Wolcott, 1994b, p. 113).

- The overall format is descriptive (case description of each candidate), analysis (the three "dimensions" [Wolcott, 1994a, p. 140]), and interpretation ("note of reflection" [Wolcott, 1994a, p. 144]).

- The article concludes with a question, asking us not whether principals are agents of change but rather whether they are "advocates of constraint" (Wolcott, 1994a, p. 146).

A CASE STUDY
(Asmussen & Creswell, 1995; see Appendix F)

This qualitative case study describes a campus reaction to a gunman incident in which a student attempted to fire a gun at his classmates. The case study begins with a detailed description of the gunman incident, a chronology of the first 2 weeks of events following the incident, and details about the city, the campus, and the building in which the incident occurred. Data collection through the multiple sources of information such as interviews, observations, documents, and audio-visual materials is presented. We did not interview the gunman or the students who were in counseling immediately following the incident, and our petition to the Institutional Review Board for Human Subjects Research guaranteed these restrictions. From the data analysis emerges denial, fear, safety, retriggering, and campus planning. We combine these narrower themes into two overarching perspectives, an organizational and a psychological or social-psychological response, and we relate these to the literature, thus providing "layers" of analysis in the study and broader interpretations of the meaning of the case. We suggest that campuses plan for their responses to campus violence, and we advance key questions to be addressed in preparing these plans.

Case study aspects. In this case study, we try to follow Lincoln and Guba's (1985) case study structure—the problem, the context, the issues, and the "lessons learned." We also add our own personal stamp by presenting tables with information about the extent of our data collection and the questions necessary to be addressed in planning a campus response to an incident. The epilogue at the end of the study brings our personal experiences into the narrative without disrupting the flow of the narrative in the study. With our last theme on the need for the campus to design a plan for responding to another incident, we advance this study as both practical and useful for personnel on campuses.

Several features mark this project as a case study:

- We identify the "case" for the study, the entire campus and its response to a potentially violent crime.

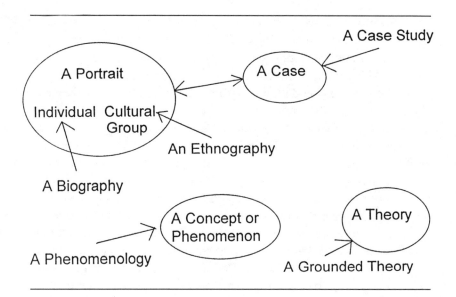

Figure 3.1 Differentiating Traditions by Foci

- This case is a "bounded system," bounded by time (6 months data collection) and place (a single campus).

- We use extensive, multiple sources of information in data collection to provide the detailed in-depth picture of the campus response.

- We spend considerable time describing the context or setting for the case, situating the case within a peaceful midwestern city, a tranquil campus, a building, and a classroom, along with the detailed events during a 2-week period following the incident.

DIFFERENTIATING THE TRADITIONS BY FOCI

A useful perspective to begin the process of differentiating among the five traditions is to assess the central purpose or focus for the tradition. As shown in Figure 3.1, the focus of a biography is on the life of an individual, and the focus of a phenomenology is on understanding a concept or phenomenon. In grounded theory, one develops a theory, whereas a portrait is drawn of a cultural group or people in an ethnography. In a case study, a specific case is examined. Turning to the five studies, the foci of the traditions become more evident.

Using Vonnie Lee (Angrosino, 1994) as a case in point, one decides to write a biography or life history when a single individual needs to be studied as suggested by the literature or when that individual can illuminate a specific issue, such as the issue of being intellectually challenged. Furthermore, the researcher needs to make a case for the need to study this particular individual—someone who illustrates a problem, someone who has had a distinguished career, someone in the national spotlight, or someone who lives an ordinary life. The process of data collection involves gathering material about the person, either historically or from present-day sources, such as conversations or observations in the case of Vonnie Lee. A key consideration is whether the material is available and accessible. In the case of Vonnie Lee, Angrosino is able to win his confidence and encourage him to talk. This occurs first when Angrosino helps him with his reading assignments and then makes a mental note "to see if he would at some later time be amenable to telling me the 'story of my life' " (p. 17).

The phenomenological study, on the other hand, focuses not on the life of an individual but rather on a concept or phenomenon, such as the psychological meaning of a caring interaction (Riemen, 1986), and this form of study seeks to understand the meaning of experiences of individuals about this phenomenon. Furthermore, in the Riemen study, the researcher talks with several individuals who experience the phenomenon, 10 individuals who submit to interviews. And the author includes a philosophical discussion about the principles of exploring the meaning of individual experiences and how these meanings can be reduced into a specific description of the experiences.

Whereas the phenomenological project focuses on the meaning of people's experience toward a phenomenon, researchers in grounded theory have a different objective—to generate a substantive theory, such as a model about women surviving and coping with abuse in the Morrow and Smith study (1995). In the introductory passages, the authors describe the need for a "theoretical framework." Thus, grounded theorists undertake research to develop theory. The data collection method involves primarily interviewing (although other data collection procedures were used). Also, the researchers use systematic procedures for analyzing and developing this theory, procedures such as open coding and axial coding, and they represent the relationship among categories with a visual model. The overall tone of this study is one of rigor and scientific credibility.

An ethnographic design is chosen when one wants to study the behaviors of a culture-sharing group, such as the Principal Selection Committee in Wolcott's (1994a) study. This design requires considerable time observing and interviewing in the school and with the committee. This involves several meetings and the recording of specific details; as Wolcott mentions, "The ethnographer's task is the recording of human behavior in cultural terms" (p. 116). Wolcott chooses three cultural terms—the role of the principal and professional knowledge about it, personal feelings, and variety-reducing behavior to record, describe, and interpret what he sees.

Finally, a case study is chosen to study a case with clear boundaries, such as the campus in our study (Asmussen & Creswell, 1995). It is important, too, for the researcher to have contextual material available to describe the setting for the case. Also, the researcher needs to have a wide array of information about the case to provide an in-depth picture of it. In our gunman case, we went to great lengths to paint this picture for the reader through our table of information sources in the article and to illustrate our wide array of data collection procedures. With these data, we construct a picture of the incident and the campus reaction to it through several themes.

With these thoughts, I focus attention on a chief characteristic that distinguishes each tradition from the others—the study of an individual, the examination of the meaning of experiences toward a phenomenon, the generation of a theory, the description and interpretation of a culture-sharing group, and the in-depth study of a single case. In addition, other factors need to be considered in a choice of a tradition:

- *The audience question:* What tradition is frequently used by gatekeepers in the field (e.g., committee members, advisers, editorial boards of journals)?

- *The background question:* What training does the researcher have in the inquiry approach?

- *The scholarly literature question:* What is needed most as contributing to the scholarly literature in the field (e.g., a study of an individual, an exploration of the meaning of a concept, a theory, a portrait of a culture-sharing group, an in-depth case study)?

■ *The personal approach questions:* Is the researcher more comfortable with a more structured approach to research or with a storytelling approach? Is the researcher more comfortable with a firmer, more well-defined approach to research or with a flexible approach?

SUMMARY

This chapter presented five different short articles to illustrate good models for writing a biography (life history), a phenomenology, a grounded theory study, an ethnography, and a case study. These articles show basic characteristics of each tradition and enable one to see differences in composing and writing varieties of qualitative studies. Choose a biography to study a single individual when material is available and accessible and the individual is willing (assuming that he or she is living) to share information. Choose a phenomenology to examine a phenomenon and the meaning it holds for individuals. Be prepared to interview the individuals, ground the study in philosophical tenets of phenomenology, follow set procedures, and end with the "essence" of the meaning. Choose a grounded theory study to generate or develop a theory. Gather information through interviews (primarily), and use systematic procedures of data gathering and analysis built on procedures such as open, axial, and selective coding. Although the final report will be "scientific," it can still address sensitive and emotional issues. Choose an ethnography to study the behavior of a culture-sharing group (or individual). Be prepared to observe and interview, and explore themes that emerge from studying human behaviors. Choose a case study to examine a "case," bounded in time or place, and look for contextual material about the setting of the "case." Gather extensive material from multiple sources of information to provide an in-depth picture of the "case."

These are important distinctions among the five traditions of inquiry. By studying each tradition in detail, we can learn more about how to proceed and how to narrow our choice of which tradition to use. With this chapter, you have an introduction to each of the five traditions, an introduction grounded in specific studies and in my descriptions of the basic elements of each. In Chapter 4, I will provide more details about each tradition.

▼ ADDITIONAL READINGS

Following is a sampling of research studies that illustrate each of the traditions of inquiry. For journal articles that report biographical research studies, see Angrosino's (1989b) study of a recovering alcoholic; Bertaux and Bertaux-Wiame's (1981) study of the bakers' trade; Geiger's (1986), Johnson and Ferraro's (1984), and Karen's (1990) studies about women's life histories; Nelson's (1990) oral life narrative of African American women; and Smith's (1987) biography of Darwin.

Angrosino, M. V. (1989b). Freddie: The personal narrative of a recovering alcoholic—Autobiography as case history. In M. V. Angrosino, *Documents of interaction: Biography, autobiography, and life history in social science perspective* (pp. 29-41). Gainesville: University of Florida Press.

Bertaux, D., & Bertaux-Wiame, I. (1981). Life stories in the bakers' trade. In D. Bertaux (Ed.), *Biography and society: The life history approach in the social sciences* (pp. 169-190). Beverly Hills, CA: Sage.

Geiger, S. N. G. (1986). Women's life histories: Method and content. *Signs: Journal of Women in Culture and Society, 11*, 334-351.

Johnson, J. M., & Ferraro, K. J. (1984). The victimized self: The case of battered women. In J. A. Kotarba & A. Fontane (Eds.), *The existential self in society* (pp. 119-130). Chicago: University of Chicago Press.

Karen, C. S. (1990, April). *Personal development and the pursuit of higher education: An exploration of interrelationships in the growth of self-identity in returning women students—Summary of research in progress.* Paper presented at the annual meeting of the American Educational Research Association, Boston.

Nelson, L. W. (1990). Code-switching in the oral life narratives of African-American women: Challenges to linguistic hegemony. *Journal of Education, 172*, 142-155.

Smith, L. M. (1987). The voyage of the Beagle: Fieldwork lessons from Charles Darwin. *Educational Administration Quarterly,* 23(3), 5-30.

For phenomenological research studies, examine Aanstoos's study of thinking in chess; Drew's (1986) study of patients' experiences with caregivers; Grigsby and Megel's (1995) study of caring experiences between nurse faculty and students; Harper's (1981) study of leisure; Heinrich's (1995) study of doctoral advisement relationships between women; and Lauterbach's (1993) study of mothers' experiences with deaths of wished-for babies.

Aanstoos, C. M. (1985). The structure of thinking in chess. In A. Giorgi (Ed.), *Phenomenology and psychological research* (pp. 86-117). Pittsburgh, PA: Duquesne University Press.

Drew, N. (1986). Exclusion and confirmation: A phenomenology of patients' experiences with caregivers. *Image: Journal of Nursing Scholarship, 18*(2), 39-43.

Grigsby, K. A., & Megel, M. E. (1995). Caring experiences of nurse educators. *Journal of Nursing Research, 34,* 411-418.

Harper, W. (1981). The experience of leisure. *Leisure Sciences, 4,* 113-126.

Heinrich, K. T. (1995). Doctoral advisement relationships between women. *Journal of Higher Education, 66,* 447-469.

Lauterbach, S. S. (1993). In another world: A phenomenological perspective and discovery of meaning in mothers' experience with death of a wished-for baby: Doing phenomenology. In P. L. Munhall & C. O. Boyd (Eds.), *Nursing research: A qualitative perspective* (pp. 133-179). New York: National League for Nursing Press.

Further specific research studies using grounded theory procedures include Conrad's (1978) study of academic change in universities; Creswell and Brown's (1992) analysis of how academic chairpersons enhance faculty research; Frontman and Kunkel's (1994) study of counselors' success with clients; Hutchinson's (1986) study of nursing in an intensive care unit; and Kearney, Murphy, and Rosenbaum's (1994) study of mothering on crack concaine.

Conrad, C. F. (1978). A grounded theory of academic change. *Sociology of Education, 51,* 101-112.

Creswell, J. W., & Brown, M. L. (1992). How chairpersons enhance faculty research: A grounded theory study. *Review of Higher Education, 16*(1), 41-62.

Frontman, K. C., & Kunkel, M. A. (1994). A grounded theory of counselors' construal of success in the initial session. *Journal of Counseling Psychology, 41,* 492-499.

Hutchison, S. A. (1986). Creating meaning: A grounded theory of NICU nurses. In W. C. Chenitz & J. M. Swanson (Eds.), *From practice to grounded theory* (pp. 191-204). Menlo Park, CA: Addison-Wesley.

Kearney, M. H., Murphy, S., & Rosenbaum, M. (1994). Mothering on crack cocaine: A grounded theory analysis. *Social Science Medicine, 38*(2), 351-361.

For ethnographic studies, see Bruckerhoff's (1991) book-length work on the culture of a high school; Geertz's (1973) classic notes on the Balinese cockfight; Rhoads' (1995) study of college fraternity life; Sells, Smith, Coe, Yoshioka, and Robbins' (1994) study of reflective team practice in family theraphy; Trujillo's (1992) study of the culture of baseball; and Wolcott's (1983) well-known study of the "sneaky kid."

Bruckerhoff, C. E. (1991) *Between classes: Faculty life at Truman High.* New York: Columbia University, Teachers College Press.

Geertz, C. (1973). Deep play: Notes on the Balinese cockfight. In C. Geertz (Ed.), *The interpretation of cultures: Selected essays* (pp. 412-435). New York: Basic Books.

Rhoads, R. A. (1995). Whales tales, dog piles, and beer goggles: An ethnographic case study of fraternity life. *Anthropology and Education Quarterly, 26,* 306-323.

Sells, S. P., Smith, T. E., Coe, J. J., Yoshioka, M., & Robbins, J. (1994). An ethnography of couple and therapist experiences in reflecting team practice. *Journal of Marital and Family Therapy, 20,* 247-266.

Trujillo, N. (1992). Interpreting (the work and the talk of) baseball. *Western Journal of Communication, 56,* 350-371.

Wolcott, H. F. (1983). Adequate schools and inadequate education: The life history of a sneaky kid. *Anthropology and Education Quarterly, 14*(1), 2-32.

Finally, for specific case study research, see Boyle and McKay's (1995) study of the exploitation of older women in the sport of lawn bowling; Brickhous and Bodner's (1992) study of the beginning science teacher; Cottle's (1991) step-by-step process by which members of a family prepare to send their child off to college; Hill, Vaughn, and Harrison's (1995) case study of five American Indian women teachers; Johnson, Holcombe, Simms, and Wilson's (1992) study of the use of writing by home economics teachers; Martens' (1992) study of change in teaching elementary science; and Medoff and Sklar's (1994) case study about an urban neighborhood.

Boyle, J., & McKay, J. (1995). "You leave your troubles at the gate": A case study of the exploitation of older women's labor and "leisure" in sport. *Gender & Society, 9*, 556-575.

Brickhous, N., & Bodner, G. M. (1992). The beginning science teacher: Classroom narratives of convictions and constraints. *Journal of Research in Science Teaching, 29*, 471-485.

Cottle, T. J. (1991). A family prepares for college. *Journal of Higher Education, 62*(1), 79-86.

Hill, B., Vaughn, C., & Harrison, S. B. (1995, September/October). Living and working in two worlds: Case studies of five American Indian women teachers. *The Clearinghouse, 69*(1), 42-48.

Johnson, J., Holcombe, M., Simms, G., & Wilson, D. (1992). Writing in the classroom: Case studies of three home economics teachers. *Journal of Vocational Home Economics Education, 10*(1), 46-58.

Martens, M. L. (1992). Inhibitors to implementing a problem-solving approach to teaching elementary science: Case study of a teacher in change. *Social Science and Mathematics, 93*, 150-156.

Medoff, P., & Sklar, H. (1994). *Streets of hope: The fall and rise of an urban neighborhood.* Boston: South End.

EXERCISES

1. Begin to focus, now, the plan for your project identified in the exercises in Chapter 2. Take your two-page summary developed and add a paragraph stating the tradition you plan to use. For your tradition of inquiry, mention the following. For a biography, what individual do you plan to study? And do you have access to information about this individual's life and a historical context of it? For a phenomenology, what is the phenomenon of interest that you plan to study? And do you have access to people who have experienced it? For a grounded theory, what social science concept, action, or process do you plan to explore as the basis for your theory? For an ethnography, what cultural group or people do you plan to study? For a case study, what is the case you plan to examine?

2. Select one of the journal articles listed in the Additional Readings section. Determine the tradition being used by the author(s) and discuss why the author(s) may have used it.

Five Qualitative Traditions of Inquiry

The five articles described in the preceding section provide examples of the varieties of qualitative research. Hopefully, the reader can see that research in the five traditions differs in form, terms, and focus. In this chapter, I add other dimensions for distinguishing among the five traditions of inquiry. For each tradition, I pose a definition, briefly trace its history, explore variants, introduce procedures involved in conducting a study, and indicate potential challenges in using the tradition.

Questions for Discussion

▼ How is each of the five traditions defined, what is its origin, what variants exist in the approach, what procedures are used, and what challenges exist in applying it?

A BIOGRAPHY

A **biographical study** is the study of *an individual* and her or his experiences as told to the researcher or found in documents and archival material. Denzin (1989a) defines the biographical method as the "studied use and collection of life documents that describe turning-point moments in an individual's life" (p. 69). These accounts explore lesser lives, great lives, thwarted lives, lives cut short, or lives miraculous in their unapplauded achievement (Heilbrun, 1988). Regardless of the type of life, I use the term *biography* to denote the broad genre of biographical writings (Smith, 1994) that includes individual biographies, autobiographies, life histories, and oral histories. I also rely on Denzin's (1989a) approach to biography, called an **interpretive biography**, because the writer tells and inscribes the **stories** of others: "We create the persons we write about, just as they create themselves when they engage in storytelling practices" (p. 82).

Biographical writing has roots in different disciplines and has found renewed interest in recent years. The intellectual strands of this tradition are found in literary, historical, anthropological, psychological, and sociological perspectives as well as in interdisciplinary views from feminist and cultural thinking (see Smith, 1994, who discusses these variants).

My particular interest is in exploring the sociological perspective, and thus I rely on writers such as Plummer (1983) and especially Denzin (1989a, 1989b). Evoking a "baseline" from the humanities, Plummer (1983), for example, discusses the evolution of "documents of life" research from the great literary works of Dostoevski, Dickens, Balzac, and Austen with a focus on human-centered research. Plummer ties biographical writings to the early works of the Department of Sociology at the University of Chicago in the 1920s and 1930s through works such as Thomas and Znaniecki's (1958) *The Polish Peasant in Europe and America*, a study of some 2,200 pages of Polish immigrants to Chicago. Other books are instrumental across anthropology, psychology, and sociology in laying the foundation for social science biographical writing such as Dollard's (1935) *Criteria for the Life History*, the psychological approaches in Allport's (1942) *The Uses of Personal Documents in Psychological Science* and, more recently, Edel's (1984) *Writing Lives* and anthropologist Langness's (1965) *The Life History in Anthropological Science*. I could mention many other authors who have influenced biographical writing in the social sciences in general and in sociology in particular (Smith, 1994); however, in my biographical discussions, I rely on Denzin (1989a), who not only constructs the classical approach to biography but also espouses an interpretive approach.

Procedurally, then, a qualitative researcher faces several decisions in undertaking a biographical type of study (and I would not go so far as to imply an order to these decisions). The first issue is to select the type of biographical study to be undertaken. Denzin (1989a) reviews the various types and their characteristics. Although biographical forms of research vary and the terms reflect different discipline perspectives, all forms represent an attempt to construct the history of a life.

- In a ***biographical study***, the life story of an individual is written by someone other than the individual being studied using archival documents and records (Denzin, 1989a). Subjects of biographies may be living or deceased. Throughout this book, I focus attention on this form because of its popularity with graduate students and social and human science writers.

- In an ***autobiography***, the life story is written by persons about themselves (Angrosino, 1989a). This form seldom is found in graduate student research.

- Another form, the **life history**, is an approach found in the social sciences and anthropology where a researcher reports on an individual's life and how it reflects cultural themes of the society, personal themes, institutional themes, and social histories (Cole, 1994). The investigator collects data primarily through interviews and conversations with the individual (see Bailey, 1978; Geiger, 1986). For a sociological definition, Plummer (1983) states that a life history is "the full length book's account of one person's life in his or her own words. Usually, it will be gathered over a number of years with gentle guidance from the social scientist, the subject either writing down episodes of life or tape recording them. At its best, it will be backed up with intensive observation of the subject's life, interviews with friends and perusals of letters and photographs" (p. 14).

- An **oral history** is an approach in which the researcher gathers personal recollections of events, their causes, and their effects from an individual or several individuals. This information may be collected through tape recordings or through written works of individuals who have died or who are still living.

In addition to these broader forms, specific biographies may be written "objectively," with little researcher interpretation; "scholarly," with a strong historical background of the subject and a chronological organization; "artistically," from the perspective of presenting details in a lively and interesting manner; or in a "narrative" form, a fictionalized account of scenes and characters (Smith, 1994).

One needs to decide whether he or she is going to approach the biography from the more classical traditional stance (Denzin, 1970; Helling, 1988; Plummer, 1983) or from the interpretive approach (Denzin, 1989a, 1989b). In a **classical biography**, the researcher uses statements about theory, concerns with validity and criticism of documents and materials, and the formulation of distinct hypotheses, all drawn from the perspective of the researcher (Denzin, 1989a). The **interpretive biography**, my preferred approach to biographical writing, operates on an entirely different set of assumptions and is well identified in a slim volume by Denzin (1989a) on *Interpretive Biography*. This form of biographical writing challenges the traditional approaches and asks that biographers be cognizant of how studies are both read and written.

In the interpretive view, biographies are, in part, written autobiographies of the writers, thus blurring the lines between fact and fiction and leading the authors to "create" the subject in the text. Biographers cannot partial out their own biases and values; thus, biographies become gendered class productions reflecting the lives of the writers. These points, Denzin (1989a) alleges, need to be acknowledged by the biographers and reflected in the written biographies.

▼ Given these central assumptions, Denzin (1989a) advances several procedural steps:

1. The investigator begins with an objective set of experiences in the subject's life noting **life course stages and experiences**. The stages may be childhood, adolescence, early adulthood, or old age, written as a **chronology**, or as experiences such as education, marriage, and employment.

2. Next, the researcher gathers concrete contextual biographical materials using interviewing (e.g., the subject recounts a set of life experiences in the form of a story or narrative). Thus, a focus is on gathering **stories**.

3. These stories are organized around themes that indicate pivotal events (or **epiphanies**) in an individual's life.

4. The researcher explores the meaning of these **stories**, relying on the individual to provide explanations and searching for multiple meanings.

5. The researcher also looks for larger structures to explain the meanings, such as social interactions in groups, cultural issues, ideologies, and **historical context**, and provides an interpretation for the life experiences of the individual (or cross-interpretations if several individuals are studied).

▼ Given these procedures and the characteristics of a biography, it is challenging for the following reasons:

■ The researcher needs to collect extensive information from and about the subject of the biography.

■ The investigator needs to have a clear understanding of historical, contextual material to position the subject within the larger trends in society or in the culture.

■ It takes a keen eye to determine the particular **stories**, slant, or angle that "works" in writing a biography and to uncover the "figure under the carpet" (Edel, 1984) that explains the multilayered context of a life.

■ The writer, using an interpretive approach, needs to be able to bring himself or herself into the narrative and acknowledge his or her standpoint.

A PHENOMENOLOGICAL STUDY

Whereas a biography reports the life of a **single individual**, a **phenomenological study** describes the meaning of the **lived experiences** for several individuals about a concept or **the phenomenon**. Phenomenologists explore the structures of consciousness in human experiences (Polkinghorne, 1989). It has roots in the **philosophical perspectives** of

Edmund Husserl (1859-1938) and philosophical discussions to follow
by Heidegger, Sartre, and Merleau-Ponty (Spiegelberg, 1982), and it
has been used in the social and human sciences, especially in sociology
(Borgatta & Borgatta, 1992; Swingewood, 1991), psychology (Giorgi,
1985; Polkinghorne, 1989, 1994), nursing and the health sciences (Nieswiadomy, 1993; Oiler, 1986), and education (Tesch, 1988).

The history of phenomenology starts with German mathematician
Edmund Husserl (1859-1938) and his extensive writings addressing
phenomenological philosophy from 1913 until his retirement (Stewart
& Mickunas, 1990). Husserl's ideas are abstract, and, as late as 1945,
Merleau-Ponty (1962) raises the question "What is phenomenology?"
in his *Phenomenology of Perception*. In fact, Husserl is known to call any
project currently under way "phenomenology" (Natanson, 1973).

Husserl emphasizes many points (Moustakas, 1994; Natanson,
1973). Researchers search for the *essential, invariant structure (or essence)*
or the central underlying meaning of the experience and emphasize
the *intentionality of consciousness* where experiences contain both the
outward appearance and inward consciousness based on memory,
image, and meaning. *Phenomenological data analysis* proceeds through
the methodology of reduction, the analysis of specific statements and
themes, and a search for all possible meanings. The researcher also
sets aside all prejudgments, *bracketing* (see *epoche*) his or her experiences (a return to "natural science") and relying on intuition, imagination, and universal structures to obtain a picture of the experience.
From these philosophical tenets, four themes are discernible (Stewart
& Mickunas, 1990):

1. *A return to the traditional tasks of philosophy.* By the end of the 19th
   century, philosophy had become limited to exploring a world by
   empirical means, called "scientism." The return to the traditional
   tasks of philosophy is a return to the Greek conception of philosophy as a search for wisdom before philosophy became enamored
   with empirical science.

2. *A philosophy without presuppositions.* Phenomenology's approach is
   to suspend all judgments about what is real—the "natural attitude"—until they are founded on a more certain basis. This sus-
   pension is called *epoche* by Husserl.

3. *The **intentionality of consciousness***. This idea is that consciousness always is directed toward an object. Reality of an object, then, is inextricably related to one's consciousness of it. Thus, reality, according to Husserl, is not divided into subjects and objects, thus shifting the Cartesian duality to the meaning of an object that appears in consciousness.

4. *The refusal of the subject-object dichotomy.* This theme flows naturally from the **intentionality of consciousness**. The reality of an object is only perceived within the meaning of the experience of an individual.

The individuals who embrace these tenets and carry them forward in intellectual thought come from many social science areas, especially sociology and psychology, and form different philosophical camps such as reflective/transcendental phenomenology, dialogical phenomenology, empirical phenomenology, existential phenomenology, hermeneutic phenomenology, and social phenomenology (Barritt, 1986; Tesch, 1990). I briefly mention social phenomenology and focus attention on psychological phenomenology as expressed through empirical/***transcendental phenomenology***.

The sociological perspective, social phenomenology, owes much to Schutz, who articulates the essence of phenomenology for studying social acts (Swingewood, 1991). Schutz is interested in how ordinary members of society constitute the world of everyday life, especially how individuals consciously develop meaning out of social interactions (people interacting with each other). As an extension of Schutz's thinking, a man by the name of Garfinkel calls this approach "ethnomethodology," a way in which to examine how individuals in society make meanings of their everyday lives. Often drawing on ethnography and cultural themes, ethnomethodology relies on methods of analyzing everyday talk (Swingewood, 1991).

My preferred approach, the ***psychological approach***, also focuses on the meaning of experiences but has found individual experiences, not group experiences, central. Coming from the Duquesne Studies in Phenomenology, the central tenets of this thinking are

to determine what an experience means for the persons who have had the experience and are able to provide a comprehensive description of it. From the individual descriptions, general or universal meanings are derived, in other words, the essences of structures of the experience. (Moustakas, 1994, p. 13)

Moustakas (1994) proceeds to elaborate on a type of phenomenology, **transcendental phenomenology**, that traces back to Husserl but places more emphasis on bracketing out preconceptions (**epoche or bracketing**) and developing universal structures based on what people experience and how.

The conduct of psychological phenomenology has been addressed in a number of writings including Dukes (1984), Tesch (1990), Giorgi (1985, 1994), Polkinghorne (1989), and, most recently, Moustakas (1994), and there is general consensus about how to proceed (Oiler, 1986). But these methods, "based on phenomenological principles . . . function as general guidelines or outlines, and researchers are expected to develop plans of study especially suited to understanding the particular experiential phenomenon that is the object of their study" (Polkinghorne, 1989, p. 44). With this caveat in mind, I summarize the major procedural issues in using phenomenology:

▼ *The researcher needs to understand the **philosophical perspectives** behind the approach, especially the concept of studying how people experience a phenomenon.* The concept of **epoche** is central, where the researcher brackets his or her own preconceived ideas about **the phenomenon** to understand it through the voices of the informants (Field & Morse, 1985).

▼ *The investigator writes research questions that explore the meaning of that experience for individuals and asks individuals to describe their everyday **lived experiences**.*

▼ *The investigator then collects data from individuals who have experienced **the phenomenon** under investigation.* Typically, this information is collected through long interviews (augmented with researcher self-reflection and previously developed descriptions from artistic works) with informants ranging in number from 5 to 25 (Polkinghorne, 1989).

▼ *The **phenomenological data analysis** steps are generally similar for all psychological phenomenologists who discuss the methods.* According to Moustakas (1994) and Polkinghorne (1989), all psychological phenomenologists employ a similar series of steps. The original protocols are divided into statements or **horizonalization**. Then, the units are transformed into **clusters of meanings** expressed in psychological and phenomenological concepts. Finally, these transformations are tied together to make a general description of the experience, the **textural description** of what was experienced and the **structural description** of how it was experienced. Some phenomenologists vary this approach by incorporating personal meaning of the experience (Moustakas, 1994), by using single-subject analysis before intersubject analysis, and by analyzing the role of the context in the process (Giorgi, 1975).

▼ *The phenomenological report ends with the reader understanding better the* **essential, invariant structure (or essence)** *of the experience, recognizing that a single unifying meaning of the experience exists.* For example, this means that all experiences have an underlying "structure" (grief is the same whether the loved one is a puppy, a parakeet, or a child). The reader of the report should come away with the feeling that "I understand better what it is like for someone to experience that" (Polkinghorne, 1989, p. 46). The actual format for the report might follow Moustakas's (1994) outline of the phenomenological model or chapters in a phenomenological study.

A **phenomenological study** may be challenging to use for the following reasons:

- The researcher requires a solid grounding in the philosophical precepts of phenomenology.

- The participants in the study need to be carefully chosen to be individuals who have experienced **the phenomenon**.

- Bracketing personal experiences by the researcher may be difficult.

- The researcher needs to decide how and in what way his or her personal experiences will be introduced into the study.

A GROUNDED THEORY STUDY

Although a phenomenological study emphasizes the meaning of an experience for a number of individuals, the intent of a **grounded theory** *study* is to *generate or discover a theory*, an abstract analytical schema of a phenomenon, that relates to a particular situation. This situation is one in which individuals interact, take actions, or engage in a process in response to a phenomenon. To study how people act and react to this phenomenon, the researcher collects primarily interview data, makes multiple visits to the field, develops and interrelates categories of information, and writes theoretical propositions or hypotheses or presents a visual picture of the theory.

Two sociologists, Barney Glaser and Anselm Strauss, first articulated grounded theory research in 1967 and later elaborated on it through subsequent books (Glaser, 1978; Glaser and Strauss, 1967; Strauss, 1987; Strauss and Corbin, 1990). In contrast to the a priori theoretical orientation in sociology, they held that theories should be "grounded" in data from the field, especially in the actions, interactions, and social process of people. Despite a rich history of collaboration between Glaser and Strauss that produced works such as *Awareness of Dying* (Glaser & Strauss, 1965) and *Time for Dying* (Glaser & Strauss, 1968), they have differed about grounded theory in recent years, leading Glaser (1992) to launch vitriolic attacks against Strauss. However, both Glaser and Strauss continue to write about grounded theory approaches, and it has gained popularity in sociology, nursing, education, and other social science fields.

The centerpiece of grounded theory research is the development or generation of a theory closely related to the context of the phenomenon being studied. Strauss and Corbin (1994), for example, mention that a theory is a plausible relationship among concepts and sets of concepts. This theory, developed by the researcher, is articulated toward the end of a study and can assume the form of a narrative statement (Strauss & Corbin, 1990), a visual picture (Morrow & Smith, 1995), or a series of hypotheses or *propositions* (Creswell & Brown, 1992).

The researcher typically conducts 20-30 interviews based on several visits "to the field" to collect interview data to *saturate* (or find information that continues to add until no more can be found) the categories. A *category* represents a unit of information composed of events, happenings, and instances (Strauss & Corbin, 1990). The researcher also collects and analyzes observations and documents, but these data forms are atypical. While the researcher collects data, she or he begins analysis. In fact, my image for data collection in a grounded theory study is a "zigzag" process—out to the field to gather information, analyze the data, back to the field to gather more information, analyze the data, and so forth. The participants interviewed are theoretically chosen—in **theoretical sampling**—to help the researcher best form the theory. How many passes one makes to the field depends on whether the categories of information become **saturated** and whether the theory is elaborated in all of its complexity. This process of taking information from data collection and comparing it to emerging categories is called the **constant comparative** method of data analysis.

The process of data analysis in grounded theory research is systematic and follows a standard format:

▼ *In* **open coding**, *the researcher forms initial categories of information about the phenomenon being studied by segmenting information.* Within each **category**, the investigator finds several **properties**, or subcategories, and looks for data to **dimensionalize**, or show the extreme possibilities on a continuum of, the property.

▼ *In* **axial coding**, *the investigator assembles the data in new ways after open coding.* This is presented using a **coding paradigm or logic diagram** in which the researcher identifies a **central phenomenon** (i.e., a central category about the phenomenon), explores **causal conditions** (i.e., categories of conditions that influence the phenomenon), specifies **strategies** (i.e., the actions or interactions that result from the central phenomenon), identifies the **context** and **intervening conditions** (i.e., the narrow and broad conditions that influence the strategies), and delineates the **consequences** (i.e., the outcomes of the strategies) for this phenomenon.

▼ *In* **selective coding**, *the researcher identifies a "story line" and writes a story that integrates the categories in the axial coding model.* In this phase, conditional **propositions** (or hypotheses) are typically presented.

▼ *Finally, the researcher may develop and visually portray a* **conditional matrix** *that elucidates the social, historical, and economic conditions influencing the central phenomenon.* This phase of analysis is not frequently found in grounded theory studies.

The result of this process of data collection and analysis is a theory, a **substantive-level theory**, written by the researchers close to a specific problem or population of people. This theory is subjected to further empirical testing because now we know the variables or categories from field-based data, although the study may end at this point because the generation of a theory is a legitimate outcome of the study.

A **grounded theory study** challenges researchers for the following reasons:

- The investigator needs to set aside, as much as possible, theoretical ideas or notions so that the analytic, substantive theory can emerge.

- Despite the evolving, inductive nature of this form of qualitative inquiry, the researcher must recognize that this is a systematic approach to research with specific steps in data analysis.

- The researcher faces the difficulty of determining when categories are saturated or when the theory is sufficiently detailed.

- The researcher needs to recognize that the primary outcome of this study is a theory with specific components: a central phenomenon, causal conditions, strategies, conditions and context, and consequences. These are prescribed categories of information in the theory.

AN ETHNOGRAPHY

An **ethnography** is a description and interpretation of a cultural or social group or system. The researcher examines the group's observable and learned patterns of **behavior**, customs, and ways of life (Harris, 1968). As both a process and an outcome of research (Agar, 1980), an ethnography is a product of research, typically found in book-length form. As a process, ethnography involves prolonged observation of the group, typically through **participant observation** in which the researcher is **immersed** in the day-to-day lives of the people or through one-on-one interviews with members of the group. The researchers studies the meanings of **behavior, language**, and interactions of the **culture-sharing group**.

Ethnography has its genesis in cultural anthropology through early 20th-century anthropologists such as Boas, Malinowski, Radcliffe-

Brown, and Mead and their studies of comparative cultures. Although they took the natural sciences as a model for research, they differed from traditional scientific approaches through the firsthand collection of data of existing "primitive" cultures (Atkinson & Hammersley, 1994). In the 1920s and 1930s, sociologists such as Park, Dewey, and Mead at the University of Chicago adapted the anthropological field methods to study cultural groups in the United States (Bogdan & Biklen, 1992). Recently, scientific approaches to ethnography have expanded to include "schools" or subtypes of ethnography with different theoretical orientations and aims such as structural function-alism, symbolic interactionism, cultural and cognitive anthropology, feminism, Marxism, ethnomethodology, critical theory, cultural stud-ies, and postmodernism (Atkinson & Hammersley, 1994). This has led to a distinct lack of orthodoxy in ethnography as a general approach to the description and interpretation of a cultural or social group, and authors need to be explicit about what school they espouse when they discuss this approach, especially as it has been embraced by re-searchers in many fields outside anthropology and sociology such as the health sciences and education.

My approach is to rely mainly on procedures found in the socio-logical approach of Hammersley and Atkinson (1995) and to draw on the educational anthropology of Wolcott (1994b) and Fetterman (1989). Through these texts, one finds that the ethnographer begins the study by looking at people in interaction in ordinary settings and by attempting to discern pervasive patterns such as life cycles, events, and cultural themes (H. F. Wolcott, personal communication, October 10, 1996). **Culture** is an amorphous term, not something "lying about" (Wolcott, 1987, p. 41) but rather something the researcher attributes to a group as he or she looks for patterns of daily living. It is inferred from the words and actions of members of the group and is assigned to this group by the researcher. It consists of looking for what people do (**behaviors**), what they say (**language**), and some tension between what they really do and what they ought to do as well as what they make and use (**artifacts**) (Spradley, 1980). Thus, the ethnographer gathers artifacts and physical trace evidence; finds stories, rituals, and myths; and/or uncovers cultural themes. Such themes are diverse, as illustrated in Winthrop's (1991) *Dictionary of Concepts in Cultural An-thropology*. Fetterman (1989), for example, suggests that the themes of structure and function guide research of social organizations. **Structure** refers to the social structure or configuration of the group, such as the kinship or political structure of the social-cultural group. **Function** refers to patterns of the social relations among members of the group that help regulate behavior.

To establish these patterns, the ethnographer engages in extensive work in the field, called **fieldwork**, gathering information through observations, interviews, and materials helpful in developing a portrait and establishing "cultural rules" of the culture-sharing group. As Wolcott (1996) comments, "They [researchers] establish what a stranger would have to know in order to understand what is going on here or, more challenging still, what a stranger would have to know in order to be able to participate in a meaningful way" (p. 6). The ethnographer is sensitive to **fieldwork** issues (Hammersley & Atkinson, 1995) such as gaining access to the group through **gatekeepers**, individuals who can provide entrance to a research site. The ethnographer locates **key informants**, individuals who provide useful insights into the group and can steer the researcher to information and contacts. The field researcher also is concerned about **reciprocity** between the investigator and the subjects being studied, so that something will be returned to the people being studied in exchange for their information, and **reactivity**, the impact of the researcher on the site and the people being studied. In accord with ethical standards, the ethnographer makes his or her presence known so that **deception** about the purpose or intent of the study is not practiced.

Sensitive to these field issues, the procedures in ethnography call for a detailed **description of the culture-sharing group** or individual, an **analysis of the culture-sharing group** by themes or perspectives, and some **interpretation of the culture-sharing group** for meanings of social interaction and generalizations about human social life (Wolcott, 1994b). The amounts of weight researchers give to these three aspects vary. The final product of this effort is a **holistic** cultural portrait of the social group that incorporates both the views of the actors in the group (**emic**) and the researcher's interpretation of views about human social life in a social science perspective (**etic**). By **holistic**, I mean that the ethnographer attempts to describe as much as possible about a cultural system or social group, and this might include the group's history, religion, politics, economy, and environment (Fetterman,

1989). By *cultural portrait*, I refer to an overview of the entire cultural scene by pulling together all aspects learned about the group and showing its complexity.

The ethnography is challenging to use for the following reasons:

■ The researcher needs to have a grounding in cultural anthropology and the meaning of a social-cultural system as well as the concepts typically explored by ethnographers.

■ The time to collect data is extensive, involving prolonged time in the field.

■ In many ethnographies, the narratives are written in a literary, almost storytelling approach, an approach that may limit the audience for the work and may be challenging for authors accustomed to traditional approaches to writing social and human science research.

■ There is a possibility that the researcher will "go native" and be unable to complete the study or be compromised in the study. This is but one issue in the complex array of fieldwork issues facing ethnographers who venture into an unfamiliar cultural group or system.

A CASE STUDY

Whereas some consider "the *case*" an object of study (Stake, 1995) and others consider it a methodology (e.g., Merriam, 1988), a *case study* is an exploration of a "bounded system" or a case (or multiple cases) over time through detailed, in-depth data collection involving multiple sources of information rich in context. This *bounded system* is bounded by time and place, and it is the *case* being studied—a program, an event, an activity, or individuals. For example, several programs (*multi-site* study) or a single program (*within-site* study) might be selected for study. *Multiple sources of information* include observations, interviews, audio-visual material, and documents and reports. The *context of the case* involves situating the case within its setting, which may be a physical setting or the social, historical, and/or economic setting for the case. The focus may be on the case that, because of its uniqueness, requires study (*intrinsic case study*), or it may be on an issue or issues, with the case used instrumentally to illustrate the issue (an *instrumental case study*) (Stake, 1995). When more than one case is studied, it is referred to as a *collective case study* (Stake, 1995).

Many of my students choose the case study as their preferred approach to qualitative research. Their rationale often is that a case study is familiar; they undoubtedly have read case studies in psychology (Freud), medicine (case analysis of a problem), law (case law), and/or political science (case reports). Case study research holds a long, distinguished history across many disciplines. Hamel (1993) traces the origin of modern social science case studies through anthropology and sociology. He cites anthropologist Malinowski's study of the Trobriand Islands, French sociologist LePlay's study of families, and the case studies of the University of Chicago's Department of Sociology in the 1920s and 1930s (e.g., Thomas & Znaniecki's [1958] study, *The Polish Peasant in Europe and America*) as antecedents of qualitative case study research. Today, the case study writer has a large array of texts and approaches from which to choose to develop a case study. Yin (1989), for example, espouses both quantitative and qualitative approaches to case study development and discusses the exploratory and descriptive *qualitative* case studies. Merriam (1988) advocates a general approach to qualitative case studies in the field of education. Hamel (1993), a sociologist, provides a historical and problem-centered discussion of qualitative case studies. Stake (1995), the approach I use extensively, systematically establishes procedures for case study research and uses Stake's own case study of Harper School as an example.

In conducting case study research, I recommend that investigators first consider what type of case study is most promising and useful. The case can be single or collective, multi-sited or within-site, focused on a case or on an issue (intrinsic, instrumental) (Stake, 1995; Yin, 1989). In choosing what case to study, an array of possibilities for *purposeful sampling* is available. I prefer to select cases that show different perspectives on the problem, process, or event I want to portray, but I also may select ordinary cases, accessible cases, or unusual cases.

The data collection is extensive, drawing on *multiple sources of information* such as observations, interviews, documents, and audio-visual materials. For example, Yin (1989) recommends six types of information: documentation, archival records, interviews, direct observations, participant observations, and physical artifacts. The type of analysis of these data can be a *holistic analysis* of the entire case or an *embedded analysis* of a specific aspect of the case (Yin, 1989). Through this data collection, a detailed *description* of the case emerges, as do an *analysis of themes* or issues and an interpretation or *assertions* about the case by the researcher (Stake, 1995). This analysis is rich in the *context of the case* or setting in which the case presents itself (Merriam, 1988). The investigator narrates the study through techniques such as a chronology of major events followed by an up-close or a detailed perspective about a few incidents. When multiple cases are chosen, a typical format is to first provide a detailed description of each case and themes within the case, called a *within-case analysis*, followed by a thematic analysis across the cases, called a *cross-case analysis*, as well as assertions or an interpretation of the meaning of the case. In the final interpretive phase, the researcher reports, as Lincoln and Guba (1985) mention, the "lessons learned" from the case.

Some of the challenges inherent in qualitative case study development are as follows:

■ The researcher must identify his or her case. I can pose no clear solution for the researcher; he or she must decide what bounded system to study, recognizing that several might be possible candidates for this selection and realizing that either the case itself or an issue, for which a case or cases are selected to illustrate, is worthy of study.

■ The researcher must consider whether to study a single case or multiple cases. I am reminded how the study of more than one case dilutes the overall analysis; the more cases an individual studies, the greater the lack of depth in any single case. When a researchers chooses multiple cases, the issue becomes "How many?"—which I cannot answer except to indicate the lack of depth issue. Typically, however, the researcher chooses no more than four cases. What motivates the researcher to consider a large number of cases is the idea of *generalizability*, a term that holds little meaning for most qualitative researchers (Glesne & Peshkin, 1992).

- Selecting the case requires that the researcher establish a rationale for his or her purposeful sampling strategy for selecting the case and for gathering information about the case.

- Having enough information to present an in-depth picture of the case limits the value of some case studies. In planning a case study, I have individuals develop a data collection matrix in which they specify the amount of information they are likely to collect about the case.

- Deciding the "boundaries" of a case—how it might be constrained in terms of time, events, and processes—may be challenging. Some case studies may not have clean beginning and ending points, and the researcher will need to work with contrived boundaries.

THE FIVE TRADITIONS COMPARED

From these sketches of the five traditions, I can identify fundamental differences among these types of qualitative research. As shown in Table 4.1, I present several dimensions for distinguishing among the five. At a most fundamental level, the five differ in what they are trying to accomplish—their foci or the primary objectives of the studies. Exploring a life is different from generating a theory or describing the behavior of a cultural group. Moreover, although overlaps exist in discipline origin, some traditions have single-disciplinary traditions (e.g., grounded theory originating in sociology, ethnography founded in anthropology or sociology), and others have a broad interdisciplinary evolution (e.g., biography, case study). The data collection varies in terms of emphasis (e.g., more observations in ethnography, more interviews in grounded theory) and extent of data collection (e.g., only interviews in phenomenology, multiple forms in case study research to provide the in-depth case picture). At the data analysis stage, the differences are most marked. Not only is the distinction one of specificity of the analysis phase (e.g., grounded theory most specific, biography less well defined), but the number of steps to be undertaken also varies (e.g., extensive steps in phenomenology, few steps in ethnography). The result of each tradition, its narrative form, takes shape from all the processes before it. A detailed picture of an individual's life forms a biography; a description of the

TABLE 4.1 Dimensions for Comparing Five Research Traditions in Qualitative Research

Dimension	Biography	Phenomenology	Grounded Theory	Ethnography	Case Study
Focus	• Exploring the life of an individual	• Understanding the essence of experiences about a phenomenon	• Developing a theory grounded in data from the field	• Describing and interpreting a cultural and social group	• Developing an in-depth analysis of a single case or multiple cases
Discipline origin	• Anthropology • Literature • History • Psychology • Sociology	• Philosophy, sociology, Psychology	• Sociology	• Cultural anthropology Sociology	• Political science, sociology, evaluation, urban studies, other social sciences
Data collection	• Primarily interviews and documents	• Long interviews with up to 10 people	• Interviews with 20-30 individuals to "saturate" categories and detail a theory	• Primarily observations and interviews with additional artifacts during extended time in the field (e.g., 6 months to a year)	• Multiple sources - documents, archival records, interviews, observations, physical artifacts
Data analysis	• Stories • Epiphanies • Historical content	• Statements • Meanings • Meaning themes • General description of the experience	• Open coding • Axial coding • Selective coding • Conditional matrix	• Description • Analysis • Interpretation	• Description • Themes • Assertions
Narrative form	• Detailed picture of an individual's life	• Description of the "essence" of the experience	• Theory or theoretical model	• Description of the cultural behavior of a group or an individual	• In-depth study of a "case" or "cases"

essence of the experience of the phenomenon becomes a phenomenology; a theory, often portrayed in a visual model, emerges in grounded theory; a holistic view of a social-cultural group or system results in an ethnography; and an in-depth study of a bounded system or a case (or several cases) becomes a case study.

In a comparison of the five traditions, two issues of overlap that need clarification arise. The first issue is that an apparent overlap exists between an ethnography and a case study. In the former, we examine a cultural system; in the latter, we examine a bounded system. Thus, confusion exists when studying both as systems. In my mind, however, there are some fundamental differences. In an ethnography, an entire cultural or social system is the focus of attention (except in a microethnography). In a case study, on the other hand, a system of people is typically not the case. In case study research, one works with a smaller unit such as a program, an event, an activity, or individuals and explores a range of topics, only one of which might be cultural behavior, language, or artifacts. Furthermore, in an ethnography, the researcher studies a culture-sharing group using anthropological concepts (e.g., myths, stories, rituals, social structure). These concepts may or may not be present in a case study.

The second issue of overlap arises when one studies an individual. In a biography, the researcher studies a single individual; in a case study, either a single individual or a number of individuals may be the case. Although it certainly is possible to conduct a case study of a single individual, I only recommend such a practice when the researcher can obtain substantial contextual material about the individual (e.g., the individual's family, daily life, work life). For the researcher desiring to study a single individual, I recommend a biographical approach. More accepted, I believe, are case studies of several individuals, usually three or four, in which one can establish depth through both within- and among-case analysis.

Regardless of overlap, relating the dimensions of Table 4.1 to research design within the five traditions will be the focus of chapters to follow. But it might be useful at this point to take the narrative form I have described in general terms and suggest a preliminary structure for the content of a study within each of the five traditions. As shown in Table 4.2, I advance an outline for each type of study. These outlines may be used in designing a journal article-length study; however, because of the numerous steps in each, they also have applicability as

TABLE 4.2   Reporting Approaches for Each Tradition

Reporting Approaches	Biography	Phenomenology	Grounded Theory	Ethnography	Case Study
General structure of study	• Introduction (problem, questions) • Research procedures (a biography, significance of individual, data collection, analysis outcomes) • Report of objective experiences • Individuals theorize about their lives • Narrative segments identified • Patterns of meaning identified (events, processes, epiphanies, themes) • Summary (Adapted from Denzin, 1989a, 1989b)	• Introduction (problem, questions) • Research procedures (a phenomenology and philosophical assumptions, data collection, analysis, outcomes) • Significant statements • Meanings of statements • Themes of meanings • Exhaustive description of phenomenon (Adapted from Moustakas, 1994)	• Introduction (problem, questions) • Research procedures (grounded theory, data collection, analysis, outcomes) • Open coding • Axial coding • Selective coding and theoretical propositions and models • Discussion of theory and contrasts with extant literature (Adapted from Strauss & Corbin, 1990)	• Introduction (problem, questions) • Research procedures (ethnography, data collection, analysis, outcomes) • Description of culture • Analysis of cultural themes • Interpretation, lessons learned, questions raised (Adapted from Wolcott, 1994b)	• Entry vignette • Introduction (problem, questions, case study, data collection, analysis, outcomes) • Description of the case(s) and its (their) context • Development of issues • Detail about selected issues • Assertions • Closing vignette (Adapted from Stake, 1995)

NOTE: Table shows general structure of study. Bulleted points might be a separate section in a journal article or book or a separate chapter in a dissertation.

chapters of a dissertation or a book-length work. I introduce them here because the reader, with an introductory knowledge of each tradition, now can sketch the general "architecture" of a study. Certainly, this architecture will emerge and be shaped differently by the conclusion of the study, but it provides a framework for the design issues to follow. I recommend these outlines as general templates at this time.

SUMMARY

In this chapter, I took the reader through each of my five traditions—biography, phenomenology, grounded theory, ethnography, and case study—and identified a definition for the tradition, offered a few remarks about origin and history of the type, specified varieties within the tradition, and detailed useful procedures for conducting the form of research. Finally, I identified challenges for individuals choosing each form of qualitative research. In concluding the chapter, I presented a matrix of dimensions on which the five traditions differ: focus, discipline origin, data collection, data analysis, and final narrative outcome of the study. Finally, I went one step further about the narrative outcome and suggested and advanced outlines for drafting a study within each tradition.

▼ ADDITIONAL READINGS

Several readings extend this brief overview of each of the five traditions of inquiry. The two books by Denzin (1989a, 1989b) provide the interpretive biographical perspective. For a more traditional approach to biographical writings, see Bowen (1969), Plummer (1983), Lomask (1986), Angrosino (1989a), and Barzun and Graff (1992). A procedural guide to the more traditional biographical approach is found in Helling (1988).

Angrosino, M. V. (1989a). *Documents of interaction: Biography, autobiography, and life history in social science perspective.* Gainesville: University of Florida Press.

Barzun, J., & Graff, H. (1992). *The modern researcher* (5th ed.). New York: Harcourt Brace Jovanovich.

Bowen, C. D. (1969). *Biography: The craft and the calling.* Boston: Little, Brown.

Denzin, N. K. (1989a). *Interpretive biography.* Newbury Park, CA: Sage.

Denzin, N. K. (1989b). *Interpretive interactionism.* Newbury Park, CA: Sage.

Helling, I. K. (1988). The life history method: A survey and discussion with Norman K. Denzin. *Studies in Symbolic Interaction, 9,* 211-243.

Lomask, M. (1986). *The biographer's craft.* New York: Harper & Row.

Plummer, K. (1983). *Documents of life: An introduction to the problems and literature of a humanistic method.* London: George Allen and Unwin.

For phenomenology, a solid grounding in the philosophical assumptions is essential, and one might examine Husserl (1931, 1970), Merleau-Ponty (1962), Natanson (1973), and Stewart and Mickunas (1990) for this background. I feel that the best procedural discussions of psychological phenomenology are found in Giorgi (1985), Polkinghorne (1989), and Moustakas (1994), with additional remarks in Van Kaam (1966), Colaizzi (1978), Spiegelberg (1982), Dukes (1984), Oiler (1986), and Tesch (1990). Giorgi (1985) in psychology and Tesch (1990) in education provide useful references to specific phenomenological studies.

Colaizzi, P. F. (1978). Psychological research as the phenomenologist views it. In R. Vaile & M. King (Eds.), *Existential phenomenological alternatives for psychology* (pp. 48-71). New York: Oxford University Press.

Dukes, S. (1984). Phenomenological methodology in the human sciences. *Journal of Religion and Health, 23,* 197-203.

Giorgi, A. (Ed.). (1985). *Phenomenology and psychological research.* Pittsburgh, PA: Duquesne University Press.

Husserl, E. (1931). *Ideas: General introduction to pure phenomenology* (D. Carr, Trans.). Evanston, IL: Northwestern University Press.

Husserl, E. (1970). *The crisis of European sciences and transcendental phenomenology* (D. Carr, Trans.). Evanston, IL: Northwestern University Press.

Merleau-Ponty, M. (1962). *Phenomenology of perception* (C. Smith, Trans.). London: Routledge & Kegan Paul.

Moustakas, C. (1994). *Phenomenological research methods.* Thousand Oaks, CA: Sage.

Natanson, M. (Ed.). (1973). *Phenomenology and the social sciences.* Evanston, IL: Northwestern University Press.

Oiler, C. J. (1986). Phenomenology: The method. In P. L. Munhall & C. J. Oiler (Eds.), *Nursing research: A qualitative perspective* (pp. 69-82). Norwalk, CT: Appleton-Century-Crofts.

Polkinghorne, D. E. (1989). Phenomenological research methods. In R. S. Valle & S. Halling (Eds.), *Existential-phenomenological perspectives in psychology* (pp. 41-60). New York: Plenum.

Spiegelberg, H. (1982). *The phenomenological movement* (3rd ed.). The Hague, Netherlands: Martinus Nijhoff.

Stewart, D., & Mickunas, A. (1990). *Exploring phenomenology: A guide to the field and its literature* (2nd ed.). Athens: Ohio University Press.

Tesch, R. (1990). *Qualitative research: Analysis types and software tools.* Bristol, PA: Falmer.

Van Kaam, A. (1966). *Existential foundations of psychology.* Pittsburgh, PA: Duquesne University Press.

In grounded theory research, consult the most recent and highly readable book by Strauss and Corbin (1990) before reviewing earlier works such as Glaser and Strauss (1967), Glaser (1978), Strauss (1987), or Glaser (1992). For brief methodological overviews of grounded theory, examine Charmaz (1983), Strauss and Corbin (1994), and the book by Chenitz and Swanson (1986).

Charmaz, K. (1983). The grounded theory method: An explication and interpretation. In R. Emerson (Ed.), *Contemporary field research* (pp. 109-126). Boston: Little, Brown.

Chenitz, W. C., & Swanson, J. M. (1986). *From practice to grounded theory: Qualitative research in nursing.* Menlo Park, CA: Addison-Wesley.

Glaser, B. G. (1978). *Theoretical sensitivity.* Mill Valley, CA: Sociology Press.

Glaser, B. G. (1992). *Basics of grounded theory analysis.* Mill Valley, CA: Sociology Press.

Glaser, B., & Strauss, A. (1967). *The discovery of grounded theory.* Chicago: Aldine.

Strauss, A. (1987). *Qualitative analysis for social scientists.* New York: Cambridge University Press.

Strauss, A., & Corbin, J. (1990). *Basics of qualitative research: Grounded theory procedures and techniques.* Newbury Park, CA: Sage.

Strauss, A., & Corbin, J. (1994). Grounded theory methodology: An overview. In N. Denzin & Y. Lincoln (Eds.), *Handbook of qualitative research* (pp. 273-285). Thousand Oaks, CA: Sage.

For a detailed overview of ethnographic research, see Spradley (1979, 1980), Fetterman (1989), and Hammersley and Atkinson (1995) and examine the methodological procedures by Wolcott (1987, 1994b). Spindler and Spindler's (1970) fieldwork studies in eleven cultures provide some of the best examples of contemporary ethnographic research.

Fetterman, D. M. (1989). *Ethnography: Step by step.* Newbury Park, CA: Sage.

Hammersley, M., & Atkinson, P. (1995). *Ethnography: Principles in practice* (2nd ed.). New York: Routledge.

Spindler, G. D., & Spindler, L. (1970). *Being an anthropologist: Fieldwork in eleven cultures.* New York: Holt, Rinehart & Winston.

Spradley, J. P. (1979). *The ethnographic interview.* New York: Holt, Rinehart & Winston.

Spradley, J. P. (1980). *Participant observation.* New York: Holt, Rinehart & Winston.

Wolcott, H. F. (1987). On ethnographic intent. In G. Spindler & L. Spindler (Eds.), *Interpretive ethnography of education: At home and abroad* (pp. 37-57). Hillsdale, NJ: Lawrence Erlbaum.

Wolcott, H. F. (1994b). *Transforming qualitative data: Description, analysis, and interpretation.* Thousand Oaks, CA: Sage.

Finally, for case study research, consult Stake (1995) or earlier books such as Lincoln and Guba (1985), Merriam (1988), and Yin (1989). Stake (1994) provides a good overview of qualitative case study research.

Lincoln, Y. S., & Guba, E. G. (1985). *Naturalistic inquiry.* Beverly Hills, CA: Sage.

Merriam, S. (1988). *Case study research in education: A qualitative approach.* San Francisco: Jossey-Bass.

Stake, R. (1994). Case studies. In N. K. Denzin & Y. S. Lincoln (Eds.), *Handbook of qualitative research* (pp. 236-247). Thousand Oaks, CA: Sage.

Stake, R. (1995). *The art of case study research.* Thousand Oaks, CA: Sage.

Yin, R. K. (1989). *Case study research: Design and method.* Newbury Park, CA: Sage.

EXERCISES

1. Continue to develop your study begun in the Exercises in Chapter 2 and refined in the Exercises in Chapter 3. Build on your section where you specify a tradition of inquiry. Provide a definition for your choice, key references about it, and the major characteristics and procedures of the tradition.

2. In this chapter, I have provided only a brief summary of each tradition. For your tradition of choice, select one of the books mentioned in the Additional Readings section and summarize the major concepts of the tradition including the procedures to be used to conduct a study.

5

▼

Philosophical and
Theoretical Frameworks

In this chapter, I begin examining the relationship between the five traditions of inquiry and phases of research design. An initial phase of design, then, is to consider not only whether a qualitative study is suitable for the study of a problem (as discussed in Chapter 2) but also to frame the study within the philosophical and theoretical perspectives. The philosophical or theoretical lenses range from broad perspectives, such as epistemological and ontological assumptions, to ideological stances, such as postmodernism and critical perspectives, to more narrowly defined "theories" (Flinders & Mills, 1993) composed of propositions and hypotheses found in the social and human sciences.

In this chapter, I begin with five assumptions that guide the design and are central to all good qualitative studies: the multiple nature of reality, the close relationship of the researcher to that being researched, the value-laden aspect of inquiry, the personal approach to writing the narrative, and the emerging inductive methodology of the process of research. For each assumption, I identify its central characteristics, discuss its application in research, and illustrate it with examples from the five traditions of inquiry.

These assumptions operate at a broad abstract level in guiding the design of all qualitative studies. In addition, the researcher may employ an ideological perspective popular today. In this chapter, I address three of these perspectives—the postmodern, critical, and feminist approaches—and illustrate their use in the five traditions. Regardless of tradition, these perspectives represent a conscious choice by the researcher (Schwandt, 1993).

At a less abstract level, researchers may employ a social science theory to guide their qualitative studies. Central to this issue is whether they should use a theoretical framework to guide their studies and, if so, to what extent, recognizing that all researchers begin with some hunches, ideas, and frameworks from past experiences and readings. In this chapter, I discuss the extent to which investigators use a social science theory *before* they pose questions and collect data and after data collection in each of the five traditions of inquiry.

Questions for Discussion

▼ What philosophical assumptions guide all qualitative studies?
▼ What are examples of ideological perspectives that qualitative researchers employ?
▼ How is social science theory used by authors in each of the five traditions of inquiry?

FIVE PHILOSOPHICAL ASSUMPTIONS

Qualitative researchers approach their studies with a certain **paradigm or worldview**, a basic set of beliefs or assumptions that guide their inquiries. These assumptions are related to the nature of reality (the ontology issue), the relationship of the researcher to that being researched (the epistemological issue), the role of values in a study (the axiological issue), and the process of research (the methodological issue) (see Table 5.1). The assumptions in Table 5.1 are adapted from the "axiomatic" issues advanced by Guba and Lincoln (1988). However, my discussion departs from their analysis in three ways. I do not contrast the qualitative or naturalistic assumptions with conventional

TABLE 5.1 Philosophical Assumptions With Implications for Practice

Assumption	Question	Characteristics	Implications for Practice (examples)
Ontological	What is the nature of reality?	Reality is subjective and multiple, as seen by participants in the study	Researcher uses quotes and themes in words of participants and provides evidence of different perspectives
Epistemological	What is the relationship between the researcher and that being researched?	Researcher attempts to lessen distance between himself or herself and that being researched	Researcher collaborates, spends time in field with participants, and becomes an "insider"
Axiological	What is the role of values?	Researcher acknowledges that research is value laden and that biases are present	Researcher openly discusses values that shape the narrative and includes own interpretation in conjunction with interpretation of participants
Rhetorical	What is the language of research?	Researcher writes in a literary, informal style using the personal voice and uses qualitative terms and limited definitions	Researcher uses an engaging style of narrative, may use first-person pronoun, and employs the language of qualitative research
Methodological	What is the process of research?	Researcher uses inductive logic, studies the topic within its context, and uses an emerging design	Researcher works with particulars (details) before generalizations, describes in detail the context of the study, and continually revises questions from experiences in the field

or positive assumptions as they do, acknowledging that qualitative research is legitimate in its own right and does not need to be compared to achieve respectability. I add to their issues one of my own concerns, the rhetorical assumption, recognizing that one needs to attend to the language and terms of qualitative inquiry. Finally, I discuss the practical implications of each assumption and attempt to bridge philosophy with practice.

Briefly, the **ontological** issue addresses the nature of reality for the qualitative researcher; reality is constructed by individuals involved in the research situation. Thus, multiple realities exist, such as the realities of the researcher, those of individuals being investigated, and those of the reader or audience interpreting a study. The qualitative researcher needs to report these realities, rely on voices and interpretations of informants through extensive quotes, present themes that reflect words used by informants, and advance evidence of different perspectives on each theme. Thus, for example, in a phenomenological study, one reports multiple statements representing the diverse perspectives on the phenomenon being explored (Moustakas, 1994). In one of my grounded theory studies on balance between the personal and work lives of academic chairpersons, I attempt to find multiple perspectives within each theme and report divergent views (Creswell & Urbom, 1997).

On the **epistemological** assumption, the relationship of the researcher to that being researched, qualitative researchers interact with those they study, whether this interaction assumes the form of living with or observing informants over a prolonged period of time or actual collaboration. In short, the researcher tries to minimize the "distance" or "objective separateness" (Guba & Lincoln, 1988, p. 94) between himself or herself and those being researched. Thus, in ethnographic research, prolonged time in the field for the investigator minimizes the distance as the investigator's observational role shifts from that of an "outsider" to that of an "insider" during his or her stay in the field.

Undoubtedly, this role and the close distance between the researcher and the participants have implications for the **axiological** assumption, the role of values in a study. In a qualitative study, the investigator admits the value-laden nature of the study and actively reports his or her values and biases as well as the value-laden nature of information gathered from the field. In an interpretive biography, for example, the researcher's presence is apparent in the text, and the author admits that the stories voiced represent an interpretation and presentation of the author as much as the subject of the study.

Literary forms of writing such as the use of metaphors, the use of first-person "I," and a focus on stories pervade qualitative inquiries. Basing research on the **rhetorical** assumption means that the qualitative investigator uses specific terms and a personal and literary narrative in the study. Hence, instead of terms such as *internal validity, external validity, generalizability,* and *objectivity,* the qualitative researcher writing a case study may employ terms such as *credibility, transferability, dependability,* and *confirmability* (Lincoln & Guba, 1985) as well as naturalistic generalizations (Stake, 1995). Words such as *understanding, discover,* and *meaning* form the glossary of emerging qualitative terms and are important rhetorical markers in writing purpose statements and research questions to be discussed later. Moreover, the language of qualitative studies becomes personal, literary, and based on definitions that evolve during a study rather than being defined by the researcher at the beginning of a study. Seldom does one see an extensive "Definition of Terms" section in a qualitative study because the terms as defined by informants are of primary importance.

From these distinctions about reality, the relationship between the researcher and that being researched, the role of values, and the rhetoric of the study emerges the **methodological** assumption, how one conceptualizes the entire research process. In a qualitative methodology, the researcher *starts* inductively, although in grounded theory, for example, the initial inductive logic of generating open coding and generating a theory evolves into the deductive process of examining the theory against existing and new databases. But overall, the qualitative researcher works inductively, such as when he or she develops categories from informants rather than specifying them in advance of the research. In a case study, for example, the researcher details the description of the case and its setting or context before mentioning the more abstract themes. The investigator may "layer the analysis," presenting numerous themes initially, followed by grouping these themes into broader and more abstract categories later. In phenomenology, the researcher first details the individual statements of informants about experiences with the phenomenon before moving to meanings and clusters of meanings. This inductive approach to developing the qualitative narrative shows that the process is one of an emerging design. For example, a researcher begins a qualitative study with general questions and refines them as the study proceeds. In addition, the process of qualitative research includes a discussion of the context of the subject or case being studied. Nowhere is the context more apparent than in a qualitative case study, where one describes the setting for the case from the more general description to the specific description. Thus, in our gunman study (Asmussen & Creswell, 1995), we first present the city, the campus, the building, and finally the classroom and the gunman incident.

IDEOLOGICAL PERSPECTIVES

These philosophical assumptions mark all qualitative studies. In addition, the researcher may elect to use ideological perspectives to draw attention to the needs of people and social action. For example, a study may include a postmodern critique as a way of thinking about socially responsive research, a critical theory orientation toward action, or a feminist approach to research *for* women with gender issues of primary concern. The researcher may include one or more of these perspectives (or others related to cultural or marginalized groups) in different aspects of a study, such as in a conceptual perspective at the beginning of a study, in the approach to data collection, in self-disclosing comments throughout the qualitative narrative, or in issues chosen to study.

Why would a researcher use one of these perspectives? Ultimately, it turns, I believe, on the personal concerns of the researcher. These personal concerns may reflect a heartfelt need to promote social action, to lift the "voices" of marginalized or oppressed people, to explore gender issues that have served to dominate and repress women, or to bring about general change in our society. One of these perspectives may be ideal to use for studying certain groups such as marginalized minorities, oppressed gays and lesbians, or street people without a voice. Regardless of the reasons, these perspectives provide one more philosophical and conceptual framework that might guide a study.

Postmodernism

Thomas (1993) calls postmodernists "armchair radicals" (p. 23) who focus their critiques on changing ways of thinking rather than on calling for action based on these changes. Rather than viewing **post-modernism** as a theory, it might be considered a family of theories and perspectives that have something in common (Slife & Williams, 1995). Postmodernists advance a reaction to or critique of the 19th-century Enlightenment and early 20th-century emphasis on technology, rationality, reason, universals, science, and the positivist, scientific method (Bloland, 1995; Stringer, 1993). In response, postmodern thinking emerged in the humanities in the 1960s, gained momentum in the 1970s, and permeated the social sciences in the 1980s and 1990s. The basic concept is that knowledge claims must be set within the conditions of the world today and in the multiple perspectives of class, race, gender, and other group affiliations. These conditions are well articulated by individuals such as Foucault, Derrida, Lyotard, Giroux, and Freire (Bloland, 1995). These are negative conditions, and they show themselves in the presence of hierarchies, power and control by individuals in these hierarchies, and the multiple meanings of language. Also included in the conditions are the importance of different discourses, the importance of marginalized people and groups (the "other"), the presence of "meta-narratives" or universals that hold true regardless of the social conditions, and the need to "deconstruct" texts in terms of both reading and writing, examining and bringing to the surface concealed hierarchies as well as dominations, oppositions, inconsistencies, and contradictions (Bloland, 1995; Stringer, 1993). Denzin's (1989a) approach to "interpretive" biography, for example, draws on postmodernism in that his method is designed to study the turning points or problematic situations in which people find themselves during transition periods (Borgatta & Borgatta, 1992).

Thus, postmodernism is characterized by a number of interrelated characteristics rather than by a single definition (Thomas, 1993), and this thinking attunes empirical social researchers to the assumptions underlying their own empiricism and encourages a reading of all qualitative narratives as rhetoric, a certain state of social being (Agger, 1991). These interrelated characteristics can form, for example, the ideological base for ethnographies, biographies, or case studies. For example, regarding a "postmodern-influenced ethnography," Thomas (1993) writes that such a study might "confront the centrality of media-created realities and the influence of information technologies" (p. 25). Thomas also comments that narrative texts need to be challenged (and written), according to the postmodernists, for their "subtexts" of dominant meanings, a topic I address further in Chapter 9.

The postmodern perspective challenges meta-narratives or theories and is considered a "post-theory" perspective (Bloland, 1995). However, the postmodern perspective has found application in qualitative research through "solutions" (Bloland, 1995), and two are mentioned here: critical theory and feminist theory. These approaches form a conceptual lens for designing a qualitative study. Investigators might employ critical theory to bring about planned change, and feminist researchers might explore issues of gender and marginalization (for other types, such as Marxist and ethnic approaches, see Denzin & Lincoln, 1994). Although these solutions may support themes of postmodern thinking, not all critical theorists and feminist writers consider themselves postmodernist, and their solutions depart from postmodern thinking in the form of action-oriented research and their support for meta-narratives or theories.

Critical Theory

Critical theory first developed from the thinking of a group of German scholars in the 1920s, collectively called the Frankfurt School (Morrow & Brown, 1994). Variants of *critical theory* abound in all of the social science disciplines, but central themes that a critical researcher might explore include the scientific study of social institutions and their transformations through interpreting the meanings of social life; the historical problems of domination, alienation, and social struggles; and a critique of society and the envisioning of new possibilities (Fay, 1987; Morrow & Brown, 1994). These themes have methodological implications, and they privilege some methods over others. As Morrow and Brown (1994) claim,

As a research program ultimately linked to a critical-emancipatory knowledge interest, critical theory is distinguished clearly by a distinctive approach to methodology as a set of metatheoretical assumptions and privileged research design strategies, a core set of substantive commitments related to the analysis of crisis tendencies in advanced capitalism, and an explicit approach to normative theory and its relation to critique of ideologies. (p. 242)

What is this "distinctive approach to methodology"? Critical theory can be "defined by the particular configuration of methodological postures it embraces" (p. 241). The critical researcher might, for example, design an ethnographic study to include changes in how people think, encourage people to interact, form networks and action-oriented groups, and help individuals examine the conditions of their existence (Thomas, 1993). The end goal of the study might be social theorizing, which Morrow and Brown define as "the desire to comprehend and, in some case, transform (through praxis) the underlying orders of social life—those social and systemic relations that constitute society" (p. 211). The investigator accomplishes this, for example, through an intensive case study or across a small number of historically comparable cases of specific actors (biographies), mediations, or systems and through "ethnographic accounts (interpretive social psychology), componential taxonomies (cognitive anthropology), and formal models (mathematical sociology)" (p. 212). In critical action research in teacher education, for example, Kincheloe (1991) recommends the following steps:

1. The teacher looks for philosophical guidance for his or her research and teaching from perspectives of critical theory, feminist theory, postmodern analysis, liberation theology, Deweyan educational theory, Afrocentric epistemology, or indigenous people's knowledge.

2. The "critical teacher" then exposes the assumptions of existing research orientations, critiques of the knowledge base, and through these critiques reveals ideological effects on teachers, schools, and the culture's view of education.

3. The researcher then selects what to study—to see the schools and classrooms from unique angles.

4. The researcher employs a variety of research strategies, making sense of information collected in light of the system of meaning, gaining awareness of the theories and assumptions that guide practice, and viewing himself or herself as part of a wider cultural panorama.

5. In the end, this research involves a pedagogy of personal and social transformation.

The design of research within a critical theory approach, according to sociologist Agger (1991), falls into two broad categories: *methodological*, in that it affects the ways in which people write and read, and *substantive*, in the theories and topics of the investigator (e.g., theorize about the role of the state and culture in advanced capitalism). Methodologically, a qualitative researcher might do the following:

1. Write about the taken-for-granted interests of perspective, polemic, and politics and be explicit about them in the text.

2. Write about challenges to prevailing positivist approaches that conceal and hide key assumptions.

3. Write about the assumptions behind the literary presentation of the qualitative study.

4. Write about how the researcher's language presents his or her own voice.

5. Emphasize multiple methodologies (qualitative and quantitative) and multiple perspectives (class, race, and gender) on problems.

One example of critical theory research is the classical ethnography from Willis (1977) of the "lads" who participated in behavior (e.g., opposition to authority, informal groups, "having a laff" [p. 29]) as a form of resistance to their school. As a study of the reproduction of class identity, this research begins with an ethnography of the male white working class counter-school culture. The lads reject the system that oppressed them, and the study captures the moment of failed resistance among working class male youths in the transition from school to work. The final analysis by Willis is a discussion about the "processes of self-induction into the labour process [that] constitute an aspect of the regeneration of working class culture in general, and an important example of how this culture is related in complex ways to regulative state institutions" (p. 3). As a study of the manifestations of resistance and state regulation, it is a model study of the ways in which actors come to terms with and struggle against cultural forms that dominated them (Morrow & Brown, 1994).

Feminist Approaches

The theme of domination prevails in the feminist literature as well, but the subject matter is gender domination within a patriarchal society. Feminist research also embraces many of the tenets of postmodern critiques as a challenge to current society. In **feminist research approaches**, the goals are to establish collaborative and nonexploitative relationships, to place the researcher within the study so as to avoid objectification, and to conduct research that is transformative. It is a complex area of inquiry, with numerous frameworks (e.g., male oriented, white feminist oriented, able-bodied female oriented) and difficult issues (e.g., the absence and invisibility of women, who can be "knowers") (Olesen, 1994).

One of the leading scholars of this approach, Lather (1991), comments on the essential perspectives of this framework. Feminist researchers see gender as a basic organizing principle that shapes the conditions of their lives. It is "a lens that brings into focus particular questions" (Fox-Keller, 1985, p. 6). The questions feminists pose relate to the centrality of gender in the shaping of our consciousness. The aim of this ideological research is to "correct both the invisibility and distortion of female experience in ways relevant to ending women's unequal social position" (Lather, 1991, p. 71). Given these goals, the foci of questions, and themes, the feminist researcher might engage in procedures such as the following:

▼ *Conduct sequential interviews in an interactive, dialogic manner that entails self-disclosure on the part of the researcher and fosters a sense of collaboration.*

▼ *Conduct group interviews that provide potential for deeper probing and reciprocally educative encounters.*

▼   *Negotiate meanings of results with participants in the study.*

▼   *Strive to address issues of false consciousness and conceptual determinism.*

▼   *Be self-reflexive about what researchers experience as they conduct research.*

Another writer, Stewart (1994), translates feminist critiques and methodology into procedural guides. She suggests that researchers need to look for what has been left out in social science writing and to study women's lives and issues such as identities, sex roles, domestic violence, abortion activism, comparable worth, affirmative action, and the way in which women struggle with their social devaluation and powerlessness within their families. Also, researchers need to consciously and systematically include their own roles or positions and assess how they impact their understandings of a woman's life. In addition, she views women as having agency, the ability to make choices and resist oppression, and she suggests that researchers need to inquire into how a woman understands her gender, acknowledging that gender is a social contract that differs for each individual. Stewart highlights the importance of studying power relationships and an individual's social position and how they impact women. Finally, she sees each woman as different and recommends that scholars avoid the search for a unified or coherent self or voice.

THEORY USE AND THE FIVE TRADITIONS

Another perspective that researchers might use is that of theories. These **social science theories** provide an explanation, a predication, and a generalization about how the world operates. They may be posed by researchers at the broad philosophical level or at the more concrete substantive level. I now address the question: To what extent do qualitative researchers use a social science theory to guide their studies or frame questions in each of the five traditions of inquiry? Flinders and Mills (1993) ask a similar question: Should a theoretical lens frame the study, thus "raising questions and suggesting points of view"?

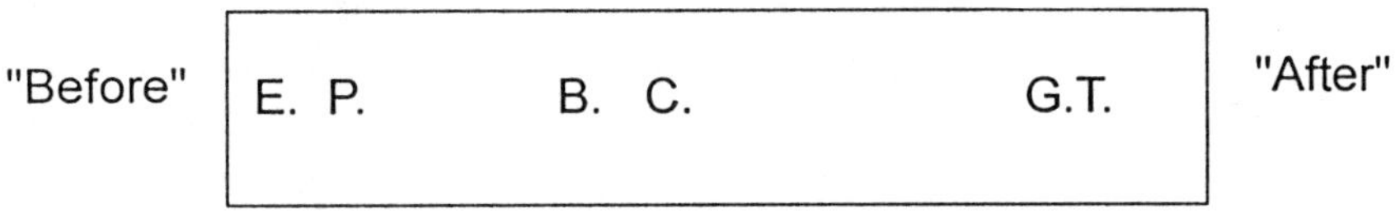

"Before" | E. P.   B. C.   G.T. | "After"

Figure 5.1 Extent of Theory Use in the Five Traditions
NOTE: B = biography; P = phenomenology; GT = grounded theory; E = ethnography;
C = case study.

(p. 49). Undoubtedly, I can only answer this question within the context of a particular study. But it is helpful, I believe, for anyone designing a study to consider how theory is used, broadly speaking, within each of the five traditions of inquiry. I think that some general guidelines can be advanced, and I illustrate these guidelines with the five article reviews presented in Chapter 3.

I conceptualize the five traditions of inquiry on a continuum, as shown in Figure 5.1. Taking a cue from a discussion with Wolcott (personal communication, February 13, 1993), I can array the traditions on this continuum according to whether they are used before the study (i.e., before asking questions and gathering data) or after the study (i.e., after data collection).

A biography. I position biography toward the middle of the continuum because theory use varies considerably in biographical studies. For example, Heilbrun (1988) believes the biographies should be framed at the outset by feminist theory. Moreover, Willis's (1977) study draws heavily on cultural theory at the beginning. Traditional models of biographical writing rely on studies that add to the theoretical knowledge in the social science (Denzin, 1989a; Helling, 1988). Perhaps less obvious, Angrosino (1994), in his sketch of Vonnie Lee, draws on anthropological-cultural themes. On the other hand, as an alternative to the traditional model, the interpretive approach of Denzin (1989a, 1989b) relies less on social science theories and turns to the meaning of experiences by the persons who experience them. Thus, in this approach, the investigator may not begin the study with a theoretical perspective that guides the study.

A phenomenology. On the continuum, I place phenomenology at the "before" end. For a phenomenologist, an a priori decision is made that he or she will examine the *meaning of experiences* for individuals. Thus, an individual starts into the field with a strong orienting framework, albeit more of a philosophical perspective than a distinct social science theory, although both provide explanations for the real world. This perspective, however, informs what will be studied and how it will be studied. I already have reviewed these core ideas in Chapter 4, but they are based on the premise that human experience makes sense to those who live it, prior to all interpretations and theorizing. Objective understanding is mediated by subjective experience, and that human experience is an inherent structural property of the experience itself, not constructed by an outside observer (Dukes, 1984). For example, in the Riemen (1986) study of caring interaction, the author specifies early in the study the philosophical grounds of phenomenology that guide the study.

A grounded theory study. At the most extreme end of the continuum, toward the "after" end, I place grounded theory. Strauss and Corbin (1990) are clear that one collects and analyzes data before using theory in a grounded theory study. This explains, for example, the women's sexual abuse study by Morrow and Smith (1995) in which they generate the theory through data collection, pose it at the end, and eschew prescribing a theory at the beginning of the study. In my own studies, I have refrained from advancing a theory at the beginning of my grounded theory research, generated the theory through data collection and analysis, posed the theory as a logic diagram, and introduced contending and contrasting theories with the model I generate at the end of my study (Creswell & Brown, 1992; Creswell & Urbom, 1997).

An ethnography. I see ethnography as an approach in which researchers bring a strong cultural lens to their study. Although this lens shapes their initial observations and questions in the field, it may be moderated and changed during fieldwork. Thus, I place ethnography at the "before" end of the continuum. For example, as mentioned by Fetterman (1989), most ethnographers use one of two cultural theories: ideational theories, which suggest that change is a result of mental activities and ideas, or materialistic theories, which hold that material conditions, such as resources, money, and modes of production, are prime movers. In Wolcott's (1994a) Principal Selection Committee study, he explores the cultural theme of the role behavior of both the prospective principals being interviewed and the committee conducting the interviews. Later, at the end of the study, we learn that one behavior exhibited by the committee was "variety-reducing" behavior.

A case study. I see qualitative case studies that employ theory in different ways, and so I position case studies at the midpoint on the continuum. Social science theories might be absent from the study with a focus on a description of the case and its issues (e.g., Stake, 1995), used to guide the study in an explanatory way (e.g., Yin, 1989), or employed toward the end of a study (e.g., Asmussen & Creswell, 1995). Stake's (1995) qualitative case study of reform in Harper School illustrates a descriptive, issue-oriented case study. The study begins by addressing issues of school reform and then a description of the school, the community, and the neighborhood. The format of description and issues continues throughout the study, and my assessment is that theory does not come into the study. On the other hand, a theory shapes the direction of McCormick's (1994) study. The study begins with the definition of a "nonreader" and then proceeds to the "theoretical bases for the study" (p. 158), framed within an interactive theory of reading ability and disability that predicts that failures and successes in literacy learning are related to external and internal factors. The study then proceeds to explore the experiences of an $8\frac{1}{2}$-year-old child. In our gunman case (Asmussen & Creswell, 1995), we do not position the study within any particular theoretical camp before data collection. However, after data collection, analysis, and formation of a theoretical model, we introduce theoretical perspectives of psychosocial and organizational perspectives to compare and contrast with our theoretical model, thus advancing a "theory-after" perspective.

SUMMARY

In this chapter, I situated qualitative research within the larger discussion about philosophical and theoretical frameworks that investigators bring to their studies. It is a complex area, and one that I can only begin to sketch with some clarity. I see, however, that the basic philosophical assumptions relate to ontology, epistemology, axiology, rhetoric, and methodology as central features of all qualitative studies. Furthermore, ideological perspectives often guide such studies, drawn broadly from postmodern concerns and specifically from orientations such as critical theory and feminism. These perspectives create issues for examination as well as procedures for conducting research. Finally, looking across the five types of traditions discussed in this book, I see that authors use social science theories to guide their studies in varying degrees. I find them at various points on a continuum representing whether the theory is used before the investigator poses questions and collects data or after data collection. As a general guide, I position the five traditions on a continuum and discuss the use of theory for each, reflecting on studies introduced in Chapter 3 and other illustrations of qualitative inquiry.

▼ ADDITIONAL READINGS

Several writers, in addition to Guba and Lincoln (1988), discuss the paradigm assumptions of qualitative research. In counseling psychology, Hoshmand (1989) reviews these assumptions. In education, see Sparkes (1992) or Cunningham and Fitzgerald (1996). In management, see Burrell and Morgan (1979) or Gioia and Pitre (1990).

Burrell, G., & Morgan, G. (1979). *Sociological paradigms and organizational analysis*. London: Heinemann.

Cunningham, J. W., & Fitzgerald, J. (1996). Epistemology and reading. *Reading Research Quarterly, 31*(1), 36-60.

Gioia, D. A., & Pitre, E. (1990). Multiparadigm perspectives on theory building. *Management Review, 15*, 584-602.

Guba, E., & Lincoln, Y. S. (1988). Do inquiry paradigms imply inquiry methodologies? In D. M. Fetterman (Ed.), *Qualitative approaches to evaluation in education* (pp. 89-115). New York: Praeger.

Hoshmand, L. L. S. T. (1989). Alternative research paradigms: A review and teaching proposal. *The Counseling Psychologist, 17*(1), 3-79.

Sparkes, A. C. (1992). The paradigms debate: An extended review and celebration of differences. In A. C. Sparkes (Ed.), *Research in physical education and sport: Exploring alternative visions* (pp. 9-60). London: Falmer.

For an introduction to postmodern thinking in the social sciences, see Rosenau (1992), Slife and Williams (1995), and the journal article by Bloland (1995).

Bloland, H. G. (1995). Postmodernism and higher education. *Journal of Higher Education, 66*, 521-559.

Rosenau, P. M. (1992). *Post-modernism and the social sciences: Insights, inroads, and intrusions.* Princeton, NJ: Princeton University Press.

Slife, B. D., & Williams, R. N. (1995). *What's behind the research? Discovering hidden assumptions in the behavioral sciences.* Thousand Oaks, CA: Sage.

For critical theory, see the following articles that provide an introduction to the subject: Bloland (1995), Agger (1991), and Carspecken and Apple (1992). For book-length works, see Morrow and Brown (1994), a useful book for drawing the connection between critical theory and methodology. Another book-length work that takes the critical theory discussion into ethnography is Thomas (1993).

Agger, B. (1991). Critical theory, poststructuralism, postmodernism: Their sociological relevance. In W. R. Scott & J. Blake (Eds.), *Annual review of sociology* (Vol. 17, pp. 105-131). Palo Alto, CA: Annual Reviews.

Bloland, H. G. (1995). Postmodernism and higher education. *Journal of Higher Education, 66*, 521-559.

Carspecken, P. F., & Apple, M. (1992). Critical qualitative research: Theory, methodology, and practice. In M. L. LeCompte, W. L.

Millroy, & J. Preissle (Eds.), *The handbook of qualitative research in education* (pp. 507-553). San Diego: Academic Press.

Morrow, R. A., & Brown, D. D. (1994). *Critical theory and methodology*. Thousand Oaks, CA: Sage.

Thomas, J. (1993). *Doing critical ethnography*. Newbury Park, CA: Sage.

For an introduction to feminist research and social science methods, see the articles or chapters by Roman (1992), Olesen (1994), and Stewart (1994). For book-length works, examine Harding (1987), Nielsen (1990), Lather (1991), Reinharz (1992), and Ferguson and Wicke (1994).

Ferguson, M., & Wicke, J. (1994). *Feminism and postmodernism*. Durham, NC: Duke University Press.

Harding, S. (1987). *Feminism and methodology*. Bloomington: Indiana University Press.

Lather, P. (1991). *Getting smart: Feminist research and pedagogy with/in the postmodern*. New York: Routledge.

Nielsen, J. M. (Ed.). (1990). *Feminist research methods: Exemplary readings in the social sciences*. Boulder, CO: Westview.

Olesen, V. (1994). Feminisms and models of qualitative research. In N. K. Denzin & Y. S. Lincoln (Eds.), *Handbook of qualitative research* (pp. 158-174). Thousand Oaks, CA: Sage.

Reinharz, S. (1992). *Feminist methods in social research*. New York: Oxford University Press.

Roman, L. G. (1992). The political significance of other ways of narrating ethnography: A feminist materialist approach. In M. L. LeCompte, W. L. Millroy, & J. Preissle (Eds.), *The handbook of qualitative research in education* (pp. 555-594). San Diego: Academic Press.

Stewart, A. J. (1994). Toward a feminist strategy for studying women's lives. In C. E. Franz & A. J. Stewart (Eds.), *Women creating lives: Identities, resilience and resistance* (pp. 11-35). Boulder, CO: Westview.

To examine the issue of the role of theory in qualitative research, I recommend the chapter in Merriam (1988), the compilation of chapters in the edited book by Flinders and Mills (1993), and the chapter in Creswell (1994).

Creswell, J. W. (1994). *Research design: Qualitative and quantitative approaches*. Thousand Oaks, CA: Sage.

Flinders, D. J., & Mills, G. E. (1993). *Theory and concepts in qualitative research*. New York: Columbia University, Teachers College Press.

Merriam, S. (1988). *Case study research in education: A qualitative approach*. San Francisco: Jossey-Bass.

EXERCISES

1. In the study you are planning to conduct, you may or may not use an ideological perspective. But it is good practice to consider how you might design this component into your proposed study. Take the study you have designed thus far (through the Exercises in Chapter 2-4) and select either a postmodern, critical theory, or feminist perspective. In the introduction to your proposed study and in your research questions, add this proposed perspective and discuss, specifically, how it will guide your study.

2. Take the five philosophical assumptions and design a matrix like Table 5.1 that includes a column for how you plan to address each assumption in your proposed study.

6
▼

Introducing and
Focusing the Study

The design of a qualitative study proceeds beyond the philosophical assumptions, perspectives, and theories into the introduction of a study. This introduction consists of stating the problem or issue leading to the study, formulating the central purpose of the study, and providing the research questions. Consistent with my view in this book, all three aspects of an introduction need to be related to a researcher's tradition of inquiry. To accomplish this, I return to two ideas mentioned in Chapter 1. In writing the problem, the purpose, and the questions, researchers have an opportunity for **encoding** with terms that signal to a reader the specific tradition being used. Also, researchers can use **foreshadowing** of ideas to be developed later within the specific data analysis procedures of a tradition. In this chapter, I develop how this might be accomplished and provide several examples from qualitative studies.

Questions for Discussion

▼ How does the problem statement, the issue or need for the study, reflect different "sources" of information, frame the existing literature, and relate to the foci of the traditions of inquiry in qualitative research?

▼ How does one pose the central research question in a study so that it encodes a tradition and foreshadows it?

▼ How can subquestions be presented in a study to both reflect the issues being explored and foreshadow the topics that will be presented in the analysis and qualitative report?

THE PROBLEM STATEMENT

In the first few paragraphs of a study, the researcher introduces the "problem" leading to the study. The term problem may be a misnomer, and individuals unfamiliar with writing research may struggle with this writing passage. Rather than calling this passage the "problem statement," it might be clearer if we call it the "need for the study." Why is this study needed, I ask? I address considering the "source" for the problem, framing it within the extant literature, and encoding and foreshadowing the text for a tradition of inquiry.

Research methods books (e.g., Marshall & Rossman, 1995) advance several needs or sources for conducting scholarly research. These needs may be based on personal experience with an issue, job-related problems, an adviser's research agenda, and/or the scholarly literature. Often the paragraphs denoting the problem will refer to one or more of these rationales. The strongest and most scholarly rationale for a study, I believe, follows from a documented need in the literature for increased understanding and dialogue about an issue. As suggested by Barritt (1986), the rationale

> is not the discovery of new elements, as in natural scientific study, but rather the heightening of awareness for experience which has been forgotten and overlooked. By heightening awareness and creating dialogue, it is hoped research can lead to better understanding of the way things appear to someone else and through that insight lead to improvements in practice. (p. 20)

Besides dialogue and understanding, a qualitative study may fill a void in existing literature, establish a new line of thinking, or assess an issue with an understudied group or population.

Researchers also situate or frame their studies within the larger existing literature. Although opinions differ about the extent of literature needed before a study begins, the qualitative texts I have read (e.g., Marshall & Rossman, 1995) all refer to the need to review the literature so that one can describe the studies about the problem to date and position one's study and ground it within this literature. I have found it helpful to visually depict where my study fits into the larger literature. For example, one might develop a research map (Creswell, 1994) of extant literature, organizing thoughts from the broader literature to the specific topic of study. Alternatively, concept mapping (Maxwell, 1996) or a conceptual framework (Miles & Huberman, 1994) present two comparable visual renderings of ideas.

In addition to determining the source of the problem and framing it within the literature and concepts, qualitative researchers need to encode the problem discussion with language that foreshadows their tradition of inquiry. This can be done, I believe, by mentioning the foci of the tradition of choice (see Chapter 3 for the discussion of foci). In a problem statement for a biographical study, for example, I would expect the writer to mention the need for learning from an individual and why this particular individual is important to study. For a phenomenological study, I should hear from the author that we need to know more about the "experiences" of individuals about a phenomenon and the meaning they ascribe to these experiences. For a grounded theory study, a theory takes center stage, and I would expect to learn how we need to modify an existing theory because it ill suits a population or issue or how we need to generate a theory because no existing theoretical perspective fits a particular issue. In an ethnographic study, the problem statement might include thoughts about why we need to describe and interpret the cultural behavior of a group of people. For a case study, the researcher should focus on an event, process, or program for which we have no in-depth perspective on this "case." Conducting the case study provides a picture to help inform our practice or to see unexplored details of the case. Thus, the need for the study, or the problem leading to it, can be related to the specific focus of the tradition of choice.

THE PURPOSE STATEMENT

This interrelationship between design and tradition continues with the purpose statement, the major objective or intent for the study that provides an essential "road map" for the reader. As a critical statement in the entire qualitative study, it needs to be given careful attention and be written in clear and concise language. Unfortunately, all too many writers leave this statement implicit, causing readers extra work in deciphering the central thrust of a project. This need not be the case, and I offer a "script" of this statement (Creswell, 1994), a statement containing several sentences and blanks that an individual fills in:

> The purpose of this _____ (biographical, phenomeno-
> logical, grounded theory, ethnographic, case) study is (was? will be?)
> to _____ (understand? describe? develop? discover?) the
> _____ (central focus for the study) for _____
> (the unit of analysis: a person? processes? groups? site?). At this stage in
> the research, the _____ (central focus being studied)
> will be generally defined as _____ (provide a gen-
> eral definition of the central concept).

Notice immediately that I have used several terms to encode the passage for a specific tradition of inquiry:

▼ *The writer identifies the specific tradition of inquiry being used in the study by mentioning the type.* The name of the tradition comes first in the passage, thus foreshadowing the inquiry approach for data collection, analysis, and report writing.

▼ *The writer encodes the passage with words that indicate the* action *of the researcher and the* focus *of the tradition.* For example, I associate words such as *understand* (useful in biographical studies), *describe* (useful in case studies, ethnographies, and phenomenologies), *develop* or *generate* (useful in grounded theory), and *discover* (useful in all traditions) with the traditions. As shown in Figure 6.1, I identify several words that researchers include in their purpose statements to encode the purpose statements for their traditions. These words indicate not only the researchers' actions but also the foci and outcomes of the studies.

▼ *The writer foreshadows data collection in this statement, whether he or she plans to study an individual (i.e., biography, possibly case study or ethnography), several individuals (i.e., grounded theory or phenomenol-*

Biography	Phenomenology	Grounded Theory	Ethnography	Case Study
• Biography (or oral history or life history) • Classical • Interpretive • Individual • Stories • Epiphanies	• Phenomenolog- ical study • Describe • Experiences • Meaning • Essence	• Gounded theory • Generate • Develop • Propositions • Process • Substantive theory	• Ethnography • Culture- sharing group • Cultural behavior and language • Cultural portrait • Cultural themes	• Case study • Bounded • Single or collective case • Event, process, program, individual

Figure 6.1 Words to Use in Encoding the Purpose Statement

ogy), a group (i.e., ethnography), or a site (i.e., program, event, activity, or place in a case study).

▼ *I include the central focus and a general definition for it in the purpose statement.* This focus may be difficult to determine in any specificity in advance. But, for example, in a biography, a writer might define or describe the specific aspect of the life to be explored (e.g., life stages, childhood memories, the transition from adolescence to adulthood, attendance at an Alcoholics Anonymous meeting). In a phenomenology, the central phenomenon to be explored might be specified such as the meaning of grief, anger, or even chess playing (Aanstoos, 1985). In grounded theory, the central phenomenon might be identified, although it is likely to change or be modified during data collection and analysis. In an ethnography, the writer might identify the key cultural concepts being examined such as roles, behaviors, acculturation, communication, myths, stories, or other concepts that the researcher plans to take into the field at the beginning of the study. Finally, in a case study such as an "intrinsic" case study, the writer might define the boundaries of the case, specifying how the case is bounded in time and place. If an "instrumental" case study is desired, then the researcher might specify and define generally the issue being examined in the case.

Several examples of purpose statements follow that illustrate the encoding and foreshadowing of traditions:

Example 6.1   A Biographical Example

From a biography of Charles Darwin and field lessons learned while studying his documents:

> In this essay, I raise nearly a dozen "interpretive asides," perhaps better called "speculations" (if not conjectures), that arose as I read and reflected upon the letters Darwin wrote to his family. (Smith, 1987, p. 9)

Example 6.2   A Phenomenological Example

From a study of doctoral advisement relationships between women:

> Given the intricacies of power and gender in the academy, what are doctoral advisement relationships between women advisors and women advisees really like? Because there were few studies exploring women doctoral students' experiences in the literature, a phenomenological study devoted to understanding women's lived experiences as advisees best lent itself to examining this question. (Heinrich, 1995, p. 449)

Example 6.3   A Grounded Theory Example

From a grounded theory study of academic change in higher education:

> The primary purpose of this article is to present a grounded theory of academic change that is based upon research guided by two major research questions: What are the major sources of academic change? What are the major processes through which academic change occurs? For purposes of this paper, grounded theory is defined as theory generated from data systematically obtained and analyzed through the constant comparative method. (Conrad, 1978, p. 101)

Example 6.4   An Ethnographic Example

From an ethnography of "ballpark" culture:

> This article examines how the work and the talk of stadium employees reinforce certain meanings of baseball in society, and it reveals how this

work and talk create and maintain ballpark culture. (Trujillo, 1992, p. 351)

Example 6.5   A Case Study Example

From a case study using a feminist perspective to examine how men exploit women's labor in the sport of lawn bowls at the "Roseville Club":

> Although scholars have shown that sport is fundamental in constituting and reproducing gender inequalities, little attention has been paid to sport and gender relations in later life. In this article we demonstrate how men exploit women's labor in the sport of lawn bowls, which is played predominately by older people. (Boyle & McKay, 1995, p. 556)

THE RESEARCH QUESTIONS

Several of these examples illustrate the interweaving of problems, research questions, and purpose statements. For purposes of this discussion, I separate them out, although in practice some researchers combine them. But, in many instances, the research questions are distinct and easily found in a study. Once again, I find these questions to provide an opportunity to encode and foreshadow a tradition of inquiry.

The Central Question

Several writers offer suggestions for writing qualitative research questions (e.g., Creswell, 1994; Miles & Huberman, 1994). These questions are open-ended, evolving, and nondirectional; restate the purpose of the study in more specific terms; start with words such as "what" or "how" rather than "why"; and are few in number (five to seven). They are posed in various forms, from the "grand tour" (Spradley, 1979, 1980) that asks, "Tell me about yourself," to more specific questions.

I recommend that a researcher reduce her or his entire study to a single, overarching question and several subquestions. Drafting this central question often takes considerable work because of its breadth and the tendency of some to form specific questions based on traditional training. To reach the overarching question, I ask qualitative researchers to state the broadest question they could possibly pose about their studies.

This central question can be encoded with the language of a tradition of inquiry. Morse (1994) speaks directly to this issue as she reviews the types of research questions. Although she does not refer to biographies or case studies, she mentions that one finds "descriptive" questions of cultures in an ethnography, "process" questions in grounded theory studies, and "meaning" questions in phenomenological studies. For example, I reviewed the five studies presented in Chapter 3 for their central research questions.

In the life history of Vonnie Lee, Angrosino (1994) does not pose a central question, but I can infer from statements about the purpose of the study that the central question might be, "How would the life history of a man with mental retardation be described and analyzed?" In the phenomenological study of the caring interactions between nurse and patient, Riemen (1986) poses the central question succinctly in the opening of the article: "From the perspective of the client, what is the essential structure of a caring nurse-client interaction?" (p. 86). In the grounded theory study of 11 women's survival and coping with childhood sexual abuse, Morrow and Smith (1995) do not present a central question in the introduction, but they mention several broad questions that guided their interviewing of the women: "Tell me, as much as you are comfortable sharing with me right now, what happened to you when you were sexually abused" and "What are the primary ways in which you survived?" (p. 25). In the ethnographic account of the Principal Selection Committee, Wolcott (1994a) states his purpose for conducting the study rather than presenting a central question, but his question might have been, "How might the episode of the behavior of a small group of individuals selecting a principal be described and interpreted?" Finally, in our case study of a campus response to a gunman incident (Asmussen & Creswell, 1995), we asked five central guiding questions in our introduction: "What happened? Who was involved in response to the incident? What themes of response emerged during the eight-month period that followed this incident? What theoretical constructs helped us understand the campus response, and what constructs were unique to this case?" (p. 576).

Subquestions

An author typically presents a small number of subquestions that follow the central question. One model for conceptualizing these subquestions is to present them in two sets: issue questions and topical questions. According to Stake (1995), *issue subquestions* address the major concerns and perplexities to be resolved. The issue-oriented questions, for example,

> are not simple and clean, but intricately wired to political, social, historical, and especially personal contexts. . . . Issues draw us toward observing, even teasing out the problems of the case, the conflictual outpourings, the complex backgrounds of human concern. (Stake, 1995, p. 17)

Topical subquestions cover the anticipated needs for information. These questions, "call for information needed for description of the case. . . . A topical outline will be used by some researchers as the primary conceptual structure and by others as subordinate to the issue structure" (Stake, 1995, p. 25). I extend Stake's concept of topical questions to include specific procedures of data analysis and presentation in a tradition of inquiry. These "topics to be covered" can mirror the procedures the researcher intends to use in their tradition of inquiry and foreshadow what the reader will find later in the study. Several illustrations in the following present the issue and topical subquestion format for a study.

In writing a *biography*, Denzin (1989b) suggests that research questions follow an interpretive format and be formulated into a single statement, beginning with why, not how, and starting with one's own personal history and building on other information. From his own studies, Denzin illustrates types of issue questions: "How is emotion, as a form of consciousness, lived, experienced, articulated and felt?" "How do ordinary men and women live and experience the alcoholic self active alcoholism produces?" (p. 50).

Then, one could pose topical questions that relate to the manner or procedure in which the "substantive" questions are to be analyzed. These questions might include the following:

- What are the object experiences in this individual's life?

- What is the story that can be told from these experiences?

- What are some narrative segments that illustrate the meanings of this individual's life?

- What are some theories that relate to this individual's life?

In an example of a *phenomenological* study, Riemen (1986) poses this question in the nursing-caring interaction study: "What is essential for the experience to be described by the client as being a caring interaction?" (p. 91). Although this is a central question, it also is issue oriented. By adding a set of topical questions, one foreshadows the steps in the data analysis. For example, following Moustakas's (1994, p. 99) procedures, one might ask the following questions:

- What are the possible structural meanings of the experience?

- What are the underlying themes and contexts that account for the experience?

- What are the universal structures that precipitate feelings and thoughts about the experience?

- What are the invariant structural themes that facilitate a description of the experience?

To illustrate both issue and topical questions in a study, Gritz (1995, p. 4) models this approach. She develops a phenomenological project to construct an understanding of "teacher professionalism" as it is understood by practicing elementary classroom teachers. She poses two sets of questions, one issue-oriented and the other topical:

Issue questions:

1. What does it mean (to practitioners) to be a professional teacher?

   a. What are the structural meanings of teacher professionalism?
   b. What are the underlying themes and contexts that account for this view of teacher professionalism?
   c. What are the universal structures that precipitate feelings and thoughts about "teacher professionalism"?
   d. What are the invariant structural themes that facilitate a description of "teacher professionalism" as it is experienced by practicing elementary classroom teachers?

Topical questions:

2. What do professional teachers do?

3. What don't professional teachers do?

4. Describe one person who exemplifies the term *teacher professionalism*.

5. What is difficult/easy about being a professional educator?

6. How/when did you first become aware of being a professional?

For a *grounded theory study*, the topical subquestions might be posed as aspects of the coding steps such as open coding, axial coding, selective coding, and the development of propositions:

- What are the general categories to emerge in a first review of the data? (open coding)

- Given the phenomenon of interest, what caused it? What contextual and intervening conditions influenced it? What strategies or outcomes resulted from it? What were the consequences of these strategies? (axial coding)

For example, in Mastera's (1995) dissertation proposal, she advances a study of the process of revising the general education curriculum in three private baccalaureate colleges. Her plan calls for both issue and topical questions. The issue questions that guide her study are "What is the theory that explains the change process in the revision of general education curricula on three college campuses?" and "How does the chief academic officer participate in the process on each campus?" She then poses several topical subquestions specifically related to open and axial coding:

1. How did the process unfold?

2. What were the major events or benchmarks in the process?

3. What were the obstacles to change?

4. Who were the important participants? How did they participate in the process?

5. What were the outcomes?

In another study, Valerio (1995) uses grounded theory questions directly related to the steps in grounded theory data analysis:

> The overarching question for my grounded theory research study is: What theory explains why teenage girls become pregnant? The sub-questions follow the paradigm for developing a theoretical model. The questions seek to explore each of the interview coding steps and include: What are the general categories to emerge in open coding? What central phenomenon emerges? What are its causal conditions? What specific interaction issues and larger conditions have been influential? What are the resulting associated strategies and outcomes? (p. 3)

In an *ethnography*, one might present topical subquestions that relate to (a) a description of the context, (b) an analysis of the major themes, and (c) the interpretation of cultural behavior (Wolcott, 1994b). Alternatively, using Spradley (1979, 1980), these topical subquestions might reflect Spradley's 12 steps in his "decision research sequence." They might be as follows:

- What is the social situation to be studied?

- How does one go about observing this situation?

- What is recorded about this situation?

- What is observed about this situation?

- What cultural domains emerge from studying this situation?

- What more specific, focused observations can be made?

- What taxonomy emerges from these focused observations?

- Looking more selectively, what observations can be made?

- What components emerge from these observations?

- What themes emerge?

- What is the emerging cultural inventory?

- How does one write the ethnography?

In using good question format for our gunman *case study* (Asmussen & Creswell, 1995), I would redraft our questions as presented in the article. To foreshadow the case of a single campus and individuals on it, I would pose the central question, "What was the campus response to the gunman incident at the midwestern university?" and then I would present the issue subquestions guiding my study (although we present these questions more as central questions, as already noted):

1. What happened?

2. Who was involved in response to the incident?

3. What themes of response emerged during the 8-month period that followed this incident?

4. What theoretical constructs helped us understand the campus response?

5. What constructs were unique to this case? (p. 576)

Then, I would present the topical procedural questions:

1. How might the campus (case), and the events following the incident, be described? (description of the case)

2. What themes emerge from gathering information about the case? (analysis of the case materials)

3. How would I interpret these themes within larger social and psychological theories? (lessons learned from the case surrounded by the literature)

These illustrations show that, in a qualitative study, one can write subquestions that address issues on the topic being explored and use terms that encode the work within a tradition. Also, topical subquestions can foreshadow the steps in the procedures of data collection, analysis, and narrative format construction.

SUMMARY

In this chapter, I addressed three topics related to introducing and focusing a qualitative study: the problem statement, the purpose statement, and the research questions. Although I discussed general features of designing each section in a qualitative study, I related the topic to traditions of inquiry. The problem statement should indicate the source of the issue leading to the study, be framed in terms of existing literature, and be related to the focus of a specific tradition of inquiry. The purpose statement also should include terms that encode the statement for a specific tradition. By including comments about the site or people to be studied, it foreshadows the tradition as well. The research questions continue this encoding for a tradition in the central question, the overarching question being addressed in the study. Following the central question are subquestions, and I expand a model presented by Stake (1995) that groups subquestions into two sets: issue subquestions, which address the major concerns in the study, and topical subquestions, which anticipate needs for information. These anticipated needs, I further contend, can be presented as steps or phases in data analysis and reporting the study. Thus, they foreshadow how the researcher will be presenting and analyzing the information within a tradition of inquiry. Examples show how both issue and topical subquestions can be designed with each of the five traditions of inquiry.

▼ ADDITIONAL READINGS

For writing problem statements in general, examine Marshall and Rossman (1995). For several basic principles in writing purpose statements, explore Creswell (1994) and references mentioned in my chapter on writing purpose statements. For a good overview of writing research questions, I recommend Miles and Huberman (1994). Also, in standard qualitative texts, most authors address qualitative research questions (e.g., Glesne and Peshkin, 1992; Maxwell, 1996). I particularly like the conceptualization of issue and topical questions by Stake (1995). Also, the reader should examine qualitative journal articles and reports to find good illustrations of problem statements, purpose statements, and research questions.

Creswell, J. W. (1994). *Research design: Qualitative and quantitative approaches*. Thousand Oaks, CA: Sage.

Glesne, C., & Peshkin, A. (1992). *Becoming qualitative researchers: An introduction*. White Plains, NY: Longman.

Marshall, C., & Rossman, G. B. (1995). *Designing qualitative research* (2nd ed.). Thousand Oaks, CA: Sage.

Maxwell, J. (1996). *Qualitative research design: An interactive approach*. Thousand Oaks, CA: Sage.

Miles, M. B., & Huberman, A. M. (1994). *Qualitative data analysis: A sourcebook of new methods* (2nd ed.). Thousand Oaks, CA: Sage.

Stake, R. (1995). *The art of case study research*. Thousand Oaks, CA: Sage.

WRITING EXERCISES

EXERCISES

1. For the study you are designing, rewrite the central question you designed in the Exercises in Chapter 2 for your tradition of inquiry, following the guidelines in this chapter for good question construction.

2. In this chapter, I have presented a model for writing the subquestions in an issue and topical format. Write five to seven issue-oriented subquestions and five to seven topical or procedural subquestions in your tradition of inquiry for your study.

7

▼

Data Collection

Data collection offers one more instance for assessing research design within each tradition of inquiry. However, before exploring this point, I find it useful to visualize the phases of data collection common to all traditions. A "circle" of interrelated activities best displays this process, a process of engaging in activities that include but go beyond collecting data.

I begin this chapter by presenting this circle of activities, briefly introducing each activity. These activities are locating a site or individual, gaining access and making rapport, sampling purposefully, collecting data, recording information, exploring field issues, and storing data. Then I explore how these activities vary by tradition of inquiry, advance a table that summarizes these differences, and end with a few summary comments about comparing the data collection activities across the five traditions.

Questions for Discussion

▼ How might the data collection process and the activities in the process be visualized?

▼ What are typical access and rapport issues in each tradition?

▼ How does one select people or places to study in each tradition?

▼ What type of information typically is collected in each tradition?

▼ How is information recorded in each tradition?

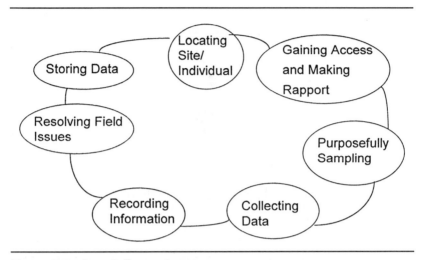

Figure 7.1 Data Collection Activities

▼ What are common issues in collecting data in each tradition?

▼ How is information typically stored in each tradition?

▼ How do the five traditions differ in the activities of data collection?

A DATA COLLECTION CIRCLE

I visualize data collection as a series of interrelated activities aimed at gathering good information to answer emerging research questions. As shown in Figure 7.1, a qualitative researcher engages in a series of activities in the process of collecting data. Although I start with locating a site or an individual to study, an investigator may begin at another entry point in the circle. Most important, I want the researcher to consider the multiple phases in collecting data, phases that extend beyond the typical reference point of conducting interviews or making observations.

An important step in the process is to find people or places to study and to gain access and establish rapport so that participants will provide good data. A closely interrelated step in the process involves determining a strategy for the purposeful sampling of individuals or sites. This is not a probability sampling so that statistical inferences can be made; rather, it is sampling so that one can best study the problem under examination. The researcher needs to determine the type of purposeful sampling from the array of possibilities and present a rationale for the selected approach.

Once the investigator selects the sites or people, decisions need to be made about the most appropriate data collection approaches. Increasingly, a qualitative inquirer faces newer and more innovative approaches such as e-mail messages, and usually a study involves more than a single source of data. To collect this information, the researcher develops protocols or written forms for recording the information and needs to assess the logistics of this recording process. Also, noting and being aware of potentially difficult field issues that may compromise the data, lead to premature exit from the field or site, and/or contribute to lost information is an important consideration. Finally, an investigator must decide how he or she will store data to find them easily and to protect them from damage or loss.

I now turn to each of these data collection activities, and I address each for general procedures and approaches within each tradition of inquiry. As shown in Table 7.1, these activities are both different and similar across the five traditions of inquiry.

THE SITE OR INDIVIDUAL

In a *biographical study*, one needs to find an individual to study, an individual who is accessible, willing to provide information, and distinctive for her or his accomplishments and ordinariness or who sheds light on a specific phenomenon or issue being explored. Plummer (1983) recommends two sources of subjects to study. The pragmatic approach is where an individual is met on a chance encounter, a subject of interest emerges from a wider study, or an individual volunteers. Alternatively, one might identify a "marginal person" who lives in conflicting cultures, a "great person" who impacts the age in which he or she lives, or an "ordinary person" who provides an example of a large population.

In a *phenomenological study*, the participants may be located at a single site, although they need not be. Most important, they must be individuals who have experienced the phenomenon being explored and can articulate their conscious experiences. Likewise, in a *grounded theory study*, the individuals may not be located at a single site; in fact,

TABLE 7.1 Data Collection Activities and the Five Traditions

Data Collection Activity	Biography	Phenomenology	Grounded Theory	Ethnography	Case Study
What is traditionally studied? (site/individual[s])	Single individual, accessible and distinctive	Multiple individuals who have experienced the phenomenon	Multiple individuals who have responded to action or participated in a process about a central phenomenon	Members of a culture-sharing group or individuals representative of the group	A bounded system such as a process, activity, event, program, or multiple individuals
What are typical access and rapport issues? (access and rapport)	Gaining permission from individuals, obtaining access to information in archives	Finding people who have experienced the phenomenon	Locating a homogeneous sample	Gaining access through gatekeeper, gaining confidence of informants	Gaining access through gatekeeper, gaining confidence of participants
How does one select sites or individuals to study? (purposeful sampling strategies)	Several strategies depending on person (e.g., convenient, politically important, typical, a critical case)	Finding individuals who have experienced the phenomenon, a "criterion" sample	Finding a homogeneous sample, a "theory-based" sample, a "theoretical" sample	Finding a cultural group to which one is a "stranger," a "representative" sample	Finding a "case" or "cases," an "atypical" case, or a "maximum variation" or "extreme" case

What type of information typically is collected? (forms of data)	Documents and archival material, open-ended interviews, subject journaling, participant observation, casual chatting	Interviews with up to 10 people	Primarily interviews with 20-30 people to achieve detail in the theory	Participant observations, interviews, artifacts, and documents	Extensive forms such as documents and records, interviews, observation, and physical artifacts
How is information recorded? (recording information)	Notes, interview protocol	Long interview protocol	Interview protocol, memoing	Fieldnotes, interview and observational protocols	Field notes, interview and observational protocols
What are common data collection issues? (field issues)	Access to materials, authenticity of account and materials	Bracketing one's experiences, logistics of interviewing	Interviewing issues (e.g., logistics, openness)	Field issues (e.g., reflexivity, reactivity, reciprocality, "going native," divulging private information, deception)	Interviewing and observing issues
How is information typically stored? (storing data)	File folders, computer files	Transcriptions, computer files	Transcriptions, computer files	Field notes, transcriptions, computer files	Fieldnotes, transcriptions, computer files

if they are dispersed, then they can provide important contextual information useful in the axial coding phase of research. They need to be individuals who have taken an action or participated in a process that is central to the grounded theory study. For example, in Creswell and Brown (1992), we interview 32 department chairpersons located across the United States.

In an *ethnographic study*, however, a single site is important where an intact culture-sharing group has developed shared values, beliefs, and assumptions. The researcher needs to select a group (or an individual or individuals representative of a group) to study, preferably one to which the investigator is a "stranger" (Agar, 1986) and can gain access. For a *case study*, the site (or sites) also is important, but it is much more circumscribed than an entire cultural system in an ethnography. These sites may be programs, events, processes, activities, or multiple individuals. Although Stake (1995) refers to an individual as an appropriate "case," I turn to the biographical approach or the life history approach in studying a single individual. However, the study of multiple individuals, each defined as a case and considered a collective case study, seems acceptable practice.

I need to register a cautionary note, as do ethnographers such as Glesne and Peshkin (1992), about studying a site or people in whom one has a vested interest. Glesne and Peshkin question research that examines "your own *backyard*—within your own institution or agency, or among friends or colleagues" (p. 21; emphasis added). This form of qualitative research attracts many students of qualitative research because studying one's own backyard provides easy access to informants and information at minimal cost. Undoubtedly, qualitative researchers bring their values, biases, and understandings to a project, and intimate knowledge of a setting may be an asset. But the negatives outweigh the positives. Studying such people or sites establishes expectations for data collection that may severely compromise the value of the data; individuals might withhold information, slant information toward what they want the researcher to hear, or provide "dangerous knowledge" that is political and risky for an "inside" investigator (Glesne & Peshkin, 1992). Also, especially in ethnographic research, the investigator tracks norms and values of which participants in the culture may not be aware; being an insider may not yield this information. Unless a compelling argument can be made for studying the "backyard," I would advise against it. In the Principal Selection Committee study, Wolcott (1994a) mentions that he might have studied the role of the principal by obtaining a principal's position, but, he cautions, "I had become acutely aware of the limitations on one's ability to objectively observe processes in which . . . [he or she] . . . is deeply involved as a participant" (p. 117).

ACCESS AND RAPPORT

Gaining access to the site or individual(s) also involves several steps. Regardless of the tradition of inquiry, permissions need to be sought from a human subjects review board, a process in which a campus committee reviews research studies for their potential harmful impact on subjects (or participants). This process involves submitting a proposal to the board that details the procedures in the project. Most qualitative studies are exempt from a lengthy review (e.g., the expedited or full review), but studies involving individuals as minors (i.e., 18 years or under) or studies of sensitive populations (e.g., HIV-positive individuals) require the expedited or full review, a process involving detailed, lengthy applications and an expanded time for review. Because many review boards are more familiar with the *quantitative* approaches to social and human science research than they are to *qualitative* approaches, the qualitative project description may need to conform to standard procedures and language in positivist research (e.g., hypotheses, subjects, results) as well as information about the protection of human subjects. As shown in Figure 7.2, the actual consent form that participants complete in a study addresses the following:

■ Their right to voluntarily withdraw from the study at any time.

■ The central purpose of the study and the procedures to be used in data collection.

■ Comments about protecting the confidentiality of the respondents.

■ A statement about known risks associated with participation in the study.

"Experiences in Learning Qualitative Research: A Qualitative Case Study"

The following information is provided for you to decide whether you wish to participate in the present study. You should be aware that you are free to decide not to participate or to withdraw at any time without affecting your relationship with this department, the instructor, or the University of Nebraska–Lincoln.

The purpose of this study is to understand the process of learning qualitative research in a doctoral-level college course. The procedure will be a single, holistic case study design. At this stage in the research, process will be generally defined as perceptions of the course and making sense out of qualitative research at different phases in the course.

Data will be collected at three points—at the beginning of the course, at the midpoint, and at the end of the course. Data collection will involve documents (journal entries made by students and the instructor, student evaluations of the class and the research procedure), audio-visual material (a videotape of the class), interviews (transcripts of interviews between students), and classroom observation field notes (made by students and the instructor). Individuals involved in the data collection will be the instructor and the students in the class.

Do not hesitate to ask any questions about the study either before participating or during the time that you are participating. We would be happy to share our findings with you after the research is completed. However, your name will not be associated with the research findings in any way, and your identity as a participant will be known only to the researchers.

There are no known risks and/or discomforts associated with this study.

The expected benefits associated with your participation are the information about the experiences in learning qualitative research, the opportunity to participate in a qualitative research study, and co-authorship for those students who participate in the detailed analysis of the data. If submitted for publication, a byline will indicate the participation of all students in the class.

Please sign your consent with full knowledge of the nature and purpose of the procedures. A copy of this consent form will be given to you to keep.

_____   _____

Signature of Participant   Date

John W. Creswell, Ed. Psy., UNL, Principal Investigator 402-472-2248

Figure 7.2   Sample Human Subjects Consent to Participate Form

- The expected benefits to accrue to the participants in the study.

- A place for them to sign and date the form (a place for the researcher to sign and date also may be offered).

For a *biographical study,* inquirers gain information from individuals by obtaining their permission to participate in the study. Study subjects should be appraised of the motivation of the researcher for their selection, granted anonymity (if they desire it), and told by the researcher about the purpose of the study. This disclosure helps build rapport. Access to biographical documents and archives requires permission and perhaps travel to distant libraries.

In a *phenomenological study,* the access issue is limited to finding individuals who have experienced the phenomenon and gaining their written permission to be studied. In Riemen's (1986) study, for example, she found 10 nonhospitalized adults over 18 years of age who had prior interactions with registered nurses and who could articulate their experiences. Because of the in-depth nature of extensive and multiple interviews with participants, it is convenient for the researcher to obtain people who are easily accessible.

The access through individual permission to be studied also is part of a *grounded theory study.* This group needs to provide permission to be studied and needs to have rapport with the researcher to disclose detailed perspectives about responding to an action or process. The grounded theorist starts with a homogeneous sample, individuals who have commonly experienced the action or process. In an *ethnography,* access typically begins with a *"gatekeeper,"* an individual who is a member of or has insider status with a cultural group. This gatekeeper is the initial contact for the researcher and leads the researcher to other informants (Hammersley & Atkinson, 1995). Approaching this gatekeeper and the cultural system slowly is sage advice for "strangers" studying the culture. Gaining access through the gatekeeper and establishing rapport with the case being studied also are important for a *case study.* For both ethnographies and case studies, gatekeepers require information about the studies that includes the following points (usually submitted in writing), as Bogdan and Biklen (1992) suggest:

- Why was the site chosen for study?

- What will be done at the site during the research study? (time and resources required by participants and amount of time to be spent at the site by the researcher)

- Will the researcher's presence be disruptive?

■ How will the results be reported?

■ What will the gatekeeper gain from the study?

PURPOSEFUL SAMPLING STRATEGY

The purposeful selection of participants represents a key decision point in a qualitative study. Researchers designing qualitative studies need clear criteria in mind and need to provide rationales for their decisions. I recommend that qualitative researchers, regardless of tradition, examine the typology of 16 strategies for purposeful sampling advanced by Miles and Huberman (1994). As shown in Figure 7.3, the authors identify the purpose for each sampling option. I especially like when writers can identify their specific strategies, offer definitions for them, and provide brief rationales for their use. I illustrate this approach for each of the five traditions.

In a *biographical study*, the individual may be "convenient" to study because she or he is available, may be a "politically important case" who attracts attention or is marginalized, or may be a "typical" case, the ordinary person. Inquirers may select several options depending on whether the person is marginal, great, or ordinary (Plummer, 1983). Vonnie Lee, who consented to participate and provide insightful information about the mentally retarded (Angrosino, 1994), was convenient to study but also was a "critical case" who permitted generalization and application to individuals with mental retardation.

I find, however, a much more narrow range of sampling strategies for a *phenomenological study*. It is essential that all participants experience the phenomenon being studied. "Criterion" sampling works well when all individuals studied represent people who have experienced the phenomenon. All individuals meet this criterion. For a *grounded theory study*, the investigator chooses participants based on their ability to contribute to an evolving theory. Using the terms of Miles and Huberman (1994), this process is "theory based," but in grounded theory the term is **theoretical sampling**, which means that the investigator examines individuals who can contribute to the evolving theory. This begins with selecting and studying a homogeneous sample of individuals (e.g., all women who have experienced childhood abuse) and then, after developing the theory, selecting and studying a heterogeneous sample (e.g., types of support groups other than

Type of Sampling	Purpose
Maximum variation	Documents diverse variations and identifies important common patterns
Homogeneous	Focuses, reduces, simplifies, and facilitates group interviewing
Critical case	Permits logical generalization and maximum application of information to other cases
Theory based	Find examples of a theoretical construct and thereby elaborate on and examine it
Confirming and disconfirming cases	Elaborate on initial analysis, seek exceptions, looking for variation
Snowball or chain	Identifies cases of interest from people who know people who know what cases are information-rich
Extreme or deviant case	Learn from highly unusual manifestations of the phenomenon of interest
Typical case	Highlights what is normal or average
Intensity	Information-rich cases that manifest the phenomenon intensely but not extremely
Politically important cases	Attracts desired attention or avoids attracting undesired attention
Random purposeful	Adds credibility to sample when potential purposeful sample is too large
Stratified purposeful	Illustrates subgroups and facilitates comparisons
Criterion	All cases that meet some criterion; useful for quality assurance
Opportunistic	Follow new leads; taking advantage of the unexpectecd
Combination or mixed	Triangulation, flexibility; meets multiple interests and needs
Convenience	Saves time, money, and effort, but at the expense of information and credibility

Figure 7.3 Typology of Sampling Strategies in Qualitative Inquiry
SOURCE: Miles and Huberman (1994, p. 28). Reprinted with permission from Miles, M. B., & Huberman, A. M. (1994). *Qualitative data analysis: A sourcebook of new methods* (2nd ed.). Thousand Oaks, CA: Sage.

women who have experienced childhood abuse). The rationale for studying this heterogeneous sample is to confirm or disconfirm the conditions, both contextual and intervening, under which the model holds (see Creswell & Urbom, 1997, for this procedure).

In an *ethnography*, once the investigator selects a site with a cultural group, the next decision is who and what will be studied. Thus, within-culture sampling proceeds, and several authors offer suggestions for this procedure. Fetterman (1989) recommends proceeding with the "big net approach" (p. 42), where at first the researcher mingles with everyone. Ethnographers rely on their judgment to select members of the subculture or unit based on their research questions. They take advantage of opportunities ("opportunistic" sampling [Miles & Huberman, 1994]) or establish criteria for studying select individuals (criterion sampling). The criteria for selecting who and what to study for Hammersley and Atkinson (1993) are based on gaining some perspective on time in the social life of the group, people representative of the culture-sharing group in terms of demographics, and the contexts that lead to different forms of behavior.

In a *case study*, the investigator might consider any one of the strategies for sampling identified by Miles and Huberman (1994). I prefer to select unusual cases in collective case studies and employ "maximum variation" as a strategy to represent diverse cases to fully display multiple perspectives about the cases. "Extreme and deviant cases" may comprise my collective case study, such as our study of the campus response to the gunman (Asmussen & Creswell, 1995).

FORMS OF DATA

Although approaches to data collection continually expand in the qualitative area (see Creswell, 1994), there are four basic types of information to collect: observations (ranging from nonparticipant to participant), interviews (ranging from semistructured to open-ended), documents (ranging from private to public), and audio-visual materials (including materials such as photographs, compact disks, and videotapes). In Figure 7.4, I present a compendium of approaches under these four categories. In recent years, new forms of data have emerged such as journaling in narrative story writing, using text from e-mail messages, and observing through videotapes and photographs. I encourage individuals designing qualitative projects to pursue information from sources generally unfamiliar to the reader. For example, I like the technique of "photo elicitation" in which participants are shown pictures (their own or those taken by the researcher)

Observations:

- Gather fieldnotes by conducting an observation as a participant.
- Gather fieldnotes by conducting an observation as an observer.
- Gather fieldnotes by spending more time as a participant than as an observer.
- Gather fieldnotes by spending more time as an observer than as a participant.
- Gather fieldnotes first by observing as an "outsider" and then moving into the setting and observing as an "insider."

Interviews:

- Conduct an unstructured, open-ended interview and take interview notes.
- Conduct an unstructured, open-ended interview, audiotape the interview, and transcribe the interview.
- Conduct a semistructured interview, audiotape the interview, and transcribe the interview.
- Conduct a focus group interview, audiotape the interview, and transcribe the interview.

Documents:

- Keep a journal during the research study.
- Have a participant keep a journal or diary during the research study.
- Collect personal letters from participants.
- Analyze public documents (e.g., official memos, minutes, records, archival material).
- Examine autobiographies and biographies.
- Have informants take photographs or videotapes (i.e., photo elicitation).

Audio-visual materials:

- Examine physical trace evidence (e.g., footprints in the snow).
- Videotape or film a social situation or an individual/group.
- Examine photographs or videotapes.
- Collect sounds (e.g., musical sounds, a child's laughter, car horns honking).
- Collect e-mail or electronic messages.
- Examine possessions or ritual objects.

Figure 7.4 A Compendium of Data Collection Approaches in Qualitative Research

and asked by the researcher to discuss the contents of the pictures (Denzin & Lincoln, 1994). Ziller (1990), for example, handed a Polaroid camera, loaded with film, to each of 40 male and 40 female 4th graders in Florida and West Germany and asked them to take pictures of images that represented war and peace.

The tradition of inquiry directs an investigator's attention toward preferred approaches to data collection, although these approaches are not rigid guidelines. For a *biography*, for example, the portrait of an individual's life is created from documents, interviews, and perhaps observations. For a life history of a living individual, Plummer (1983) discusses having the individual write down his or her history, a form of journaling. Also, the researcher conducts unstructured, open-ended interviews, with a "mixture of participant observation and almost casual chatting with notes taken" (p. 95). The cornerstone for life history writing for Plummer, however, is the open-ended interview.

For a *phenomenological study*, the process of collecting information involves primarily in-depth interviews (see, e.g., the discussion about the long interview in McCracken, 1988) with as many as 10 individuals. I have seen the number of interviewees referenced in studies range from 1 (Dukes, 1984) up to 325 (Polkinghorne, 1989). Dukes (1984) recommends studying 3 to 10 subjects, and the Riemen (1986) study included 10. The important point is to describe the meaning of a small number of individuals who have experienced the phenomenon. With an in-depth interview lasting as long as 2 hours (Polkinghorne, 1989), 10 subjects in a study represents a reasonable size. Added to 10 in-depth interviews might be the self-reflection of the researcher as a preparatory step to interviewing (Polkinghorne, 1989) or as the initial step in the analysis (Moustakas, 1994). Besides interviewing and self-reflection, Polkinghorne (1989) adds gathering information from depictions of the experience outside the context of the research projects such as descriptions drawn from novelists, poets, painters, and choreographers.

Interviews play a central role in the data collection in a *grounded theory study*. With the intent of developing a model or theory and saturating categories, I recommend that a grounded theorist interview 20 to 30 individuals. In our study of academic chairpersons (Creswell & Brown, 1992), each of our interviews with 33 individuals lasted approximately 1 hour. Other data forms besides interviewing, such as participant observation, researcher reflection or journaling (memoing), participant journaling, and focus groups, may be used to help develop the theory (see Morrow & Smith's [1995] use of these forms in their study of women's childhood abuse). However, in my experience, these multiple data forms play a secondary role to interviewing in grounded theory studies.

In an *ethnographic study*, the investigator collects descriptions of behavior through observations, interviewing, documents, and artifacts (Hammersley & Atkinson, 1995; Spradley, 1980), although observing and interviewing appear to be the most popular forms of data collection. **Participant observation**, for example, offers possibilities for the researcher on a continuum from being a complete outsider to being a complete insider (Jorgensen, 1989). The approach of changing roles from that of an outsider to an insider through the course of the ethnographic study is well documented in field research (Jorgensen, 1989). Wolcott's (1994b) study of the Principal Selection Committee illustrates an outsider perspective as he observed and recorded events in the process without becoming an active participant in the committee's conversations and activities.

A *case study* involves the widest array of data collection as the researcher attempts to build an in-depth picture of the case. I am reminded of the multiple forms of data collection recommended by Yin (1989) in his book about case studies. He refers to six forms: documents, archival records, interviews, direct observation, participant observation, and physical artifacts.

Because of the extensive data collection in our gunman case study (Asmussen & Creswell, 1995), we presented a matrix of information sources for the reader. This matrix contains four types of data (interviews, observations, documents, and audio-visual materials) for the columns and specific forms of information (e.g., students at large, central administration) in the rows. Our intent was to convey through this matrix the depth and multiple forms of data collection, thus suggesting the complexity of our case. The use of a matrix, especially applicable in an information-rich case study, might serve the inquirer equally well in all traditions of inquiry.

In an examination of the data collection forms of the five traditions in Table 7.1, interviewing and observing are central to all traditions and deserve additional attention. Because of the extensive discussions of these topics in the literature, I highlight only basic procedures that I recommend to prospective interviewers and observers.

Interviewing

One might view interviewing as a series of steps in a procedure:

▼ *Identify interviewees based on one of the purposeful sampling procedures mentioned in the preceding (Miles & Huberman, 1994).*

▼ *Determine what type of interview is practical and will net the most useful information to answer research questions.* Assess the types available such as a telephone interview, a focus group interview, or a one-on-one interview. A telephone interview provides the best source of information when the researcher does not have direct access to individuals. The drawbacks of this approach are that the researcher cannot see the informal communication, and the phone expenses. Focus groups are advantageous when the interaction among interviewees will likely yield the best information, when interviewees are similar and cooperative with each other, when time to collect information is limited, and when individuals interviewed one on one may be hesitant to provide information (Krueger, 1994; Morgan, 1988; Stewart & Shamdasani, 1990). With this approach, however, care must be taken to encourage all participants to talk and to monitor individuals who may dominate the conversation. For one-on-one interviewing, the researcher needs individuals who are not hesitant to speak and share ideas and needs to determine a setting in which this is possible. The less articulate, shy interviewee may present the researcher with a challenge and less than adequate data.

▼ *Whether conducting one-on-one or focus group interviews, I recommend the use of adequate recording procedures, such as a lapel mike for both the interviewer and interviewee or an adequate mike sensitive to the acoustics of the room.*

▼ *Design the interview protocol, a form about four or five pages in length, with approximately five open-ended questions and ample space between the questions to write responses to the interviewee's comments.*

▼ *Determine the place for conducting the interview.* Find, if possible, a quiet location free from distractions. Ascertain that the physical setting lends itself to audiotaping, an essential necessity, I believe, in accurately recording information.

▼ *After arriving at the interview site, obtain consent from the interviewee to participate in the study.* Have the interviewee complete a consent form for the human relations review board. Go over the purpose of the study, the amount of time that will be needed to complete the interview, and plans for using the results from the interview (offer a copy of the report or an abstract of it to the interviewee).

▼ *During the interview, stick to the questions, complete within the time specified (if possible), be respectful and courteous, and offer few questions and advice.* This last point may be the most important, and I am reminded how a good interviewer is a listener rather than a speaker during an interview. Also, record information on the interview protocol in the event that the audio-recording does not work. Recognize that quickly inscribed notes may be incomplete and partial because of the difficulty of asking questions and writing answers at the same time.

Observing

Observing in a setting is a special skill that requires management of issues such as the potential deception of the people being interviewed, impression management, and the potential marginality of the researcher in a strange setting (Hammersley & Atkinson, 1995). Like interviewing, I also see observing as a series of steps:

▼ *Select a site to be observed.* Obtain the required permissions needed to gain access to the site.

▼ *At the site, identify who or what to observe, when, and for how long.* A **gatekeeper** or **key informants** help in this process.

▼ *Determine, initially, a role as an observer.* This role can range from that of a complete participant (going native) to that of a complete observer. I especially like the procedure of being an outsider initially followed by becoming an insider over time.

▼ *Design an observational protocol as a method for recording notes in the field.* Include in this protocol both descriptive and reflective notes (i.e., notes about your experiences, hunches, and learnings).

▼ *Record aspects such as portraits of the informant, the physical setting, particular events and activities, and your own reactions (Bogdan & Biklen, 1989).*

▼ *During the observation, have someone introduce you if you are an outsider, be passive and friendly, and start with limited objectives in the first few sessions of observation.* The early observational sessions may be times in which to take few notes and confine attention to observing.

▼ *After observing, slowly withdraw from the site, thanking the partici-*
pants and informing them of the use of the data and their accessibility to
the study.

RECORDING PROCEDURES

For both observing and interviewing, data collection forms used in all five traditions of inquiry, I mention the use of protocols, a predetermined sheet on which one logs information learned during the observation or interview. Interview protocols enable a person to take notes during the interview about the responses of the interviewee. They also help a researcher organize thoughts on items such as headings, information about starting the interview, concluding ideas, information on ending the interview, and thanking the respondent. In Figure 7.5, I provide the interview protocol used in our gunman case study (Asmussen & Creswell, 1995). Besides the five open-ended questions in the gunman case study, this form contains several features I recommend:

▼ *Use a header to record essential information about the project and as a*
reminder to go over the purpose of the study with the interviewee. This heading might also include information about confidentiality and address aspects included in the consent form.

▼ *Place space between the questions in the protocol form.* Recognize that an individual may not always respond directly to the questions being asked. For example, while you ask Question 2, the interviewee may respond to Question 4. Be prepared to write notes to all of the questions as the interviewee speaks.

▼ *Memorize the questions and their order to minimize losing eye contact.* Provide appropriate verbal transitions from one question to the next.

▼ *Write out the closing comments that thank the individual for the inter-*
view and request follow-up information, if needed, from them.

Interview Protocol
Project: University Reaction to a Terrorist Incident

Time of interview:
Date:
Place:
Interviewer:
Interviewee:
Position of interviewee:

(Briefly describe the project)

Questions:
1. What has been your role in the incident?

2. What has happened since the event that you have been involved in?

3. What has been the impact on the university community of this incident?

4. What larger ramifications, if any, exist from the incident?

5. To whom should we talk to find out more about campus reaction to the incident?

(Thank individual for participating in this interview. Assure him or her of confidentiality of responses and potential future interviews.)

Figure 7.5 Sample Interview Protocol

During an observation, use an observational protocol to record information. As shown in Figure 7.6, this protocol records information by one of my students on a class visit by Harry Wolcott. I provide only one page of the protocol, but one can see that it has a header describing information about the observational session and then includes "descriptive notes" where the researcher records a description of activities and a drawing of the physical setting. Moreover, the researcher provides "reflective notes"—notes about the process, reflections on activities, and summary conclusions about activities for later theme development. A line down the center of the page divides descriptive notes from reflective notes. A visual sketch of the setting and a header provide additional useful information.

Whether the investigator is using an observational or interview protocol, the essential process is recording information or, as Lofland and Lofland (1995) put it, "logging data" (p. 66). This process involves recording information through various forms such as observational fieldnotes, interview write-ups, mapping, census taking, photographing, sound recording, and collecting and organizing documents. An informal process may occur in recording information composed of initial "jottings" (Emerson, Fretz, & Shaw, 1995), daily logs or summaries, and descriptive summaries (see Sanjek, 1990, for examples of fieldnotes). These forms of recording information are popular in biographies, ethnographies, and case studies.

FIELD ISSUES

Researchers engaged in studies within all five traditions face issues in the field when gathering data. During the last several years, I have systematically collected notes from students and colleagues about the issues they encounter. Some common issues are the need to change or adjust the form of data collection once they enter the field. An overwhelming response is surprise by beginning qualitative researchers about the amount of time needed to collect extensive data. For practice, I recommend limited data collection, such as one or two interviews or observations, so that researchers can estimate the time needed to collect data. Along with the time issue is the concern about the amount of energy and focus required to establish a substantial database.

Length of Activity: 90 Minutes	
Descriptive Notes	*Reflective Notes*
General: What are the experiences of graduate students as they learn qualitative research in the classroom?	
See classroom layout and comments about physical setting at the bottom of this page.	*Overhead with flaps: I wonder if the back of the room was able to read it.*
Approximately 5:17 p.m., Dr. Creswell enters the filled room, introduces Dr. Wolcott. Class members seem relieved.	*Overhead projector not plugged in at the beginning of the class: I wonder if this was a distraction (when it took extra time to plug it in).*
Dr. Creswell gives brief background, concentrating on his international experiences; features a comment about the educational ethnography *The Man in the Principal's Office.*	*Lateness of the arrival of Drs. Creswell and Wolcott: Students seemed a bit anxious. Maybe it had to do with the change in starting time to 5 p.m. (some may have had 6:30 classes or appointments to get to).*
Dr. Wolcott begins by telling the class he now writes out educational ethnography and highlights this primary occupation by mentioning two books: *Transferring Qualitative Data* and *The Art of Fieldwork.*	*Drs. Creswell and Wolcott seem to have a good rapport between them, judging from many short exchanges that they had.*
While Dr. Wolcott begins his presentation by apologizing for his weary voice (due to talking all day, apparently), Dr. Creswell leaves the classroom to retrieve the guest's overhead transparencies.	
Seemed to be three parts to this activity: (1) the speaker's *challenge* to the class of detecting pure ethnographical methodologies, (2) the speaker's *presentation* of the "tree" that portrays various stategies and substrategies for qualitative research in education, and (3) the relaxed "elder statesman" *fielding* class questions, primarily about students' potential research projects and prior studies Dr. Wolcott had written.	SKETCH OF CLASSROOM
The first question was "How do you look at qualitative research?" followed by "How does ethnography fit in?"	

Figure 7.6 Sample Observational Protocol

In Figure 7.7, I enumerate other field issues and group them into topical areas. These issues span access/site problems to observations, interviews, document research, journals, video materials, and general ethical issues.

Issues of locating and obtaining permission to use materials present a challenge to biographical writers. The issues related to interviewing surface during phenomenological studies and grounded theory studies, whereas ethnographers struggle with access concerns and with sharing information with interviewees and participants in the cultural group. Case study writers, who gather extensive information, struggle with the time commitment and the details of interviewing.

Conducting interviews is taxing, especially for inexperienced researchers engaged in studies that require extensive interviewing, such as phenomenology, grounded theory, and case study research. Equipment issues loom large as a problem in interviewing, and both recording equipment and transcribing equipment need to be organized in advance of the interview. The process of questioning during an interview (e.g., saying "little," handling "emotional outbursts," using "ice-breakers") includes problems that an interviewer must address. Many inexperienced researchers express surprise at the difficulty of conducting interviews and the lengthy process involved in transcribing audiotapes from the interviews. In addition, in phenomenological interviews, asking appropriate questions and relying on informants to discuss the meaning of their experiences require patience and skill on the part of the researcher. In document research, the issues involve locating materials, often at sites far away, and obtaining permission to use the materials. For biographers, the primary form of data collection might be archival research from documents.

When the researcher asks participants in a study to keep journals, additional field issues surface. Journaling is a popular data collection process in case studies. What instructions should be given to individuals prior to writing in their journals? Are all participants equally comfortable with journaling? Is it appropriate, for example, with small children who express themselves well verbally but have limited writing skills? The researcher also may have difficulty reading the handwriting of participants who journal. Recording videotapes raises issues for the qualitative researcher such as keeping disturbing room sounds to a minimum, deciding on the best location for the camera,

Access/site questions:

- Difficulty making initial contact with person in the field
- Building trust or credibility at the field site (feeling like intruder)
- Gaining access to the site and individuals
- Getting people to respond to requests for information
- Deciding whether to collect information in the natural site
- Determining whether one can understand a setting when one is close to it

Observations:

- Determining whether fieldnotes are credible
- Writing down "jottings"
- Incorporating "quotes" into fieldnotes
- Assuming an observer role and how to change roles
- Learning how to best collect information from early field visits in case studies
- Learning how to "funnel" from broad observations to narrow ones

Interviews:

- Saying "little" during interview
- Having tapes that will work in the transcribing machine
- Scheduling a time for all to participate in a group interview
- Matching the "level" of questions to the ability of informants
- Realizing the costliness and lengthy process of transcribing data
- Using an appropriate level of questioning at the beginning of the interview
- Interruptions during an interview
- Difficulty scheduling an interview
- Having confidence in interviewing skills
- Having difficulty taking notes while interviewing
- Conducting interview with two or more individuals
- Encouraging all participants to talk in a group interview
- Asking appropriate questions
- Learning to listen rather than talking in interviews
- Handling emotional outbursts
- Addressing participants who do not want to be audiotaped
- Finding a transcriptionist and the right type of equipment in a case study and grounded theory project
- Moving from ice-breakers to questions in interview
- Addressing when interviewees stray from the interview questions
- Giving the interview questions to participants before the interview
- Working with the logistics of the tape-recording equipment
- "Bracketing" personal bias
- Focusing the questions to ask in a group interview

(continued)

Figure 7.7 Field Issues in Qualitative Research

Document research:
- Having difficulty locating materials
- Having difficulty obtaining permission to use materials
- Questioning the value of materials

Journals:
- Having people write complete journal entries
- Having difficulty reading handwritten journals
- Having informants express the difficulty of journaling
- Having informants express questions about how one might journal

Video materials:
- Having disturbing room sounds
- Having problems videotaping in a small room
- Having difficulties focusing and positioning the camera

Ethical issues:
- Protecting the anonymity of the informants
- Disclosing (or not) the purpose of the research
- Deciding whether (or how) to use information "shared off the record" in an interview in a case study
- Determining whether the researcher should share personal experiences

Figure 7.7 Continued

and determining whether to provide close-up shots versus distant shots.

Regardless of tradition of inquiry, a qualitative researcher faces many ethical issues that surface during data collection in the field and in analysis and dissemination of qualitative reports. The criteria of the American Anthropological Association (see Glesne & Peshkin, 1992) reflect appropriate standards. A researcher protects the anonymity of the informants, for example, by assigning numbers or aliases to individuals. A researcher develops case studies of individuals that represent a composite picture rather than an individual picture. Furthermore, to gain support from participants, a qualitative researcher conveys to participants that they are participating in a study, explains the purpose of the study, and does not engage in **deception** about the nature of the study. What if the study is on a sensitive topic and the participants decline to be involved if they are aware of the topic? This issue of disclosure of the researcher, widely discussed in cultural anthropology (e.g., Hammersley & Atkinson, 1995), is handled by the researcher by presenting *general* information, not specific information about the study. Another issue likely to develop is when participants share information "off the record." Although in most instances this information is deleted from analysis by the researcher, the issue becomes problematic when the information harms individuals. I am reminded of a researcher who studied incarcerated Native Americans in prisons and learned about a potential "breakout" during one of the interviews. This researcher concluded that it would be a breach of faith with the informant if she reported the matter, and she kept quiet. Fortunately, the breakout was not attempted. A final ethical issue is whether the researcher shares experiences with informants in an interview setting such as in a case study, phenomenology, or ethnography. This sharing minimizes the "bracketing" that is essential to construct the meaning of participants in phenomenology and reduces information shared by informants in case studies and ethnographies.

STORING DATA

I am surprised at how little attention is given in books and articles about storing qualitative data. The approach to storage will reflect the type of information collected, which varies by tradition of inquiry. In writing a biographical life history, the researcher needs to develop a filing system for the "wad of handwritten notes or a tape" (Plummer, 1983, p. 98). Although his ideas are based on *quantitative* data, Davidson's (1996) suggestions about backing up information collected and noting changes made to the database represent sound advice for *qualitative* researchers. With the advent of the use of computers in qualitative research, more attention will likely be given to how qualitative data are organized and stored, whether the data are fieldnotes, transcripts, or rough jottings. With extremely large databases being used by some qualitative researchers, this aspect assumes major importance. A computer program, such as Folio VIEWS, provides a program for organizing, sorting, and making subsets of text data. As one example of a textbase managing program, Folio VIEWS enables the investigator to search and retrieve various combinations of words, phrases, coded segments, memos, or other material (Weitzman & Miles, 1995).

Some principles about data storage and handling that are especially well suited for qualitative research include the following:

- Always develop backup copies of computer files (Davidson, 1996).

- Use high-quality tapes for audio-recording information during interviews. Also, make sure that the size of the tapes fits the transcriber's machine.

- Develop a master list of types of information gathered.

- Protect the anonymity of participants by masking their names in the data.

- Convert word processing files over to ASCII files for easy entry into some qualitative computer programs (this topic will be addressed further in Chapter 8).

- Develop a data collection matrix as a visual means of locating and identifying information for a study.

FIVE TRADITIONS COMPARED

Returning again to Table 7.1, there are both differences and similarities among the activities of data collection for the five traditions of inquiry. Turning to differences, first, the diversity of forms of data collection is great. For case studies, the researcher uses multiple forms of data to build the in-depth case. For grounded theory studies, phenomenological projects, and biographies, investigators rely primarily on interviews. Ethnographers rely heavily on participant observation. Unquestionably, some mixing of forms occurs, but in general these patterns of collection by tradition hold true.

Second, the unit of data collection varies. Biographers, phenomenologists, and ground theorists study individuals; case study researchers examine groups of individuals participating in an event or activity or an organization; and ethnographers study entire cultural systems or some subcultures of the systems. Third, I found the amount of discussion about field issues to vary. Ethnographers have written extensively about field issues (e.g., Hammersley & Atkinson, 1995), thus reflecting the concerns of a stranger going into the field. Biographers are less specific about field issues (e.g., Denzin, 1989b), although concerns about sources of bias surface in discussions about the classical approach to biographical writings (Plummer, 1983).

Fourth, the traditions vary in their intrusiveness of data collection. Conducting interviews seems less intrusive in phenomenological projects and grounded theory studies than does the high level of access needed in personal biographies, the prolonged stays in the field in ethnographies, and the immersion into programs or events in case studies.

In my review of the five traditions and data collection, I found overlap in several areas. A number of these were highlighted earlier in the chapter. All qualitative studies conducted in public organizations need to be approved by a human subjects review board. Also, the use of interviews and observations is central to many of the traditions. Furthermore, the recording devices such as observational and interview protocols can be similar regardless of tradition (although specific questions on each protocol will reflect the language of the tradition). Finally, the issue of storage of information is closely related to the form of data collection, and the basic objective of researchers, regardless of tradition, is to develop some filing and storing system for organized retrieval of information.

SUMMARY

In this chapter, I addressed several components of the data collection process. The researcher attends to locating a site or person to study, gaining access and building rapport at the site or with the individual, sampling purposefully using one of the many approaches to sampling in qualitative research, collecting information through as many as four forms (interviews, observations, documents, and audio-visual material), establishing approaches for recording information such as the use of interview or observational protocols, resolving field issues ranging from access to ethical concerns, and developing a system for storing and handling the databases. Applied to the five traditions of inquiry, the traditions differ in the diversity of information collected, the unit of study being examined, the extent of field issues, and the intrusiveness of the data collection effort. Researchers, regardless of tradition, need approval from review boards, engage in similar data collection of interviews and observations, and use similar recording protocols and forms for storing data.

▼ ADDITIONAL READINGS

For a discussion about purposeful sampling strategies, I recommend Miles and Huberman (1994).

Miles, M. B., & Huberman, A. M. (1994). *Qualitative data analysis: A sourcebook of new methods* (2nd ed.). Thousand Oaks, CA: Sage.

For interviewing, I direct researchers to Kvale (1996), McCracken (1988), Rubin and Rubin (1995), Seidman (1991), and Weiss (1992).

Kvale, S. (1996). *InterViews: An introduction to qualitative research interviewing*. Thousand Oaks, CA: Sage.

McCracken, G. (1988). *The long interview*. Newbury Park, CA: Sage.

Rubin, H. J., & Rubin, I. S. (1995). *Qualitative interviewing*. Thousand Oaks, CA: Sage.

Seidman, I. E. (1991). *Interviewing as qualitative research*. New York: Columbia University, Teachers College Press.

Weiss, R. S. (1992). *Learning from strangers: The art and method of qualitative interview studies*. New York: Free Press.

For discussions about making observations and taking fieldnotes, I suggest several writers: Bernard (1994), Bogdewic (1992), Emerson et al. (1995), Hammersley and Atkinson (1995), Jorgensen (1989), and Sanjek (1990).

Bernard, H. R. (1994). *Research methods in anthropology: Qualitative and quantitative approaches* (2nd ed.). Thousand Oaks, CA: Sage.

Bogdewic, S. P. (1992). Participant observation. In B. F. Crabtree & W. L. Miller (Eds.), *Doing qualitative research* (pp. 45-69). Newbury Park, CA: Sage.

Emerson, R. M., Fretz, R. I., & Shaw, L. L. (1995). *Writing ethnographic fieldnotes*. Chicago: University of Chicago Press.

Hammersley, M., & Atkinson, P. (1995). *Ethnography: Principles in practice* (2nd ed.). New York: Routledge.

Jorgensen, D. L. (1989). *Participant observation: A methodology for human studies*. Newbury Park, CA: Sage.

Sanjek, R. (1990). *Fieldnotes: The makings of anthropology*. Ithaca, NY: Cornell University Press.

For a discussion of field relations and issues, see Hammersley and Atkinson (1995) and Lofland and Lofland (1995).

Hammersley, M., & Atkinson, P. (1995). *Ethnography: Principles in practice* (2nd ed.). New York: Routledge.

Lofland, J., & Lofland, L. H. (1995). *Analyzing social settings: A guide to qualitative observation and analysis* (3rd ed.). Belmont, CA: Wadsworth.

EXERCISES

1. Gain some experience in collecting data for your project. Conduct either an interview or an observation and record the information on a protocol form. After this experience, identify issues that posed challenges in data collection.

2. It is helpful to design the data collection activities for a project. Examine Table 7.1 for the seven activities. Develop a matrix that describes data collection for all seven activities for your project.

WRITING EXERCISES

Data Analysis and Representation

Analyzing text and multiple forms of data presents a formidable task for qualitative researchers. Deciding how to represent the data in tables, matrices, and narrative form is challenging as well. I feel that it is important in this chapter to first discuss several general procedures for analysis of data before detailing the differences in analysis and representing data by tradition of inquiry.

I begin by summarizing three general approaches to analysis provided by leading authors. I then present a visual model—a data analysis spiral—that I find useful to conceptualize the data analysis process in qualitative research. I use this spiral as a conceptualization to further explore each tradition of inquiry, and I examine specific data analysis procedures within each tradition and compare these procedures. I end with the use of computers in qualitative analysis and assess the use of one program, NUD·IST (non-numerical data indexing, searching, and theorizing), useful in analysis generally and within the traditions specifically.

Questions for Discussion

▼ What are common data analysis strategies used in qualitative research regardless of tradition of inquiry?

▼ How might the overall data analysis be conceptualized in qualitative research?

▼ What are specific data analysis procedures within each tradition
of inquiry, and how do they differ?

▼ How can one represent the analysis using a computer program,
and how would this representation differ by tradition of inquiry?

THREE ANALYSIS STRATEGIES

Undoubtedly, no consensus exists for the analysis of the forms of
qualitative data. But, at the outset, it might be useful to explore
common features espoused by several writers. In Table 8.1, I present
the general data analysis strategies advanced by three qualitative
authors (Bogdan & Biklen, 1992; Huberman & Miles, 1994; Wolcott,
1994b). These three authors advocate many similar processes, as well
as a few different processes, in the analytic phase of qualitative
research.

They recommend, first, a general review of all information, often
in the form of jotting down notes in the margins of text (e.g., observational fieldnotes, interview transcriptions, notes about photographs
or videotapes). I personally favor reading through all collected information to obtain a sense of the overall data, a procedure also advo-
cated by Tesch (1990). In addition, writing findings in the form of
memos and reflective notes is an initial sorting-out process. One also
might begin to write summaries of field notes.

At this point, the researcher might obtain feedback on the initial
summaries by taking information back to informants, a procedure to
be discussed later as a key verification step in research as well as an
analysis step. Also at this point, a researcher looks closely at the words
used by participants in the study, such as the metaphors they use, or
the researcher translates participants' ideas into metaphors. The process of reducing the data begins. It is followed by creating displays of
information such as diagrams, tables, or graphs—means for visualizing the information and representing it by case, by subject, or by
theme.

Another important approach to reducing the data is to develop
codes or categories and to sort text or visual images into categories. I
think about "winnowing" the data here; not all information is used in

TABLE 8.1 General Data Analysis Strategies by Authors

Analytic Strategy	Bogdan & Biklen (1992)	Huberman & Miles (1994)	Wolcott (1994b)
Sketching ideas	Jot down ideas in margins of fieldnotes	Write margin notes in fieldnotes	Highlight certain information in description
Taking notes	Write memos, write observer's comments	Write reflective passages in notes	
Summarize field notes		Draft a summary sheet on fieldnotes	
Getting feedback on ideas	Try out themes on subjects		
Working with words	Play with metaphors, analogies, concepts	Make metaphors	
Display data	Develop diagrams, continua, tables, matrices, and graphs	Make contrasts and comparisons	Display findings in tables, charts, diagrams, and figures; compare cases; compare with a standard
Identify codes	Develop coding categories	Write codes, memos	
Reduce information	Sort material into categories	Note patterns and themes	Identify patterned regularities
Count frequency of codes		Count frequency of codes	
Relating categories		Factoring, noting relations among variables, building a logical chain of evidence	
Use systematic procedures of tradition of inquiry			Follow fieldwork procedures in ethnography
Relate to analytic framework in literature			Contextualize in framework from literature
Redesign study			Propose a redesign of the study

a qualitative study, and some may be discarded (Wolcott, 1994b). Researchers develop a short list of tentative codes (e.g., 12 or so) that match a text segment, regardless of the length of the database. Beginning researchers tend to develop elaborate lists of codes when they review their databases. I proceed differently. I begin with a short list—5 or 6 categories with shorthand labels or codes—and then I expand the categories as I continue to review and re-review my database. Typically, regardless of the size of the database, I do not develop more than 25-30 categories of information, and I find myself working to reduce these to the 5 or 6 that I will use in the end to write my narrative. Those researchers who end up with 100 or 200 categories—and it is easy to find this many in a complex database—struggle to reduce the picture to the 5 or 6 that they must end with for most publications.

As another technique, Huberman and Miles (1994) suggest that investigators make preliminary "counts" of data and determine how frequently codes appear in the database. Finally, researchers relate categories and develop analytic frameworks, procedures found in grounded theory research (Corbin & Strauss, 1990). Such comparisons and contrasts may lead to the redesign of a study or to the generation of a new framework.

THE DATA ANALYSIS SPIRAL

Data analysis is not off-the-shelf; rather, it is custom-built, revised, and "choreographed" (Huberman & Miles, 1994). Qualitative researchers "learn by doing" (Dey, 1993, p. 6). This leads critics to claim that qualitative research is largely intuitive, soft, and relativistic or that qualitative data analysts fall back on the three "I's"—"insight, intuition, and impression" (Dey, 1995, p. 78). Undeniably, qualitative researchers preserve the unusual and serendipitous, and writers craft each study differently, using analytic procedures that evolve in the field. But given this perspective, I believe that the analysis process conforms to a general contour.

The contour is best represented in a spiral image, a data analysis spiral. As shown in Figure 8.1, to analyze qualitative data, the researcher engages in the process of moving in analytic circles rather than using a fixed linear approach. One enters with data of text or images (e.g., photographs, videotapes) and exits with an account or a narrative. In between, the researcher touches on several facets of analysis and circles around and around.

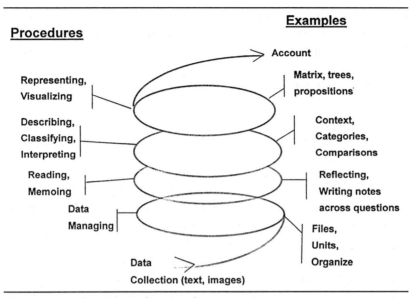

Figure 8.1 The Data Analysis Spiral

Data management, the first loop in the spiral, begins the process. At an early stage in the analysis process, researchers organize their data into file folders, index cards, or computer files. Besides organizing files, researchers convert their files to appropriate text units (e.g., a word, a sentence, an entire story) for analysis either by hand or by computer. Materials must be easily located in large databases of text (or images). As Patton (1980) says,

> The data generated by qualitative methods are voluminous. I have found no way of preparing students for the sheer massive volumes of information with which they will find themselves confronted when data collection has ended. Sitting down to make sense out of pages of interviews and whole files of field notes can be overwhelming. (p. 297)

Computer programs help with this phase of analysis, and their role in this process will be addressed later.

Following the organization and conversion of the data, researchers continue analysis by getting a sense of the whole database. Agar (1980), for example, suggests that researchers "read the transcripts in their entirety several times. Immerse yourself in the details, trying to get a sense of the interview as a whole before breaking it into parts"

(p. 103). Writing memos in the margins of fieldnotes or transcripts or under photographs helps in this initial process of exploring a database. These memos are short phrases, ideas, or key concepts that occur to the reader.

With the data in our gunman case study (Asmussen & Creswell, 1995), we scanned all of our databases to identify major organizing ideas. Looking over our fieldnotes from observations, interview data, physical trace evidence, and audio and visual images, we disregarded predetermined questions to "hear" what interviewees said. We reflected on the larger thoughts presented in the data and formed initial categories. These categories were few in number (about 10), and we looked for multiple forms of evidence to support each. Moreover, we found evidence that portrayed multiple perspectives about each category.

This process I have described consists of moving from the reading and memoing loop into the spiral to the describing, classifying, and interpreting loop. In this loop, category formation represents the heart of qualitative data analysis. Here researchers describe in detail, develop themes or dimensions through some classification system, and provide an interpretation in light of their own views or views of perspectives in the literature. Authors employ descriptive detail, classification, or interpretation or some combination of these analysis procedures. Detailed description means that authors describe what they see. This detail is provided in situ, that is, within the context of the setting of the person, place, or event. Description becomes a good place to start in a qualitative study (after reading and managing data), and it plays a central role in ethnographic studies.

Classifying pertains to taking the text or qualitative information apart, looking for categories, themes, or dimensions of information. As a popular form of analysis, classification involves identifying five or six general themes. These themes, in turn, I view as a "family" of themes with children, or subthemes, and grandchildren represented by segments of data. It is difficult, especially in a large database, to reduce the information down into five or six "families," but my process involves winnowing the data, reducing them to a small, manageable set of themes to write into my final narrative.

Interpretation involves making sense of the data, the "lessons learned" as described by Lincoln and Guba (1985). Several forms exist,

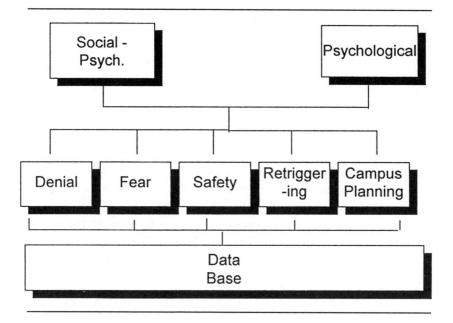

Figure 8.2 Layers of Analysis in Gunman Case (Asmussen & Creswell, 1995)

such as interpretation based on hunches, insights, and intuition. It also might be an interpretation within a social science construct or idea or a combination of personal views as *contrasted* with a social science construct or idea. At this point in their analyses, researchers step back and form larger meanings of what is going on in the situations or sites.

In the final phase of the spiral, researchers present the data, a packaging of what was found in text, tabular, or figure form. For example, creating a visual image of the information, a researcher may present a "comparison" table (see Spradley, 1980) or a matrix—for example, a 2 × 2 table that compares men and women in terms of one of the themes or categories in the study (see Miles & Huberman, 1994). The cells contain text, not numbers. A hierarchical tree diagram represents another form of presentation. This shows different levels of abstraction, with the boxes in the top of the tree representing the most abstract information and those at the bottom representing the least abstract themes. Figure 8.2 illustrates the levels of abstraction that we used in the gunman case (Asmussen & Creswell, 1995). Although I have presented this figure at conferences, we did not include it in the published journal article version of the study. This illustration shows inductive analysis that begins with the raw data consisting of multiple sources of information and then broadens to several specific themes (e.g., safety, denial) and on to the most general themes represented by the two perspectives of social-psychological and psychological factors.

Hypotheses or propositions that specify the relationship among categories of information also represent information. In grounded theory, for example, investigators advance propositions that interrelate the causes of a phenomenon with its context and strategies. Finally, authors present metaphors to analyze the data, literary devices in which something borrowed from one domain applies to another (Hammersley & Atkinson, 1995). Qualitative writers may compose entire studies shaped by analyses of metaphors.

ANALYSIS WITHIN TRADITIONS OF INQUIRY

Beyond these general spiral analysis processes, I can now relate the procedures to each of the five traditions of inquiry and highlight specific differences in analysis and representing data. My organizing framework for this discussion is found in Table 8.2. I address each tradition and discuss specific analysis and representing characteristics. At the end of this discussion, I return to significant differences and similarities among the five traditions.

Biography

Denzin (1989b) suggests that a researcher begin analysis by identifying an objective set of experiences in the subject's life. Having the individual journal a sketch of his or her life may be a good beginning point for analysis. In this sketch, the researcher looks for life-course stages or experiences (e.g., childhood, marriage, employment) to develop a *chronology* of the individual's life. Stories and epiphanies will emerge from the individual's journal or from interviews. The researcher looks in the database (typically interviews or documents) for concrete, contextual biographical materials. An interviewer prompts a subject to expand on various sections of the stories and asks the interviewee to theorize about his or her life. These theories may relate to career models, processes in the life course, models of the social world, relational models of biography, and natural history models of the life course. Then, narrative segments and categories within the interview-story are isolated by the researcher, and larger *patterns* and *meanings* are determined.

Finally, the individual's biography is reconstructed, and the researcher identifies factors that have shaped the life. This leads to the writing of an analytic abstraction of the case that highlights (a) the processes in the individual's life, (b) the different theories that relate to these life experiences, and (c) the unique and general features of the life.

In the life history of Vonnie Lee (Angrosino, 1994), the reader finds many of these forms of analysis in the **chronology** of the bus trip, the specific **stories** such as the logo on the bus, and the theorizing (at least by the author) about the meaning of the bus trip as a metaphor for Vonnie Lee's experiences in life as an individual with mental retardation.

Phenomenology

I see the biographical approach by Denzin (1989b) as a general template for analysis in contrast to the detailed, specific approaches to phenomenological analysis advanced by Moustakas (1994). Moustakas reviews two approaches, but I see his second approach, called a modification of the Stevick-Colaizzi-Keen method, being used frequently in phenomenological studies. The steps are as follows:

▼ *The researcher begins with a full description of his or her own experience of the phenomenon.*

▼ *The researcher then finds statements (in the interviews) about how individuals are experiencing the topic, lists out these significant statements (**horizonalization** of the data) and treats each statement as having equal worth, and works to develop a list of nonrepetitive, nonoverlapping statements.*

TABLE 8.2 Data Analysis and Representation by Research Traditions

Data Analysis and Representation	Biography	Phenomenology	Grounded Theory Study	Ethnography	Case Study
Data managing	• Create and organize files for data	• Create and organize files for data	• Create and organize files for data	• Create and organize files for data	• Create and organize files for data
Reading, memoing	• Read through text, make margin notes, form initial codes	• Read through text, make margin notes, form initial codes	• Read through text, make margin notes, form initial codes	• Read through text, make margin notes, form initial codes	• Read through text, make margin notes, form initial codes
Describing	• Describe objective set of experiences—chronology of life	• Describe the meaning of the experience for researcher		• Describe the social setting, actors, events; draw picture of setting	• Describe the case and its context
Classifying	• Identify stories • Locate epiphanies • Identify contextual materials for life	• Find and list statements of meaning for individuals • Group statements into meaning units	• Engage in axial coding—causal condition, context, intervening conditions, strategies, consequences • Engage in open coding—categories, properties, dimension-alize properties	• Analyze data for themes and patterned regularities	• Use categorical aggregation • Establish patterns of categories

Interpreting	• Theorize toward developing patterns and meanings	• Develop a textural description, "What happened" • Develop a structural description, "How" the phenomenon was experienced • Develop an overall description of the experience, the "essence"	• Engage in selective coding and development of stories • Develop a conditional matrix	• Interpret and make sense of the findings	• Use direct interpretation • Develop naturalistic generalizations
Representing, visualizing	• Present narration focusing on processes, theories, and unique and general features of the life	• Present narration of the "essence" of the experience; use tables or figures of statements and meaning units	• Present a visual model or theory • Present propositions	• Present narrative presentation augmented by tables, figures, and sketches	• Present narrative augmented by tables, and figures

▼   *These statements are then grouped into "meaning units," the researcher lists these units, and he or she writes a description of the "textures"* **(textural description)** *of the experience—what happened—including verbatim examples.*

▼   *The researcher next reflects on his or her own description and uses* **imaginative variation or structural description***, seeking all possible meanings and divergent perspectives, varying the frames of reference about the phenomenon, and constructing a description of how the phenomenon was experienced.*

▼   *The researcher then constructs an overall description of the meaning and the* **essence** *of the experience.*

▼   *This process is followed first for the researcher's account of the experience and then for that of each participant.* After this, a "composite" description is written.

In the nursing-patient caring interaction study by Riemen (1986), the researcher presents significant statements of caring and noncaring interactions for both males and females. Furthermore, Riemen formulates meaning statements from these significant statements and presents them in tables as well. Finally, Riemen advances two "exhaustive" descriptions for the **essence** of the experience—two short paragraphs—and sets them apart by enclosing them in tables.

Grounded Theory

Similar to phenomenology, grounded theory uses set procedures for analysis. It consists of **open, axial**, and **selective coding** as advanced by Corbin and Strauss (1990). Grounded theory provides a procedure for developing categories of information (**open coding**), interconnecting the categories (**axial coding**), building a "story" that connects the categories (**selective coding**), and ending with a discursive set of theoretical **propositions** (Strauss & Corbin, 1990).

In the **open coding** phase, the researcher examines the text (e.g., transcripts, fieldnotes, documents) for salient categories of information supported by the text. Using the **constant comparative** approach, the researcher attempts to **"saturate"** the categories—to look for instances that represent the **category** and to continue looking (and interviewing) until the new information obtained does not further provide insight into the category. These categories are composed of subcategories, called **properties**, representing multiple perspectives about the categories. Properties, in turn, are **dimensionalized** and presented on a continuum. Overall, this is the process of reducing the database to a small set of themes or categories that characterize the process or action being explored in the grounded theory study.

Once an initial set of categories is developed, the researcher identifies a *single* **category** as the **central phenomenon** of interest and begins exploring the interrelationship of categories, called **axial coding—causal conditions** that influence the central phenomenon, the **strategies** for addressing the phenomenon, the **context** and **intervening conditions** that shape the strategies, and the **consequences** of undertaking the strategies. In this phase of analysis, the researcher creates a **coding paradigm**, or a theoretical model that visually portrays the interrelationship of these axial coding categories of information. A theory is built or generated. At the broadest level of analysis, the researcher can create a **conditional matrix**. This matrix is an analytical aid—a diagram—that helps the researcher visualize the wide range of conditions and **consequences** related to the **central phenomenon** (Strauss & Corbin, 1990). Seldom have I found this broad level of analysis in grounded theory studies.

The specific form for presenting the theory differs. In our study of department chairs, we present it as hypotheses (Creswell & Brown, 1992); in their study of coping strategies of sexually abused women, Morrow and Smith (1995) advance a visual model; and in our study of balance between work and personal life (Creswell & Urbom, 1997), we offer a visual model and three stories.

The grounded theory study of survival and coping from childhood abuse by Morrow and Smith (1995) reflects several of these phases of data analysis. They present results of the **axial coding** by discussing **causal conditions** that influence the **central phenomenon**, threatening or dangerous feelings as well as helplessness, powerlessness, and lack of control. They specify two groups of **strategies** these women used and indicate the narrower **context** in which these strategies occurred as well as the broader **intervening conditions** such as family dynamics and the victim's age. They detail the **consequences** of using the strategies such as coping, healing, and empowerment. They present these categories in a visual model, called a "theoretical model for surviving and coping with childhood sexual abuse" (p. 27).

Ethnography

For ethnographic research, I recommend the three aspects of data transformation advanced by Wolcott (1994b): *description, analysis,* and *interpretation of the culture-sharing group*. Wolcott (1990b) believes that a good starting point for writing an ethnography is to describe the *culture-sharing group* and setting:

> Description is the foundation upon which qualitative research is built. . . . Here you become the storyteller, inviting the reader to see through your eyes what you have seen. . . . Start by presenting a straightforward description of the setting and events. No footnotes, no intrusive analysis—just the facts, carefully presented and interestingly related at an appropriate level of detail. (p. 28)

This *description* may be analyzed by presenting information in chronological order or by using the researcher or narrator order (as seen in Wolcott's [1994a] Principal Selection Committee study). The writer describes through progressively focusing the description or chronicling a "day in the life" of the group or individual. Finally, other techniques involve focusing on a critical or key event, developing a "story" complete with a plot and characters, writing it as a "mystery," examining groups in interaction, following an analytical framework, or showing different perspectives through the views of informants.

Analysis for Wolcott (1994b) is a sorting procedure—"the quantitative side of qualitative research" (p. 26). This involves highlighting specific material introduced in the descriptive phase or displaying findings through tables, charts, diagrams, and figures. The researcher also analyzes through using systematic procedures such as those advanced by Spradley (1979, 1980), who calls for building taxonomies, generating comparison tables, and developing semantic tables. Perhaps the most popular analysis procedure, also mentioned by Wolcott (1994b), is the search for *patterned regularities* in the data. Other forms of analysis consist of comparing the cultural group to others, evaluating the group in terms of standards, and drawing connections between the ***culture-sharing group*** and larger theoretical frameworks. Other analysis steps include critiquing the research process and proposing a redesign for the study.

Making an ethnographic ***interpretation of the culture-sharing group*** is a data transformation step as well. Here the researcher goes beyond the database and probes "what is to be made of them" (Wolcott, 1994b, p. 36). The researcher speculates outrageous, comparative interpretations that raise doubts or questions for the reader. The researcher draws inferences from the data or turns to theory to provide structure for his or her interpretations. The researcher also personalizes the interpretation: "This is what I make of it" or "This is how the research experience affected me" (p. 44). Finally, the investigator forges an interpretation through expressions such as poetry, fiction, or performance.

Wolcott (1994b) includes the ethnography of the Principal Selection Committee in the section on "description" in his book *Transforming Qualitative Data: Description, Analysis, and Interpretation*. In this ethnography, Wolcott details the procedures of this committee as its members interviewed seven candidates. He does not make explicit his steps in analysis, but they can be easily seen. He isolates a single episode, describes the interviews with six of the seven candidates, analyzes and presents three themes (i.e., lack of professional knowledge, an esteem for personal feelings, and a proclivity toward variety-reducing behavior), and reflects or interprets these themes as to their impact on education, change, and the principalship.

Case Study

For a case study, as in ethnography, analysis consists of making a detailed ***description*** of the case and its setting. If the case presents a chronology of events, then I recommend analyzing the multiple sources of data to determine evidence for each step or phase in the evolution of the case. Moreover, the setting is particularly important. In our gunman case (Asmussen & Creswell, 1995), we analyzed the information to determine how the incident fit into the setting—in our situation, a tranquil, peaceful midwestern community.

In addition, Stake (1995) advocates four forms of data analysis and interpretation in case study research. In ***categorical aggregation***, the researcher seeks a collection of instances from the data, hoping that issue-relevant meanings will emerge. In **direct interpretation**, on the other hand, the case study researcher looks at a single instance and draws meaning from it without looking for multiple instances. It is a process of pulling the data apart and putting them back together in more meaningful ways. Also, the researcher establishes **patterns** and looks for a correspondence between two or more categories. This correspondence might take the form of a table, possibly a 2 × 2 table, showing the relationship between two categories. Finally, the researcher develops **naturalistic generalizations** from analyzing the data, generalizations that people can learn from the case either for themselves or for applying it to a population of cases.

To these analysis steps I would add **description** of the case, a detailed view of aspects about the case—the "facts." In our gunman case study (Asmussen & Creswell, 1995), we describe the events following the incident for 2 weeks, highlighting the major players, the sites, and the activities. We then aggregate the data into about 20 categories (categorical aggregation) and collapse them into 5 patterns. In the final section of the study, we develop generalizations about the case in terms of the patterns and how they compare and contrast with published literature on campus violence.

COMPARING THE FIVE TRADITIONS

Returning to Table 8.2, data analysis and representation have several common and distinctive features among the five traditions. Across all five traditions, the researcher typically begins with creating and organizing files of information. Next, the process of a general reading and memoing of information occurs to develop a sense of the data and to begin the process of making sense of them. Then, all traditions have a phase of description with the exception of grounded theory, in which the investigator seeks to begin building toward a theory of the action or process. Now the analysis procedures begin to depart.

Grounded theory and phenomenology have the most detailed, explicated procedure for data analysis. Ethnography and case studies have analysis procedures that are common, and biography represents the least structured procedure. Also, the terms used in the phase of classifying show distinct language among these traditions; what is called *open coding* in grounded theory is similar to the first stage of classifying (*statements*) in phenomenology or *categorical aggregation* in case study research. The researcher needs to become familiar with the definition of these terms of analysis and employ them correctly depending on tradition of inquiry. The presentation of the data, in turn, reflects the data analysis steps, and it varies from a narration in biography to tabled statements, meanings, and description in phenomenology, to a visual model or theory in grounded theory.

COMPUTERS, ANALYSIS, AND TRADITIONS

Overall, authors overlook the specific application of computer programs in analysis for traditions of inquiry except for a short discussion by Lonkila (1995) about programs and grounded theory and the suggestion that some programs are best suited for one approach than another (e.g., the program Ethnography was designed for ethnographic studies; NUD·IST, a theory-generation program, was designed for grounded theory).

The link between computer programs to analyze text and traditions of inquiry needs to be established. It is especially important because not all qualitative researchers see such programs as relevant to their needs. I feel, however, that computer programs help in the analysis of qualitative data, especially in understanding a large (e.g., 500 or more pages) text database. For those studies employing especially large databases, such as ethnographies with extensive fieldnotes and interviews, grounded theory studies comprised of 20-30 extensive interviews, or case studies with multiple types of information, computer programs provide an invaluable aid in research. Following are some of these advantages:

■ The computer program provides an organized storage "file" system so that the researcher can quickly and easily locate material and store it in one place. This aspect becomes especially important in locating entire cases or cases with specific characteristics.

■ The computer program helps a researcher locate material easily, whether this material is an idea, a statement, a phrase, or a word.

No longer do we need to "cut and paste" material onto file cards and sort and resort the cards according to themes. No longer do we need to develop an elaborate "color code" system for text related to themes or topics. The search for text can be easily accomplished with a computer program.

■ A computer program "forces" the researcher to look at the database line for line and think about the meaning of each sentence and idea. Without a program, the researcher is likely to casually read through the text files or transcripts and not analyze each idea carefully.

The disadvantages of using a computer program go beyond their cost and maintenance:

■ Computer programs require a researcher to learn how to use the programs, a sometimes daunting task that is above and beyond learning required for understanding the procedures of qualitative research. Granted, some people learn computer programs more easily than do others, and prior experience with programs shortens the learning time.

■ Computer programs may take the place of a careful analysis of the material. As such, they should not be a substitute for a close reading of the material to obtain a sense of the whole; they should be an *adjunctive* procedure in the analysis process.

■ As one builds categories of information from databases, computer programs "fix" those categories and researchers label the categories. An individual may reluctantly change categories, relabel information, or organize it under different categories because he or she believes that data are fixed or set by the program (Kelle, 1995).

■ The manuals for qualitative computer programs describe the steps in "running" the programs. They provide little assistance in qualitative data analysis, in procedures used in writing narratives, and in the use of the computer to aid in this process.

■ Computer programs vary in their features. Accordingly, a prospective buyer should assess the features of programs as discussed in Weitzman and Miles (1995) or Miles and Huberman (1994).

Using NUD·IST and Analysis Features

Several programs are available for both the PC and the MAC platforms (see Weitzman & Miles, 1995, for a review of 24 programs). The basic feature of all of these programs is that they enable the researcher to "tag" text information and place it into a category, called *code and retrieve programs* by Weitzman and Miles. This category is then labeled by the researcher. Also, many programs enable one to search for certain words or a string of words in the text databases, called *text retrievers*. Other programs are good at organizing a large number of files (*textbase managers* such as Folio VIEWS, as mentioned in Chapter 7), whereas still others provide for testing a hypothesis of the relationship of categories in a text database, called *code-based theory builders*. A final set of programs enables one to draw networks or diagrams that function to conceptualize relationships among categories, called *conceptual network builders*.

I focus on one of these programs, a theory-building program called NUD·IST (non-numerical unstructured data indexing, searching, and theorizing; Richards & Richards, 1994). This program was developed in Australia in 1991, and it is a popular qualitative analysis package available for both the MAC and PC platforms. My interest is not to market NUD·IST but rather to use it to illustrate the workings of one program and to discuss its features that aid in data analysis and qualitative report writing. NUD·IST requires at least 4 megabytes of RAM and space for data files (at least 2 megabytes), depending on the size of the database to be analyzed. For the PC, it operates under Windows. It is being marketed by Scolari under Sage Publications for approximately $300, and Scolari has produced a demonstration program available for downloading from the World Wide Web.

NUD·IST helps researchers by providing a system for the following:

- *Storing and organizing files.* I can establish "document" files (converted from a word processing program to DOS, ASCII, or text in some programs) and *store information* with the NUD·IST program. These document files consist of information from one discrete unit of information such as a transcript from one interview, my set of observational notes, or one article scanned from a newspaper. I need, however, to establish the appropriate unit for a document (e.g., a line, a sentence, a paragraph) in the project.

- *Searching for themes.* I tag segments of text from all of the documents that relate to a single idea and query the database for all *information pertaining to a single theme.* For example, assume that all individuals in a study of balancing one's personal and professional lives (Creswell & Urbom, 1997) talk about the role of the family in this balancing act. I create a category (or "node" in NUD·IST) called "family role," select text in my 18 transcripts where individuals talk about this role, and merge it into the "family role" node. I then retrieve information in this node, and I print out the different ways in which people talk about their family roles.

- *Crossing themes.* I take my example of "family role" one step further. I can *relate this node to other nodes.* Assume that I have another node titled "marital status." In "marital status," I have two categories: "single-family parent" and "two-parent family." I ask NUD·IST to cross the two categories, "family role" with "marital status," to see, for example, whether single-family parents talk differently about their family roles than do two-parent families. NUD·IST then generates information for a matrix with information in the cells reflecting the different perspectives.

- *Diagramming.* In the process of categorizing the information, categories are identified, and these are developed into a *visual picture* of the categories that displays their interconnectedness. In NUD·IST, this is called a *tree diagram*, a hierarchical tree of categories based on a "root" node at the top and parents and siblings in the tree. Thus, I generate a "picture" of the analysis, the major categories, the minor categories, and how the information from the text is grouped. I find such a picture to be a useful device for discussing my data analysis in conference presentations or for portraying my material for journal articles.

- *Creating a template.* The visual picture or tree diagram is a useful heuristic within the different traditions of inquiry, and I can relate the NUD·IST nodes in the tree to each of the five traditions addressed in this book. At the beginning of my data analysis, for example, I create a *template*—basically, an a priori codebook for organizing information—based on the type of tradition I am using

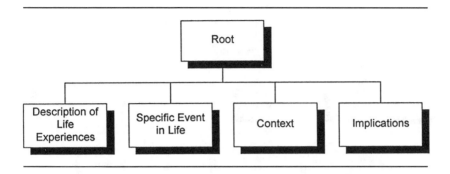

Figure 8.3 Tree Diagram for Biography Using NUD·IST Program

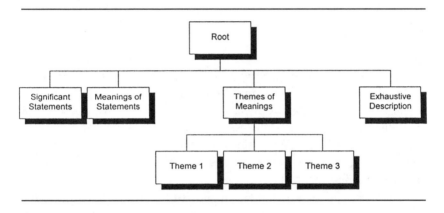

Figure 8.4 Tree Diagram for Phenomenology Using NUD·IST Program

in my study. This template advances a preliminary visual picture of my overall study and my process of data analysis.

To help visualize this template, I present several hypothetical templates as tree diagrams in NUD·IST. As shown in Figures 8.3 to 8.7, I suggest a tree diagram for the data analysis procedures in each of the five traditions of inquiry. For the template of a biography (as shown in Figure 8.3), I use material from Denzin's (1989a) approach, and I examine my text database to determine where I can select text that conveys a description of the individual, specific events, my own personal interpretation of events, and implications for the reader. I then select text that relates to these nodes and merge it into the node. My template for a phenomenology study (Figure 8.4) follows Mous-

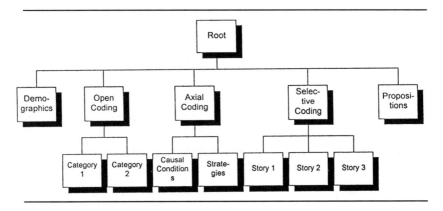

Figure 8.5 Tree Diagram for Grounded Theory Study Using NUD·IST Program

takas (1994) closely by grouping text in my analysis into significant statements, developing larger meanings that occur related to the statements, grouping the meanings into themes, and writing my exhaustive description (the essence). By specifying the nodes in advance of analysis, I work simultaneously on several categories in my tree (e.g., tagging text segments for statements while I write the exhaustive description).

The template for a grounded theory study (Figure 8.5) follows the coding process recommended by Strauss and Corbin (1990). While I tag information into my demographic nodes, I also identify open coding categories, begin to specify my axial coding paradigm, and write a story that interconnects my axial coding categories. Also, during the text analysis process, I identify propositions or hypotheses useful in connecting the axial coding categories. For the template for an ethnography (Figure 8.6), I visualize data analysis and establish nodes about the three transformation steps recommended by Wolcott (1994b)—description of the culture-sharing group, analysis of themes of the culture, and interpretation. Accordingly, I create my template so that I can tag and place information from my field notes or interviews into one of these three categories as I review my documents. A case study template (Figure 8.7) includes contextual material about my case such as the information in our gunman case (Asmussen & Creswell, 1995) about the city, the campus, and the classroom in which

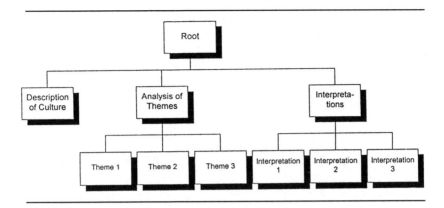

Figure 8.6 Tree Diagram for Ethnography Using NUD·IST Program

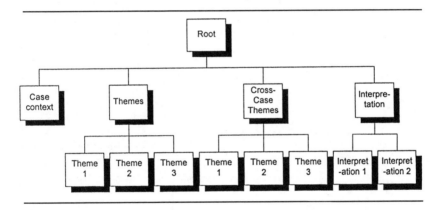

Figure 8.7 Tree Diagram for Case Study Using NUD·IST Program

the event took place. It also contains information about the themes building in my case analysis such as the themes of denial, safety, and need for campus planning in our gunman case study. If multiple cases are used, then this template reflects themes that cross cases. Finally, in my case study template, I want to provide an interpretation of this case or the lessons learned from it. Thus, I create a node in my tree for these reflections.

- *Analyzing and reporting.* At a more specific level, NUD·IST helps in the analysis and narrative reporting stage of writing qualitative

TABLE 8.3 Data Analysis Elements, Writing Objectives, and NUD·IST Procedures

Data Analysis Element	Writing Objective	NUD·IST Procedure
Create a template for analysis	Develop a visual of data analysis plan	Create a tree of steps in analysis into which data segments are placed
Create headings in the manuscript for major themes	Create four or five major themes in the study in words of participants	Create a node for each heading and put text that applies into the node
Title the manuscript	Create a title in the words of the participants—to make report realistic, to catch attention of readers	Create a node based on short phrases found in the text; create alternative titles in this node as they appear in analyzing the texts
Include quotes in the manuscript	Identify good quotes that provide sound evidence for the themes, description, interpretation, and so forth	Create a general node and place all good quotes in that node; create a node for quotes under each theme or category of information
Phrase study in words of participants	Locate commonly used words or phrases and develop them into themes	Use word search procedure, string or pattern search, and place contents into a node; spread text around the word (or phrase) to capture the context of the word (or phrase)
Create a comparison table	Compare categories of information	Use matrix feature of program
Show levels of abstraction in the analysis	Present a visual of the categories in the analysis	Present the "tree" diagram
Discuss metaphors	Find text in which metaphors are presented and group into categories	Set up one node for metaphors with children of different types of metaphors; place text in nodes by types of metaphors

studies by locating useful words, phrases, or dialogue. I find it helpful to consider the interrelationship of specific data analysis elements, objectives for my writing, and specific procedures in NUD·IST. The templates, for example, illustrate developing a visual model for analysis of the data to frame the analysis within a tradition of inquiry. But a template is only one way in which to interconnect analysis, writing, and NUD·IST. As shown in Table 8.3, I see others:

- *Headings* in a study reflect the major themes identified by the writer. These themes, best stated in the words of participants of the study, are called *in vivo codes* in grounded theory and are specified as nodes in NUD·IST. Thus, I like to phrase the study in the words of participants and use NUD·IST to search for common words found in my initial reading of a document. These words may, moreover, be frequently used metaphors by participants in the study.

- When I write a study, the *title* keeps evolving (also see Glesne & Peshkin's [1992] discussion of this phenomenon). I create a node with my "working" title and continually revise it, thus tracking the evolution of the central idea I explore in my study.

- *Quotes* provide a realistic, immediate feel to a qualitative study. I establish a node called "quotes" and merge good quotable material into it as I analyze my documents. A variation on this approach is to create several "quotes" nodes under each theme.

- *Comparison tables* provide useful visuals to present information that crosses nodes.

- *Levels of abstraction* show the complexity of a study and help a reader understand the evolution of the study from specific data-bases to increasingly broader themes. The tree diagram or my template portrays these levels and my process of data analysis.

SUMMARY

This chapter presented data analysis and representation. I began with a review of data analysis procedures advanced by three authors and noted the general process that starts with sketching ideas and taking notes, and I moved to broad analytic frameworks. I then advanced a spiral of analysis that captures the general process. This spiral contains aspects of data management; reading and memoing; describing, classifying, and interpreting; and representing and visualizing data. I next introduced the traditions of inquiry and related them to this spiral, and I presented procedures of analysis found in discussions about biography, phenomenology, grounded theory, ethnography, and case studies. Finally, I suggested that computer programs aid in the analysis and representation of data and discussed one program, NUD·IST, as an illustration of using computer analysis within traditions to write qualitative narratives. To show the utility of NUD·IST, I created a template for each of the five traditions of inquiry, and I suggested procedures that interrelate data analysis, writing objectives, and use of NUD·IST.

▼ ADDITIONAL READINGS

Perhaps the classic on qualitative data analysis is Miles and Huberman (1994), now in its second edition. Also for general approaches to coding text information, I recommend Tesch (1990).

Miles, M. B., & Huberman, A. M. (1994). *Qualitative data analysis: A sourcebook of new methods* (2nd ed.). Thousand Oaks, CA: Sage.

Tesch, R. (1990). *Qualitative research: Analysis types and software tools.* Bristol, PA: Falmer.

Specific data analysis strategies with each of the five traditions of inquiry are available in Denzin (1989a) for biography, Moustakas (1994) for phenomenology, Stake (1995) for case studies, Strauss and Corbin (1990) for grounded theory, and Wolcott (1994b) for ethnography.

Denzin, N. K. (1989a). *Interpretive biography.* Newbury Park, CA: Sage.

Moustakas, C. (1994). *Phenomenological research methods.* Thousand Oaks, CA: Sage.

Stake, R. (1995). *The art of case study research.* Thousand Oaks, CA: Sage.

Strauss, A., & Corbin, J. (1990). *Basics of qualitative research: Grounded theory procedures and techniques.* Newbury Park, CA: Sage.

Wolcott, H. F. (1994b). *Transforming qualitative data: Description, analysis, and interpretation.* Thousand Oaks, CA: Sage.

For a review of computer programs available for analyzing text data, I recommend Kelle (1995), Tesch (1990), and Weitzman and Miles (1995).

Kelle, E. (Ed.). (1995). *Computer-aided qualitative data analysis.* Thousand Oaks, CA: Sage.

Tesch, R. (1990). *Qualitative research: Analysis types and software tools.* Bristol, PA: Falmer.

Weitzman, E. A., & Miles, M. B. (1995). *Computer programs for qualitative data analysis.* Thousand Oaks, CA: Sage.

EXERCISES

1. Analyze data from your data collection in the Exercises in Chapter 7. Analyze them using the steps or phases for your tradition of inquiry. Present a summary of findings.

2. Plan the data analysis steps for your project. Using Table 8.2 as a guide, discuss how you plan to describe, classify, and interpret your information.

3. Gain some experience using a computer software program. Obtain a copy of the NUD·IST demonstration program from Sage Publications, complete the tutorial, and submit printouts of the output at all four phases of the tutorial.

Writing the
Narrative Report

Writing and composing the narrative report brings the entire study together. Borrowing a term from Strauss and Corbin (1990), I am fascinated by the "architecture" of a study, how it is composed and organized by writers. I also like their suggestion that writers use a "spatial metaphor" (p. 231) to visualize their full reports or studies. To consider a study "spatially," they ask the following questions. Do you come away with an idea like walking slowly around a statue, studying it from a variety of interrelated views? Like walking downhill step by step? Like walking through the rooms of a house?

In this chapter, I assess the general architecture of a qualitative study, and then I invite the reader to enter specific rooms of the study to see how they are composed. In this process, I begin with four rhetorical issues in the rendering of a study regardless of tradition: audience, encoding, quotes, and authorial representation. Then I take each tradition of inquiry and assess two rhetorical structures: the overall structure (i.e., overall organization of the report or study) and the embedded structure (i.e., specific narrative devices and techniques that the writer uses in the report). I return once again to the five examples of studies in Chapter 3 to illustrate overall and embedded structures. Finally, I compare the narrative structures for the five traditions in terms of four dimensions.

Questions for Discussion

▼ For what audience is the qualitative study being written?

▼ How does a writer encode the study for an audience?

▼ How are quotes used in a qualitative study?

▼ How does the author represent herself or himself in the narrative?

▼ What are the overall rhetorical structures for writing a study within each of the five traditions of inquiry?

▼ What are the embedded rhetorical structures for writing a study within each of the five traditions of inquiry?

▼ How do the narrative structures for the five traditions differ?

SEVERAL RHETORICAL ISSUES

Unquestionably, the narrative forms are extensive in qualitative research. In reviewing the forms, Glesne and Peshkin (1992) note that narratives in "storytelling" modes blur the lines between fiction, journalism, and scholarly studies. Other forms engage the reader through a chronological approach as events unfold slowly over time, whether the subject is a study of a culture-sharing group, the narrative of the life of an individual, or the evolution of a program or an organization. Another technique is to narrow and expand the focus, evoking the metaphor of a camera lens that pans out, zooms in, then zooms out again. Some reports rely heavily on description of events, whereas others advance a small number of "themes" or perspectives. A narrative might capture a "typical day in the life" of an individual or a group. Some reports are heavily oriented toward theory, whereas others, such as Stake's (1995) "Harper School," employ little literature and theory. Regardless of form, qualitative researchers in all these studies wrestle with rhetorical issues.

Audience

A basic axiom holds that all writers write for an audience. Thus, writers consciously think about their audience or multiple audiences for their studies (Richardson, 1990, 1994). Tierney (1995), for example, identifies four potential audiences: colleagues, those involved in the interviews and observations, policymakers, and the general public. In short, how the findings are presented depends on the audience with whom one is communicating (Giorgi, 1985). For example, because Fischer and Wertz (1979) disseminated information about their phenomenological study at public forums, they produced several expressions of their findings, all responding to different audiences. They used a general structure, four paragraphs in length, an approach that they admitted lost its richness and concreteness. Another form consisted of case synopses, each reporting the experiences of one individual and each two and one half pages in length.

Encoding

A closely related topic is the encoding of the report for specific audiences. Earlier, in Chapter 6, I presented encoding the problem, purpose, and research questions; now I consider encoding the entire narrative report. Richardson's (1990) study of women in affairs with married men illustrates how a writer can shape a work for a trade audience, an academic audience, or a moral/political audience. For a trade audience, she encoded her work with literary devices such as

> jazzy titles, attractive covers, lack of specialized jargon, marginalization of methodology, common-world metaphors and images, and book blurbs and prefatory material about the "lay" interest in the material. (p. 32)

For the moral/political audience, she encoded through devices such as

> in-group words in the title, for example, woman/women/feminist in feminist writing; the moral or activist "credentials" of the author, for example, the author's role in particular social movements; references to moral and activist authorities; empowerment metaphors, and book blurbs and prefatory material about how this work relates to real people's lives. (pp. 32-33)

Finally, for the academic publications (e.g., journals, conference papers, academic books), she marked it by a prominent display of academic credentials of author, references, footnotes, methodology sections, use of familiar academic metaphors and images (such as "exchange theory," "roles," and "stratification"), and book blurbs and prefatory material about the science or scholarship involved. (p. 32)

Although I emphasize academic writing here, researchers encode qualitative studies for audiences other than academics. For example, in the social and human sciences, policymakers may be a primary audience, and this necessitates writing with less methods, more parsimony, and a focus on practice and results.

Richardson's (1990) ideas triggered my own thoughts about how one might encode a qualitative narrative. Such encoding might include the following:

- *An overall structure that does not conform to the standard quantitative introduction, methods, results, and discussion format.* Instead, the methods might be called "procedures," and the results might be called "findings." In fact, the heading might be phrased in the words of participants in the study as they discuss "denial," "retriggering," and so forth, as I did in our gunman case (Asmussen & Creswell, 1995).

- *A writing style that is personal, familiar, perhaps "up-close," highly readable, friendly, and applied for a broad audience.*

- *A level of detail that makes the work come alive (**verisimilitude** comes to mind [Richardson, 1994, p. 521]), a criterion for a good literary study where the writing seems "real" and "alive," transporting the reader directly into the world of the study, whether this world is the cultural setting of principals discussing the specifics of candidates they interviewed (Wolcott, 1994a) or women expressing emotion about their abusive childhoods (Morrow & Smith, 1995).*

Quotes

In addition to encoding text with the language of qualitative research, authors bring in the voice of participants in the study. Writers use ample quotes, and I find Richardson's (1990) discussion about three types of quotes most useful. The first consists of short eye-catching quotations. These are easy to read, take up little space, and stand out from the narrator's text but verify it—piled up and indented, and indented to signify different perspectives. For example, in the caring interaction phenomenological study by Riemen (1986), tables contain short quotes containing statements of significance from participants in the study. Dialogue, a variation of quotes, may be used, such as in the Principal Selection Committee study by Wolcott (1994a) in which he states conversation between candidates (e.g., "Mr. Fifth") and the interviewing principals.

The second consists of embedded quotes, briefly quoted phrases within the analyst's narrative. These quotes, according to Richardson (1990), prepare a reader for a shift in emphasis or display a point and allow the writer (and reader) to move on. We use embedded quotes extensively in our gunman study (Asmussen & Creswell, 1995) because they consume little space and provide specific concrete evidence, in the informants' words, to support a theme. Embedded quotes also are used extensively in the childhood sexual abuse grounded theory study by Morrow and Smith (1995).

A third type is the longer quotation, used to convey more complex understandings. These are difficult to use because of space limitations in publications and because longer quotes may contain many ideas and so the reader needs to be guided both "into" the quote and "out of" the quote to focus his or her attention on the controlling idea that the writer would like the reader to see. In the Vonnie Lee biography, Angrosino (1994) states several long quotes to provide complete answers to questions posed to Vonnie Lee and to develop for the reader a sense of Vonnie Lee's voice, questions such as "Why do you like the bus so much?" (p. 21).

Authorial Representation

How much of the "self," the researcher, is present in the narrative? What is the authorial stance of the writer (Richardson, 1994; Tierney, 1995)? How does the writer give "voice" to the researcher or what Derrida (1981) calls the "metaphysics of presence"?

When the writer is omniscient, postmodern thinkers "deconstruct" the narrative, challenging that every text is contested terrain and cannot be understood without references to ideas being concealed by the author and contexts within the author's life (Agger, 1991). This theme was espoused in my earlier discussion of Denzin's (1989a) "interpretive" approach to biographical writing.

How should an author proceed? According to Richardson (1994), the best writing acknowledges its own "undecidability" forthrightly, that all writing has "subtexts" that "situate" or "position" the material within a particular historical and locally specific time and place. In this perspective, no writing has "privileged status" (Richardson, 1994, p. 518) or superiority over other writings. Strategies to convey the position of the writer include disclosure by the author of his or her biases, values, and context that may have shaped the narrative. Also, the writer can be "present" in the narrative report through devices such as an epilogue (see Asmussen & Creswell, 1995), reflective footnotes, interpretive commentaries, or a section on the role of the researcher (see Marshall & Rossman, 1995).

In addition to these rhetorical issues, the writer needs to address how he or she is going to compose the overall narrative structure of the report and use embedded structures within the report to provide a narrative within the tradition of choice. I offer Table 9.1 as a guide to the discussion to follow, recognizing that I raise many overall and embedded structural approaches as they apply to the five traditions of inquiry.

BIOGRAPHY

Turning to biography, I am reminded of Edel (1984), who commented that "every life takes its own form and a biographer must find the ideal and unique literary form to express it. In structure, a biography need no longer be chronological" (p. 30). Edel's comment suggests that the traditional approach of a chronological treatment of the subject may have given way to more diversity in the form and structure of a biography. This has been my experience as I examine individual biographies and explore the literature about the narrative structure of them.

TABLE 9.1 Overall and Embedded Rhetorical Structures and the Five Traditions of Inquiry

Tradition of Inquiry	Overall Rhetorical Structures	Embedded Rhetorical Structures
Biography	• Extent of author interpretation (Clifford, 1970) • Extent of voice to subject (Denzin, 1989b) • Progressive-regressive method (Denzin, 1989b)	• Epiphany (Denzin, 1989b) • Theme or key event (Smith, 1994) • Transitions (Lomask, 1986)
Phenomenology	• Chapters in a "research manuscript" (Moustakas, 1994) • The "research report" (Polkinghorne, 1989)	• Figure or table for essence (Grigsby & Megel, 1995) • Discussion about philosophy (Harper, 1981) • Creative closing (Moustakas, 1994)
Grounded theory study	• Components of a grounded theory study (May, 1986) • Parameters of a grounded theory study (Strauss & Corbin, 1990)	• Extent of analysis (Chenitz & Swanson, 1986) • Form of propositions (Strauss & Corbin, 1990) • Use of visual diagram (Morrow & Smith, 1995)
Ethnography	• Types of tales (Van Maanen, 1988) • Description, analysis, and interpretation (Wolcott, 1994b) • "Thematic narrative" (Emerson et al., 1995)	• Tropes (Hammersley & Atkinson, 1995) • "Thick" description (Denzin, 1989b) • Dialogue (Nelson, 1990) • Scenes (Emerson et al., 1995) • Literary devices (Richardson, 1990)
Case study	• Report format with vignettes (Stake, 1995) • Substantive case report format (Lincoln & Guba, 1985) • Types of cases (Yin, 1989)	• Funnel (Asmussen & Creswell, 1995) • Amount of description (Merriam, 1988)

Overall Rhetorical Structure

At the larger structural level, the biographer needs to discern the degree to which there is "intrusion of the author into the manuscript" (Smith, 1994, p. 292). This issue, the extent of author interpretation in a biography, varies from one study to another. Clifford (1970)

organizes the possibilities. With minimal author interpretation, an "objective" biography is written, typically in the form of a collation of facts held together by a chronological theme. Next, although considered popular writing, the "artistic and scholarly" form is a presentation in a lively and interesting manner. Alternatively, in a "narrative" biography, the writer fictionalizes scenes and conversations based on letters and documents. Finally, in the "fictionalized" biography, the study reads like a historical novel with minimum attention to original research and primary documents.

Another large structural issue in a biography is the amount of voice given to the subject in the study. Denzin (1989b), for example, writes about the interpretive model of biographical writing. The researcher might write from the *subject's perspective*, with the narrative resting on the edited transcripts of interviews and minimal interpretation by the researcher. A *subject-produced biography* actually is an autobiography, an "instance of life," (p. 61) without being shaped by the investigator.

Finally, to study the "meaning structures" (Denzin, 1989b, p. 67), Denzin employs making sense of an individual's life using a **progressive-regressive method** whereby the biographer begins with a key event in the subject's life and then works forward and backward from that event, such as in Denzin's study of alcoholics.

Embedded Rhetorical Structure

Denzin (1989b) describes the "key event" or the "epiphany," defined as interactional moments and experiences that mark people's lives. He distinguishes four types: the major event that touches the fabric of the individual's life; the cumulative or representative events, experiences that continue for some time; the minor epiphany, which represents a moment in an individual's life; and episodes or relived epiphanies, which involve reliving the experience. Similar to Denzin's key event, Smith (1994) recommends another embedded structure: finding a theme to guide the development of the life to be written. This theme emerges from preliminary knowledge or a review of the entire life, although researchers often experience difficulty in distinguishing the major theme from lesser minor themes.

Other embedded rhetorical devices include the use of transitions, at which biographers excel. Lomask (1986) refers to these as built into the narratives in natural chronological linkages. Writers insert them through words or phrases, questions (which Lomask calls being "lazy"), and time-and-place shifts moving the action forward or backward. In addition to transitions, biographers employ foreshadowing, the frequent use of narrative hints of things to come or of events or themes to be developed later.

Angrosino's (1994) study of Vonnie Lee, for example, illustrates many biographical writing structures. At the outset, we are told that this is "explorations in life history and metaphor" (p. 14) as the type of biographical writing. Although difficult to classify according to Clifford's (1970) taxonomy of biographies, it has elements of the artistic and scholarly biography where Angrosino tells a compelling story of Vonnie Lee within the scholarly context of Vonnie Lee's life, his bus ride, and the thematic meanings of this bus ride. Certainly, Angrosino focuses on a key event, perhaps a minor epiphany in Vonnie Lee's life of the bus ride. When Angrosino joins Vonnie Lee on his bus ride, the reader gains a sense of movement from one bus stop to another until they reach Vonnie Lee's place of employment. The transitions of this journey are natural, and his struggles in life are foreshadowed early in the story through the recapitulation of his abusive early life. This bus journey, on several levels, becomes a metaphor for Vonnie Lee's life of empowerment and stability.

PHENOMENOLOGY

Those who write about phenomenology (e.g., Moustakas, 1994) provide more extensive attention to overall structures than to embedded ones. However, as in all forms of qualitative research, one can learn much from a careful study of research reports in journal article, monograph, or book form.

Overall Rhetorical Structure

The highly structured approach to analysis by Moustakas (1994) presents a detailed form for composing a phenomenological study.

These analysis steps—horizonalizing individual statements, creating meaning units, clustering themes, advancing textural and structural descriptions, and presenting an integration of textural and structural descriptions into an exhaustive description of the essential invariant structure (or essence) of the experience—provide a clearly articulated procedure for organizing a report (Moustakas, 1994). In my experience, individuals are quite surprised to find highly structured approaches to phenomenological studies on sensitive topics (e.g., "being left out," "insomnia," "being criminally victimized," "life's meaning," "voluntarily changing one's career during midlife," "longing," "adults being abused as children" [Moustakas, 1994, p. 153]). But the data analysis procedure, I think, guides a researcher in that direction and presents an overall structure for analysis and ultimately the organization of the report.

Consider the overall organization of a report as suggested by Moustakas (1994). He recommends specific chapters in "creating a research manuscript":

- *Chapter 1: Introduction and statement of topic and outline.* Topics include an autobiographical statement about experiences of the author leading to the topic, incidents that lead to a puzzlement or curiosity about the topic, the social implications and relevance of the topic, new knowledge and contribution to the profession to emerge from studying the topic, knowledge to be gained by the researcher, the research question, and the terms of the study.

- *Chapter 2: Review of the relevant literature.* Topics include a review of databases searched, an introduction to the literature, a procedure for selecting studies, the conduct of these studies and themes that emerged in them, a summary of core findings and statements as to how the present research differs from prior research (in question, model, methodology, and data collected).

- *Chapter 3: Conceptual framework of model.* Topics include the conceptual framework including theory to be used as well as the concepts and processes related to the research design (Chapters 3 and 4 might be combined).

- *Chapter 4: Methodology.* Topics include the methods and procedures in preparing to conduct the study, in collecting data, and in organizing, analyzing, and synthesizing the data.

- *Chapter 5: Presentation of data.* Topics include verbatim examples of data collection, data analysis, a synthesis of data, horizonalization, meaning units, clustered themes, textural and structural descriptions, and a synthesis of meanings and essences of the experience.

- *Chapter 6: Summary, implications, and outcomes.* Topics include a summary of the study, statements about how the findings differ from the literature review, recommendations for future studies, the identification of limitations, a discussion about implications, and the inclusion of a creative closure that speaks to the essence of the study and its inspiration for the researcher.

A second model, not as specific, is found in Polkinghorne (1989) where he discusses the "research report." In this model, the researcher describes the procedures to collect data and the steps to move from the raw data to a more general description of the experience. Also, the investigator includes a review of previous research, the theory pertaining to the topic, and implications for psychological theory and application. I especially like Polkinghorne's comment about the impact of such a report:

> Produce a research report that gives an accurate, clear, and articulate description of an experience. The reader of the report should come away with the feeling that "I understand better what it is like for someone to experience that." (p. 46)

Embedded Rhetorical Structure

Turning to embedded rhetorical structures, the literature provides the best evidence. A writer presents the "essence" of the experience for participants in a study through sketching a short paragraph about it in the narrative or by enclosing this paragraph in a figure. This latter approach is used effectively in a study of the caring experiences of nurses who teach (Grigsby & Megel, 1995). Another structural device is to "educate" the reader through a discussion about phenomenology and its philosophical assumptions. Harper (1981) uses this approach and describes several of Husserl's major tenets as well as the advantages of studying the meaning of "leisure" in a phenomenology.

Finally, I personally like Moustakas's (1994) suggestion: "Write a brief creative close that speaks to the essence of the study and its inspiration to you in terms of the value of the knowledge and future directions of your professional-personal life" (p. 184). Despite the phenomenologist's inclination to bracket himself or herself out of the narrative, Moustakas introduces the *reflexivity* that psychological phenomenologists can bring to a study, such as casting their initial problem statement within an autobiographical context.

Riemen's (1986) nursing research study of the caring interaction of nurses and their clients portrays many of the overall and embedded structural forms of a phenomenological study. Riemen presents this study as a "scientific report" complete with the sections identified earlier by Moustakas (1994). She also identifies the problem, the design, the review of the literature, a definition of terms, procedures for collecting and treating data, an analysis through the steps—statements, meanings, clusters of themes, and exhaustive descriptions—based on a procedure similar to that of Moustakas by Colaizzi (1978), and a discussion in light of the literature, conclusions, and summary. The end point of the findings is several exhaustive descriptions for a caring and noncaring interaction. She places these descriptions in tables in the text rather than in figures. The study also includes a discussion about the philosophical perspectives of phenomenological research.

GROUNDED THEORY

From reviewing grounded theory studies in journal article form, qualitative researchers can deduce a general form (and variations) for composing the narrative. The problem with journal articles is that the authors present truncated versions of the studies to fit within the parameters of the journals. Thus, a reader emerges from a review of a particular study without a full sense of the entire project.

Overall Rhetorical Structure

Most important, authors need to present the theory in any grounded theory narrative. As May (1986) comments, "In strict terms, the findings are the theory itself, i.e., a set of concepts and propositions which link them" (p. 148). May continues to explicate the overall structure of a grounded theory report and contrasts this structure with a "hypothetico-deductive" (hypothesis-testing) research in a quantitative project:

- *A study includes the major research question, how it evolved, and the definitions of key terms.* In a grounded theory study, this question is broad, and it will change several times during data collection and analysis.

- *The writer includes a literature review, but this review "neither provides key concepts nor suggests hypotheses as it does in hypothetico-deductive research" (May, 1986, p. 149).* Instead, this literature review shows gaps or bias in existing knowledge, thus providing a rationale for a grounded theory study. A researcher does not provide a theoretical framework in this review inasmuch as the intent of grounded theory is to generate or develop a theory.

- *Writing the methodology early in a study poses difficulties because it evolves during the course of the study.* However, the researcher begins somewhere, and she or he can describe preliminary ideas about the sample, the setting, and the data collection procedures.

- *The findings section presents the theoretical scheme.* The writer includes references from the literature to show outside support for the theoretical model. Also, segments of actual data in the form of vignettes and quotes provide useful explanatory material. This material helps the reader form a judgment about how well the theory is grounded in the data.

- *A final section discusses the relationship of the theory to other existing knowledge and the implications of the theory for future research and practice.*

Strauss and Corbin (1990) also provide broad parameters for their grounded theory studies. They suggest the following:

- *Develop a clear analytic story.* This is to be provided in the selective coding phase of the study.

- *Write on a conceptual level, with description kept secondary to concepts and the analytic story.* This means that one finds little description of the phenomenon being studied and more analytic theory at an abstract level.

- *Specify the relationships among categories.* This is the theorizing part of grounded theory found in axial coding when the researcher tells the story and advances propositions.

- *Specify the variations and the relevant conditions, consequences, and so forth for the relationships among categories.* In a good theory, one finds variation and different conditions under which the theory holds. This means that the multiple perspectives or variations in each component of axial coding are developed fully. For example, the consequences in the theory are multiple and detailed.

Embedded Rhetorical Structure

In grounded theory studies, the researcher varies the narrative report based on the extent of data analysis. Chenitz and Swanson (1986), for example, present six grounded theory studies that vary in the types of analysis reported in the narrative. In a preface to these examples, they mention that the analysis (and narrative) might address one or more of the following: description; the generation of categories through open coding; linking categories around a core category in axial coding, thus developing a substantive, low-level theory; and a substantive theory linked to a formal theory.

I see grounded theory studies that include one or more of these analyses. For example, in a study of gays and their "coming out" process, Kus (1986) uses only open coding in the analysis and identifies four stages in the process of coming out: identification in which the gay undergoes a radical identity transformation; cognitive changes in which the individual changes negative views about gays into positive ideas; acceptance, a stage in which the individual accepts being gay as a positive life force; and action, the process of engaging in behavior that results from accepting being gay such as self-disclosure, expanding friends to include gays, becoming politically involved in gay causes, and volunteering for gay groups. By contrast, Creswell and Brown (1992) examine the faculty development practices of chairpersons who enhance the research productivity of their faculties. We take the reader through most of the coding procedures of Strauss and Corbin (1990). We begin with open coding, move to axial coding complete with a logic diagram, and state a series of explicit propositions in directional (as opposed to the null) form.

Another embedded narrative feature is to examine the form for stating propositions or theoretical relationships in grounded theory studies. Sometimes, these are presented in "discursive" form, or describing the theory in narrative form. Strauss and Corbin (1990) present such a model in their theory of "protective governing" (p. 134) in the health care setting. Another example is seen in Conrad (1978) with formal propositions about academic change in the academy.

A final embedded structure is the presentation of the "logic diagram," the "mini-framework," or the "integrative" diagram where the researcher presents the actual theory in the form of a visual model. The elements of it are identified by the researcher in the axial coding phase, and the "story" in axial coding is a narrative version of it. How is this visual model presented? A good example of this diagram is found in the Morrow and Smith (1995) study of women who have survived childhood sexual abuse. Their diagram shows a theoretical model that contains the axial coding categories of causal conditions, the central phenomenon, the context, intervening conditions, strategies, and consequences. It is presented with directional arrows indicating the flow of causality from left to right, from causal conditions to consequences. Arrows also show that the context and intervening conditions directly impact the strategies. Presented near the end of the study, visual form represents the culminating theory for the study.

ETHNOGRAPHY

Ethnographers write extensively about narrative construction, such as how the nature of the text shapes the subject matter, to the "literary" conventions and devices used by authors (Atkinson & Hammersley, 1994). The general shape of ethnographies and embedded structures are well detailed in the literature.

Overall Rhetorical Structure

For example, Van Maanen (1988) provides the alternative ways in which "tales" can be told in an ethnography. Many ethnographies are written in the realist tale, reports that provide direct, matter-of-fact portraits of studied cultures without much information about how the ethnographers produced the portraits. In this type of tale, a writer uses an impersonal point of view, conveying a "scientific" and "objective" perspective. A confessional tale takes the opposite approach, and the researcher focuses more on his or her fieldwork experiences than on the culture. The final type, the impressionistic tale, is a personalized account of "fieldwork case in dramatic form" (p. 7). It has elements of both realist and confessional writing and, in my mind, presents a compelling and persuasive story. In both the confessional and impressionistic tales, the first-person point of view is used, conveying a personal style of writing. Van Maanen states that other, less frequently written tales also exist—critical tales focusing on large social, political, symbolic, or economic issues; formalist tales that build, test, generalize, and exhibit theory; literary tales in which the ethnographers write like journalists, borrowing fiction-writing techniques from novelists; and jointly told tales in which the production of the studies is jointly authored by the fieldworkers and the informants, opening up shared and discursive narratives.

On a slightly different note, but yet related to the larger rhetorical structure, Wolcott (1994b) provides three components of a good qualitative inquiry that are a centerpiece of good ethnographic writing as well as steps in data analysis. First, an ethnographer writes a "description" of the culture that answers the question, "What is going on here?" (p. 12). Wolcott offers useful techniques for writing this description: chronological order, the researcher or narrator order, a progressive focusing, a critical or key event, plots and characters, groups in interaction, an analytical framework, and a story told through several perspectives. Second, after describing the culture using one of these approaches, the researcher "analyzes" the data. Analysis includes highlighting findings, displaying findings, reporting fieldwork procedures, identifying patterned regularities in the data, comparing the case with a known case, evaluating the information, contextualizing the information within a broader analytic framework, critiquing the research process, and proposing a redesign of the study. Of all these analytic techniques, the identification of "patterns" or themes is central to much ethnographic writing. Third, interpretation should be involved in the rhetorical structure. This means that the researcher can extend the analysis, make inferences from the information, do as directed or as suggested by gatekeepers, turn to theory, refocus the interpretation itself, connect with personal experience, analyze or interpret the interpretive process, or explore alternative formats. Of these interpretive strategies, I personally like the approach of interpreting the findings both within the context of the researcher's experiences and within the larger body of scholarly research on the topic.

A more detailed, structured outline for an ethnography is found in Emerson et al. (1995). They discuss developing an ethnographic study as a "thematic narrative," a story "analytically thematized, but often in relatively loose ways . . . constructed out of a series of thematically organized units of fieldnote excerpts and analytic commentary" (p. 170). This thematic narrative builds inductively from a main idea or thesis that incorporates several specific analytic themes and is elaborated throughout the study. It is structured into the following:

■ *First is an introduction that engages the reader's attention and focuses the study, then proceeds to link the researcher's interpretation to wider issues of scholarly interest in the discipline.*

■ *After this, the researcher introduces the setting and the methods for learning about it.* In this section, too, the ethnographer relates details about entry into and participation in the setting as well as advantages and constraints of the ethnographer's research role.

■ *Analytic claims come next, and Emerson et al. (1995) indicate the utility of "excerpt commentary" units, whereby an author incorporates an analytic point, provides orientation information about the point, presents the excerpt or direct quote, and then advances analytic commentary about the quote as it relates to the analytic point.*

■ *In the conclusion, the author reflects and elaborates on the thesis advanced at the beginning.* This interpretation may extend or modify the thesis in light of the materials examined, relate the thesis to general theory or a current issue, or offer a meta-commentary on the thesis, methods, or assumptions of the study.

Embedded Rhetorical Structure

Ethnographers use embedded rhetorical devices such as figures of speech or "tropes" (Hammersley & Atkinson, 1995). Metaphors, for example, provide visual and spatial images or dramaturgical characterizations of social actions as theater. Another trope is the synecdoche, in which ethnographers present examples, illustrations, cases, and/or vignettes that form a part but stand for the whole. Ethnographers present storytelling tropes examining cause and sequence that follow grand narratives to smaller parables. A final trope is irony, in which researchers bring to light contrasts of competing frames of reference and rationality.

More specific rhetorical devices depict scenes in an ethnography (Emerson et al., 1995). Writers can incorporate details or "write lushly" (Goffman, 1989, p. 131) or "thickly," description that creates verisimilitude and produces for readers the feeling that they experience, or perhaps could experience, the events described (Denzin, 1989b). Denzin (1989b) talks about the importance of using "thick description" in writing qualitative research. By this, he means that the narrative "presents detail, context, emotion, and the webs of social relationships . . . [and] evokes emotionality and self-feelings. . . . The voices, feelings, actions, and meanings of interacting individuals are heard" (p. 83). He further contrasts thin description with thick description:

- *Thin description:* "I had trouble learning the piano keyboard" (Denzin, 1989b, p. 85).

- *Thick description:* "Sitting at the piano and moving into the production of a chord, the chord as a whole was prepared for as the hand moved toward the keyboard, and the terrain was seen as a field relative to the task. . . . There was chord A and chord B, separated from one another. . . . A's production entailed a tightly compressed hand, and B's . . . an open and extended spread. . . . The beginner gets from A to B disjointly" (Sudnow, 1978, pp. 9-10).

Also, ethnographers present dialogue, and the dialogue becomes especially vivid when written in the dialect and natural language of the culture (see, e.g., the articles on Black English vernacular or "code switching" in Nelson, 1990). Writers also rely on characterization in which human beings are shown talking, acting, and relating to others. Longer scenes take the form of sketches, a "slice of life" (Emerson et al., 1995, p. 85), or larger episodes and tales.

Enthographic writers tell "a good story" (Richardson, 1990). Thus, one of the forms of "evocative" experimental qualitative writing for Richardson (1990) is the fictional representation form in which writers draw on the literary devices such as flashback, flashforward, alternative points of view, deep characterization, tone shifts, synecdoche, dialogue, interior monologue, and sometimes omniscient narrator.

In Wolcott's (1994a) Principal Selection Committee study, for example, time is altered as a literary device as one hears first not about the successful candidate in the selection process but rather about Candidate No. 7 ("Mr. Seventh"). Also, in terms of the larger structure, with an introduction, "the ethnographic approach" (p. 116), and the "results," in the proceedings of the Principal Selection Committee, Wolcott tells a realist tale with several elements included in the thematic narrative as described by Emerson et al. (1995). Within the larger framework of his book, *Transforming Qualitative Data*, Wolcott (1994b) includes this principal selection story as an example of emphasis on description as he takes the reader through the details of the process of interviewing each of the candidates for the principal's position. Toward the end of this study, however, Wolcott analyzes three themes and notes in the conclusion his reflecting comments on the role of the principal in public schools. Thus, Wolcott follows his own model of description, analysis, and interpretation as an overall guiding structure for his composition. In addition, he refers to his story of the search process as an "episode," a longer scene as discussed by Emerson et al. (1995). He also refers to the "variety-reducing" behavior of the Principal Selection Committee, spoken of metaphorically as a cybernetic system, and mentions the paradox of both encouraging and managing change that falls on a principal. Wolcott (1994a) packs the study with quotes and provides a vivid picture of the committee deliberations. These pictures show his use of thick description, for example, his discussion about "Mr. First," the principal finally selected by the committee, and this individual's comments about his junior high:

> Mr. First described programs and problems at his junior high school. He explained how he had tried to break down the resistance of those parents who "have the attitude that the school only calls once a year and that's when the kid is in trouble." He cited several aspects of secondary school administration which he disliked: "I don't like the sports emphasis in high school, the problems with buses and scheduling, the court cases. Last year

I spent one day out of every two weeks in court. I'd rather be working with kids earlier in their lives, not in the kind of conference I sat in recently with a parent when a doctor told the mother her alternatives are either to give the daughter 'The Pill' or lock her up in a cage." (p. 138)

CASE STUDY

Turning to case studies, I am reminded by Merriam (1988) that "there is no standard format for reporting case study research" (p. 193). Unquestionably, some case studies generate theory, some are simply descriptions of cases, and others are more analytical in nature and display cross-case or inter-site comparisons. The overall intent of the case study undoubtedly shapes the larger structure of the written narrative. Still, I find it useful to conceptualize a general form, and I turn to key texts on case studies to receive guidance.

Overall Rhetorical Structure

One can open and close with vignettes to draw the reader into the case. This approach is suggested by Stake (1995), who provides a complete outline for the flow of ideas in a case study. These ideas are staged as follows:

- *The writer opens with a vignette so that the reader can develop a vicarious experience to get a feel for the time and place of the study.*

- *Next, the researcher identifies the issue, the purpose, and the method of the study so that the reader learns about how the study came to be, the background of the writer, and the issues surrounding the case.*

- *This is followed by an extensive description of the case and its context—a body of relatively uncontested data—a description the reader might make if he or she had been there.*

- *Issues are presented next, a few key issues, so that the reader can under-stand the complexity of the case.* This complexity builds through references to other research or the writer's understanding of other cases.

- *Next, several of the issues are probed further. At this point, too, the writer brings in both confirming and disconfirming evidence.*

- *Assertions are presented, a summary of what the writer understands about the case and whether initial naturalistic generalizations, conclusions arrived at through personal experience or offered as vicarious experiences for the reader, have been changed conceptually or challenged.*

- *Finally, the writer ends with a closing vignette, an experiential note, reminding the reader that this report is one person's encounter with a complex case.*

I like this general outline because it provides description of the case; presents themes, assertions, or interpretations of the researcher; and begins and ends with realistic scenarios.

A similar model is found in Lincoln and Guba's (1985) substantive case report. They describe a need for the explication of the problem, a thorough description of the context or setting, a description of the transactions or processes observed in that context, saliences at the site (elements studied in depth), and outcomes of the inquiry ("lessons learned").

At a more general level yet, I find Yin's (1989) 2 × 2 table of types of case studies helpful. Case studies can be either single-case or multiple-case design and either holistic (single unit of analysis) or embedded (multiple units of analysis) design. He comments further that a single case is best when a need exists to study a critical case, an extreme or unique case, or a revelatory case. Whether the case is single or multiple, the researcher decides whether to study the entire case, a holistic design, or multiple subunits within the case (the embedded design). Although the holistic design may be more abstract, it captures the entire case better than the embedded design. However, the embedded design starts with an examination of subunits and allows for the detailed perspective should the questions begin to shift and change during fieldwork.

Embedded Rhetorical Structures

What specific narrative devices, embedded structures, do case study writers use to "mark" their studies? One might approach the description of the context and setting for the case from a broader picture to a narrower one. For example, in our gunman case (Asmussen & Creswell, 1995), we describe the actual campus incident first in terms of the city in which the situation developed, followed by the campus and, more narrow yet, the actual classroom on campus. This funneling approach narrows the setting from that of a calm city environment to a potentially volatile campus classroom and seems to launch the study into a chronology of events that occur.

We also are cognizant of the amount of description in our case study versus the amount of analysis and interpretation or assertions. In comparing description versus analysis, Merriam (1988) suggests that the proper balance might be 60%/40% or 70%/30% in favor of description. In our gunman case, we balance in equal thirds (33%-33%-33%)—a concrete description of the setting and the actual events (and those that occurred within 2 weeks after the incident); the five themes; and our interpretation, the lessons learned, reported in the discussion section. In our case study, the description of the case and its context did not loom as large as in other case studies. But these matters are up to writers to decide, and it is conceivable that a case study might contain mainly descriptive material, especially if the bounded system, the case, is quite large and complex.

Our gunman study (Asmussen & Creswell, 1995) also represents a single-case study (Yin, 1989), with a single narrative about the case, its themes, and its interpretation. In another study, the case presentation might be that of multiple cases, with each case discussed separately, or multiple case studies with no separate discussions of each case but an overall cross-case analysis (Yin, 1989). Another Yin (1989) narrative format is to pose a series of questions and answers based on the case study database.

Within any of these formats, one might consider structures for building ideas. For example, in our gunman study (Asmussen & Creswell, 1995), we descriptively present the chronology of the events during the incident and immediately after it. The chronological approach seems to work best when events unfold and follow a process; case studies often are bounded by time and cover events over time (Yin, 1989). In addition to this approach, one might build a theory composed of identifying variables (or themes) that are interrelated; use a "suspense" structure with an "answer" to the outcome of the case presented first, followed by the development of an explanation for this outcome; or use an "unsequenced" structure consisting of events, processes, or activities not necessarily presented in the order in which they unfolded in the case (Yin, 1989).

A COMPARISON OF NARRATIVE STRUCTURES

Looking back over Table 9.1, I present many diverse structures for writing the qualitative report. What major differences exist in the structures depending on one's choice of tradition?

First, I am struck by the diversity of discussions about narrative structures. I found little crossover or sharing of structures among the five traditions, although, in practice, this undoubtedly occurs. The narrative troupes and the literary devices, discussed by ethnographers, have applicability regardless of tradition. Second, the narrative structures are highly related to data analysis procedures. A phenomenological study and a grounded theory study follow closely the data analysis steps. In short, I am reminded once again that it is difficult to separate the activities of data collection, analysis, and report writing in a qualitative study. Third, the emphasis given to writing the narrative, especially the embedded narrative structures, varies among the traditions. Ethnographers lead the group in their extensive discussions about narrative and text construction. Phenomenologists and grounded theory writers spend little time on this topic. Fourth, the overall narrative structure in some traditions is clearly specified (e.g., a grounded theory study, a phenomenological study, and perhaps a case study), whereas it is open to interpretation in others (e.g., a biography, an ethnography). Perhaps this conclusion reflects the more structured approach versus the less structured approach, overall, among the five traditions of inquiry,

SUMMARY

In this chapter, I discussed writing the narrative report. I began by discussing several rhetorical issues the writer must address. These issues include the audience for the writing, the encoding for that audience, the use of quotes, and an assessment of the representation of the author in the text. Then I turned to each of the five traditions of inquiry and presented overall rhetorical structures for organizing the entire study as well as specific embedded structures, writing devices, and techniques that the researcher incorporates into the study. A table of these structures shows the diversity of perspectives about structure that reflects different data analysis procedures and discipline affiliations. I concluded with observations about the differences in narrative structures among the five traditions, differences reflected in the variability of approaches, the relationships between data analysis and report writing, the emphasis in the literature of each tradition on narrative construction, and the amount of structure in the overall architecture of a study within each tradition.

▼ ADDITIONAL READINGS

A good, thoughtful book on writing qualitative research is Wolcott's (1990b) popular book. For examining the issue of authorial presence, I recommend Geertz's (1995) recent book in anthropology and an earlier book by Clifford and Marcus (1986). For general principles in writing scholarly research, examine Creswell (1994). For a discussion about encoding texts for audiences, see Richardson (1990). For the types of tales that can be told, the Van Maanen (1988) book is applicable in all the traditions of inquiry. Readers also are advised to examine qualitative studies found in journal articles and books as well as comments addressed by writers such as Denzin (1989b), Moustakas (1994), Strauss and Corbin (1990), Emerson et al. (1995), Hammersley and Atkinson (1995), Stake (1995), and Yin (1989).

Clifford, J., & Marcus, G. E. (Eds.). (1986). *Writing culture: The poetics and politics of ethnography*. Berkeley: University of California Press.

Creswell, J. W. (1994). *Research design: Qualitative and quantitative approaches*. Thousand Oaks, CA: Sage.

Denzin, N. K. (1989b). *Interpretive interactionism*. Newbury Park, CA: Sage.

Emerson, R. M., Fretz, R. I., & Shaw, L. L. (1995). *Writing ethnographic fieldnotes*. Chicago: University of Chicago Press.

Geertz, C. (1995). *After the fact: Two countries, four decades, one anthropologist.* Cambridge, MA: Harvard University Press.

Hammersley, M., & Atkinson, P. (1995). *Ethnography: Principles in practice* (2nd ed.). New York: Routledge.

Moustakas, C. (1994). *Phenomenological research methods.* Thousand Oaks, CA: Sage.

Richardson, L. (1990). *Writing strategies: Reaching diverse audiences.* Newbury Park, CA: Sage.

Stake, R. (1995). *The art of case study research.* Thousand Oaks, CA: Sage.

Strauss, A., & Corbin, J. (1990). *Basics of qualitative research: Grounded theory procedures and techniques.* Newbury Park, CA: Sage.

Van Maanen, J. (1988). *Tales of the field: On writing ethnography.* Chicago: University of Chicago Press.

Wolcott, H. F. (1990b). *Writing up qualitative research.* Newbury Park, CA: Sage.

Yin, R. K. (1989). *Case study research: Design and method.* Newbury Park, CA: Sage.

EXERCISES

1. Show that you understand the overall and embedded rhetorical structures for writing within your tradition of inquiry by drafting a complete narrative for your project. You might model your narrative after a journal article format using your tradition.

2. Develop a plan for the narrative structure for a study within your tradition of inquiry. To do this, design a matrix with two columns and seven rows. In the first column, list several writing criteria: the overall writing approach, the intended audience for the study, the encoding to be used in the narrative, the approach to using quotes, the strategies to display authorial presence, the general outline of the flow of the ideas in the manuscript, and the embedded rhetorical devices. In the second column, add information about how each criterion will be addressed in your project.

10

▼

Standards of Quality and Verification

Qualitative researchers strive for "understanding," that deep structure of knowledge that comes from visiting personally with informants, spending extensive time in the field, and probing to obtain detailed meanings. During or after a study, qualitative researchers ask, "Did we get it right?" (Stake, 1995, p. 107) or "Did we publish a 'wrong' or inaccurate account?" (Thomas, 1993, p. 39). To answer these questions, they ask participants in the study or, better yet, reflect on the question personally. And qualitative researchers look to the multivocal discourse communities such as constructivists and interpretivists to raise the questions and pose the answers (Denzin & Lincoln, 1994; Kvale, 1996; Lather, 1993).

In this chapter, I address the central question: "How do we know that the qualitative study is believable, accurate, and 'right'?" To answer this question introduces standards of quality in qualitative research and the approaches to verification. Unquestionably, this is a complex and emerging area (Lincoln, 1995) within qualitative research—to sort out, for example, where the discussion of *verification* ends and

AUTHOR'S NOTE: The original version of this chapter was co-authored with Dana Miller, Doane College, and was presented at the Midwest Educational Research Association, Chicago, October 13, 1995. Several comments presented in this chapter were modified from Creswell and Miller (1997).

that of *standards* begins. As a case in point, when Peshkin (1993) discusses "worthy research outcomes" (p. 28) for qualitative research, he places verification as one category amid others such as description, interpretation, and evaluation. As a working definition, I view verification as a *process* that occurs throughout the data collection, analysis, and report writing of a study and standards as *criteria* imposed by the researcher and others after a study is completed.

In this chapter, I begin by mentioning several issues currently being discussed about the standards to be employed for judging qualitative research. Then I turn to the topic of verification and examine the perspectives, terms, and procedures for assessing it. Finally, I take the discussion into the five traditions of inquiry and examine both the standards and the verification approaches being used by select authors.

Questions for Discussion

▼ What general standards exist for judging the quality of a qualitative study?

▼ What perspectives and terms are used by qualitative researchers for verification?

▼ What are eight popular verification procedures used in qualitative research?

▼ What verification procedures are used in each of the five traditions of inquiry?

▼ What standards exist for assessing the quality of a study within each of the five traditions of inquiry?

▼ How do the five traditions compare in terms of standards of quality and verification?

ISSUES IN THE DISCUSSION OF STANDARDS

Do standards exist for assessing the quality of qualitative research, standards at either the abstract or the specific level? Given the evolution of methodological priorities and concerns, Howe and Eisenhardt (1990) suggest that only broad, abstract standards are possible for qualitative (and quantitative) research. Moreover, to determine, for example, whether a study is a good ethnography cannot be answered apart from whether the study contributes to our understanding of important educational questions. Howe and Eisenhardt elaborate further, suggesting that five standards be applied to all research. First, they assess a study in terms of whether the research questions drive the data collection and analysis rather than the reverse being the case. Second, they examine the extent to which the data collection and analysis techniques are competently applied in a technical sense. Third, they ask whether the researcher's assumptions are made explicit, such as the researcher's own subjectivity. Fourth, they wonder whether the study has overall warrant, such as whether it is robust, uses respected theoretical explanations, and discusses disconfirmed theoretical explanations. Fifth, the study must have "value" both in informing and improving practice (the "So what?" question) and in protecting confidentiality, privacy, and truth telling of participants (the ethical question).

Within a postmodern, interpretive framework comes a second perspective, from Lincoln (1995), who thinks about the quality issue in terms of *emerging* criteria. She tracks her own thinking (and that of her colleague, Guba) from early approaches of developing parallel methodological criteria (Lincoln & Guba, 1985) to establishing the criteria of "fairness" (a balance of stakeholder views), sharing knowledge, and fostering social action (Guba & Lincoln, 1989), to her current stance. The new emerging approach to quality is based on three new commitments: to emergent relations with respondents, to a set of stances, and to a vision of research that enables and promotes justice. Based on these commitments, she then proceeds to identify eight standards:

- There are standards set in the *inquiry community* such as guidelines for publication. These guidelines admit that within diverse traditions of research, inquiry communities have developed their own traditions of rigor, communication, and ways of working toward consensus. These standards, she also maintains, serve to exclude and legitimate research knowledge and social science researchers.

■ The standard of *positionality* guides interpretive or qualitative research. Drawing on those concerned about standpoint epistemology, this means that the "text" should display honesty or authenticity about its own stance and about the position of the author.

■ Another standard is under the rubric of *community*. This standard acknowledges that all research takes place in, is addressed to, and serves the purposes of the community in which it was carried out. Such communities might be feminist thought, Black scholarship, Native American studies, or ecological studies.

■ Interpretive or qualitative research must give *voice* to participants so that their voice is not silenced, disengaged, or marginalized. Moreover, alternative or multiple voices need to be heard in a text.

■ *Critical subjectivity* as a standard means that the researcher needs to have heightened self-awareness in the research process and create personal and social transformation. This "high-quality awareness" enables the researcher to understand his or her psychological and emotional states before, during, and after the research experience.

■ High-quality interpretive or qualitative research involves a *reciprocity* between the researcher and those being researched. This means that intense sharing, trust, and mutuality exist.

■ The researcher should respect the *sacredness* of relationships in the research-to-action continuum. This means that the researcher respects the collaborative and egalitarian aspects of research and "make[s] spaces for the lifeways of others" (Lincoln, 1995, p. 284).

■ *Sharing of the privileges* acknowledges that in good qualitative research, the researcher shares her or his rewards with persons whose lives they portray. This sharing may be in the form of royalties from books or the sharing of rights to publication.

When the Howe and Eisenhardt (1990) criteria are compared to the Lincoln (1995) criteria, I am reminded of the emerging discourse on this subject of standards and the gulf of distance among those discussing standards in the qualitative area. I am also reminded of how these discussions largely take place *outside* of our traditions of inquiry approach, although Lincoln does acknowledge that inquiry communities within disciplines often shape the criteria. Before I explore these criteria *within* traditions, I turn to verification, which can become another criterion for assessing the quality of a study.

PERSPECTIVES, TERMS, AND PROCEDURES OF VERIFICATION

Exploring Perspectives and Terms

Multiple perspectives exist regarding the importance of verification in qualitative research, the definition of it, and procedures for establishing it. For example, writers search for and find *qualitative equivalents that parallel* traditional quantitative approaches to validity. LeCompte and Goetz (1982) display this approach when they compare issues of validity and reliability to their counterparts in experimental design and survey research. They contend that qualitative research has garnered much criticism in the scientific ranks for its failure to "adhere to canons of reliability and validity" (p. 31) in the traditional sense. They apply threats to internal validity in experimental research to ethnographic research (e.g., history and maturation, observer effects, selection and regression, mortality, spurious conclusions). They further identify threats to external validity as "effects that obstruct or reduce a study's comparability or translatability" (p. 51).

Some writers argue that authors who continue to use positivist terminology facilitate the acceptance of qualitative research in a quantitative world. Ely et al. (1991) believe that using quantitative terms tends to be a defensive measure that muddies the waters and that "the language of positivistic research is not congruent with or adequate to qualitative work" (p. 95). For example, Lincoln and Guba (1985) use *alternative terms* that, they contend, adhere more to naturalistic axioms. To establish the "trustworthiness" of a study, Lincoln and Guba use the terms "credibility," "transferability," "dependability," and "confirmability" as "the naturalist's equivalents" for "internal validity," "external validity," "reliability," and "objectivity" (p. 300). To operationalize these new terms, they propose techniques such as prolonged engagement in the field and the triangulation of data of sources, methods, and investigators to establish credibility. To make sure that the findings are transferable between the researcher and those being studied, thick description is necessary. Rather than reliability, one seeks dependability that the results will be subject to change and instability. The naturalistic researcher looks to confirmability rather than objectivity in establishing the value of the data. Both dependability and confirmability are established through an auditing of the research process.

As another example, rather than using the term *validity*, Eisner (1991) discusses the credibility of qualitative research. He constructs standards such as structural corroboration, consensual validation, and referential adequacy. In structural corroboration, the researcher relates multiple types of data to support or contradict the interpretation. As Eisner states, "We seek a confluence of evidence that breeds credibility, that allows us to feel confident about our observations, interpretations, and conclusions" (p. 110). He further illustrates this point with an analogy drawn from detective work; the researcher compiles bits and pieces of evidence to formulate a "compelling whole." At this stage, the researcher looks for recurring behaviors or actions and considers disconfirming evidence and contrary interpretations. Moreover, he recommends that to demonstrate credibility, the weight of evidence should become persuasive. Consensual validation seeks the opinion of others, and Eisner refers to "an agreement among competent others that the description, interpretation, and evaluation and thematics of an educational situation are right" (p. 112). Referential adequacy suggests the importance of criticism, and Eisner describes the goal of criticism as illuminating the subject matter and bringing about more complex and sensitive human perception and understanding.

Verification also has been *reconceptualized* by qualitative researchers with a postmodern sensibility; it is an "incitement to discourse." Lather (1991) comments that current "paradigmatic uncertainty in the human sciences is leading to the re-conceptualizing of validity" and calls for "new techniques and concepts for obtaining and defining trustworthy data which avoids the pitfalls of orthodox notions of validity" (p. 66). For Lather, the character of a social science report changes from that of a closed narrative with a tight argument structure to a more open narrative with holes and questions and an admission of situatedness and partiality.

In *Getting Smart*, Lather (1991) advances a "reconceptualization of validity." She identifies four types of validity including triangulation (multiple data sources, methods, and theoretical schemes), construct validity (recognizing the constructs that exist rather than imposing theories/constructs on informants or the context), face validity as "a 'click of recognition' and a 'yes, of course,' instead of 'yes, but' experience" (Kidder, 1982, p. 56), and catalytic validity that energizes participants toward knowing reality to transform it.

In a later article, Lather's (1993) terms become more unique and closely related to feminist research in "four frames of validity." The first, "ironic" validity, is where the researcher presents truth as a problem. The second, "paralogic" validity, is concerned with undecidables, limits, paradoxes, and complexities, a movement away from theorizing things and toward providing direct exposure to other voices in an almost unmediated way. The third, "rhizomatic" validity, pertains to questioning proliferations, crossings, and overlaps without underlying structures or deeply rooted connections. The researcher also questions taxonomies, constructs, and interconnected networks whereby the reader jumps from one assemblage to another and consequently moves from judgment to understanding. The fourth type is situated, embodied, or "voluptuous" validity, which means that the researcher sets out to understand more than one can know and to write toward what one does not understand.

Another postmodern perspective emerges from Richardson's (1994) metaphorical description of validity. She challenges the traditional central image of "validity" as a rigid, fixed, two-dimensional object. Rather,

> The central image is the crystal, which combines symmetry substances, transmutations, multidimensionalities, and angles of approach. Crystals grow, change, alter, but are not amorphous. Crystals are prisms that reflect externalities and refract within themselves, creating different colors, patterns, arrays, casting off in different directions. What we see depends on our angle of repose. . . . Crystallization, without losing structure, deconstructs the traditional idea of "validity" (we feel how there is no single truth, we see how texts validate themselves); and crystallization provides us with a deepened, complex, thoroughly partial understanding of the topic. Paradoxically, we know more and doubt what we know. (p. 522)

Another individual who shares a reconceptualization of validity is Wolcott (1990a). He suggests that "validity neither guides nor informs" his work (p. 136). He does not dismiss validity but rather

TABLE 10.1 Selected Studies, Perspectives, and Terms About Verification

Study	Perspective	Terms
LeCompte & Goetz (1982)	Parallel qualitative equivalents: Compare issues of validity to counterparts in experimental and survey research	Internal validity External validity Reliability Objectivity
Lincoln & Guba (1985)	Alternative terms: Pose alternative terms that apply more to naturalistic axioms	Credibility Transferability Dependability Confirmability
Eisner (1991)	Alternative terms: Reasonable standards for judging the credibility of qualitative research	Structural corroboration Consensual validation Referential adequacy
Lather (1993)	Reconceptualized: Four frames of validity	Ironic validity Paralogic validity Rhizomatic validity Situated/embedded voluptuous validity
Richardson (1990)	Reconceptualized: Metaphor of a crystal	Crystals: Grow, change, alter, reflect externalities, refract within themselves
Wolcott (1994)	Distraction: Neither guides nor informs	Understanding better than validity

places it in a broader perspective. Wolcott's goal is to identify "critical elements" and write "plausible interpretations from them" (p. 146). He ultimately tries to understand rather than convince and voices the view that *validity distracts* from his work of understanding what is really going on. Wolcott claims that the term *validity* does not capture the essence of what he seeks, adding that perhaps someone will coin a term appropriate for the naturalistic paradigm. But for now, he says, the term *understanding* seems to encapsulate the idea as well as any other.

The multiple views of verification, as shown in Table 10.1, show that writers view it from a quantitative perspective to find equivalents, employ a distinct language to provide a legitimacy for it in naturalistic research, reconceptualize it within a postmodern framework, or suggest that it is a distraction to good research. Overall, my approach to verification is to do the following:

■ View verification as a distinct strength of qualitative research in that the account made through extensive time spent in the field, the detailed thick description, and the closeness to participants in the study all add to the value of a study.

■ Use the term *verification* instead of *validity* because verification underscores qualitative research as a distinct approach, a legitimate mode of inquiry in its own right.

■ Employ the Lincoln and Guba (1985) terms of *trustworthiness* and *authenticity* as general concepts to use in establishing the credibility of a study.

■ Employ different frames of verification (validity) if using a post-modern perspective, such as those advanced by Lather (1991, 1993).

■ Recognize that the verification of a study has procedural implications and can be assessed by the researcher.

Exploring Procedures

It is not enough to gain perspectives and terms; ultimately, these ideas are translated into practice. From a review of major studies, my colleague and I (Creswell & Miller, 1997) present a classification of procedures found irrespective of perspectives and terms. Lincoln and Guba (1985) describe these as techniques "whereby the naturalist's alternative trustworthiness criteria may be operationalized" (p. 301). Our discussion turns to eight verification procedures often discussed in the literature, and they are not presented in any specific order of importance.

■ *Prolonged engagement* and *persistent observation* in the field include building trust with participants, learning the culture, and checking for misinformation that stems from distortions introduced by the researcher or informants (Ely et al., 1991; Erlandson, Harris, Skipper, & Allen, 1993; Glesne & Peshkin, 1992; Lincoln & Guba, 1985; Merriam, 1988). In the field, the researcher makes decisions about what is salient to the study, relevant to the purpose of the study, and of interest for focus. Fetterman (1989) contends that "working with people day in and day out, for long periods of time, is what gives ethnographic research its validity and vitality" (p. 46).

■ In *triangulation*, researchers make use of multiple and different sources, methods, investigators, and theories to provide corroborating evidence (Ely et al., 1991; Erlandson et al., 1993; Glesne & Peshkin, 1992; Lincoln & Guba, 1985; Merriam, 1988; Miles & Huberman, 1994; Patton, 1980, 1990). Typically, this process involves corroborating evidence from different sources to shed light on a theme or perspective.

■ *Peer review or debriefing* provides an external check of the research process (Ely et al., 1991; Erlandson et al., 1993; Glesne & Peshkin, 1992; Lincoln & Guba, 1985; Merriam, 1988), much in the same spirit as interrater reliability in quantitative research. Lincoln and Guba (1985) define the role of the peer debriefer as a "devil's advocate," an individual who keeps the researcher honest; asks hard questions about methods, meanings, and interpretations; and provides the researcher with the opportunity for catharsis by sympathetically listening to the researcher's feelings. This reviewer may be a peer, and both the peer and the researcher keep written accounts of the sessions, called *peer debriefing sessions* (Lincoln & Guba, 1985).

■ In *negative case analysis*, the researcher refines working hypotheses as the inquiry advances (Ely et al., 1991; Lincoln & Guba, 1985; Miles & Huberman, 1994; Patton, 1980, 1990) in light of negative or disconfirming evidence. The researcher revises initial hypotheses until all cases fit, completing this process late in data analysis and eliminating all outliers and exceptions.

■ *Clarifying researcher bias* from the outset of the study is important so that the reader understands the researcher's position and any biases or assumptions that impact the inquiry (Merriam, 1988). In this clarification, the researcher comments on past experiences, biases, prejudices, and orientations that have likely shaped the interpretation and approach to the study.

■ In *member checks*, the researcher solicits informants' views of the credibility of the findings and interpretations (Ely et al., 1991; Erlandson et al., 1993; Glesne & Peshkin, 1992; Lincoln & Guba, 1985; Merriam, 1988; Miles & Huberman, 1994). This technique is considered by Lincoln and Guba (1985) to be "the most critical technique for establishing credibility" (p. 314). This approach, writ large in most qualitative studies, involves taking data, analyses, interpretations, and conclusions back to the participants so that they can judge the accuracy and credibility of the account. According to Stake (1995), participants should "play a major role directing as well as acting in case study" research. They should be asked to examine rough drafts of the researcher's work and to provide alternative language, "critical observations or interpretations" (p. 115).

- *Rich, thick description* allows the reader to make decisions regarding transferability (Erlandson et al., 1993; Lincoln & Guba, 1985; Merriam, 1988) because the writer describes in detail the participants or setting under study. With such detailed description, the researcher enables readers to transfer information to other settings and to determine whether the findings can be transferred "because of shared characteristics" (Erlandson et al., 1993, p. 32).

- *External audits* (Erlandson et al., 1993; Lincoln & Guba, 1985; Merriam, 1988; Miles & Huberman, 1994) allow an external consultant, the auditor, to examine both the process and the product of the account, assessing their accuracy. This auditor should have no connection to the study. In assessing the product, the auditor examines whether or not the findings, interpretations, and conclusions are supported by the data. Lincoln and Guba (1985) compare this, metaphorically, with a fiscal audit, and the procedure provides a sense of interrater reliability to a study.

Examining these eight procedures as a whole, I recommend that qualitative researchers engage in at least two of them in any given study. Unquestionably, procedures such as triangulating among different data sources (assuming that the investigator collects more than one), writing with detailed and thick description, and taking the *entire written narrative* back to participants in member checking all are reasonably easy procedures to conduct. They also are the most popular and cost-effective procedures. Other procedures are more rigorous in their application, such as peer audits and external audits, and may involve not only time but also costs to the researcher.

STANDARDS AND VERIFICATION WITHIN
TRADITIONS OF INQUIRY

Regardless of the procedures used and the general standards employed by investigators, they assume more specific meaning when viewed within the context of our five traditions of inquiry. What is the process of verification, and what standards hold for biographical, phenomenological, grounded theory, ethnography, and case study research?

Biography

From among many authors who have written about biographical studies (e.g., Barzun & Graff, 1992; Bertaux, 1981; Edel, 1984; Lomask, 1986; Plummer, 1983), I have chosen Denzin (1970, 1989a, 1989b) to illustrate one author's stance on the question of verification in biographical writing. Denzin is especially important because his works illustrate how a single author modifies his or her perspective over time. I contrast his earlier writings in the well-known book *The Research Act*, which was published in 1970 and went through several editions, with two of his books to appear during 1989, *Interpretive Interactionism* and *Interpretive Biography*. In these writings, Denzin shifts from the classical, traditional approach to the interpretive approach.

Looking back on the "classic formulation" of biography, Denzin (1989a) offers the following procedures:

1. Select a series of research hypotheses and problems to be answered.

2. Record the objective events and experiences in the subject's life that pertain to the research problem.

3. *Triangulate* these events by source and point of view so that contradictions, irregularities, and discontinuity can be established.

4. Obtain the subject's interpretations of these events in their chronological or natural order.

5. Analyze these reports in terms of *internal validity, internal criticism, external validity,* and *external criticism.*

6. Resolve the validity of these sources and establish the priority of the sources for testing hypotheses.

7. Test the hypotheses while searching for negative evidence.

8. Organize the draft of the entire life history, submitting this to the subject for reactions.

9. Rework the report in its natural sequence and conclude with a statement concerning theory.

This approach is based on the assumption that lives have natural histories, unfold over time, and are marked with objective events and experiences. As Denzin (1989a) states, "A life is pictured as an orderly production" (p. 50). His perspective and language parallel those of quantitative research, and Denzin (1970) reflects on issues well known in experimental designs such as historic factors, maturational variables, subject bias, and subject mortality. This perspective on the critical assessment of documents also is reinforced in the biographical perspective of Edel (1984).

By 1989, Denzin's views had changed to incorporate methods inextricably related to the interpretive process. Denzin's (1989a, 1989b) books in that year are a good case in point. Gone are the comments about validity and reliability. Instead, Denzin (1989a) is primarily interested in the problem of "how to locate and interpret the subject in biographical materials" (p. 26). He advances several guidelines for writing an interpretive biography:

■ The lived experiences of interacting individuals are the proper subject matter of sociology.

■ The meanings of these experiences are best given by the persons who experience them; thus, a preoccupation with method, validity, reliability, generalizability, and theoretical relevance of the biographical method must be set aside in favor of a concern for meaning and interpretation.

■ Students of the biographical method must learn how to use the strategies and techniques of literary interpretation and criticism (i.e., bring their method in line with the concern about reading and writing of social texts, where texts are seen as "narrative fictions" [Denzin, 1989a, p. 26]).

■ When an individual writes a biography, he or she writes himself or herself into the life of the subject about whom the individual is writing; likewise, the reader reads through her or his perspective.

On validity, Denzin's position is best summarized by his following statement:

A concern with the very terms reliability, validity methods of data generation, hypotheses generation, validation and testing reveals a commitment to a "positivistic" philosophy of science. . . . The belief that somehow sociology can be scientific and humanistic at the same time reflects a compromising bias that inevitably places the scientific over the humanistic. (p. 6)

Thus, within a humanistic, interpretive stance, Denzin (1989b) identifies "criteria of interpretation" as a standard for judging the quality of a biography. These criteria are based on respecting the researcher's perspective as well as on thick description. He advocates the ability of the researcher to illuminate the phenomenon in a thickly contextualized manner (i.e., thick description of developed context) so as to reveal the historical, processual, and interactional features of the experience. Also, the researcher's interpretation must engulf what is learned about the phenomenon and incorporate prior understandings while always remaining incomplete and unfinished.

This focus on interpretation and thick description is in contrast to criteria established within the more traditional approach to biographical writing. For example, Plummer (1983) asserts that three sets of questions related to sampling, the sources, and the validity of the account should guide a researcher to a good life history study:

■ Is the individual representative? Edel (1984) asks a similar question: How has the biographer distinguished between the reliable and unreliable witnesses?

■ What are the sources of bias (about the informant, the researcher, and the informant-researcher interaction)? Or, as Edel (1984) questions, how has the researcher avoided making himself or herself simply the voice of the subject?

■ Is the account valid when subjects are asked to read it, when it is compared to official records, and when it is compared to accounts from other informants?

Phenomenology

Similar to interpretive biographers, phenomenologists view verification and standards as largely related to the researcher's interpretation. To illustrate different conceptions of verification in psychological approaches to phenomenology, neither empirical nor transcendental phenomenologists place substantial emphasis on verification beyond the perspective of the researcher. Still, Dukes (1984) goes further than Moustakas (1994).

For Dukes (1984), distinct procedures exist for "verification" in a study and include the lens of both the researcher and outside reviewers. First, the data can be submitted for confirmation to a different researcher who looks for "identical patterns." Second, an outside reader can recognize the logic of the experience and how it matches his or her own experience. Dukes refers to reader verification as the "eureka factor" (p. 201). Third, further verification occurs through "rational analysis of spontaneous recognition" (p. 201) where the researcher asks whether the patterns fit together logically and whether the same elements could be arranged to constitute an entirely different pattern. Finally, the strength of the results depends, in part, on whether the researcher can subsume them under other data. The experience of grief, for example, sheds some light on similar experiences such as separation or divorce.

For Moustakas (1994), "establishing the truth of things" (p. 57) begins with the researcher's perception. One must reflect, first, on the meaning of the experience for oneself; then, one must turn outward, to those being interviewed, and establish "intersubjective validity," the testing out of this understanding with other persons through a back-and-forth social interaction. But the investigator need not stop at this point. Moustakas discusses verification using informant feedback and illustrates his point using Humphrey's (1991) study of "searching for life's meaning." Humphrey requests that each participant carefully examine the unified description of the search for life's meaning and make corrections in the description. This approach, however, leads Humphrey to look more closely at his *own* fear of the existential void. Thus, judging the accuracy of a report falls to the researcher in phenomenological studies as well as to reviews by other researchers outside the study.

What criteria should be used to judge a phenomenological study? From the many readings about phenomenology, one can infer criteria from the discussions about steps (Giorgi, 1985) or the "core facets" of transcendental phenomenology (Moustakas, 1994, p. 58). I have found direct discussions of the criteria to be missing, but perhaps Polkinghorne (1989) comes the closest in my readings when he discusses whether the findings are "valid" (p. 57). To him, validity refers to the notion that an idea is well grounded and well supported. He asks, "Does the general structural description provide an accurate portrait of the common features and structural connections that are manifest in the examples collected?" (p. 57). He then proceeds to identify five questions that researchers might ask themselves:

1. Did the interviewer influence the contents of the subjects' descriptions in such a way that the descriptions do not truly reflect the subjects' actual experience?

2. Is the transcription accurate, and does it convey the meaning of the oral presentation in the interview?

3. In the analysis of the transcriptions, were there conclusions other than those offered by the researcher that could have been derived? Has the researcher identified these alternatives?

4. Is it possible to go from the general structural description to the transcriptions and to account for the specific contents and connections in the original examples of the experience?

5. Is the structural description situation specific, or does it hold in general for the experience in other situations? (Moustakas, 1994, p. 57)

Grounded Theory

Grounded theorists, too, believe that the responsibility for establishing verification in a study rests with the researcher. But verification in grounded theory research is an active part of the process of research and becomes part of the standards one should use to judge the quality of the study. Strauss and Corbin (1990) pose the question, "Under what conditions [does] the theory . . . fit with 'reality,' give understanding, and be useful [practically and in theoretical terms?]" (p. 257). This perspective underscores the importance of fit, understanding, and utility. Furthermore, in comments about verification, they alternate between the terms *verification* and *validity*. Their procedures for examining verification lie at different stages in conducting research. For example, one important step in grounded theory research is to develop open coding categories and then, through axial coding, to interrelate these categories. Here an important verification step takes place. The researcher poses questions that relate the categories and then returns to the data and looks for evidence, incidents, and events that support or refute the questions, thereby verifying the data. This procedure is called **discriminant sampling**.

Then, after the researcher writes the theory, the literature is used for "supplemental validation"; the researcher references the literature to give validation for the accuracy of the findings or how the findings differ from the published literature. Finally, for outside reviewers to judge the quality of a grounded theory study, judgments are made about the "validity, reliability, and credibility" of the data (Strauss & Corbin, 1990) within the standard canons of scientific research. Thus, a tone of quantitative standards permeates their writings, and the researcher's lens becomes critical in the process of establishing the verification of the data.

Strauss and Corbin (1990) go a step further and identify the criteria by which one judges the quality of a grounded theory study. They advance seven criteria related to the general research process:

Criterion #1: How was the original *sample* selected? What grounds?

Criterion #2: What major *categories* emerged?

Criterion #3: What were some of the events, incidents, actions, and so on (as indicators) that pointed to some of these major *categories?*

Criterion #4: On the basis of what categories did *theoretical sampling* proceed? Guide data collection? Was it representative of the categories?

Criterion #5:   What were some of the *hypotheses* pertaining to concep-
                tual relations (that is, among categories), and on what
                grounds were they formulated and tested?

Criterion #6:   Were there instances when *hypotheses* did not hold up
                against what was actually seen? How were these discrep-
                ancies accounted for? How did they affect the hypothe-
                ses?

Criterion #7:   How and why was the *core category* selected (sudden,
                gradual, difficult, easy)? On what grounds? (p. 253; em-
                phases added)

They also advance six criteria related to the empirical grounding of a
study:

Criterion #1:   Are *concepts* generated?

Criterion #2:   Are the concepts *systematically related?*

Criterion #3:   Are there many conceptual *linkages*, and are the catego-
                ries *well developed?* With density?

Criterion #4:   Is much *variation* built into the theory?

Criterion #5:   Are the *broaden conditions* . . . built into its explanation?

Criterion #6:   Has *process* (change or movement) been taken into
                account? (pp. 254-256; emphases added)

These criteria, related to the process of research and the grounding of
the study in the data, represent benchmarks for assessing the quality
of a study that the author can mention in his or her study. For example,
in a grounded theory dissertation, Landis (1993) not only presents
these standards but also assesses for her readers the extent to which
her study meets the criteria.

Ethnography

Ethnographers, such as Wolcott (1990a), show little interest in
verification of their studies. Likewise, Fetterman (1989) devotes only
scant attention to validity, calling it "ethnography validity." He embeds it within his comments about data analysis, referring to it as
"triangulation" of data sources, an approach in which the researcher
tests one source of information against another to strip away alterna-

tive rival explanations. By using this approach, he feels that researchers can "improve the quality of data and the accuracy of ethnographic findings" (p. 91). In a similar manner, mainstream ethnographers Hammersley and Atkinson (1995) use as a "crucial test for their accounts" (p. 228) triangulation and "respondent validation." The first calls for more than comparing different sources of information; the researcher compares information from different phases of the fieldwork, from different points in the temporal cycles occurring in the setting, and from different researchers. Respondent validation consists of determining whether the actors whose beliefs and behavior are being described recognize the validity of their accounts. These actors may have access to specific knowledge of the contexts of events, motives, and times, although this knowledge may be false, misinterpreted, misdescribed, or influenced by their social position or their perceptions of the research process.

Turning to Thomas (1993), what distinguishes a "critical" ethnography from a conventional ethnography is the former's emphasis on research with a political purpose to challenge research, policy, and other forms of human activity. Critical ethnographers further speak "on behalf" of their subjects as a means of empowering them, giving them "voice." The critical ethnographer begins with the assumption that all cultural members experience unnecessary repression to some extent. Thomas continues with thoughts about verification. He discusses two points where verification occurs in a study: data collection and writing the narrative. In data collection, the ethnographer exercises care in observing, recording, and analyzing the data. Bringing evidence to bear from several sources—triangulation—enriches the evidence and guards against potential errors. Having informants or other researchers read drafts of the report and replicate studies also illuminates whether the evidence is accurate and the concepts are fruitful. Finally, personal reflection is needed by the researcher. Having said this, Thomas then turns to the writing of the narrative and embeds the discussion of verification squarely within a critical discourse perspective. He asks the questions: What is the truth quotient of the study? and What are the social implications of our findings and how we present them? The first question relates to the need for the researcher to be reflective about how our values and ideologies influence our work so that we do not inadvertently exclude counter-examples. The second addresses whether the study challenges injustices and calls for reform.

From Fetterman (1989), Hammersley and Atkinson (1995), and Thomas (1993), one sees limited attention to verification and brief discussions about the importance of triangulation of data, using informant feedback, personal reflection, feedback from other researchers, and attending to the social implications of a study. Moreover, one gains a sense from studying ethnography that the interest is primarily in the fieldwork phase of the research in which one checks his or her data sources and relies on building an account in collaboration with informants.

This same fieldwork emphasis finds its way into the standards of quality advanced by ethnographers. For example, Spindler and Spindler (1987) emphasize that the most important requirement for an ethnographic approach is to explain behavior from the "native's point of view" (p. 20) and to be systematic in recording this information using note taking, tape recorders, and cameras. This requires that the ethnographer be present in the situation and engage in constant interaction between observation and interviews. These points are reinforced in nine criteria for a "good ethnography":

Criterion I.   Observations are contextualized.

Criterion II.   Hypotheses emerge in situ as the study goes on.

Criterion III.   Observation is prolonged and repetitive.

Criterion IV.   Through interviews, observations, and other eliciting procedures, the native view of reality is obtained.

Criterion V.   Ethnographers elicit knowledge from informant-participants in a systematic fashion.

Criterion VI.   Instruments, codes, schedules, questionnaires, agenda for interviews, and so forth are generated in situ as a result of inquiry.

Criterion VII.   A transcultural, comparative perspective is frequently an unstated assumption.

Criterion VIII. The ethnographer makes explicit what is implicit and tacit to informants.

Criterion IX.   The ethnographic interviewer must not predetermine responses by the kinds of questions asked. (Spindler & Spindler, 1987, p. 18)

This list, grounded in fieldwork, leads to a strong ethnography. Moreover, as Lofland (1974) contends, the study is located in wide conceptual frameworks; presents the novel but not necessarily new; provides evidence for the framework(s); is endowed with concrete, eventful interactional events, incidents, occurrences, episodes, anecdotes, scenes, and happenings without being "hyper-eventful"; and shows an interplay between the concrete and analytical and the empirical and theoretical.

Case Study

As compared to an ethnography, a case study, as viewed by Stake (1995), requires extensive verification. In fact, Stake devotes an entire chapter to triangulation. He asks the question, "Do we have it right?" and then proceeds to underscore the importance of validity in a qualitative study. He expands on two procedural concepts: triangulation and member checking. He suggests that **triangulation of information**—searching for the convergence of information—relates directly to "data situations" in developing a case study. For "uncontestable description," the researcher should expend little effort toward triangulation, whereas "dubious and contested description" requires confirmation through triangulation. When "assertions" are made and "key interpretations" are offered, the researcher needs to provide extra effort toward confirmation. However, for the "author's persuasions," little effort toward confirmation and triangulation is needed. To discuss how these confirmations are addressed, Stake offers the triangulation protocol suggested by Denzin (1970): data sources, investigator, theory, and methodological.

For member checking, Stake (1995) recommends that the researcher ask actors or participants to examine rough drafts of writing in which the actions or words of the actor are featured. This typically is done after data collection, and Stake comments that he usually receives little back from the actors in this process. Finally, to complete his discussion of verification, Stake provides a "critique checklist" (p. 131) for a case study report and shares 20 criteria for assessing a good case study report:

1. Is the report easy to read?

2. Does it fit together, each sentence contributing to the whole?

3. Does the report have a conceptual structure
   (i.e., themes or issues)?

4. Are its issues developed in a serious and scholarly way?

5. Is the case adequately defined?

6. Is there a sense of story to the presentation?

7. Is the reader provided some vicarious experience?

8. Have quotations been used effectively?

9. Are headings, figures, artifacts, appendixes, and indexes used
   effectively?

10. Was it edited well, then again with a last-minute polish?

11. Has the writer made sound assertions, neither over- nor
    under-interpreting?

12. Has adequate attention been paid to various contexts?

13. Were sufficient raw data presented?

14. Were data sources well chosen and in sufficient number?

15. Do observations and interpretations appear to have been
    triangulated?

16. Is the role and point of view of the researcher nicely apparent?

17. Is the nature of the intended audience apparent?

18. Is empathy shown for all sides?

19. Are personal intentions examined?

20. Does it appear that individuals were put at risk?
    (Stake, 1995, p. 131)

COMPARING THE TRADITIONS

As shown in Table 10.2, I make several distinctions about issues of quality and verification across the five traditions of inquiry. The perspectives differ, as do the terms used to describe verification. The procedures (e.g., triangulation, member checks) cover many of the approaches I review, and a substantial emphasis is on the personal interpretation of the researcher in several traditions. At times, the procedures are embedded within the data analysis steps (e.g., grounded theory); at other times, they are employed after completion of the study (e.g., phenomenology). Thus, verification, as mentioned earlier, can be both part of the process of research and a standard or criterion for judging the quality of a study. Some authors reconceptualize the traditional concept of validity as used by quantitative researchers (e.g., postmodern and interpretive writers), whereas others stay close to the positivist tradition (e.g., grounded theory). Others outright dismiss verification checks or shift their perspectives on validity in their writings (e.g., see Lather, 1991, 1993).

Also, the focus of verification may be either an "external" standard (e.g., asking informants to comment, looking to other researchers to verify, determining whether it appeals to audiences) or an "internal" standard (e.g., determining whether the research make sense to the individual or is consistent with the researcher's sense of meaning). The perspective for validity also varies. It might be the researcher, the reader, the audience, or some combination of these. This shapes the central question asked about validity. Furthermore, the extent to which "standards" exist and are explicated in some orderly fashion— and perhaps are indistinguishable from the verification question— also differs among the traditions, perhaps underscoring varying degrees of interest in the question of quality.

Given this diversity in perspectives and views, I recommend that qualitative writers strongly consider how they plan to substantiate the accuracy of their accounts and employ multiple procedures, even within a tradition of inquiry. Moreover, it is useful to ground the procedures in practices, and here I describe the practices within a few selected perspectives. Finally, I recommend that one find standards of quality *within a tradition* and present them in the qualitative report and reflect on how the study meets these standards. This practice may be difficult to follow in those traditions where only general guidelines exist.

TABLE 10.2   Perspectives, Terms, Procedures, and Standards Within Five Traditions of Inquiry

Tradition	Author(s)	Perspective	Terms	Procedures	Standards
Biography	Denzin (1989b)	Postmodern	Interpretation	• Thick description • Reflexivity	Not well detailed
Phenomenology	Dukes (1984)	Different terms	Verification Spontaneous recognition	• Confirmed by other researchers • Reflexivity	Not well detailed
	Mouslakas (1994)	Different terms	Truth Intersubjective validity	• Individual perceptions • Testing out with others	Not well detailed
Grounded theory	Strauss & Corbin (1990)	Parallel terms	Verification/ validity Supplemental validity	• Relating data to categories • Comparing findings to literature	See process and empirical grounding in Strauss & Corbin (1990)
Ethnography	Fetterman (1989)	Parallel terms	Ethnographic validity	• Triangulation of data sources • Informant feedback	See Spindler & Spinder (1987)
	Hammersley & Atkinson (1995)	Parallel terms	Triangulation Respondent validity	• Triangulation (multiple forms) • Member checking	See Lofland (1974)
	Thomas (1993)	Postmodern	Truth quotient	• Reflexivity • Social implications	
Case study	Stake (1995)	Parallel term	Validity	• Triangulation • Member checking	See Stake (1995) for 20 points

SOURCE: Adapted from a table presented in Creswell and Miller (1997).

I present only a small picture into the larger window of perspectives on this issue of standards and verification. The evolving perspective on qualitative validity is consistent with my views; it is impossible to reach a consensus. In addition, rather than a standard protocol for qualitative validity, I am moving toward a better understanding of multiple perspectives so that students and researchers can choose from among many types.

SUMMARY

In this chapter, I first assessed two general standards for judging the quality of qualitative research, noting that standards vary and evolve. Then I reviewed several perspectives on the verification or validity question, perspectives that ranged from authors creating parallels to positivistic thinking, to new terms, to a reluctance to embrace this question as important. Turning to procedures, I assessed eight approaches authors use to establish verification or the accuracy of their accounts, and I related these approaches to the five traditions of inquiry as well as standards espoused by writers within the traditions.

▼ ADDITIONAL READINGS

The two perspectives on standards, Howe and Eisenhardt (1990) and Lincoln (1995), show the variety of approaches to the quality question.

Howe, K., & Eisenhardt, M. (1990). Standards for qualitative (and quantitative) research: A prolegomenon. *Educational Researcher, 19*(4), 2-9.

Lincoln, Y. S. (1995). Emerging criteria for quality in qualitative and interpretive research. *Qualitative Inquiry, 1*, 275-289.

Key readings on the issue of verification or validity can be found in Goetz and LeCompte (1984) and in Lincoln and Guba (1985), a classic in the field.

Goetz, J. P., & LeCompte, M. D. (1984). *Ethnography and qualitative design in educational research.* Orlando, FL: Academic Press.

Lincoln, Y. S., & Guba, E. G. (1985). *Naturalistic inquiry.* Beverly Hills, CA: Sage.

For specific procedures within the traditions of inquiry, I recommend books by Denzin (1989a), Fetterman (1989), Hammersley and Atkinson (1995), Moustakas (1994), Stake (1995), Strauss and Corbin (1990), and Thomas (1993).

Denzin, N. K. (1989a). *Interpretive biography*. Newbury Park, CA: Sage.

Fetterman, D. M. (1989). *Ethnography: Step by step*. Newbury Park, CA: Sage.

Hammersley, M., & Atkinson, P. (1995). *Ethnography: Principles in practice* (2nd ed.). New York: Routledge.

Moustakas, C. (1994). *Phenomenological research methods*. Thousand Oaks, CA: Sage.

Stake, R. (1995). *The art of case study research*. Thousand Oaks, CA: Sage.

Strauss, A., & Corbin, J. (1990). *Basics of qualitative research: Grounded theory procedures and techniques*. Newbury Park, CA: Sage.

Thomas, J. (1993). *Doing critical ethnography*. Newbury Park, CA: Sage.

EXERCISES

1. Identify one of the eight procedures for verification mentioned in this chapter and use it in your study. Also, indicate whether your study changed as a result of its use or remained the same.

2. For the tradition you used or are planning to use, identify the criteria for assessing the quality of the study and present an argument for each criterion as to how the study meets or will meet each criterion.

11
▼

"Turning the Story" and Conclusion

▼ In this book, I suggest that researchers be cognizant of the procedures of qualitative research and of the differences in traditions of qualitative inquiry. This is not to suggest a preoccupation with method or methodology; indeed, I see two parallel tracks in a study: the substantive content of the study and the methodology. With increased interest in qualitative research, it is important that studies being conducted go forward with rigor and attention to the procedures developed within traditions of inquiry.

The traditions are many, and their procedures for research are well documented within books and articles. A few writers classify the

AUTHOR'S NOTE: I am indebted to Harry Wolcott for never quite being able to communicate what the scenario for an ethnography was supposed to look like but always making me think I was right on the verge of getting it (H. F. Wolcott, personal communication, October 10, 1996).

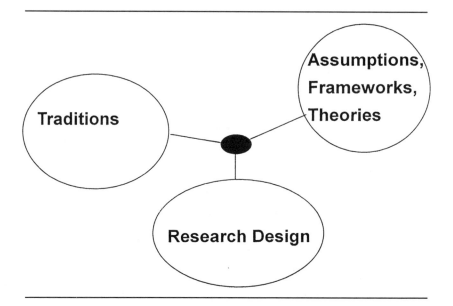

Figure 11.1 Visual Image of Conducting Qualitative Research

traditions, and some authors mention their favorites. Unquestionably, qualitative research cannot be characterized as of one type, attested to by the multivocal discourse surrounding qualitative research today. Adding to this discourse are perspectives about philosophical, theoretical, and ideological stances. To capture the essence of a good qualitative study, I visualize such a study as comprised of three interconnected circles. As shown in Figure 11.1, these circles include the tradition of inquiry, research design procedures, and philosophical and theoretical frameworks and assumptions. The interplay of these three factors contributes to a complex, rigorous study.

TURNING THE STORY

In this chapter, I again sharpen the distinctions among the traditions of inquiry, but I depart from my side-by-side approach used in prior chapters. I focus the lens in a new direction and "turn the story" of our gunman case (Asmussen & Creswell, 1995) into a biography, a phenomenology, a grounded theory, and an ethnography. Before continuing on with this chapter, the reader is advised to reexamine the gunman case study as presented in Appendix F and reviewed in Chapter 3.

Turning the story through different traditions of inquiry raises the issue of whether one *should* match a particular problem to a tradition of inquiry. Much emphasis is placed on this relationship in social and human science research. I agree this needs to be done. But for purposes of this book, my way around this issue is to pose a *general* problem— "How did the campus react?"—and then construct scenarios for *specific* problems. For instance, the specific problem of studying a single individual's reaction to the gun incident is different from the specific problem of how the students reacted, but both scenarios are reactions to the *general* issue of campus reaction to the incident. The general problem that I address is that we know little about how campuses respond to violence and even less about how different constituent groups on campus respond to a potentially violent incident. This was the central problem in our gunman case study (Asmussen & Creswell, 1995), and I briefly review the major dimensions of this study.

A CASE STUDY

This qualitative case study (Asmussen & Creswell, 1995) presents a campus reaction to a gunman incident in which a student attempted to fire a gun at his classmates. We titled this study "Campus Response to a Student Gunman," and we composed this case study with the "substantive case report" format of Lincoln and Guba (1985) in mind. This format calls for an explication of the problem, a thorough description of the context or setting and the processes observed, a discussion of important elements, and, finally, "lessons to be learned" (p. 362). After introducing the case study with the problem of violence on college campuses, this study provides a detailed description of the setting and a chronology of events immediately following the incident and events during the following 2 weeks. Then we turn to important themes to emerge in this analysis—themes of denial, fear, safety, retriggering, and campus planning. We construct a "layering of themes" building from the specific to the more general. These themes merge into two overarching themes: an organizational theme and a psychological or social-psychological theme. We gathered data through interviews with informants, observations, documents, and audio-visual materials. From the case emerges a proposed plan for campuses, and the case ends with an implied lesson for the specific midwestern campus and a specific set of questions this campus or other campuses might use to design a plan for handling future campus terrorist incidents.

Turning to specific research questions in this case, we asked the following. What happened? Who was involved in response to the incident? What themes of response emerged during an 8-month period? What theoretical constructs helped us understand the campus response and what constructs developed that were unique to this case? We entered the field 2 days after the incident and did not use any a priori theoretical lens to guide our questions or the results. The narrative first described the incident, analyzed it through levels of abstraction, and provided some interpretation by relating the context to larger theoretical frameworks. We verified our case by using multiple data sources for the themes and by checking the final account with select informants or "member checking."

A BIOGRAPHY

How might I approach this same general problem as an interpretive biographical study? Rather than identify responses from multiple campus constituents, I focus on one individual such as the instructor of the class involved in the incident. I sketch the working title, "Confrontation of Brothers: An Interpretive Biography of an Afro-American Professor." This instructor, like the gunman, is Afro-American, and his response to such an incident is situated within racial and cultural contexts. Hence, as an interpretive biographer, I might ask the following research question: What are the life experiences for the instructor of the class, and how do these experiences form and shape his reaction to the incident? This biographical approach relies on studying a single individual and situating this individual within his historic background. I would examine life events or "epiphanies" culled from stories he tells me. As a theoretical perspective, I might bring to the study the issues of race, discrimination, and marginality and how these issues play out both within the Afro-American culture and between Black and other cultures. These perspectives may shape how the instructor views the student gunman in the class. I also might compose this report by discussing my own situated beliefs followed by those of the instructor and the changes he brings about as a result of his experiences. For instance, did he continue teaching? Did he talk with the class about his feelings? For verification, my biography of this instructor would contain a detailed description of the context to reveal the historical and interactional features of the experience (Denzin, 1989b). I also would acknowledge that any interpretation of the instructor's reaction would be incomplete, unfinished, and a rendering from my own perspective as a non-Afro-American.

A PHENOMENOLOGY

Rather than study a single individual as in a biography, I would study several individual students and examine a psychological concept in the tradition of psychological phenomenology. My working title might be "The Meaning of Fear for Students Caught in a Near Tragedy on Campus." Assume that this concept is the "fear" of the students expressed during the incident, immediately after it, and several weeks later. I might pose the following questions. What fear did the students experience, and how did they experience it? What meanings did they ascribe to this experience? As a phenomenologist, I assume that human experience makes sense to those who live it and that human experience can be consciously expressed (Dukes, 1984). Thus, I bring a concept to explore (fear) and a philosophical orientation (I want to study the meaning of the students' experiences). I engage in extensive interviews with up to 10 students, and I analyze the interviews using the steps described by Moustakas (1994) and illustrated in the phenomenological study by Riemen (1986). I begin with an explication of my own fears and my experience of it. Then I read through all of the students' statements and locate significant statements about their meanings of fear. I would interpret the meanings of their statements and cluster these meanings into themes. My final step is to write a long paragraph providing a narrative description of *what* they experienced and *how* they experienced it to develop the "essential structure" of their experiences. Throughout the interviews, I "bracket" my own views about fear and rely on statements supplied by the students. As a phenomenologist, I would be most interested in the meanings of the experiences for myself first and then turn outward and establish the "intersubjective validity," testing this understanding with other individuals (Moustakas, 1994).

A GROUNDED THEORY STUDY

If a theory needs to be developed (or modified) to explain the campus reaction to this incident, then I would use grounded theory. For example, I might develop a theory around the "surreal" experiences of several students immediately following the incident, experiences resulting in actions and reactions by students. The draft title of my study might be "A Theory of Surreal Experiences for Students in a Campus Incident," as indicated by the following example:

> In the debriefing by counselors, one female student commented, "I thought the gunman would shoot out a little flag that would say 'bang.'" For her, the event was like a dream.

My research questions might be as follows: What theory explains the phenomenon of the "surreal" experiences of the students immediately following the incident? What were these experiences? What caused them? What strategies did they use to cope with them? What were the consequences of their strategies? What specific interaction issues and larger conditions influenced their strategies? Consistent with grounded theory, I would not bring into the data collection and analysis a specific theoretical orientation other than to see how the students interact and respond to the incident. The narrative format would be to first identify categories of these experiences and present them as open coding, and then to pose a visual picture of a theory composed of causal conditions, intervening and context factors, and specific strategies and consequences (axial coding). I would advance theoretical propositions or hypotheses that explain surreal experiences of the students (selective coding). I would verify my account by judging the thoroughness of the research process and whether the findings are empirically grounded. Corbin and Strauss (1990) provide specific questions that I use related to these two dimensions.

AN ETHNOGRAPHY

In grounded theory, my focus is on generating a theory grounded in the data. In ethnography, I turn the focus instead to a set of incidents as a critical event that offers an opportunity to see "culture at work." To keep the study manageable, I might begin by looking at how the event, although itself unpredictable, triggered quite predictable responses among members of the campus community. These community members responded according to their roles, and thus I could look at some recognized campus microcultures. Students constitute one such microculture, and they, in turn, comprise a number of further microcultures or subcultures. Because the students in this class were together for 16 weeks during the semester, they had enough time to develop some shared patterns of behavior and might be presumed to have become a more cohesive group after the incident, and so they might tentatively be identified as a microculture. Maybe that is getting too finely detailed. Suppose I decide instead to look at the entire campus community in my ethnographic study.

The title of the study might be "Getting Back to Normal: An Ethnography of a Campus Response to a Gunman Incident," and I ask the following questions: How did this incident produce predictable role performance within affected groups? Using the entire campus as a cultural system or culture-sharing group, in what roles did the individuals and groups participate? One possibility would be that they want to get the campus back to normal after the incident by engaging in predictable patterns of behavior. Although no one anticipates the exact moment or nature of the incident itself, its occurrence sets in motion rather predictable role performances throughout the campus community. Administrators do not close the campus and start running around warning, "The sky is falling." Campus police do not offer counseling sessions, whereas the Counseling Center does—but again, predictably, those sessions serve the student population, not police or groundskeepers who feel far more threatened. In short, predictable performances by campus constituencies follow in the wake of this incident.

Indeed, campus administrators routinely hold a news conference following the incident. Also, predictably, police carry out their investigation, and students ultimately and reluctantly contact their parents. The campus slowly returns to normal—an attempt to return to day-to-day business, to steady state, or to homeostasis, as the systems thinkers say. In these predictable role behaviors, one sees culture at work.

As I enter the field, I explore cultural themes of the "organization of diversity" and "maintenance" activities of individuals and groups within the culture-sharing campus. Wallace (1970) defines the "organization of diversity" as "the actual diversity of habits, of motives, of personalities, of customs that do, in fact, coexist within the boundaries of any culturally organized society" (p. 23). My data collection consists of observations over time of predictable activities, behaviors, and roles in which people engage that help the campus return to normal. This data collection depends heavily on interviews. My ultimate narrative of the culture-sharing campus is in Wolcott's (1994b) three parts: a detailed description of the campus, an analysis of the cultural themes of "organizational diversity" and maintenance (possibly with taxonomies or comparisons [Spradley, 1979, 1980]), and my interpretation of the meaning of these themes for a campus response to the terrorist incident in light of systems thinking. Specific detail and my storytelling abilities enhance the narrative.

To end the study, I might use the "canoe into the sunset" approach or the more methodologically oriented ending of checking my account with informants. Here is the first approach:

> The newsworthiness of the event will be long past before the ethnographic study is ready, but the event itself is of rather little consequence if the ethnographer's focus is on campus culture. Still, without such an event, the ethnographer working in his or her own society (and perhaps own campus as well) might have a difficult time "seeing" people performing in predictable everyday ways simply because that is the way in which we expect them to act. For the ethnographer working "at home," one has to find ways in which to make the familiar seem strange. An upsetting event can make ordinary role behavior easier to discern as people respond in predictable ways to unpredictable circumstances. Those predictable patterns are the stuff of culture.

Here is the verification ending:

> Some of my "facts" or hypotheses may need (and be amenable to) checking or testing if I have carried my analysis in that direction. If I have tried to

be more interpretive, then perhaps I can "try out" the account on some of the people described, and the cautions and exceptions they express can be included in my final account to suggest that things are even more complex than the way I have presented them.

CONCLUSION

How have I answered my "compelling" question raised at the outset: How does the tradition of inquiry shape the design of a study? First, one of the most pronounced ways is in the focus of the study. As discussed in Chapter 3 and depicted in Figure 3.1, a theory differs from the exploration of a phenomenon or concept, from an in-depth case, and from the creation of an individual or group portrait. I find Figure 3.1 a useful orientating device for deciding which tradition I will use in a study.

However, this is not as clear-cut as it appears. A single case study of an individual can be approached either as a biography or as a case study. A cultural system may be explored as an ethnography, whereas a smaller "bounded" system, such as an event, a program, or an activity, may be studied as a case study. Both are systems, and the problem arises when one undertakes a microethnography, which might be approached either as a case study or as an ethnography. However, when one seeks to study cultural behavior, language, or artifacts, then the study of a system for me should be undertaken as an ethnography.

Second, a theoretical orientation plays a more central role in some traditions than in others. The extent to which one enters the field with a priori theories or a strong theoretical or philosophical lens varies, as discussed in Chapter 5. The "theory-before" traditions (H. F. Wolcott, personal communication, February 13, 1993) include ethnographies (i.e., cultural themes) and phenomenologies (i.e., Husserl's [1931] philosophical tenets), whereas the "theory-after" tradition is grounded theory. Case studies and biographies reside in the middle of a continuum of theory-before and theory-after, where examples of both extremes exist.

Third, the tradition shapes the language of the research design procedures in a study, especially terms used in the introduction to a study, the data collection, and the analysis phases of design. I incorporated these terms into Chapter 6 as I discussed procedures for designing the problem statement, the purpose statement, and the research questions and emphasized them in data collection and analysis. Writers encode their studies with terms specific to a tradition (Richardson, 1990). The glossary in Appendix A provides a useful list of terms within each tradition that researchers might incorporate into the language of their studies.

Fourth, the tradition influences *what* and *who* is studied, as discussed in Chapter 7. A study may consist of a single individual (i.e., biography), groups of people (i.e., phenomenology, grounded theory), or a culture (i.e., ethnography). A case study might fit into all three of these categories as one explores a single individual, an event, or a large social setting. Also in Chapter 7, I highlighted how the traditions vary in the extent of data collection, from primarily unidimensional approaches (i.e., biographies = interviews; grounded theory = interviews; phenomenology = interviews) to multidimensional approaches (i.e., ethnographies = observations, interviews, and documents; case studies = interviews, observations, documents, archival material, and video). Although these forms of data collection are not fixed, I see a general pattern that differentiates the traditions.

Fifth, the distinctions among the traditions are most pronounced in the data analysis phase, as discussed in Chapter 8. Data analysis ranges from unstructured to structured approaches. Among the more unstructured approaches, I include ethnographies (with the exception of Spradley, 1979, 1980) and biographies (especially those interpretive forms advanced by Denzin, 1989b). The more structured approaches consist of grounded theory with a systematic procedure and phenomenology (see Colazzi's [1978] approach and those of Dukes, 1984, and Moustakas, 1994) and case studies (Stake, 1995). These procedures provide direction for narrative approaches. Also, the traditions shape the amount of relative weight given to description in the analysis of the data. In ethnographies, case studies, and biographies, researchers employ substantial description; in phenomenologies, investigators use less description; and grounded theorists seem not to use it at all, choosing to move directly into analysis of the data.

Sixth, the tradition shapes the final written product as well as the embedded rhetorical structures used in the narrative. This explains why qualitative studies look so different and are composed so differently, as discussed in Chapter 9. Take, for example, the presence of the researcher. The presence of the researcher is found little in the more "objective" accounts provided in grounded theory. Alternatively, the researcher is center stage in ethnographies and possibly in case studies where "interpretation" plays a major role.

Seventh, the criteria for assessing the quality of a study differ among the traditions, as discussed in Chapter 10. Although some overlap exists in the procedures for verification, the criteria for assessing the worth of a study are available for each tradition.

In summary, when designing a qualitative study, I recommend that the author design the study within one of the traditions of qualitative inquiry. This means that components of the design process (e.g., theoretical framework, research purpose and questions, data collection, data analysis, report writing, verification) will reflect the procedures of the tradition and be composed with the encoding and composing features of that tradition. This is not to rigidly suggest that one cannot mix traditions and employ, for example, a grounded theory analysis procedure within a case study design. "Purity" is not my aim. But in this book, I suggested that the reader sort out the traditions first before combining them and see each one as a rigorous procedure in its own right. As I contrasted the five traditions, I found distinctions as well as overlap among them, but approaching a study attuned to procedures found within the tradition will enhance the sophistication of the project and convey a level of expertise of the researcher needed within qualitative inquiry.

EXERCISES

1. Take the qualitative study you have completed and turn the story into one of the other traditions of qualitative inquiry.

2. In this chapter, I presented the study of campus response to a gunman incident in five ways. Take each scenario and label the parts using the language of each tradition and the terms found in the glossary in Appendix A.

APPENDIX A

▼

An Annotated
Glossary of Terms

▼ The definitions in this glossary represent key terms as they are used and defined in this book. Many definitions exist for these terms, but the most workable definitions for me (and hopefully the reader) are those that reflect the content and references presented in this book. I group the terms by tradition of inquiry and alphabetize them within the tradition, and at the end of the glossary I define additional terms that do not conveniently relate to any specific tradition.

▼ BIOGRAPHY ▼

autobiography This form of biographical writing is the narrative account of a person's life that he or she has personally written or otherwise recorded (Angrosino, 1989a).

biographical study This is the study of a single individual and his or her experiences as told to the researcher or as found in documents

GLOSSARY/
BIOGRAPHY

and archival materials (Denzin, 1989a). I use the term to connotate the broad genre of biographical writings that includes individual biographies, autobiographies, life histories, and oral histories.

chronology   This is a common approach for undertaking a biographical form of writing in which the author presents the life in stages or steps according to the age of the individual (Denzin, 1989a).

classical biography   This form of biography reflects the author's use of a theoretical orientation, formal hypotheses or questions, and validity, reliability, and generalizability issues in a scientific tradition. It is called the "classical" approach by Denzin (1989a).

epiphanies   These are special events in an individual's life that represent turning points. They vary in their impact from minor epiphanies to major epiphanies, and they may be positive or negative in their impact (Denzin, 1989a).

historical context   This is the context in which the researcher presents the life of the subject. The context may be the subject's family, the subject's society, or the history, social, or political trends of the subject's times (Denzin, 1989a).

interpretive biography   This form of a biography is based on the author being present in the study and open recognition that biographical writing is, in part, autobiographical of the author. Thus, this writing is situated in the life experiences of the author as well as the individual being studied. As mentioned by Denzin (1989a), "We create the persons we write about, just as they create themselves when they engage in storytelling practices" (p. 82).

life course stages and experiences   These are stages in an individual's life or key events that become the focus for the biographer (Denzin, 1989a).

life history   This is a form of biographical writing in which the researcher reports an extensive record of a person's life as told to the researcher (see Geiger, 1986). Thus, the individual being studied is alive and life as lived in the present is influenced by personal, institutional, and social histories (Cole, 1994). The investigator may use different disciplinary perspectives (Smith, 1994), such as the exploration of an individual's life as representative of a culture, as in an anthropological life history.

oral history   In this biographical approach, the researcher gathers personal recollections of events and their causes and effects from an individual or several individuals. This information may be collected through tape recordings or through written works of individuals who have died or are still living. It often is limited to the distinctly "modern" sphere and to accessible people (Plummer, 1983).

progressive-regressive method   This is an approach to writing a biography in which the researcher begins with a key event in the subject's life and then works forward and backward from that event (Denzin, 1989a).

single individual   This is the person studied in a biography. This person may be an individual with great distinction or an ordinary person. This person's life may be a lesser life, a great life, a thwarted life, a life cut short, or a life miraculous in its unapplauded achievement (Heilbrun, 1988).

stories   These are aspects that surface during an interview in which the participant describes a situation, usually with a beginning, a middle, and an end, so that the researcher can capture a complete idea and integrate it, intact, into the qualitative narrative (Denzin, 1989a).

▼ PHENOMENOLOGY ▼

clusters of meanings   This is the third step in phenomenological data analysis in which the researcher clusters the statements into themes or meaning units, removing overlapping and repetitive statements (Moustakas, 1994).

epoche or bracketing   This is the first step in "phenomenological reduction," the process of data analysis in which the researcher sets aside, as far as is humanly possible, all preconceived experiences to best understand the experiences of participants in the study (Moustakas, 1994).

essential, invariant structure (or essence)   This is the goal of the phenomenologist, to reduce the textural (*what*) and structural (*how*) meanings of experiences to a brief description that typifies the experiences of all of the participants in a study. All individuals experience it; hence, it is invariant, and it is a reduction to the "essentials" of the experiences (Moustakas, 1994).

horizonalization   This is the second step in the phenomenological data analysis in which the researcher lists every significant statement relevant to the topic and gives it equal value (Moustakas, 1994).

imaginative variation or structural description   Following the textural description, the researcher writes a "structural" description of an experience, addressing *how* the phenomenon was experienced. It involves seeking all possible meanings, seeking divergent perspectives, and varying the frames of reference about the phenomenon or using imaginative variation (Moustakas, 1994).

intentionality of consciousness   Being conscious of objects always is intentional. Thus, when I perceive a tree, "My intentional experience is a combination of the outward appearance of the tree and the tree as contained in my consciousness based on memory, image, and meaning" (Moustakas, 1994, p. 55).

lived experiences   This term emphasizes in phenomenological studies the importance of individual experiences of people as conscious human beings (Moustakas, 1994).

phenomenological data analysis   Several approaches to analyzing phenomenological data are represented in the literature. Moustakas (1994) reviews these approaches and then advances his own. I rely on the Moustakas modification that includes the researcher bringing personal experiences into the study, the recording of significant statements and meanings, and the development of descriptions to arrive at the essences of the experiences.

phenomenological study   This type of study describes the meaning of experiences of a phenomenon (or topic or concept) for several individuals. In this study, the researcher reduces the experiences to a central meaning or the "essence" of the experience (Moustakas, 1994).

the phenomenon   This is the central concept being examined by the phenomenologist. It is the concept being experienced by subjects in a study, psychological concepts such as grief, anger, or love.

philosophical perspectives   Specific philosophical perspectives provide the foundation for phenomenological studies. These perspectives originated in the 1930s writings of Husserl. These perspectives include having the investigator conduct research with a broader perspective than that of traditional empirical, quantitative science; suspend his or her own preconceptions of experiences; experience an object through his or her own senses (i.e., conscious of it) as well as see it "out there" as real; and report the meaning individuals ascribe to an experience in a few statements that capture the "essence" (Stewart & Mickunas, 1990).

psychological approach   This is the approach taken by psychologists who discuss the inquiry procedures of phenomenology (e.g., Giorgi, 1994; Moustakas, 1994; Polkinghorne, 1989). In their writings, they examine psychological themes for meaning, and they may incorporate their own selves into the studies.

structural description From the first three steps in phenomenological data analysis, the researcher writes a description of "how" the phenomenon was experienced by individuals in the study (Moustakas, 1994).

textural description From the first three steps in phenomenological data analysis, the researcher writes about *what* was experienced, a description of the meaning individuals have experienced (Moustakas, 1994).

transcendental phenomenology According to Moustakas (1994), Husserl espoused this form of phenomenology, and it becomes a guiding approach to Moustakas. In this approach, the researcher sets aside prejudgments regarding the phenomenon being investigated. Also, the researcher relies on intuition, imagination, and universal structures to obtain a picture of the experience and uses systematic methods of analysis as advanced by Moustakas (1994).

GLOSSARY/
PHENOMENOLOGY

axial coding   This step in the coding process follows open coding. The researcher takes the categories of open coding, identifies one as a central phenomenon, and then returns to the database to identify (a) what caused this phenomenon to occur, (b) what strategies or actions actors employed in response to it, (c) what context (specific) and intervening conditions (broad context) influenced the strategies, and (d) what consequences resulted from these strategies. The overall process is one of relating categories of information to the central phenomenon category (Strauss & Corbin, 1990).

category   This is a unit of information analyzed in grounded theory research. It is composed of events, happenings, and instances of phenomenon (Strauss & Corbin, 1990) and given a short label. When researchers analyze grounded theory data, their analysis leads, initially, to the formation of a number of categories during the process called "open coding." Then, in "axial coding," the analyst interrelates the categories and forms a visual model.

causal conditions   In axial coding, these are the categories of conditions I identify in my database that cause or influence the central phenomenon to occur.

central phenomenon   This is an aspect of axial coding and the formation of the visual theory, model, or paradigm. In open coding, the researcher chooses a central category around which to develop the theory. I choose this central category by examining my open coding categories and selecting one that holds the most conceptual interest, is most frequently discussed by participants in the study, and is most "saturated" with information. I then place it at the center of my grounded theory model and label it "central phenomenon."

coding paradigm or logic diagram   In axial coding, the central phenomenon, causal conditions, context, intervening conditions, strategies, and consequences are portrayed in a visual diagram. This diagram is drawn with boxes and arrows indicating the process or flow of activities. It is helpful to view this diagram as more than axial coding; it is the theoretical model developed in a grounded theory study (see Morrow & Smith, 1995).

conditional matrix   This is a diagram, typically drawn late in a grounded theory study, that presents the conditions and consequences related to the phenomenon under study. It enables the researcher to both distinguish and link levels of conditions and consequences specified in the axial coding model (Strauss & Corbin, 1990). It is a step seldom seen in data analysis in grounded theory studies.

consequences   In axial coding, these are the outcomes of strategies taken by participants in the study. These outcomes may be positive, negative, or neutral (Strauss & Corbin, 1990).

constant comparative   This was an early term (Conrad, 1978) in grounded theory research that referred to the researcher identifying incidents, events, and activities and constantly comparing them to an emerging category to develop and saturate the category.

context   In axial coding, this is the particular set of conditions within which the strategies occur (Strauss & Corbin, 1990). These are specific in nature and close to the actions and interactions.

dimensionalized   This is the smallest unit of information analyzed in grounded theory research. The researcher takes the properties and places them on a continuum or dimensionalizes them to see the extreme possibilities for the property. It appears in the "open coding" analysis (Strauss & Corbin, 1990).

discriminant sampling   This is a form of sampling that occurs late in a grounded theory project after the researcher has developed a model. The question becomes, at this point: How would the model hold if I gather more information from people similar to those I initially interviewed? Thus, in verifying the model, the researcher then chooses sites, persons, and/or documents that "will maximize opportunities for verifying the story line, relationships between categories, and for filling in poorly developed categories" (Strauss & Corbin, 1990, p. 187).

generate or discover a theory Grounded theory research is the process of developing a theory, not testing a theory. Researchers might begin with a tentative theory they want to modify or no theory at all with the intent of "grounding" the study in views of participants. In either case, an inductive model of theory development is at work here, and the process is one of generating or discovering a theory grounded in views from participants in the field.

grounded theory study In this type of study, the researcher generates an abstract analytical schema of a phenomenon, a theory that explains some action, interaction, or process. This is accomplished primarily through collecting interview data, making multiple visits to the field (theoretical sampling), attempting to develop and interrelate categories (constant comparison) of information, and writing a substantive or context-specific theory (Strauss & Corbin, 1990).

in vivo codes These are codes or categories in grounded theory research where the investigator uses the exact words of the interviewee to form the names for the codes or categories. They are "catchy" and immediately draw the attention of the reader (Strauss & Corbin, 1990, p. 69).

intervening conditions In axial coding, these are the broader conditions—broader than the context—within which the strategies occur. They might be social, economic, and political forces, for example, that influence the strategies in response to the central phenomenon (Strauss & Corbin, 1990).

memoing This is the process in grounded theory research of the researcher writing down ideas about the evolving theory. It could be in the form of preliminary propositions (hypotheses), ideas about emerging categories, or some aspects of the connection of categories as in axial coding. In general, these are written records of analysis that help with the formulation of theory (Strauss & Corbin, 1990).

open coding This is the first step in the data analysis process for a grounded theorist. It involves taking data (e.g., interview transcrip-

GLOSSARY/
GROUNDED THEORY

tions) and segmenting them into categories of information (Strauss & Corbin, 1990). I recommend that researchers try to develop a small number of categories, slowly reducing the number from, say, 30 to 5 or 6 that become major themes in a study.

properties   These are other units of information analyzed in grounded theory research. Each category in grounded theory research can be subdivided into properties that provide the broad dimensions for the category. Strauss and Corbin (1990) refer to them as "attributes or characteristics pertaining to a category" (p. 61). They appear in "open coding" analysis.

propositions   These are hypotheses, typically written in a directional form, that relate categories in a study. They are written from the axial coding model or paradigm and might, for example, suggest why a certain cause influences the central phenomenon that, in turn, influences the use of a specific strategy.

saturation, saturate, or saturated   In the development of categories and data analysis phase of grounded theory research, I want to find as many incidents, events, or activities as possible to provide support for them. In this process, I finally come to a point at which the categories are "saturated"; I no longer find new information that adds to my understanding of the category.

selective coding   This is the final phase of coding the information. The researcher takes the central phenomenon and systematically re-lates it to other categories, validating those relationships and filling in categories that need further refinement and development (Strauss & Corbin, 1990). I like to develop a "story" that narrates these categories and shows their interrelationship (see Creswell & Urbom, 1997).

strategies   In axial coding, these are the specific actions or inter-actions that occur as a result of the central phenomenon (Strauss & Corbin, 1990).

substantive-level theory   This is a low-level theory that is applicable to immediate situations. This theory evolves from the study of a phenomenon situated in "one particular situational context" (Strauss & Corbin, 1990, p. 174). Researchers differentiate this form of theory from theories of greater abstraction and applicability, called midlevel theories, grand theories, or formal theories.

theoretical sampling In data collection for grounded theory research, the investigator selects a sample of individuals to study based on their contribution to the development of the theory. Often, this process begins with a homogeneous sample of individuals who are similar, and, as the data collection proceeds and the categories emerge, the researcher turns to a heterogeneous sample to see under what conditions the categories hold true.

▼ ETHNOGRAPHY ▼

analysis of the culture-sharing group   The ethnographer develops themes—cultural themes—in the data analysis. It is a process of reviewing all of the data and segmenting them into a small set of common themes, well supported by evidence in the data (Wolcott, 1994b).

artifacts   This is the focus of attention for the ethnographer as he or she determines what people make and use, such as clothes and tools (cultural artifacts) (Spradley, 1980).

behaviors   These are the focus of attention for the ethnographer as he or she attempts to understand what people do (cultural behavior) (Spradley, 1980).

cultural portrait   One key component of ethnographic research is composing a holistic view of the culture-sharing group or individual. The final product of an ethnography should be this larger portrait, or overview of the cultural scene, presented in all of its complexity (Spradley, 1979).

culture   This term is an abstraction, something that one cannot study directly. From observing and participating in a culture-sharing group, an ethnographer can see "culture at work" and provide a description and interpretation of it (H. F. Wolcott, personal communication, October 10, 1996). It can be seen in behaviors, language, and artifacts (Spradley, 1980).

culture-sharing group   This is the unit of analysis for the ethnographer as he or she attempts to understand and interpret the behavior, language, and artifacts of people. The ethnographer typically focuses on an entire group—one that shares learned, acquired behaviors—to make explicit how the group "works." Some ethnographers will focus on part of the social-cultural system for analysis and engage in a microethnography.

deception   This is another field issue that has become less and less a problem since the ethical standards were published by the American Anthropological Association. It relates to the act of the researcher intentionally deceiving the informants to gain information. This deception may involve masking the identity of the research, withholding important information about the purpose of the study, or gathering information secretively.

description of the culture-sharing group   One of the first tasks of an ethnographer is to simply record a description of the culture-sharing group and incidents and activities that illustrate the culture (Wolcott, 1994b). For example, a factual account may be rendered, pictures of the setting may be drawn, or events may be chronicled.

emic and etic   These terms refer to the type of information being reported and written into an ethnography, whether the researcher reports the views of the informants (emic) or his or her own personal views (etic) (Fetterman, 1989).

ethnography   This is the study of an intact cultural or social group (or an individual or individuals within the group) based primarily on observations and a prolonged period of time spent by the researcher in the field. The ethnographer listens and records the voices of informants with the intent of generating a cultural portrait (Thomas, 1993; Wolcott, 1987).

fieldwork   In ethnographic data collection, the researcher conducts data gathering in the "field" by going to the site or sites where the culture-sharing group can be studied. Often, this involves a prolonged period of time with varying degrees of immersion in activities, events, rituals, and settings of the cultural group (Sanjek, 1990).

function   This is a theme or concept about the social-cultural system or group that the ethnographer studies. Function refers to the social relations among members of the group that help regulate behavior. For example, the researcher might document patterns of behavior of fights within and among various inner-city gangs (Fetterman, 1989).

GLOSSARY/
ETHNOGRAPHY

gatekeeper   This is a data collection term and refers to the individual who the researcher must visit before entering a group or cultural site. To gain access, the researcher must receive this individual's approval (Hammersley & Atkinson, 1995).

holistic   The ethnographer assumes this outlook in research to gain a comprehensive and complete picture of a social group. It might include the group's history, religion, politics, economy, and/or environment. In this way, the researcher places information about the group into a larger perspective or "contextualizes" the study (Fetterman, 1989).

immersed   The ethnographic researcher becomes immersed in the field through a prolonged stay, often as long as 1 year. Whether the individual loses perspective and "goes native" is a field issue much discussed in the ethnographic literature.

interpretation of the culture-sharing group   The researcher makes an interpretation of the meaning of the culture-sharing group. This interpretation may be informed by the literature, personal experiences, or theoretical perspectives (Wolcott, 1994b).

key informants   These are individuals with whom the researcher begins in data collection because they are well informed, are accessible, and can provide leads about other information (Gilchrist, 1992).

language   This is the focus of attention for the ethnographer as he or she discerns what people say (speech messages) (Spradley, 1980).

participant observation   The ethnographer gathers information in many ways, but the primary approach is to observe the culture-sharing group and become a participant in the cultural setting (Jorgensen, 1989).

reactivity   This field issue involves the concern that the informants in a site may be responding in a dishonest or untruthful way to the researcher. It means that the researcher needs to include verifica-

GLOSSARY/
ETHNOGRAPHY

tion procedures in his or her study to check whether this issue is a problem.

reciprocity   This field issue addresses the need for the participants in the study to receive something in return for their willingness to be observed and provide information. The researcher needs to consider how he or she will reimburse participants for being allowed to study them.

reflexivity   This means that the writer is conscious of his or her biases, values, and experiences that are brought to a qualitative research study. Typically, the writer makes this explicit in the text (Hammersley & Atkinson, 1995).

structure   This is a theme or concept about the social-cultural system or group that the ethnographer attempts to learn. It refers to the social structure or configuration of the group, such as the kinship or political structure of the social-cultural group. This structure might be exemplified, for example, by an organizational chart (Fetterman, 1989).

GLOSSARY/
ETHNOGRAPHY

▼ CASE STUDY ▼

analysis of themes   Following description, the researcher then analyzes the data for specific themes, aggregating information into large clusters of ideas and providing details that support the themes. Stake (1995) calls this analysis "development of issues" (p. 123).

assertions   This is the last step in the analysis where the researcher makes sense of the data and provides an interpretation of the "lessons learned" (Lincoln & Guba, 1985; Stake, 1995). The assertions may be couched in terms of personal views or in terms of theories or constructs in the literature.

bounded system   The "case" selected for study has boundaries, often bounded by time and place. It also has interrelated parts that form a whole. Hence, the proper case to be studied is both "bounded" and a "system" (Stake, 1995).

case   This is the "bounded system" or the "object" of study. It might be an event, a process, a program, or several people (Stake, 1995). If a single individual is to be studied, then I generally refer the researcher to a biographical approach.

case study   In qualitative research, this is the study of a "bounded system" with the focus being either the case or an issue that is illustrated by the case (or cases) (Stake, 1995). A qualitative case study provides an in-depth study of this "system," based on a diverse array of data collection materials, and the researcher situates this system or case within its larger "context" or setting.

categorical aggregation   This is an aspect of data analysis in case study research where the researcher seeks a collection of instances from the data, hoping that issue-relevant meanings will emerge (Stake, 1995).

collective case study   This type of case study consists of multiple cases. It might be either intrinsic or instrumental, but its defining feature is

▼ 249

that the researcher examines several cases (e.g., multiple case study) (Stake, 1995).

context of the case   In analyzing and describing a case, the researcher sets the case within its setting. This setting may be broadly concep-tualized (e.g., large historical, social, political issues) or narrowly conceptualized (e.g., the immediate family, the physical location, the time period in which the study occurred) (Stake, 1995).

cross-case analysis   This form of analysis applies to a collective case (Stake, 1995) when the researcher examines more than one case. It involves examining themes across cases to discern themes that are common to all cases. It is an analysis step that typically follows within-case analysis when the researcher studies multiple cases.

description   This means simply stating the "facts" about the case as recorded by the investigator. This is the first step in analysis of data in a qualitative case study, and Stake (1995) calls it "narrative description" (p. 123).

direction interpretation   This is an aspect of interpretation in case study research where the researcher looks at a single instance and draws meaning from it without looking for multiple instances of it. It is a process of pulling the data apart and putting them back together in more meaningful ways (Stake, 1995).

embedded analysis   In this approach to data analysis, the researcher selects one analytic aspect of the case for presentation (Yin, 1989).

holistic analysis   In this approach to data analysis, the researcher examines the entire case (Yin, 1989) and presents description, themes, and interpretations or assertions related to the whole case.

instrumental case study   This is a type of case study with the focus on a specific issue rather than on the case itself. The case then becomes a vehicle to better understand the issue (Stake, 1995).

intrinsic case study   This is a type of case study with the focus of the study on the case because it holds intrinsic or unusual interest

GLOSSARY/
CASE STUDY

(Stake, 1995). I would consider our gunman case study (Asmussen & Creswell, 1995) to be an intrinsic case study.

multi-site/within-site When sites are selected for the "case," they might be located at different geographical locations. This type of study is considered to be "multi-site." Alternatively, the case might be at a single location and considered a "within-site" study.

multiple sources of information One aspect that characterizes good case study research is the use of many different sources of information to provide "depth" to the case. Yin (1989), for example, recommends that the researcher use as many as six different types of information in his or her case study.

naturalistic generalizations In the interpretation of a case, an investigator undertakes a case study to make the case understandable. This understanding may be what the reader learns from the case or its application to other cases (Stake, 1995).

patterns This is an aspect of data analysis in case study research where the researcher establishes patterns and looks for a correspondence between two or more categories to establish a small number of categories (Stake, 1995).

purposeful sampling This is a major issue in case study research, and the researcher needs to clearly specify the type of sampling strategy in selecting the case (or cases) and a rationale for it. It applies to both the selection of the case to study as well as the sampling of information used within the case. I use Miles and Huberman's (1994) list of sampling strategies and apply it in this book to case studies as well as to other traditions of inquiry.

triangulation of information In qualitative research, the convergence of sources of information, views of investigators, different theories, and different methodologies represents the triangulation of ideas (Denzin, 1970) to help support the development of themes. In case study research, Stake (1995) places emphasis on sources of data and suggests that the researcher triangulate differently based on "data situations" in the case.

GLOSSARY/
CASE STUDY

within-case analysis   This type of analysis may apply to either a single case or multiple collective case studies. It means that the researcher identifies themes within a single case. For collective case studies, this analysis may suggest unique themes to a case, or themes that are common to all cases studied.

GLOSSARY/
CASE STUDY

▼ OTHER TERMS ▼

axiological   This qualitative assumption holds that all research is value laden including the value systems of the inquirer, the theory, the paradigm used, and the social and cultural norms for either the inquirer or the respondents (Guba & Lincoln, 1988). Accordingly, the researcher admits and discusses these values in his or her research.

critical theory   Central themes that a critical researcher might explore include the scientific study of social institutions and their transformations through interpreting the meanings of social life; the historical problems of domination, alienation, and social struggles; and a critique of society and the envisioning of new possibilities (Fay, 1987; Morrow & Brown, 1994).

encoding   This term means that the writer places certain features in his or her writing to help a reader know what to expect. These features not only help the reader but also aid the writer, who can then draw on the habits of thought, glosses, and specialized knowledge of the reader (Richardson, 1990). Such features might be the overall organization, code words, images, and other "signposts" for the reader. As applied in this book, the features consist of terms and procedures of a tradition that become part of the language of all facets of research design (e.g., purpose statement, research subquestions, methods).

epistemological   This is another philosophical assumption for the qualitative researcher. It addresses the relationship between the researcher and that being studied as interrelated, not independent. Rather than "distance," as I call it, a "closeness" follows between the researcher and that being researched. This closeness, for example, is manifest through time in the field, collaboration, and the impact that that being researched has on the researcher.

feminist research approaches   In feminist research methods, the goals are to establish collaborative and nonexploitative relationships, to place the researcher within the study so as to avoid objectification, and to conduct research that is transformative (Stewart, 1994).

foreshadowing   This term means that writers use techniques to portend the development of ideas (Hammersley & Atkinson, 1995). In this book, I use the idea mainly in writing the problem statement, purpose statement, and research subquestions to foreshadow the data analysis procedures.

issue subquestions   These are subquestions in a qualitative study that follow the central underlying question. They are written to address the major concerns and perplexities to be resolved, the "issue" of a study (Stake, 1995). They typically are few in number and are posed as questions.

methodological   This assumption holds that a qualitative researcher conceptualizes the research process in a certain way. For example, a qualitatative inquirer relies on views of participants and discusses their views within the context in which they occur to inductively develop, from particulars to abstractions, ideas in a study (Creswell, 1994).

ontological   This is a philosophical assumption about the nature of reality. It addresses the question: When is something real? The answer provided is that something is real when it is constructed in the minds of the actors involved in the situation (Guba & Lincoln, 1988). Thus, reality is not "out there," apart from the minds of actors.

paradigm or worldview   This is the philosophical stance taken by the researcher that provides a basic set of beliefs that guides action (Denzin & Lincoln, 1994). It defines, for its holder, "the nature of the world, the individual's place in it, and the range of possible relationships to that world" (Guba & Lincoln, 1994, p. 107). Denzin and Lincoln (1994) further call this the "net that contains the researcher's epistemological, ontological, and methodological premises" (p. 13). In this discussion, I extend this "net" to also include the axiological and rhetorical assumptions.

postmodernism   This ideological perspective is considered a family of theories and perspectives that have something in common (Slife & Williams, 1995). Postmodernists advance a reaction or critique of the 19th-century Enlightenment and early 20th-century emphasis on technology, rationality, reason, universals, science, and the positivist, scientific method (Bloland, 1995; Stringer, 1993). Postmodernists assert that knowledge claims must be set within the conditions of the world today and in the multiple perspectives of class, race, gender, and other group affiliations.

qualitative research This is an inquiry process of understanding based on a distinct methodological tradition of inquiry that explores a social or human problem. The researcher builds a complex, holistic picture, analyzes words, reports detailed views of informants, and conducts the study in a natural setting.

research design I refer to the entire process of research from conceptualizing a problem to writing the narrative, not simply the methods such as data collection, analysis, and report writing (Bogdan & Taylor, 1975).

rhetorical This assumption means that the qualitative investigator uses terms and a narrative unique to the qualitative approach. The narrative is personal and literary (Creswell, 1994). For example, the researcher might use the first-person pronoun "I" instead of the impersonal third-person voice.

social science theories These are the theoretical explanations that social scientists use to explain the world (Slife & Williams, 1995). They are based on empirical evidence that has accumulated in social science fields such as sociology, psychology, education, economics, urban studies, and communication. As a set of interrelated concepts, variables, and propositions, they serve to explain, predict, and provide generalizations about phenomena in the world (Kerlinger, 1979). They may have broad applicability (grand theories) or narrow applications (minor working hypotheses) (Flinders & Mills, 1993).

topical subquestions These are subquestions in a qualitative study that follow the central underlying question. They cover the anticipated needs for information (Stake, 1995), and I have extended Stake's idea to include anticipated procedures in the study for data analysis and reporting the study. In this way, the topical subquestions foreshadow the procedures to be used in the study.

tradition of inquiry   This is an approach to qualitative research that has a distinguished history in one of the social science disciplines and that has spawned books, journals, and distinct methodologies. These traditions, as I call them, are known in other books as "strategies of inquiry" (Denzin & Lincoln, 1994) or "varieties" (Tesch, 1990).

verisimilitude   This is a criterion for a good literary study in which the writing seems "real" and "alive," transporting the reader directly into the world of the study (Richardson, 1994).

GLOSSARY/
OTHER TERMS

APPENDIX B

▼

A Biography

This article discusses the use of life history as a method of ethnographic research among stigmatized, unempowered people. The author describes and analyzes the process of eliciting the life history of a man with mental retardation. To combine life history interviewing with the detailed observation of behavior in a naturalistic setting is typical of the ethnographic tradition; interviews with people from marginalized social groups (particularly those who are considered mentally "disabled") are, however, often decontextualized and conducted in quasi-clinical settings that emphasize the retrospective reconstruction of the life. By treating a person with mental retardation as a contextualized participant in a world outside the clinical setting and by eliciting the life narrative in the course of following that person as he attempts to make sense of life outside the institution, it is possible to clarify the dynamic in the formation of a metaphor of personal identity. This technique might not be appropriate for all persons with mental disability, but when it *can* be used, it helps to demonstrate the proposition that mental retardation is not a monolithic condition whose victims are distinguished by arbitrary gradations of standardized test scores. Rather, it is only one of many factors that figure into a person's strategy for coping with the world.

ON THE BUS WITH VONNIE LEE
Explorations in Life History and Metaphor

MICHAEL V. ANGROSINO
University of South Florida

A LIFE IN PROCESS

VONNIE LEE

Vonnie Lee Hargrett celebrated his 29th birthday while I was writing this article in the summer of 1993 in the Florida city to which his parents had migrated from a rural part of the state. The family was, in Vonnie Lee's own words, "poor White trash—real crackers." His father was

SOURCE: This article originally appeared in the *Journal of Contemporary Ethnography*, 23, 14-28. Copyright 1994, Sage Publications, Inc., 1994.

mostly absent, supposedly shuttling around Florida, Georgia, and Alabama seeking work; if he ever did work ("Not like I even once believed he did," Vonnie Lee told me), he never sent any money home, and he disappeared for good ("real good," Vonnie Lee smirked) about 8 years ago. His mother is an alcoholic who has, over the course of the years, taken up with countless men, most of whom were physically abusive to everyone in the family. Several of them were apparently encouraged in their sexual abuse of Vonnie Lee's two sisters; at least two of them also sexually abused Vonnie Lee. The children were sent to school on a come-and-go basis as the mother moved from place to place around town with her different boyfriends. All three children developed serious learning deficits, although only Vonnie Lee seems to have been tagged by a counselor as mentally retarded. He was never in one school long enough to benefit from any special education programs, however, and he stopped going to school altogether by the time he was 12 years old.

During his teen years he lived mostly on the streets in the company of an older man, Lucian, who made a living by "loaning" Vonnie Lee to other men on the street. Vonnie Lee often says, "Lucian, he's like the only real father I ever had—whatever he had he shared with me. I'd-a done anything for him. *Anything.*"

Lucian was found one morning beaten to death in an empty lot. Vonnie Lee, who had been with one of Lucian's clients that night, discovered the body upon his return to their campsite. The police found him, sobbing and gesturing wildly over the body, and took him into custody. He was held briefly on suspicion of murder, but there was no hard evidence linking him to the crime and he was never charged. His disorderly behavior, however, was sufficient to have him "Baker Acted" (involuntarily committed for psychiatric observation under the provisions of the Florida Mental Health Act). He spent the next few years in and out of psychiatric facilities, developing the remarkable—and, to any number of clinicians, the thoroughly frustrating—capacity to turn into the most level-headed, socially appropriate, even intelligent young gentleman after just a short time in treatment. He would be released, make his way back to the streets, survive quite well for a time, then "break up" (a term he explicitly and consistently prefers to "break down") and be carted off to jail or the hospital.

Vonnie Lee was finally remanded to Opportunity House (OH), an agency designed for the habilitation of adults with the dual diagnosis of mental retardation and psychiatric disorder; most of them also have criminal records. There he made sustained academic, social, and vocational progress, and in June 1992 he was deemed ready for "supervised independent living."

One of the key steps in preparing OH clients for independent living is to teach them to use the public transportation system. I had been a member of OH's board of directors since 1982 (a position I was asked to fill as a result of my long-term research involvement with the program) and had also been a frequent volunteer classroom tutor. I was, however, never directly involved with the "social skills habilitation" aspect of the program until I was asked to fill in for an ailing staff member who was supposed to show Vonnie Lee the bus route from his new apartment to the warehouse where he was to begin working. I was not entirely pleased with the prospect; our city, despite its substantial size and pretensions to urban greatness, has a notoriously inadequate bus system, and I knew that even the relatively simple trip from Vonnie Lee's apartment to his work site involved several transfers and could mean long, hot waits at unshaded bus stops.

VONNIE LEE AND ME

I first met Vonnie Lee shortly after his arrival at OH in 1990. The teacher asked me to help him with his reading assignment: a paragraph about some children taking a walk with their dog. (The fact that reading materials for adults with limited reading ability are almost always about children or about topics that would typically engage the imaginations of children is a subtle but nonetheless painful insult that merits at least a parenthetical complaint here.) Vonnie Lee did not have any particular difficulty reading all the words, but he was having trouble with comprehension. After reading the paragraph, he was unable to answer questions requiring recall and synthesis of information. He seemed more depressed than angry over his failure, and so I said, "Let's put the book away for a minute. Why don't you tell me about a time you remember when *you* took a walk." My intention was to allow him to refocus on the elements constituting a simple narrative in his own words instead of on the specific details about the unfamiliar Tom, Sally, and Spot. Instead, he just said, with inexpressible and totally unexpected sadness, "Yeah. Take a walk. Story of my life." I little realized the full import of his remark but did make a mental note to see if he would at some later time be amenable to telling me the "story of my life" along with the other OH clients among whom I was conducting life history research.

We eventually got around to taping some conversations that would lead to the production of his autobiography, but I frankly was stumped. The problem was not that his discourse was jumbled; in fact, it proceeded in the most nearly linear, chronological sequence of any of the stories I worked on at OH. The problem was that even after numerous sessions I could form no clear sense of who or what Vonnie Lee thought he was. Was Vonnie Lee perhaps a person whose mental disorder was—despite his surface demeanor of reasonable intelligence and even a sense of humor—so profound that he couldn't be fitted into my emergent analytical scheme?

Like my other OH life history collaborators, Vonnie Lee worked in an anecdotal style of narrative. That is, rather than say, for example, "I was born in this city. I lived with my mother and father. I remember the house we lived in," he would say, "When I was a real little kid. Yeah. Let me tell you about that." And he would go on to relate an encapsulated anecdote that was meant to represent his life as a "real little kid." Then he would go on and say, "So then I got a little older. Yeah. Here's what it was." And he would launch into another encapsulated story. My problem, though, was that in Vonnie Lee's case the stories were almost devoid of characters, except in marginal scene-setting roles, and of plot, even of the most attenuated type. For example:

> So Hank [one of his mother's boyfriends] says, "Let's you and me go see Ronnie [a dealer in stolen auto parts for whom Hank sometimes worked]." So we're on the bus. It starts over there next to the mall, and it cuts across and then it stops on the corner where it's that hospital. It stopped there a good long while, you know. Then it goes on down 22nd Street. Past the Majik Mart. Past that gas station with the big yellow thing out front.

And on and on the story would go, except that it was essentially a description of the bus route. Vonnie Lee seemed to have a photographic memory of every convenience store, gas station, apartment complex, newspaper machine, and frontyard basketball hoop along the way. But in the process, he completely lost the point (or what I assumed was the point). There was no word about his reaction to all these sights, nor was there any mention of what Hank was doing. Indeed, they never got to Ronnie's place; the anecdote ended when they got off the bus in front of a Salvation Army thrift shop, apparently several blocks from their destination. When I asked him what happened when they got there, he shrugged and said, "Oh, nothing." I sensed that he wasn't trying to cover anything up (he had already made it perfectly clear that Hank was a thief), and I felt certain that he wasn't just goofing around. He truly believed that the point of the story was the bus ride, not the destination. Vonnie Lee was cooperative in responding to direct questions aimed, on my part, at identifying key players in his life and the events that linked them together. But on his own initiative, he was inclined only to offer what he seemed to feel were these deeply revelatory bus itineraries.

BUS TRIP

On the day I picked up Vonnie Lee at OH to show him the bus routes, we drove first to his new apartment complex. I parked my car and we walked up to the corner bus stop. Vonnie Lee was visibly excited, more animated and seemingly more happy than I had ever seen him. It was a crushingly hot Florida summer day and thunderstorms threatened, but he seemed so elated that my own spirits were lifted. "I bet you're really excited about having your own place," I ventured (violating the first rule of life history interviewing by putting words into the mouth of an informant). "Nah," he replied, "I like the streets to live on—but they won't let me or else I go back to lockup." Nothing daunted, I went on, "But it must be great to have a real job." "In that old dump? Hell no!" he retorted. So what *was* he so happy about? It dawned on me that the bus itself was the object of his joy, as I watched him bounce into the vehicle when it finally lumbered to a stop. The symbol of the city's bus line is a large red heart, and Vonnie Lee made a dash for a seat directly under a poster bearing that logo; from time to time during the ride, he would reach up and touch it lovingly.

Vonnie Lee seemed to be very familiar with the route we were taking. "Yeah, I walked it about 13 million times," he said with contempt. But now as we sat on the nearly empty bus, he kept swiveling from one side to the other, calling out local landmarks with great glee. At one point, we passed an elderly lady laboriously dragging several large plastic supermarket bags across the street. "I know her type," he sneered. "Uses up every last damn dime she got and she can't ride the bus back home. Drags her ass around like some goddam retard."

We reached the junction where we needed to transfer. "Oh, *here's* where I do it!" Vonnie Lee shouted ecstatically. "I *love* this street, but I never get a chance to come here no more!" The street in question is one of the city's shabbiest, lined with unpleasant-looking bars, sec-ondhand clothing stores, and unkempt, garagelike structures from which used furniture, carpeting "seconds," rebuilt appliances, and sundry "recyclables" are delivered. The place where Vonnie Lee was to work was on a street like this one but which required a further transfer to reach; he was, I had to admit, quite right in characterizing such a place as an "old dump," but his mood betrayed not the slightest hint of regret.

We waited for a very long time at the transfer stop. Two heavily made-up young women were lolling in front of one of the bars but were making no real attempt to secure business; they seemed stunned by the heat and shook their heads wearily at the spectacle of Vonnie Lee jumping up and down to catch a glimpse of the approaching bus. When it came at last, it was more crowded than the first had been, and Vonnie Lee's face clouded briefly when he saw that the favored seat under the heart was already taken. He resigned himself to a less desirable place but kept turning his head toward the heart as if to reassure himself, even as he resumed his practice of announcing every building on the street. He was less familiar with this street than with the first, and his litany seemed to be serving the purpose of fixing the sights in his own mind as well as of enlightening me.

Vonnie Lee seemed sorry to get off when we reached our stop, but he brightened immediately when he saw the street down which our third and final lap would take us. It was a street very much like the second, although it led off to a part of town he hardly knew at all; the thrill of the new gave him added zest. It began to rain while we waited and waited for the third bus, and we found only modest shelter in the boarded-up doorway of what had once been a storefront church. Vonnie Lee's spirits didn't sag in the least, even when the bus arrived, packed full of damp and irritable riders. He managed to find a standing spot near enough the heart logo and immediately set about his recitation of the sights. Some of the people nearby looked a little annoyed, but no one said anything. The crowd was as thoroughly depressed and defeated as Vonnie Lee was giddy.

It bears mentioning that the city's buses are *very* slow. Not only do they run infrequently, but once they do arrive they appear to obey an unstated mandate to stop at *every* marked stop, whether or not anyone wants to get on or off. As a result, the trip from the apartment to the warehouse, which might have taken at most 20 minutes by car, ended up consuming an hour and a half by bus. The other anomaly in the bus system that I had ample time to observe that day (and I had lived in the city for nearly two decades at that time without ever having ridden a city bus) was that all the riders (including my own wet and bedraggled self) looked like stereotyped versions of either very poor or mentally/physically disabled people. I came to realize that no bus route connected one "nice" part of town with another; all of them took off into and covered most of their distance within "bad" sections. (Since my trip with Vonnie Lee, the transit authority has added several routes connecting upscale residential neighborhoods with the downtown business and government districts, but they are all "express" runs that zoom right through the intervening "bad" spots.) It was clear that the bus system had been designed primarily for domestic workers going to and from the posh homes and business offices and for blue-collar workers traveling from low-rent districts to downscale factory zones.

In many big cities, going to work by bus is a perfectly appropriate thing for even the most affluent of business people to do. But in our city, the bus is the very embodiment of stigma—the slow, inconvenient transport of the poor, the powerless, and the socially marginal.

When we reached our stop, literally in front of the plumbing supply warehouse where Vonnie Lee was to work, it began pouring again. We dashed inside where Vonnie Lee's supervisor, Mr. Washington, was very gracious in showing us around and then allowing us to wait out the storm. The warehouse was cramped and dingy, but it seemed to be doing a brisk business ("People are going to need toilets, even during a recession," Mr. Washington noted), and the supervisor and most of the other workmen showed a genuine interest in Vonnie Lee's welfare. (Several other OH clients had been employed there over the years; the owner of the business had a mentally retarded brother who died young, and he looked on his employment program as a way of honoring his memory.) "I love it!" Vonnie Lee shouted as one of the other men took him through the back door to show him a tiny commissary where they could buy soft drinks and snacks.

"It's the bus he loves—coming here on the bus," Mr. Washington said to me when we were alone. I admitted that Vonnie Lee did seem to have had an unaccountably good time on the ride. "Yeah. I've seen it before. Ask him about it, why don't you?"

The return ride was a replay of the first; Vonnie Lee had already memorized all the new landmarks. "Why do you like the bus so much?" I asked at last—the question that had been obvious all day but had seemed too silly and irrational to bring up. And, as he always did when I put a direct question to him, he gave me a straightforward answer. He repeated his answer on tape later on, telling me,

Like I always said, we was dirt poor at home. Mama never had no car or nothing. Most of them guys was even more worthlesser than Daddy. Why that woman has a thing for big losers I'll never know! Now every once in a while one of 'em took me on the bus. And poor old Lucian—he didn't like to get on the bus because he said everybody looked at him funny, but still we did it now and again just to show we *could*. I mean—it's only the lowdownest who can't *never* do it.

Jeez! I'd walk a street and say, "If I was a bigshot, I'd be on the bus right now!" The bad thing—a man just can't ride one end of the street to another like he was some retard with no place to go. A man gotta go *somewheres*, and I never knew how to get *anywheres* like from one to the other one. I nearly peed my pants when they told me I could learn; they never thought I could before now. I got kinda scared when they told me Ralph couldn't take me and you was gonna do it; I thought, "Hey, he don't really work at OH. Maybe he don't know how and he'll screw me up." But then I figured you'd figure it out and then you'd show me.

THE MEANING OF THE BUS

It all became clear to me. The bus—to the "nice" people the symbol of poverty, the despised underside of the glittery urban lifestyle touted by the city's boosters—was for Vonnie Lee a potent symbol of empowerment. Coming from a family that was *too poor even to take the bus* was a humiliation that had scarred his young life. He spent his years grimly walking, walking, learning the details of the streets and yet yearning for the time when he could be chauffeured high above those streets in the style to which he felt himself entitled. For Vonnie Lee, the payoff for all his hard work in overcoming both his background and his numerous "break up" reversals was neither the apartment nor the job but the fact that he was finally deemed worthy to learn how to ride the bus between the two. So many of the OH clients with whom I spoke longed to see themselves in positions of power, and their dreams of driving fancy cars, although unrealistic, were at least recognizable ambitions. I had completely missed Vonnie Lee's ideal; because he saw escape and empowerment in the bus (something to which *anyone*, even a person with mental retardation, could reasonably aspire), I had ignored the fact that it *was* a dream for him and that it gave shape and meaning to his life.

I finally saw why, when telling his life story without specific prompts, he did so in the form of bus routes. For Vonnie Lee, those rare rides were the stuff of which his dreams were made; they embodied his values, his aspirations, and even his self-image. My other informants' stories led me to conclude that they had developed stable self-images that survived all the vicissitudes of their lives. Vonnie Lee's self-image, on the other hand, was bound up not in who he was but in who he wanted to be: a man on a bus, going somewhere. Since his earlier rides had been dry runs, as it were, they didn't add up to a consistent pattern, and he went along as someone else's adjunct (and the someone else was, at best, only a temporarily significant other); he never felt that they represented any sort of defined closure. As a result, he did not feel impelled to "finish" those stories, as the real finish—the point at which he was ready to believe himself to be someone—was in the future.

Mr. Washington had indeed seen a number of his charges who liked to ride the bus because it was so liberatingly different from the heavily supervised minivan that shuttled the OH clients around prior to their graduation. But Vonnie Lee's fixation on the bus went even further than the supervisor could have imagined. When we finally got back to OH, I took a careful look around Vonnie Lee's room as I helped him pack up some of his belongings. Taped to his mirror was an outline drawing of a heart; it had been cleanly scissored out of a coloring book about seasons and holidays that one of his "lower functioning" roommates was using in class. Vonnie Lee had carefully colored the big valentine with a neon red marker. Before that day, I would have assumed that he was, like some of my other informants, pretending to have received at least one passionate proposal of marriage on Valentine's Day. But now I knew immediately that it was not a valentine at all but the closest thing he could find to the bus company logo.

DISCUSSION

Vonnie Lee's autobiography, and the story of my interaction with him, is part of a long-term research project whose methodology and conceptual framework were described in some detail in earlier writings (Angrosino 1989, 1992; Angrosino and Zagnoli 1992). That project was designed to demonstrate three points: that individual identity is conceptualized and communicated as much through the form as through the content of autobiographical material (Crocker 1977; Hankiss 1981; Howarth 1980; Olney 1972), that autobiographies are best interpreted as extended metaphors of self (Fitzgerald 1993; Norton 1989), and that even persons with conditions that interfere with their ability to construct conventionally coherent narratives nevertheless sustain self-images (Zetlin and Turner 1984) and can communicate those images to others of the same culture by using culturally recognizable metaphorical forms.

In earlier analyses based on this research, I relied essentially on literary theory as applied to autobiography to define "metaphor." In accordance with that view, I was less concerned with specific expressive metaphors ("The house I grew up in was a toilet") than with the way in which an entire life was reconstructed in the narration around a master concept of self. The informants profiled in the other studies had adopted clearly defined social roles (the "blame attributor," the "tactical dependent," the "denier," the "passer") and told their stories in ways that marshaled rhetorical devices ("antithesis," "compensation," "allusion," "anecdote," "oratory," "dialogue") to buttress the presentation of those roles. In so doing, the roles became a dominating metaphor of the stigmatization experienced by the informants.

Although this perspective on metaphor was a useful framework for analyzing the stories of some informants who, in their various ways, perceived a continuity between their early experiences and their current lives, it was inadequate in Vonnie Lee's case. Although reasonably articulate about his past, Vonnie Lee is a person who adamantly refuses to live in the past; his orientation is so thoroughly toward the future that he resists characterizing himself in terms of what he has always been. Far from operating on the assumption that he is a product of his past (even if only in reaction to it), Vonnie Lee sees his life as beginning only when he makes a definitive break with that past. For Vonnie Lee, the past is not even prologue; it is, for all intents and purposes, irrelevant as a predictor of his future.

The dominating metaphor of Vonnie Lee's life, then, emerges not out of retrospective narrative but out of the actions he is currently taking to remake himself into his desired new image. For this reason, it is important not to limit the dialogue of discovery to retrospective interviews conducted in a time and place of their own. Rather, it is crucial to conduct what amounts to a personalized ethnography of this informant—to catch him in the act of self-creation, as it were. He does not use metaphor to symbolize the asserted continuities of his broken life as do the other informants; his metaphorical image is created in the actions that define his trajectory of "becoming."

For an ethnographer who works in an applied field (such as the formulation of policy for and the delivery of services to people with a defined disorder, such as mental retardation), this research demonstrates the benefits of the in-depth autobiographical interview methodology for establishing the human dimensions of mentally disordered persons, who are all too frequently described in terms of deviations from standardized norms. Vonnie Lee's story goes one step further: It demonstrates the desirability of contextualizing the autobiographical interview within the ongoing life experience of the subject rather than treating it as a retrospective review.

Such contextualization is, to be sure, an article of faith among anthropological ethnographers and is widely accepted by other social scientists working in the ethnographic tradition. It is, however, a conclusion that has rarely been applied to studies of "deviant," "stigmatized," or "marginalized" people.

There is a great deal of published material based on the life histories of people with mental retardation, but, as Whittemore, Langness, and Koegel (1986) point out in their critical survey of that literature, those materials are almost entirely lacking in any sense of an insider's perspective. Much of that literature is more focused on the experiences of caregivers, the assumption being that the person with retardation is unable to speak coherently on his or her own behalf. It is true that retarded people in clinical settings are interviewed with an eye to telling their life stories, but such accounts (which are rarely published) presuppose a clinically defined disorder and focus on the psychodynamics of the illness; the whole person is subsumed into the "disorder," and the interview itself is part of the process of correction and therapy.

My work is more closely allied with the tradition pioneered at the University of California, Los Angeles, by Edgerton and his colleagues in the "sociobehavioral" group, who have made it a practice to study the lives of their subjects in their entirety. "Because these lives change in response to various environmental demands, just as they develop in reaction to maturational changes, we emphasize process" (Edgerton 1984, 1-2) rather than retrospection; moreover, they do so by providing detailed descriptions of the communities where the subjects live so as to situate the life histories outside the strictly clinical milieu. Nevertheless, even this approach begins with the acceptance of clinically defined disorder, such that the contextualized life history serves mainly to illuminate the process of "adjustment" to a presumed mainstream norm.

My encounter with Vonnie Lee taught me that his worldview was not a failed approximation of how a "normal" person would cope, nor was it, when taken on its own terms, intrinsically disordered. His fixation on the bus is only "disordered" or an "attempt at adjustment" if we assume that the rest of us are not without our own idées fixes regarding the world and our place in it. Were we to suffer the misfortune of being labeled "retarded," would all of our ideas, attitudes, and practices stand up to scrutiny as being unimpeachably "normal"? Once we start looking for evidence of "disorder," then "disorder" is almost certainly what we find. If anything, Vonnie Lee's logic is more clearly worked out and better integrated than that of more sophisticated people; his "retardation" may, indeed, lie in the way he has purified his obsession down to its basics rather than veiling it in varieties of symbolic discourse as "normal" people do. Interviewing him in a way that arose out of a normal activity did not merely "contextualize" his disorder, it removed the emphasis on disorder altogether. Like a conventional anthropologist conducting participant observation in a community other than his or her own, I only began to make progress when I stopped thinking that there was something "exotic" in Vonnie Lee's approach to the world and started asking him simply what things meant to him. This insight might not come as a surprise to theoreticians who work in the autobiographical genre, or to anthropologically oriented ethnographers in general, but it is certainly a different point of view from that typically seen among professional service providers in the mental health/mental retardation field.

It is certainly true that Vonnie Lee's is only one story. I have been asked by several people who have read drafts of this article, "But is he typical of retarded people in his ability to concentrate and integrate his life experiences?" The honest answer is that I don't know. But in a larger sense, to ask the question is to assume that "mental retardation" is a defined, bounded category fixed within the parameters of clinical, statistical norms. Vonnie Lee is "retarded" in the sense that he has been so labeled and has been dealt with by "the system" as a retarded person for much of his life. And yet he copes with the world around him in a way that, although out of the statistical "norm," is not entirely dysfunctional—as long as we stop trying to see his experiences as illustrations of disorder. Mental retardation is a broad and heterogeneous category; I do not doubt that many persons so diagnosed would have great difficulty in expressing as coherent a worldview as Vonnie Lee's. This kind of methodology would almost certainly not work with all people so diagnosed.

What this fragment of a research project demonstrates is that for at least some people with mental retardation, it is possible to do what anthropological ethnographers have long done: get away from asking retrospective questions that only emphasize the "exoticism" of the subjects and, instead, allow questions to flow naturally out of observations of the subjects in their ordinary round of activities. That method has long been a way to see cultural differences as variations in human responses to certain common problems; here it is a way of seeing that a person like Vonnie Lee might be extreme in some of his responses but is still part of the same continuum of experience. Perhaps in his specialness and individual quirkiness, Vonnie Lee *is* typical after all—not of "mentally retarded persons" but of human beings who learn how to use elements of the common culture to serve their individual purposes.

REFERENCES

Angrosino, M. V. 1989. *Documents of interaction: Biography, autobiography, and life history in social science perspective.* Gainesville: University of Florida Press.

———. 1992. Metaphors of stigma: How deinstitutionalized mentally retarded adults see themselves. *Journal of Contemporary Ethnography* 21:171-99.

Angrosino, M. V., and L. J. Zagnoli. 1992. Gender constructs and social identity: Implications for community-based care of retarded adults. In *Gender constructs and social issues*, edited by T. Whitehead and B. Reid, 40-69. Urbana: University of Illinois Press.

Crocker, J. C. 1977. The social functions of rhetorical form. In *The social uses of metaphor*, edited by D. J. Sapir and J. C. Crocker, 33-66. Philadelphia: University of Pennsylvania Press.

Edgerton, R. B. 1984. Introduction. In *Lives in process: Mildly retarded adults in a large city*, edited by R. B. Edgerton. Washington, DC: American Association on Mental Deficiency.

Fitzgerald, T. K. 1993. Limitations of metaphor in the culture-communication dialogue. Paper presented at the annual meeting of the Southern Anthropological Society, Savannah, GA, 25 March.

Hankiss, A. 1981. Ontologies of the self: On the mythological rearranging of one's life history. In *Biography and society: The life history approach in the social sciences*, edited by D. Bertaux, 203-10. Beverly Hills, CA: Sage.

Howarth, W. L. 1980. Some principles of autobiography. In *Autobiography: Essays theoretical and critical*, edited by J. Olney, 86-114. Princeton, NJ: Princeton University Press.

Norton, C. S. 1989. *Life metaphors: Stories of ordinary survival*. Carbondale: Southern Illinois University Press.

Olney, J. 1972. *Metaphors of self: The meaning of autobiography*. Princeton, NJ: Princeton University Press.

Whittemore, R. D., L. L. Langness, and P. Koegel. 1986. The life history approach to mental retardation. In *Culture and retardation*, edited by L. L. Langness and H. G. Levine, 1-18. Dordrecht, Netherlands: D. Reidel.

Zetlin, A. G., and J. L. Turner. 1984. Self-perspectives on being handicapped: Stigma and adjustment. In *Lives in process: Mildly retarded adults in a large city*, edited by R. B. Edgerton, 93-120. Washington, DC: American Association on Mental Deficiency.

APPENDIX C

▼

A Phenomenology

The Essential Structure
of a Caring Interaction

Doing Phenomenology

Doris J. Riemen

The words "care" and "caring" are prevalent throughout nursing literature. There is consistent confirmation that caring is vital and, in fact, the very essence of nursing (Bendall, 1977; Leininger, 1977; Rule, 1978; Watson, 1979). Although constructs and essential ingredients that are present in caring have been posited (Leininger, 1977; Mayer-

SOURCE: The material in this appendix originally appeared as Chapter 5, "The Essential Structure of a Caring Interaction: Doing Phenomenology," in P. M. Munhall & C. J. Oiler (Eds.), *Nursing research: A qualitative perspective* (pp. 85-105). Norwalk, CT: Appleton-Century-Crofts. Used by permission.

off, 1971), very little research has been done to substantiate what constitutes the essential structure of a caring nurse-client interaction from the perspective of the client.

The use of the term "caring" has become a cliche. Slogans abound in nursing advertisements, articles, and textbooks that proclaim nurses as "caring and competent," "caring and sharing," "we care a bundle," the "final step in caring," and "to care is human." Yet books, articles, magazines, and newspapers proclaim the lack of caring that is evident in the health care system today (Howard & Strauss, 1975).

One poignant example was a letter written to the *Washington Post* in March 1977 by a mother whose 17-year-old daughter was tragically killed in an automobile accident. In an open letter to health professionals (cited in Reilly, 1978, p. v), writing of her experience in the emergency room after the accident, the mother wrote:

> Please search yourselves for resources to deal helpfully with others like us. Seek ways to make the few moments available for deeply troubled persons times of healing rather than destruction. Plan ways of staffing your facilities with people who are full of heart and wise in the administration of compassion. We need caring so desperately.

THE PROBLEM

The problem of this study was stated: From the perspective of the client, what is the essential structure of a caring nurse-client interaction?

Prior to 1982, the limited research available regarding caring interactions concentrated almost exclusively on empirical indicators of nurse caring behaviors as defined and categorized from the nurse's perspective (Amacher, 1973; Henry, 1976; McCorkle, 1974). To objectively study only empirical indicators of caring from the nurse's perspective would not get at the essential structure of the caring interaction as experienced by the client. In the final analysis, to describe caring interactions as indicated only from the nurse's point of view may not be at all congruent with the client's experience. It is primarily when the client defines the essential structure of the caring interaction for nurses that progress can be made to provide clients with the quality of nursing care that can be identified and labeled as caring.

The purpose of this study was to research the phenomenon of caring by obtaining from clients' verbal descriptions their perceptions of caring and noncaring interactions with nurses. The essential structure of a caring interaction was extracted from these descriptions by phenomenological analysis.

Justification of the Problem

Flaskerud et al. state (1979, p. 161):

> In a system where parts are emphasized instead of wholes, where cure is the focus instead of care, where processing the patient through the system takes on assembly line dimensions, nurses have neither the incentive nor the inclination to become involved with patient care in a concerned (caring) way. Apart from performing necessary tasks, interactions between nurses and patients are uninvolved and often dehumanizing.

The whole technical revolution in medicine has tended to increase the trend toward impersonal treatment. As Wexler (1976) observed, this technical revolution has "created an array of tools with which to do things *to* people, thus resulting in less and less time to do things *with* people" (p. 276).

Howard and Strauss (1975), in describing depersonalization, wrote of the tendency to treat people as things (thinging) whereby people are viewed as objects of action rather than as subjects. Thus, patients and clients are perceived as "insensitive objects, objects that psychologically, at least, do not exist at all" (p. 60).

Menninger (1975) noted that most discussions of health care quality medical literature has made occasional apologies for the omission of measuring in some way the subjective caring aspect of treatment by getting feedback from patients. Pelligrino (1974) suggested it was possible to investigate the inherent dehumanizing tendencies in today's patterns of patient care by incorporating the practice of genuine caring in each individual interaction.

THE PHENOMENOLOGICAL APPROACH

Philosophical Existential Perspectives

In the 1960s, nurses began writing about the relevancy of existentialism as a philosophy applicable to nursing, specifically the philosophies of Gabriel Marcel and Martin Buber (Ferlic, 1968; Nelson, 1978; Vaillot, 1966). Although there is a wide variation in the interpretations of existentialism, all interpretations stress the worth of the individual and the potential for change. Man *is* not but is forever becoming. The notion of growth is implicit in existentialism.

Existential Themes of Martin Buber. Buber is generally considered to be the most influential Jewish philosopher of the 20th century. His most notable contribution is his book *I and Thou*. Buber (1958) stated that the "self," or the "I," of each person comes into being in one or another of two primary relations—the I-it or the I-thou. Livingston (1971, p. 350) defined I-it as [follows]:

> The usual way of relating ourselves to other beings is by experiencing and using them, i.e., we observe a thing, examine it, and test it. Our relationship is essentially objective and instrumental. . . . [I]t is the typical way we relate to things and persons in general.

Buber stated that no man can know another simply as he knows objects. Real knowledge of another person requires openness, participation, and empathy. Buber (1958) stated that I-thou involves a "real encounter and genuine mutuality" (p. 50). He contended that what has happened is that the proper balance of I-it and I-thou has been disturbed by the increase of I-it relations (p. 56):

> In our age the I-it relation, gigantically swollen, has usurped, practically uncontested, the mastery and the rule. The I of this relation, an I that possesses all, succeeds with all, this I that is unable to say Thou, unable to meet a being essentially, is the lord of the hour.

Existential Themes of Gabriel Marcel. Like Buber, Marcel (1971) sees a first level of participation that is characterized by experiencing and utilizing.

Marcel distinguished between the kind of reflection that is appropriate for the sciences and that which is appropriate to reflect on human relations. The distinction is between a problem and a mystery. A problem is something to be solved by certain techniques, and an objective study of a problem will achieve a definite result. Yet those methods are not applicable for situations where the feelings of the persons in the situation are crucial to understanding the real problem. Questions such as love, death, and caring are examples of what he calls a mystery.

Marcel's themes of presence and availability are particularly pertinent as a framework for a caring relationship (1971, pp. 24, 26):

> When I say that a being is granted to me as a presence . . . this means that I am unable to treat him as if he were merely placed in front of me; between him and

me there arises a relationship which surpasses my awareness of him; he is not only before me, he is also with me.

The person who is at my disposal is the one who is capable of being with me with the whole of himself when I am in need; while the one who is not at my disposal seems merely to offer me a temporary loan raised on his resources. For the one I am a *presence;* for the other I am an *object.*

Marcel termed this interdependence of man as "intersubjectivity." Paterson and Zderad (1976) have defined intersubjectivity as lived dialogue, "a form of existential intersubjective relating expressed in being and doing with the other who is regarded as a presence (as opposed to an object)" (pp. 34-35).

Existential Perspectives of Caring. A differentiation must be explicit between "caring" and "taking care of." Nursing literature abounds with information on the latter. To take care of someone physically could very easily be done in an I-it relationship. Nursing interpersonal relationships of this type exist in every setting, i.e., the person in a coma, the "gall-bladder" in Room 114, "a 24-year-old male appendectomy." Nurses today are accustomed to dealing with people as nonpeople. To be involved in an existential caring relationship means the establishment of an I-thou relationship.

Gadow (1980) proposes existential advocacy as the essence of nursing and points to the nurse's participation, the give and take, the dialogue with the patient in determining the unique meaning for the patient. Gulino (1982) postulated that an exposure to existential ideas will help the nurse view the client holistically. Carper (1978) wrote of the "self-conscious reluctance . . . to include those aspects of knowing in nursing that are not the result of empirical research" (p. 16).

Phenomenological Approach to the Problem

The phenomenological approach is primarily an attempt to understand empirical matters from the perspective of those being studied. Bruyn (1966) stated [that] "phenomenology serves as the rationale behind efforts to understand individuals by entering into their field of perception in order to see life as these individuals see it" (p. 90). In order to ascertain the essential structure of a caring interaction, it would be desirable to learn the client's perceptions of the caring interactions that take place between the client and the nurse.

Whereas the majority of psychologists adhere to the behavioristic science methodology developed to predict and control, a number have opted for the phenomenological approach. Omery (1983, p. 55) listed three reasons why most psychologists pursue the more definite and structured methodology:

1. Psychology, like nursing, experiences direct competition with medicine, a science that uses natural scientific research methods effectively.
2. The development of the definitive methodology seems to have been an attempt to increase the legitimacy of the method, since psychology was already established within an academic setting where the natural scientific method dominated.
3. Possibly it was due to the sensitivity of psychology because so much of its original knowledge was rooted in philosophy.

Valle and King (1978) stated that phenomenologically oriented psychological research seeks to answer two related questions: what is the phenomenon that is experienced and lived, and how does it show itself? May (cited in Valle & King, 1978) defined existential phenomenology as meaning "ideally to take the human being as he exists, a living, acting, feeling, thinking phenomenon, at this moment in an organic relationship to us" (p. vii). Existentialism seeks not only to understand mankind in concrete lived situations and the lived moments but also man's responses to these moments.

Regardless of a phenomenon's particular variations, the same phenomenon is seen as (Valle & King, 1978, p. 15):

> having the same essential meaning when it is perceived over time in many different situations. . . . Only after seeing different reflections and varied appearances on repeated occasions does the constant unchanging structure become known to us.

As Giorgi (1970, p. 179) stated, "One of its (structure's) values for us is that it is precisely structure that is the reality that one responds to at the phenomenal level." Colaizzi (1973, p. 28) supported the importance of the phenomenological description when he stated:

> Without thereby first disclosing the foundations of a phenomenon, no progress whatsoever can be made concerning it, not even a first faltering step can be taken towards it, by science or by any other kind of cognition.

There is not *one* phenomenological methodology but rather a variety of methods that all hold to the primacy of the subjective experience. A few examples of recent studies illustrate the similar yet variable phenomenological methodologies being employed to study questions of human experience.

A phenomenological approach was used to discover the fundamental structure of aggression in middle adolescence (Munn, 1982). The experiences of ten adolescents were analyzed. The three essential constituents and their components were combined to form a fundamental structure of aggression. Heckler (1982) interviewed therapists regarding "healing episodes" and the data [were] analyzed phenomenologically. A healing episode was a moment or series of moments in which a client experienced either an insight, an emotional catharsis, or feelings of well-being. Myruk (1982) in studying self-esteem used the data from interviews to analyze for regularities and then universal themes. Colaizzi's method of analysis was used to phenomenologically analyze male executives' work experience with female executives (Simons-Kiecker, 1982).

A phenomenological methodology was used to research the question of "What is it to be fat?" (Rolfson, 1982). A six-step process was utilized to explicate a phenomenological description of being fat as a category of human experience. A phenomenological evaluation of family and child perspectives (Duffy, 1982) was designed to develop a picture of family functioning and perspectives. Families and children were interviewed about their thoughts, feelings, and actions regarding illness when the child was a patient. Interviews using open-ended questions were tape-recorded, transcribed, and analyzed for individual verbalization rates, individual family content, and group family and child content. Stanley (1978) used an adaptation of van Kaam's six-step process to explicate the necessary and sufficient components of the lived experience of "hope."

It is desirable to study caring from an existential/philosophical and phenomenological perspective in order to analyze the essential structure of client-nurse caring interactions from the client's perspective.

Assumptions

Phenomenological analysis requires the researcher to state his or her assumptions regarding the phenomenon under investigation and then bracket or suspend these preconceptions in order to fully understand the experience of the subject and not impose an a priori hypothesis on the experience. McCarthy (1980, p. 723) stated that:

> nurse-client interactions have the same chameleonic qualities as do any of the
> performing arts . . . and are as inaccessible to measurement as any whole and
> wholly human act can be.

While no performance can be exactly the same as another, it is assumed that there is an essential structure of a caring interaction that
can be extracted from the client's verbal description of this experience.
This essential structure or core of the interaction can be identified by
the absence of this quality in those interactions described as noncaring
nurse-client interactions.

THE DESIGN

Definitions of Terms

For the purposes of this study, the following terms were defined.

Essential structure of a caring nurse-client interaction—description
of the answer to the question of "What is essential for the experience
to be described by the client as being a caring interaction?" Caring and
noncaring interactions are not defined by the researcher but by the
client in his verbal descriptions.

Nurse—a registered nurse; however, it is presumed that some of the
descriptions may be a nurse who is not a registered nurse. Nonetheless, it is a person who the client has identified as being a member of
the nurse category.

Client—anyone over the age of 18 who has had a prior interaction
with a nurse, who was not hospitalized at the time of the interview,
and [who] was not personally known to the researcher prior to the
interview.

Interaction—any mutual or reciprocal action or influence between the
client [and] the nurse.

Review of the Literature

Watson (1979) called caring the "essence" of nursing, and listed ten
curative factors as primary mechanisms in caring for another human

being. In her cross-cultural studies, Leininger (1977) posited 17 major constructs that are present in caring. Fromm (1956) listed caring as one of his four components of love. Rogers (1969) equated love and caring. He stated, "I find it enriching when I can truly prize and care for or love another" (p. 233). The helping professions' literature emphasized [that] the adults who met the criteria were solicited by the investigator from students, faculty, and staff of a 2-year upper division university located in the southwestern United States. Five male names and five female names were selected at random from the pool of names.

The sample size was small because of the time involved in transcribing and analyzing the large amount of data from each subject. Each subject's verbal description was a complete description of the nurse-client interaction and as such described the essential structure of that interaction.

Data Collection. The subjects were approached and asked if they would like to participate in a research project involving the tape recording of their description of a caring and a noncaring interaction with a registered nurse. Written consent was obtained, and a second signature was recorded on the permission form to tape the description. Clients were informed that they did not have to complete the recording and could stop at any point.

The following verbal instructions were given:

- Describe a personal interaction you have had with a registered nurse who you felt was caring.
- Try to describe how you felt in that interaction.
- Describe a personal interaction you have had with a registered nurse who you felt was noncaring.
- Try to describe how you felt during that interaction.
- Please do not stop until you feel that you have discussed your feelings as completely as possible.

A description of the interaction was recorded. Questions were asked by the researcher only when it was necessary in order to clarify what the client was relating. Of special significance were the client's feelings regarding the interaction and what meaning [they] appeared to have for him or her. When the client had described his or her feelings and the total interaction and when no further clarification was required, the recording was considered complete. The length of the interviews varied from 20 to 50 minutes.

Treatment of Data

The raw data as recorded were transcribed verbatim for each subject. These transcriptions were subjected to phenomenological analysis using a methodology as developed by Colaizzi (1978). The procedural steps used were as follows:

1. All the subjects' descriptions were read in order to acquire a feeling for them.
2. Significant statements were extracted from each description, phrases and sentences that directly pertain to the investigated phenomenon. Statements were eliminated that contained the same or nearly the same statements.
3. Meanings were formulated by spelling out the meaning of each significant statement. In this difficult step, the meanings arrived at must not sever the connection with the original description. The formulations discover and bring out those meanings hidden in the various contexts of the phenomenon that are present in the original descriptions.
4. Clusters of themes were organized from the aggregate formulated meanings. This allowed for the emergence of themes common to all of the subjects' descriptions.
   a. These clusters of themes were referred back to the original descriptions in order to validate them. This was done to see if there was anything in the original that was not accounted for in the cluster of themes, and whether the cluster proposed anything which was not in the original. If either of the above was true, a re-examination was necessary.
   b. At this point discrepancies may be noted among and/or between the various clusters; some themes may flatly contradict other ones or may appear to be totally unrelated to other ones. The researcher then proceeded with the solid conviction that what was logically inexplicable might be existentially real and valid.
5. An exhaustive description of the phenomenon resulted from the integration of the above results.
6. The exhaustive description of the phenomenon is as unequivocal a statement of the essential structure of the phenomenon as possible.
7. The descriptions of the noncaring interactions were analyzed using the same process as with the caring interactions. A final validating step was achieved by returning to the subjects and

asking if the description formulated validated the original experience.

Analysis of Data

The research question was stated as follows: From the perspective of the client, what is the essential structure of a caring nurse-client interaction? Taped interviews of the ten subjects were transcribed, and the significant statements extracted from these transcriptions became the raw data for analysis. As the significant statements were being extracted from the original transcriptions, it became apparent that it would be of value to make separate lists for male and female clients because the statements differed slightly in their emphasis. In the final step of analysis, however, the essential structure of a caring interaction was drawn from both groups. After extraction of all significant statements from all ten transcriptions [was] complete duplicate statements were eliminated. The remaining significant statements are presented in Tables 5-1 and 5-2.

The same analytical process was carried out regarding the noncaring interactions. The significant statements from the noncaring interactions are listed in Tables 5-3 and 5-4.

Meanings were formulated from the significant statements. These formulated meanings are presented in Tables 5-5 and 5-6. These meanings were arrived at by reading, rereading, and reflecting upon the significant statements in the original transcriptions to get the meaning of the client's statement in the original context.

The aggregate of formulated meanings was organized into clusters of themes. These clusters represent themes that have emerged from and are common to all of the subjects' descriptions. These clusters are presented in Table 5-7. These clusters were referred back to the original descriptions in order to validate them. Each description was examined to see if there was anything in the original that was not accounted for in the cluster of themes, and whether the cluster proposed something that was not in the original.

An exhaustive description of the phenomenon was produced by the integration of the results of the analysis. The description of the caring interaction is a statement of its essential structure. The exhaustive description of a caring interaction is presented in Table 5-8.

An exhaustive description of a noncaring interaction was produced by integration of the results of analysis of the noncaring data. The exhaustive description of a noncaring interaction is presented in Table 5-9.

TABLE 5.1. FEMALE SIGNIFICANT STATEMENTS: CARING INTERACTIONS

1. Listened well—really listened
2. Empathetic
3. Understanding
4. Supportive to my concerns
5. There to talk to
6. Talked to me about things other than illness
7. Made me feel like a normal person
8. Interested in me as a person
9. Sat down on the side of my bed
10. Held my hand
11. Asked me questions
12. Looked me directly in the face
13. Verbalized some of her own insecurities
14. Let me know it was all right to be scared
15. Came back several times to see if I was comfortable
16. Felt secure with her being there
17. Felt more relaxed
18. Felt peace of mind
19. Didn't feel I was something on display
20. Felt I was human
21. Mild mannered—quiet—gentle
22. Really concerned
23. Compassionate
24. She knew something was bothering me
25. Nurse explained
26. I was very relieved
27. I felt well taken care of
28. Motherly
29. Call and see if I needed anything
30. Talked "nice"
31. Tried to give me hope
32. She knew what she was doing
33. Concerned with family also
34. I felt very warm toward her
35. I wanted to do something for her
36. I was comfortable with her
37. Understood patient and family as individuals
38. Paid attention to me
39. Paid attention to what I said

Example: Statements 9-13 are from the following transcription: "The situation that I came upon was, the *nurse listened and was very interested.* She was *interested* in my illness, also *in me as a person* and an individual. She *sat down on the side of my bed,* which I thought was good. I liked that closeness. She *listened to me,* she *held my hand,* and she *asked me questions* that really let me know that she was *really listening* to me. There's a difference between hearing something and listening, and when I talked to her she would *look me directly in the face.* She seemed to *really understand.* She didn't sympathize with me, but I could feel the *empathy between the two of us,* holding my hand and sitting on the side of the bed. She even *verbalized some of her own insecurities.*"

The following phrases from this transcription were duplications of significant statements from previous transcriptions and were therefore not repeated again in the final list of significant statements: *listened* was a duplicate of number 1 (*listened well— really listened*); *interested in me as a person* was an exact duplicate of number 8; *empathy between the two of us* was a duplicate of number 2 (*empathetic*).

A final validation was undertaken by returning to eight of the subjects (two were unavailable) and asking them if the description formulated validated their original experiences. The eight subjects contacted stated that the description they read of the caring and noncaring interactions contained the essence of their experience. Four

TABLE 5.2. MALE SIGNIFICANT STATEMENTS: CARING INTERACTIONS

1. Nurse was there	13. She looked after me all the time
2. Holding my hand and mopping my brow	14. Made me feel good
3. Make me comfortable	15. Interested in me as a person
4. Trying to comfort me	16. Give me what I need first—then do the nursing
5. Nurse would come when I rang	17. Explain to me
6. Come voluntarily	18. Ask if I needed anything
7. Sit down	19. Spent time with you
8. Talk to you	20. Pleasant
9. Really listen	21. Kind
10. Feel like it's my daughter taking care of me	22. Felt you were in good hands
11. Go out of her way	23. Soft attitude
12. Constantly coming back to see if she could help	24. Compassionate
	25. Really concerned about you feeling good

Example: Statements 6-10 are from the following transcription. "She would come *voluntarily, sit down, and talk and listen—really listen.* She was always fixing my bed and making sure I was comfortable. It made me *feel like it was my daughter that was taking care of me.*"

Because the phrase *making sure I was comfortable* was a duplication of number 3, *make me comfortable,* it was not repeated.

of the subjects stated they had not really thought of their experience in the terminology of the nurse's presence as used by the investigator. However, they further stated that the words they used in their original interviews had the same essential meaning as the terminology used by the investigator.

DISCUSSION OF THE FINDINGS

The phenomenological analysis resulted in the exhaustive description of the essential structure of a caring nurse-client interaction as stated in Table 5-8. The use of the word presence brings to mind several aspects, i.e., that of being physically present and mentally present, and being willingly and unwillingly present. As Nelson (1978) observed, "It can be safely concluded that the decision to make oneself present is rooted in the will" (p. 154). Just because the nurse is physically present, there is no guarantee that the individual is also present mentally. The nurse's existential presence means that not only

TABLE 5.3. FEMALE SIGNIFICANT STATEMENTS: NONCARING INTERACTIONS

1. I felt as though my hands were being slapped
2. Rules more important than people
3. It was an arbitrary, capricious power thing to her
4. She looked at the equipment instead of me
5. Always appeared to be in a hurry—always in a rush
6. Didn't have time to talk
7. Didn't want to talk
8. She wasn't interested in what I had to say
9. She was there to perform her duties and then go home
10. She didn't get close—stood at a distance
11. Felt as though I had a contagious disease that would rub off
12. Wouldn't look me in the eye
13. She was so snappy
14. Defensive
15. Wasn't interested in the person as a whole
16. I was not at ease
17. I was uncomfortable
18. I became depressed
19. I felt I had to keep my mouth shut
20. Super-efficient attitude
21. Nothing seemed to bother her
22. Seemed to feel she was really tough
23. She made me more tense
24. She showed she was frustrated
25. Made me frustrated and scared
26. I was upset
27. Unable to figure out what was going on
28. She didn't care what she said
29. I was almost a "basket case"
30. I was fidgeting
31. Buzz and she would not come
32. She'd say "yes-yes" and not come
33. She did not explain—"just sign"
34. Frightened me to death
35. Acted like she had a job to do
36. Didn't pay any attention when I told her—because I was older
37. Made me feel angry
38. No confidence in her
39. Afraid
40. Prancing around when the doctor was there
41. Left equipment on my bed and left the room
42. Told me to get up and take care of myself
43. I was scared and weak
44. She would not come and help
45. I fainted
46. I cried
47. I didn't want her to touch me
48. She was too busy talking to the other nurses to talk to me
49. She did not know what she was doing
50. I was not treated as a person
51. It was as though I was a nobody
52. Didn't want to go back to that hospital
53. Couldn't "care less"
54. Acted like clockwork

Example: Statements 35-38 are from the following transcription. "The nurse *acted like she had a job to do* and I should get up and take care of myself. *She didn't pay any attention when I told her* (wasn't supposed to get up) *because I was older.* Well, I ah, it *makes me feel very angry* for one thing, and it makes me have *less confidence in the nurse.*"

is the nurse present physically and mentally, but he or she is voluntarily or willingly and consciously present.

TABLE 5.4. MALE SIGNIFICANT STATEMENTS:
NONCARING INTERACTIONS

1. Didn't pay attention to what you needed
2. Just came in to do what she had to do
3. She didn't have "no pity—no mercy"
4. Talk to you a very short time
5. She just wasn't soft
6. Seemed it was just a "rum dum affair" (nursing)
7. Give you a quick answer and go about her business
8. Won't tell you what she's doing
9. Give you a simple answer as though you couldn't possibly understand
10. Act like it was an everyday affair
11. Do a job—look at you like an object
12. Watch you like you're a 10-year-old
13. Raise and shake her finger at me
14. Felt like a child being scolded
15. Not come in the room
16. Element of human contact lacking
17. Efficient—but no human element
18. Rang bell and would not come
19. Not supply any information
20. Bathed me as though she was doing a dog
21. It's insulting
22. Strapped me to the bed—never talked to me and walked out
23. Spoke loud and slow as though I'd lost my marbles
24. Could "care less" about how I was suffering
25. Very rough—like striking out at me
26. No personal awareness of my comfort
27. Sound of her voice was cold—unconcerned
28. Felt helpless
29. Washing me as though I was a toy
30. I was of no value to her

Example: Statements 7-12 are from the following transcription. "The other one, she'd bring you in a medication or something, you'd ask a question and *she'd give you a quick answer and go on about her business. She won't tell you what she's doing* or else she would *give you a simple answer as though you couldn't possibly understand.* She would *act like it* (nursing) *was an everyday affair.* When she did something like stick a thermometer in your mouth, it was *just doing a job* and she would stand there and *look at you like you were just an object.*"

For Marcel, existential presence is found in his theme of availability (disponibilite). A quote of Marcel's is appropriate for reflection at this point (1971, p. 25):

It is an undeniable fact, though hard to describe in intelligible terms, that there are some people who reveal themselves as present—that is to say, at our disposal—when we are in pain or in need to confide in someone, while there are other people who do not give us this feeling, however great is their good will. . . . [T]he most attentive and most conscientious listener may give me the impression of not being present; he gives me nothing, he cannot make room for me in himself, whatever the material favors he is prepared to grant me. The truth is that there is a way of giving, and another way of listening which is the way of refusing oneself; the material gift, the visible action, do not necessarily witness

TABLE 5.5.   FORMULATED MEANINGS OF SIGNIFICANT STATEMENTS: CARING

Female
1. Nurse really listened to what the client said, responding to the individual's uniqueness.
2. Nurse was perceptive and supportive of the client's stated and unstated concerns.
3. Nurse's physical presence of sitting, talking, direct eye contact, holding hands, and being self-disclosing made the client feel free to talk.
4. Caring interactions (encompassing behaviors and attitudes) made the client feel like a valued human being and not like an inanimate object or thing on display.
5. Nurse's voluntary and unsolicited return to the client was highly indicative of a caring attitude.
6. Individualized concern for the client made the client feel comfortable, secure, at peace, and relaxed.
7. The soft, gentle voice and mannerism impressed the client as caring, nonthreatening, and nondegrading.
8. The security felt by the client when in a caring interaction invokes feelings of being well taken care of by a family member.
9. Caring encounters evoked warm feelings in the client of wanting to do something reciprocal for the nurse.

Male
1. Nurse's physical presence of sitting, talking, and holding hands made client feel the nurse was truly concerned with him as a valued individual.
2. Nurse's voluntary and unsolicited return to the client was seen by the client as highly indicative of caring.
3. Nurse's caring made him feel comfortable, relaxed, secure, and in good hands, as though he was being taken care of by a family member.
4. Attention by the nurse to comfort and needs of the client before doing nursing "tasks" was interpreted by the client as caring.
5. A kind, soft, pleasant, gentle voice and attitude impressed the client as being caring and nondegrading.

to presence. . . . [P]resence is something which reveals itself immediately and unmistakably in a look, a smile, an intonation, or a handshake.

The client's consistent use of the term "really listening" is closely related to the notion of presence as described by Marcel. The willingness of the nurse in a caring interaction to "give" of oneself voluntarily and without solicitation from the client, is akin to what Marcel describes as availability.

For Buber (1958) the initial phase of a relationship is in the realm of I-it. In noncaring interactions, the nurses look at the clients as things to be manipulated and controlled. The degrading remarks, which

---

TABLE 5.6. FORMULATED MEANINGS OF SIGNIFICANT
STATEMENTS: NONCARING

Female
  1. The nurse's actions of always being in a hurry, without taking time to really talk or
     listen, are indicative to the client of the nurse's lack of interest in her as an
     individual.
  2. The nurse's attitude of lack of interest in her as a person is interpreted by the client
     as the nurse viewing nursing as "only a job."
  3. The nurse's physical actions and manner of speaking that belittle and degrade are
     seen by the client as noncaring.
  4. The physical behaviors exhibited by the nurse of being cold, tough, super-efficient,
     rigidly following rules, avoiding eye contact, not offering explanations, and seeing
     only parts of the client results in the client feeling frustrated, scared, depressed,
     angry, afraid, and upset.

Male
  1. The nurse who does not pay any attention to the client's needs but views nursing as
     a job is perceived by the client as noncaring.
  2. The physical absence or only short, superficial appearance of the nurse is
     interpreted by the client that the nurse does not consider him to be of any
     importance as a human being.
  3. The cold voice and rough physical actions of the nurse are interpreted by the client
     as his being treated as a nonhuman subject or as an inanimate object.
  4. The verbal and physical communication from a nurse that makes the client feel like
     a bad child is insulting and degrading and makes the client feel helpless and
     frustrated.

---

make the clients feel they are being treated like children, are used by
the nurses to manipulate and control. The noncaring interactions are
further characterized by the client being responded to as a nonhuman
being or object.

Buber's notion of "personal making present" is similar to Marcel's
theme of availability or presence. The nurse who does not hide behind
the busy schedule, the uniform, and the equipment, makes him- or
herself open to participation (Buber, 1965, p. 205).

> When I step into an elemental relation to the other . . . that is when he becomes
> present to me. Hence I designate awareness in this special sense as "personal
> making present."

In caring interactions, the client appreciates being recognized by
the nurse as a unique, thinking, feeling human being. Buber (1965,
p. 71) states that "Every human being needs confirmation because
man as man needs it." In really listening to a client's stated and

---

TABLE 5.7. CLUSTERS OF COMMON THEMES

Caring
1. Nurse's existential presence
   a. The nurse's physical and mental presences are available for the client's use.
   b. For the client, the nurse's presence is available not only when calling for it but also when needing the nurse's presence but not soliciting it.
2. Client's uniqueness
   a. The nurse recognizes the client's uniqueness by really listening and responding to him or her as a valued individual.
   b. The client perceives he or she is treated by the nurse as a human being of value.
3. Consequences
   a. The nurse's individualized concern for the client results in the client feeling comfortable, secure, at peace, and relaxed.

Noncaring
1. Nurse's presence
   a. The nurse's physical presence is to get the "job" done.
   b. For the client, the physical presence is available briefly or not at all, even when solicited.
2. Client's uniqueness
   a. The nurse does not recognize the client's uniqueness because the nurse does not "really listen" or appears "too busy" to pay attention to the client as an individual.
   b. The client is devalued as a unique individual by actions of the nurse that degrade and belittle.
3. Consequences
   a. The nurse's lack of concern for the client results in the client feeling frustrated, scared, depressed, angry, afraid, and upset.

---

unstated needs, the nurse participates in the client's world and comes to appreciate and respond to the client on the I-thou level of equality.

In the analysis, the formulated meanings from the significant statements of both male and female clients were integrated into the description of the essential structure of a caring interaction. However, in looking at the statements it will be noted there is a subtle difference. Both sexes mentioned the unsolicited caring behaviors and that of being really listened to as being of major importance. However, men mentioned nurses' physical actions of comfort and reassurance, while women noted psychological support at a deeper or more intimate level than noted by the men. From rereading the original transcriptions, the investigator concluded that women expected this deeper level of emotional support and felt very free to verbally report it. The men either did not feel the need or didn't feel as free to admit the need.

TABLE 5.8. **EXHAUSTIVE DESCRIPTION OF A CARING NURSE: CLIENT INTERACTION**

In a caring interaction, the nurse's existential presence is perceived by the client as more than just a physical presence. There is the aspect of the nurse giving of oneself to the client. This giving of oneself may be in response to the client's request, but it is more often a voluntary effort and is unsolicited by the client. The nurse's willingness to give of oneself is primarily perceived by the client as an attitude and behavior of sitting down and really listening and responding to the unique concerns of the individual as a person of value. The relaxation, comfort, and security that the client experiences both physically and mentally are an immediate and direct result of the client's stated and unstated needs being heard and responded to by the nurse.

TABLE 5.9. **EXHAUSTIVE DESCRIPTION OF A NONCARING NURSE: CLIENT INTERACTION**

The nurse's presence with the client is perceived by the client as a minimal presence of the nurse being physically present only. The nurse is viewed as being there only because it is a job and not to assist the client or answer his or her needs. Any response by the nurse is done with a minimal amount of energy expenditure and bound by the rules. The client perceives the nurse who does not respond to this request for assistance as being noncaring. Therefore, an interaction that never happened is labeled as a noncaring interaction. The nurse is too busy and hurried to spend time with the client and therefore does not sit down and really listen to the client's individual concerns. The client is further devalued as a unique person because he or she is scolded, treated as a child, or treated as a nonhuman being or an object. Because of the devaluing and lack of concern, the client's needs are not met and the client has negative feelings, that is, frustrated, scared, depressed, angry, afraid, and upset.

CONCLUSIONS AND IMPLICATIONS

Findings of this phenomenological study add credence to the limited research on caring. It is not only what the nurse does in the way of physical acts of assistance, but what the nurse is. Being existentially present or available, showing genuine interest in the client as a valued individual by really listening is considered by clients to be one of the most important aspects of caring. These findings have implications in the areas of nursing education, nursing practice, nursing research, and in building and testing nursing theory.

Nursing Education

The findings of this study have implications for the inclusion and integration of existential philosophical thought into undergraduate nursing education. With some understanding of existential philosophical concepts, students can begin to build their nursing practice on a meaningful philosophical base. If caring is valued as a base for nursing practice, the nursing educators have the responsibility to provide access to existential philosophical ways of thinking. If caring is a valued attribute for nurses, then the demonstration of this attribute must be evident for nursing students to see in nursing educators. Presence, really listening, and respect for the uniqueness of the individual are all characteristics nurse educators must live so that students can know the receptivity of caring.

Nursing Research

The findings of this study show that data can be gathered directly from individuals, analyzed, and the findings communicated so that the meanings for the person in the lived world are not distorted, reduced, or fragmented. Rather, the meanings are viewed holistically, as a part of the individual's whole experience. Quantitative data can provide information, but cannot provide what it *feels* like to be in a caring or noncaring interaction.

One consideration is that phenomenological research can never exhaust the investigated phenomenon. The results of phenomenological research are "the essence of certainty to be established with reservations" (Merleau-Ponty, 1962, p. 396). Phenomenology tells what man is all about outside the boundaries of traditional science. Nursing will enhance its research possibilities if it can learn to treat the qualitative as such, rather than seeking its transformation into quantifiable measurements.

Nursing Practice

Considering the client as the center of his or her own universe, then what is going on in the client's environment is of utmost importance to him or her. The client's perceptions are not the same as those of other individuals. It is logical to assume that the best source of information about the client is the client. Situations should, therefore, be defined from the client's point of view. In nursing, to view each client from his or her own unique individual point of view, will entail the nurse being existentially present. Existential presence in a caring interaction does not have to entail hours of time. It does mean that in interactions with clients, the nurse will truly be present in thought, word, and deed. If the existential mode of interaction became as habitual as the brisk, efficient, cliche, nonhuman type of interaction, clients would respond with the feelings of relaxation, comfort, and security. Although there is limited research to validate the notion, feelings of relaxation, comfort, and security are generally supported as hastening and promoting clients' recovery and well-being.

Nursing Theory

"Theory must as usual, wait on practice" (Griffin, 1980, p. 265). While the statement has a certain validity, the findings of this study would seem to indicate that theory development is possible concurrently with utilization of the findings in education, research, and practice.

Rogers (1970) has several assumptions within her theory: (1) man as a unified whole possess[es] his own integrity and manifest[s] characteristics that are more and different from the sum of his parts; (2) man and environment are continuously exchanging matter and energy. One of the unstated assumptions is that an observer cannot see the whole and the parts simultaneously (Rogers, 1970). Health in Rogers' theory is when the client's pattern and organization of his or her energy field is in synchrony with the pattern and organization of the environmental energy field. Nursing to Rogers is the humanistic science that has as its aim to assist people in achieving their maximum health potential. Thus, within this framework, any nursing attitudes and behaviors which assist in synchrony of pattern and organization of the client-nurse energy field, would assist clients in achieving their maximum health potential.

Findings of this study would indicate that the consequences of caring nurse-client interactions are a client who is relaxed, comfortable, and more secure—one whose energy field is in synchrony with the energy field of his or her environment. The nurse, by attitude and actions, becomes the medium by which energy is channeled to the client. It is this giving or availability—an essential of a caring interaction—that is the medium of energy exchange flowing to the client. Although research in the area of channeling energy is limited, Krieger (1979) in her investigations on therapeutic touch has recounted numerous interactions where a transfer of energy has taken place. If transfer of energy is demonstrable by the mechanism of therapeutic touch, it is possible to assume psychological energy transfer taking place within caring interactions between nurse and client.

SUMMARY

Since the research question is based on client perceptions, the phenomenological analysis of transcribed client interviews was an appropriate methodology for this study. The six-step method of analysis as described by Colaizzi (1978) was followed. Each step of the analysis was guided by two concerns: (1) to characterize the essential meaning of what the client's description reveals about the nature of a caring interaction, and (2) to remain as faithful as possible to the client's original characterization. The additional data regarding noncaring interactions [were] also collected, analyzed, and contrasted to the description of a caring interaction.

The phenomenological analytical process by which findings were arrived at was a reflective activity. This activity is similar, if not identical, to that used in everyday life. None of the subjects asked what was meant by "caring" or "noncaring." Each subject already understood what was involved in a caring and a noncaring interaction. In other words, each subject, in order to explicitly realize and describe the caring and noncaring interaction, had to be already living an understanding of the meanings of caring and noncaring.

This study sought to understand the client's way of being-in-a-situation as it was actually lived and experienced by the client in interaction with a nurse. The essential structure of a caring interaction was allowed to show itself and speak for itself. It was not translated or defined by external criteria. The research remained faithful to the being-in-the-situation of all human phenomenon.

REFERENCES

Amacher, N. J. Touch is a way of caring. *American Journal of Nursing*, 1973, *73*(5), 852-854.

Bendall, E. The future of British nurse education. *Journal of Advanced Nursing*, 1977, *2*, 171-181.

Brown, L. J. Behaviors of nurses perceived by hospitalized patients as indicators of care. *Dissertation Abstracts International*, 1982, *42*(11), 4361-B. (University Microfilms No. DA 82-09803)

Bruyn, S. R. *The human perspective in sociology.* Englewood Cliffs, N.J.: Prentice-Hall, 1966.

Buber, M. *I and thou* (2nd ed.; R. G. Smith, Ed. and Trans.). New York: Charles Scribner's Sons, 1958.

Buber, M. *Between man and man.* (R. G. Smith, Ed. and Trans.). New York: Macmillan, 1965.

Carkhuff, R. R. *Helping and human relations* (Vol. 2). New York: Holt, Rinehart, & Winston, 1969.

Carper, B. A. Practice oriented theory. Fundamental patterns of knowing in nursing: Part 1. *Advances in Nursing Science*, 1978, *1*(1), 13-23.

Colaizzi, P. F. *Reflection and research in psychology: A phenomenological study of learning.* Dubuque, Iowa: Kendall-Hunt, 1973.

Colaizzi, P. F. Psychological research as the phenomenologist views it. In R. Vaile & M. King (Eds.), *Existential phenomenological alternatives for psychology.* New York: Oxford University Press, 1978.

Combs, A. A., Avila, D. L., & Purkey, W. W. *Helping relationships* (2nd ed.). Boston: Allyn & Bacon, 1978.

Davis, A. J. The phenomenological approach in nursing research. In N. Chaska (Ed.). *The nursing profession: Views through the mist.* New York: McGraw-Hill, 1978.

Duffy, A. F. Asthma: A phenomenological evaluation of family and child perspectives. *Dissertation Abstracts International*, 1982, *42*(11), 4573-B. (University Microfilms No. DA 82-08955)

Ferlic, A. Existential approach in nursing. *Nursing Outlook*, 1968, *16*(1), 30-33.

Flaskerud, J., Halloran, E., Janken, J., et al. Avoidance and distancing: A descriptive view of nursing. *Nursing Forum*, 1979, *15*, 158-174.

Ford, M. B. Nurse professionals and the care process. *Dissertation Abstracts International*, 1992, *42*(3), 967-B. (University Microfilms No. 8119796).

Fromm, E. *The art of love.* New York: Harper & Row, 1956.

Gadow, S. Existential advocacy. In S. F. Spiker & S. Gadow (Eds.). *Nursing: Ideas and images opening dialogue with the humanities.* New York: Springer, 1980.

Gazda, G. M., Asbury, F. R., Balzer, F. J., et al. *Human relations development* (2nd ed.). Boston: Allyn & Bacon, 1977.

Gilfoyle, E. M. Caring: A philosophy for practice. *American Journal of Occupational Therapy*, 1980, *34*(8), 517-521.

Giorgi, A. *Psychology as a human science.* New York: Harper & Row, 1970.

Griffin, A. P. Philosophy and nursing. *Journal of Advanced Nursing*, 1980, *5*, 261-272.

Gulino, C. K. Entering the mysterious dimension of others: An existential approach to nursing care. *Nursing Outlook*, 1982, *30*(6), 352-357.

Heckler, R. A. Reaching for the sun: A phenomenological approach to the therapist's experience of healing in psycho-therapy. *Dissertation Abstracts International*, 1982, *43*(1), 251-B. (University Microfilms No. DA 82-13147)

Helmstadter, G. O. *Research concepts in human behavior education, psychology, sociology.* Englewood Cliffs, N.J.: Prentice-Hall, 1970.

Henry, O. M. Nurse behaviors perceived by patients as indicators of caring. *Dissertations Abstracts International*, 1976, 34-B.

Howard, J., & Strauss, A. *Humanizing health care.* New York: Wiley, 1975.

Hyde, A. The phenomenon of caring: Part VI. *American Nurses' Foundation*, 1977, *12*(1), 2.

Krieger, D. *The therapeutic touch.* Englewood Cliffs, N.J.: Prentice-Hall, 1979.

Larson, P. Oncology patients' and professional nurses' perceptions of important nurse caring behaviors. *Dissertation Abstracts International*, 1982, *42*(2), 568-B. (University Microfilms No. AAD81-16511)

Leininger, M. Caring: The essence and central focus of nursing. *Nursing Research Reports: American Nurses Foundation, Inc.*, 1977, *12*(1), 2-14.

Livingston, J. *Modern Christian thought.* New York: Macmillan, 1971.

Marcel, G. *The philosophy of existence* (R. F. Grabow, Ed. and Trans.) Philadelphia: University of Pennsylvania Press, 1971.

Mayeroff, M. *On caring.* New York: Harper & Row, 1971.

McCarthy, P. A. On the nature of the art of nursing. *Nursing Outlook*, 1980, *28*(12), 723.

McCorkle, R. Effects of touch on seriously ill patients. *Nursing Research*, 1974, *34*(2), 125-132.

McNally, S. J. M. The nurse leader: A caring administrator. *Supervisor Nurse*, 1977, *8*(10), 47-49.

Menninger, W. W. "Caring" as part of health care quality. *Journal of American Medical Association*, 1975, *234*(8), 836-837.

Merleau-Ponty, M. *Phenomenology of perception.* New York: Humanities Press, 1962.

Munn, T. L. The meaning and experience of aggression In adolescence: A phenomenological approach. *Dissertation Abstracts International*, 1982, *43*(3), 915-B. (University Microfilms No. DA 82-19420)

Myruk, C. J. Being pleased with oneself in a biographically critical way: An existential-phenomenological investigation. *Dissertation Abstracts International*, 1982, *42*(12), 4937-B. (University Microfilms No. DA 82-09397)

Nelson, M. J. Implications for existential encounters in the thoughts of Gabriel Marcel and Martin Buber. *Dissertation Abstracts International*, 1978, *39*(5), 2226 B. (University Microfilms No. 78218260)

Noddings, N. Caring. *Journal of Curriculum Theorizing*, 1981, *3*(2), 139-148.

Oiler, C. The phenomenological approach in nursing research. *Nursing Research*, 1982, *31*(3), 178-181.

Omery, A. Phenomenology: A method for nursing research. *Advances in Nursing Science*, 1983, *5*(2), 49-63.

Paterson, J. G., & Zderad, L. T. *Humanistic Nursing.* New York: Wiley Biomedical Publications, 1976.

Pelligrino, E. D. Educating the humanist physician: An ancient ideal reconsidered. *Journal of the American Medical Association*, 1974, *227*(11), 2128-2133.

Reilly, D. *Teaching and evaluating the affective domain in nursing programs.* New York: Charles Slack, 1978.

Rogers, C. *Freedom to learn.* Columbus, Ohio: Charles Merrill, 1969.

Rogers, M. *An introduction to theoretical basis of nursing.* Philadelphia: F. A. Davis, 1970.

Rolfson, M. A. Being fat: A phenomenological inquiry. *Dissertation Abstracts International*, 1982, *43*(4), 1241-B. (University Microfilms No. DA 82-21556)

Rule, M. L. The professional ethic in nursing. *Journal of Advanced Nursing*, 1978, *3*, 3-8.

Simons-Kiecker, J. Male executives' work experience with female executives: A phenomenological study. *Dissertation Abstracts International*, 1982, *42*(11), 4609-B. (University Microfilms No. DA 82-534)

Stanley, T. M. The lived experience of hope: The isolation of discreet descriptive elements common to the experience of hope in healthy young adults. *Dissertation Abstracts International*, 1978, *39*(3), 1212-1213. (University Microfilms No. DA 7816899)

Vaillot, Sister M. C. Existentialism: A philosophy of commitment. *American Journal of Nursing*, 1966, *66*(3), 500-505.

Valle, R., & King, M. *Existential phenomenological alternatives for psychology*. New York: Oxford University Press, 1978.

van Kaam, A. L. The nurse in the patient's world. *American Journal of Nursing*, 1959, *59*(12), 1708-1710.

Watson, J. *Nursing: The philosophy and science of caring*. Boston: Little, Brown, 1979.

Wexler, M. The behavioral sciences in medical education: A view from psychology. *American Psychologist*, 1976, *31*, 275-283.

Yerxa, E. J. Occupational therapy's role in creating a future climate of caring. *American Journal of Occupational Therapy*, 1980, *34*(8), 529-534.

BIBLIOGRAPHY

Rubel, Sister M. Coming to grips with the nursing process. *Supervisor Nurse*, 1976, *7*(2), 30-39.

van Kaam, A. L. Phenomenal analysis: Exemplified by a study of the experience of really feeling understood. *Journal of Psychology*, 1959, *15*, 66-72.

APPENDIX D

▼

A Grounded Theory Study

Constructions of Survival and Coping by Women Who Have Survived Childhood Sexual Abuse

Susan L. Morrow
University of Utah

Mary Lee Smith
Arizona State University

This qualitative study investigated personal constructs of survival and coping by 11 women who have survived childhood sexual abuse. In-depth interviews, a 10-week focus group, documentary evidence, and follow-up participant checks and collaborative analysis were used. Over 160 individual strategies were coded and analyzed, and a theoretical model was developed describing (a) causal conditions that underlie the development of survival and coping strategies, (b) phenomena that arose from those causal conditions, (c) context that influenced strategy development, (d) intervening conditions that influenced strategy development, (e) actual survival and coping strategies, and (f) consequences of those strategies. Subcategories of each component of the theoretical model were identified and are illustrated by narrative data. Implications for counseling psychology research and practice are addressed.

The sexual abuse of children appears to exist at epidemic levels, with estimates that 20%-45% of women and 10%-18% of men in the United States and Canada have been sexually abused as children;

SOURCE: The material in this appendix is reprinted from Morrow, S. L., & Smith, M. L. (1995). Constructions of survival and coping by women who have survived childhood sexual abuse. *Journal of Counseling Psychology, 42,* 24-33. Copyright 1995, American Psychological Association. Used by permission.

experts agree that these figures are underestimates (Geffner, 1992; Wyatt & Newcomb, 1990). Approximately one third of students seeking counseling in one university counseling center reported having been sexually abused as children (Stinson & Hendrick, 1992). Because of the breadth and severity of psychological and physical symptoms consequent to childhood sexual abuse, the confusion surrounding treatment methods, and the large number of "normal" individuals seeking counseling who display severe psychological symptoms (Courtois, 1988; Geffner, 1992; Lundberg-Love, Marmion, Ford, Geffner, & Peacock, 1992; Russell, 1986), a theoretical framework is needed to better understand the consequences of childhood sexual abuse.

Two primary modes of understanding and responding to consequences of childhood sexual abuse are symptom and construct approaches (Briere, 1989). Researchers and practitioners alike have adopted a symptom-oriented approach to childhood sexual abuse. It is characteristic of both academic and lay literatures to portray consequences of sexual abuse in lengthy lists of symptoms (Courtois, 1988; Russell, 1986). Briere (1989), however, encouraged a broader perspective, advocating the identification of overarching constructs and core effects—as opposed to symptoms—of sexual victimization.

Mahoney (1991) explicated core ordering processes—tacit, deep-structural processes of valence, reality, identity, and power—that underlie personal meanings or constructions of reality. He emphasized the importance of understanding tacit theories of self and world that guide the development of patterns of affect, thinking, and behavior. A construct-oriented approach to the study of survival and coping offers the possibility of developing a conceptual framework that will bring order into the chaos of symptomatology that currently characterizes the field, as well as relating those symptoms to core ordering processes.

A number of authors (Johnson & Kenkel, 1991; Long & Jackson, 1993; Roth & Cohen, 1986) have related coping theories (Horowitz, 1979; Lazarus & Folkman, 1984) to sexual-abuse trauma. However,

---

AUTHORS' NOTE: We thank Arlene Metha, Gail Hackett, Carole Edelsky, B. J. Moore, Lucille Pope, Helga Kansy, and the research collaborators for their valuable input related to the structure and process of this research. Susan L. Morrow conducted the research for this article while at Arizona State University, and the design and analysis were the collaborative activities of both Susan L. Morrow and Mary Lee Smith. Correspondence concerning this article should be addressed to Susan L. Morrow, Department of Educational Psychology, 327 Milton Bennion Hall, University of Utah, Salt Lake City, Utah 84112.

traditional coping theories have tended to problematize emotion-focused and avoidant coping styles commonly used by women and abuse survivors (Banyard & Graham-Bermann, 1993). Strickland (1978) stressed the importance of practitioners accurately assessing individuals' life situations in determining the efficacy of certain coping strategies. Banyard and Graham-Bermann (1993) emphasized the need to examine power as a mediator in the coping process. The child who is a victim of sexual abuse is inherently powerless; therefore, particular attention must be paid to a reexamination of coping strategies with this population.

The purpose of the present research was to understand the lived experiences of women who had been sexually abused as children and to generate a theoretical model for the ways in which they survived and coped with their abuse. As Hoshmand (1989) noted, qualitative research strategies are particularly appropriate to address meanings and perspectives of participants. In addition, she suggested that naturalistic methods offer the researcher access to deep-structural processes.

Considerable attention has been given to the truthfulness of claims of childhood sexual abuse, particularly when alleged victims have forgotten or repressed all or part of their abuse experiences. Loftus (1993) outlined the difficulties inherent in determining the veridicality of retrieved memories, urging caution on the part of psychologists working in the area of sexual abuse and calling for ongoing research into the nature of true repressed memories. While acknowledging the importance of Loftus's concerns, a constructivist approach orients toward "assessing the viability (utility) as opposed to the validity (truth) of an individual's unique worldview" (Neimeyer & Neimeyer, 1993, p. 2). In accordance with this view, each volunteer's self-identification as an abuse survivor was the criterion for inclusion in the present investigation and her definition of survival and coping the starting point for the investigation. We accepted the stories of participants at face value as their phenomenological realities.

The primary method of investigating those realities was grounded theory (Glaser & Strauss, 1967), a qualitative research method designed to aid in the systematic collection and analysis of data and the construction of a theoretical model. The data analysis was based on transcriptions of semistructured, in-depth interviews; videotapes of a 10-week group that focused on what survival and coping meant to the research participants; documentary evidence, including participants' journals and other relevant writings; and Susan L. Morrow's field notes and journals.

Method

Qualitative research methods are particularly suited to uncovering meanings people assign to their experiences (Hoshmand, 1989; Polkinghorne, 1991). Chosen to clarify participants' understandings of their abuse experiences, the methods used involved (a) developing codes, categories, and themes inductively rather than imposing predetermined classifications on the data (Glaser, 1978), (b) generating working hypotheses or assertions (Erickson, 1986) from the data, and (c) analyzing narratives of participants' experiences of abuse, survival, and coping.

Participants

Research participants were 11 women, with ages ranging from 25 to 72, who had been sexually abused as children. One woman was African American, 1 was West Indian, and the remainder were Caucasian. Three were lesbians, 1 was bisexual, and 7 were heterosexual. Three women were physically disabled. Participants' educational levels ranged from completion of the Graduate Equivalency Degree to having a master's degree. Abuse experiences varied from a single incident of molestation by a family friend to 18 years of ongoing sadistic abuse by multiple perpetrators. Age of initial abuse ranged from infancy to 12 years of age; abuse continued as late as age 19. All participants had been in counseling or recovery processes lasting from one 12-step meeting to years of psychotherapy.

Procedure

Entry into the field. Research participants were recruited in a large southwestern metropolitan area through therapists known for expertise in their work with the survivors of sexual abuse. Each therapist was sent a letter describing the study in detail; a similar letter was enclosed to give to clients who might benefit from or be interested in participating in the study. Interested clients, in turn, called Susan L. Morrow, the investigator. Of the 12 respondents, 11 became research participants. The 12th declined to participate for personal reasons.

When prospective participants contacted Morrow, the purpose and scope of the study were reviewed and an appointment was made for an initial interview. Informed consent was discussed in detail at the beginning of the interview, with an emphasis on confidentiality and the potential emotional consequences of participation. After a participant signed the consent, audio- or videotaping commenced. Each participant chose her own pseudonym for the research and was promised the opportunity to review quotes and other information about her before publication.

Data sources. Each of the 11 survivors of sexual abuse participated in a 60- to 90-min in-depth, open-ended interview, during which two questions were asked: "Tell me, as much as you are comfortable sharing with me right now, what happened to you when you were sexually abused," and "What are the primary ways in which you survived?" Morrow's responses included active listening, empathic reflection, and minimal encouragers.

After the initial interviews, 7 of the 11 interviewees became focus-group participants. Four were excluded from the group: 2 who were interviewed after the group had started and 2 who had other commitments. The group provided an interactive environment (Morgan, 1988) that focused on survival and coping. In the initial meeting, participants brainstormed about the words *victim, survivor,* and *coping.* Subsequent group sessions built on the first, with participants exploring emerging categories from the data analysis and their own research questions, which had been invited by Morrow. Morrow took a participant-observer role, moving from less active involvement in the beginning to a more fully participatory role toward the end (Adler & Adler, 1987).

A central feature of the analysis was Morrow's self-reflectivity (Peshkin, 1988; Strauss, 1987). Morrow's own subjective experiences were logged, examined for tacit biases and assumptions, and subsequently analyzed.

Documentary evidence completed the data set. These data consisted of participants' journals, kept both in conjunction with and independent of the project, artistic productions, and personal writings from earlier periods of participants' lives.

Data collection, analysis, and writing. A central concern for rigor in qualitative research is evidentiary adequacy—that is, sufficient time in the field and extensiveness of the body of evidence used as data (Erickson, 1986). The data consisted of over 220 hr of audio- and videotapes, which documented more than 165 hr of interviews, 24 hr of group sessions, and 25 hr of follow-up interactions with participants over a period of more than 16 months. All of the audiotapes and a portion of the videotapes were transcribed verbatim by Morrow. In addition, there were over 16 hr of audiotaped field notes and reflections. The data corpus consisted of over 2,000 pages of transcriptions, field notes, and documents shared by participants.

The analytic process was based on immersion in the data and repeated sortings, codings, and comparisons that characterize the grounded theory approach. Analysis began with open coding, which is the examination of minute sections of text made up of individual words, phrases, and sentences. Strauss and Corbin (1990) described open coding as that which "fractures the data and allows one to identify some categories, their properties and dimensional locations" (p. 97). The language of the participants guided the development of code and category labels, which were identified with short descriptors, known as *in vivo codes*, for survival and coping strategies. These codes and categories were systematically compared and contrasted, yielding increasingly complex and inclusive categories.

Morrow also wrote analytic and self-reflective memos to document and enrich the analytic process, to make implicit thoughts explicit, and to expand the data corpus. Analytic memos consisted of questions, musings, and speculations about the data and emerging theory. Self-reflective memos documented Morrow's personal reactions to participants' narratives. Both types of memos were included in the data corpus for analysis. Analytic memos were compiled and an analytic journal was kept for cross-referencing codes and emerging categories. Large poster boards with movable tags were used to facilitate the arranging and rearranging of codes within categories.

Open coding was followed by axial coding, which puts data "back together in new ways by *making connections between a category and its subcategories*" (italics in original, Strauss & Corbin, 1990, p. 97). From this process, categories emerged and were assigned in vivo category labels. Finally, selective coding ensued. Selective coding was the integrative process of "selecting the core category, systematically relating it to other categories, validating those relationships [by searching for confirming and disconfirming examples], and filling in categories that need[ed] further refinement and development" (Strauss & Corbin, 1990, p. 116).

Codes and categories were sorted, compared, and contrasted until saturated—that is, until analysis produced no new codes or categories and when all of the data were accounted for in the core categories of the grounded theory paradigm model. Criteria for core status were (a) a category's centrality in relation to other categories, (b) frequency of a category's occurrence in the data, (c) its inclusiveness and the ease with which it related to other categories, (d) clarity of its implications for a more general theory, (e) its movement toward theoretical power as details of the category were worked out, and (f) its allowance for maximum variation in terms of dimensions, properties, conditions, consequences, and strategies (Strauss, 1987).

In keeping with Fine's (1992) recommendations that researchers move beyond the stances of ventriloquists or mere vehicles for the voices of those being researched, we sought to engage the participants as critical members of the research team. Consequently, after completion of the group, the 7 group members were invited to become coanalysts of data from the focus group. Four elected to do so. Not choosing to extend their original commitment, 2 terminated their participation at that point; a 3rd declined because of physical problems. The 4 coanalysts (termed *participant-coresearchers*) continued to meet with Morrow for more than a year. They acted as the primary source of participant verification, analyzing videotapes of the group sessions in which they had participated, suggesting categories, and revising the emerging theory and model. Participant-coresearchers used their natural intuitive analytic skills as well as grounded theory principles and procedures that had been taught to them by Morrow to collaborate in the data analysis.

Morrow met weekly with an interdisciplinary qualitative research collective throughout the data gathering, analysis, and writing of the research account. The group provided peer examination of the analysis and writing, as recommended by LeCompte and Goetz (1982), thereby enhancing researcher and theoretical sensitivity, overcoming selective inattention, and enhancing receptiveness to the setting (Glaser, 1978; Lincoln & Guba, 1985).

Accountability was achieved through ongoing consultations with participants and colleagues and by maintaining an audit trail that outlined the research process and the evolution of codes, categories, and theory (Miles & Huberman, 1984). The audit trail consisted of chronological narrative entries of research activities, including pre-entry conceptualizations, entry into the field, interviews, group activities, transcription, initial coding efforts, analytic activities, and the evolution of the survival and coping theoretical model. The audit trail also included a complete list of the 166 in vivo codes that formed the basis for the analysis.

Because of the human cognitive bias toward confirmation (Mahoney, 1991), an active search for disconfirming evidence was essential to achieving rigor (Erickson, 1986). Data were combed to disconfirm various assertions made as a result of the analysis. Discrepant case analysis, also advised by Erickson (1986), was conducted, and participants were consulted to determine reasons for discrepancies.

Results

The grounded theory model for surviving and coping with child-hood sexual abuse, evolving from Strauss and Corbin's (1990) frame-work and developed from the present investigation, is present in Figure 1.

Causal Conditions of Phenomena
Related to Sexual Abuse

Two types of causal conditions emerged from the data, which ultimately led to certain phenomenological experiences related to sexual abuse. These causal conditions were (a) cultural norms and (b) forms of sexual abuse. Cultural norms of dominance and submission, violence, maltreatment of women, denial of abuse, and powerlessness of children formed the bedrock on which sexual abuse was perpe-trated. Paula's (all names used are pseudonyms) experiences reflected a number of these norms: Her father enforced his dominance by physically and sexually abusing Paula's mother and calling Paula and her mother "cunt," "whore," and "fat pig." He was an avid reader of pornography and regularly invited Paula into the bathroom, where he showed her pictures from his magazines. He took photographs of her in the bathtub or sunbathing by the pool. She stated that most of his abuse of her was ". . . real, real physical. [He] beat the shit out of us." His sexual abuse of her was "covert." Audre commented the following after disclosing that her sexual abuser had beaten her "only" once: "You know, he never whipped me like that again. Never again. And he never had to. . . . Whenever I would resist him at any point, he'd just look at me." Dominance, violence, and the powerless-ness of children converged in Audre's life to set the stage for her abuse, as did the denial of abuse or the potential for abuse by significant people in her life and in the lives of other victims. After being sexually abused by an elderly neighbor, Liz brought home a picture he had taken to show her parents. Liz reported, "My mother got right down in my face and said, 'He didn't do anything to you, did he?' " Fright-ened, Liz replied, "No, he didn't do anything to me."

The second causal condition consisted of the various forms of sexual abuse that had been perpetrated. Abuses ranged from innuen-dos and violations of privacy to rape and vaginal penetration with loaded guns. These forms of abuse were classified through the data analysis into five categories: (a) nonphysical sexual abuses, (b) physi-

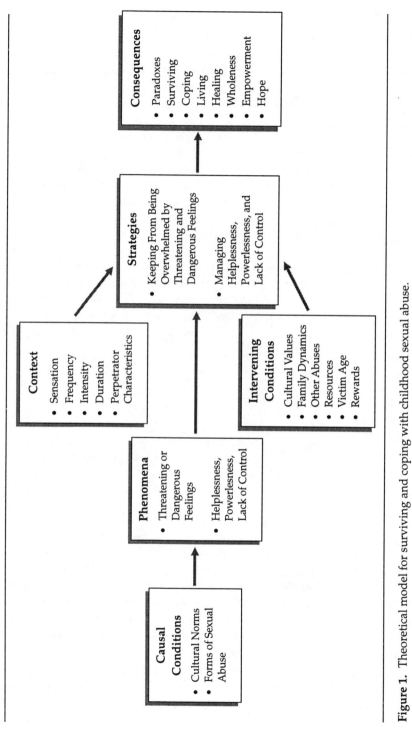

Figure 1. Theoretical model for surviving and coping with childhood sexual abuse.

cal molestation, (c) being forced to perform sexual acts, (d) penetration, and (e) sexual torture. Nonphysical sexual abuses, perpetrated on all of the victims, consisted of perpetrators engaging in sexual talk, photographing the child in sexual poses or nude, exposing the genitals to the child, engaging in sexual teasing and jokes, performing sexual activities in front of the child, and inviting the child to participate in sexual activity. Physical molestation, also experienced by all of the participants, included sexual touching, pinching, poking, tickling, and stroking the child with objects; removing the child's covers or clothes; holding the child in such a way that sexual contact was made; masturbating the child; washing and examining the child's genitals in excess of actions necessary for health and cleanliness; and performing cunnilingus on the child. Of the participants, 7 had been forced to perform sexual acts, such as masturbation, fellatio, or cunnilingus. At least 5 of the victims had been penetrated vaginally, orally, or anally with fingers, hands, penises, guns, knives, or other implements; four others were uncertain about penetration because of amnesic episodes. Six remembered being subjected to sexual tortures of a sadistic nature beyond those already described.

Phenomena Resulting From Cultural Norms and Forms of Sexual Abuse

Causal conditions—cultural norms and the forms of sexual abuse to which victims were subjected—resulted in two core categories of subjective phenomena as reported by participants: (a) being overwhelmed by feelings victims experienced as threatening or dangerous and (b) experiencing helplessness, powerlessness, and lack of control. These categories support and extend Herman's (1992) description of traumatic reactions, in which she found that "the salient characteristic of the traumatic event is its power to inspire helplessness and terror" (p. 34). This research indicates that terror is but one of the overwhelming emotions characteristic of trauma experienced by survivors of sexual abuse. Most, but not all, of the survivors in the study experienced terror; all experienced overwhelming emotions of fear, pain, or rage.

Meghan foreshadowed one of these phenomena the first night of the group, when she said, "To keep from feeling my feelings, I have become a very skilled helper of other people." Throughout the data, others echoed her words. The analytic moment in which this category emerged is illustrated in the following analytic memo written by Morrow (in vivo codes are in italics):

> I'm reaching a higher level of abstraction. Is the overarching category *protection from feelings?* Many categories are subsumed under it: One *talks* to get out the *stories;* the *feelings* are less intense. Fake orgasm (*sex*) because you don't have any physical *feelings. Art* was used to deal with *feelings,* express *anger, release* the pressure of the *feelings,* use *chemicals* to deal with *feelings* (and a whole complex interaction here) . . .

Existing and emergent codes and categories were compared and contrasted with this category; the category was modified to accommodate the data, producing the phenomenon that was labeled *being overwhelmed by threatening or dangerous feelings*—feelings that participants described as subjectively threatening or dangerous.

In addition to being overwhelmed by feelings, participants experienced what was termed *helplessness, powerlessness, and lack of control.* Lauren provided an exemplar of the second category, illustrating the pervasiveness of her perpetrator's power:

> He stands there. A silhouette at first and then his face and body come into view. He is small, but the backlighting intensifies his figure and he seems huge, like a prison guard. He is not always there but it feels like he might as well be. When he's not there, I search the distance for him and he appears. He seems to be standing there for hours. As if he's saying, you are weak, I am in control.

Not only did Lauren experience powerlessness during her abuse, but her lack of control invaded her dreams and her moments alone.

Context in Which Survival and Coping Strategies Developed

Strategies for survival and coping were developed in response to being overwhelmed by threatening or dangerous feelings and experiencing helplessness, powerlessness, and lack of control. These strategies were influenced by particular contextual markers related to both the causal conditions—particularly the forms of sexual abuse—and the resultant phenomena. These contextual markers included (a) sensations, (b) frequency, (c) intensity, (d) duration, and (e) perpetrator characteristics.

Sensations experienced by victims during sexual abuse ranged from arousal to pain, varying from mild to severe intensity. The frequency and duration of sexual abuse ranged from a single instance to years of ongoing sexual abuse, which occurred as often as daily or as infrequently as once every summer. Perpetrator characteristics varied from one to multiple perpetrators of both genders, who were always older and larger than their victims and ranged in relationship from blood relatives to strangers. The phenomena—being overwhelmed by threatening or dangerous feelings and experiencing helplessness, powerlessness, and lack of control—also varied as to types of physical and emotional sensations; ranged in intensity, frequency, and duration; and frequently continued for years after the original abuse had ended.

Intervening Conditions Influencing Survival and Coping Strategies

In addition to context, there were also intervening conditions, which were broad, general conditions that influenced participants' choices of survival and coping strategies. Intervening conditions included (a) cultural values, (b) family attitudes, values, beliefs, and dynamics, (c) other abuses present, (d) age of the victim, (e) rewards that accompanied the abuse, and (f) outside resources. Cultural values that were particularly influential were those of a religious nature related to sex and sexual abuse: "Guilt, I believe, is the driving force in Catholicism. . . . I felt guilt after I was molested. . . . I see the Catholic stuff as running in tandem with the issues of being a sexual-abuse survivor." One woman uncovered a family norm that condoned incest when her uncle bragged, "We were one big fuckin' family. . . . Everybody screwed everybody." Alcohol and alcoholic dynamics were part of almost every family, and it was rare that emotional or physical abuse was not an accompaniment of sexual violation. When perpetrators provided rewards or favors to their victims, victims were more likely to cooperate but expressed more confusion than did those who were not rewarded.

The ages at which participants had been abused ranged from infancy through 19 years of age. The data analysis revealed only one pattern related to the age of the victim when she was abused. In keeping with the literature on dissociation (Kluft, 1985), all of the participants who had developed severe dissociative patterns had been sexually abused in infancy or early childhood.

Only one participant experienced outside intervention in her abuse, although all had since turned to and found emotional support from friends, partners, or therapists. As in Liz's case ("He didn't do anything to you, did he?"), potential helpers were unwilling or unable to see that abuse was happening. However, in one case, a grandmother—who knew of and was powerless to stop the abuse—provided the support that the survivor now believes saved her life and sanity.

Strategies for Surviving and Coping
With Childhood Sexual Abuse

In the presence of the context and intervening conditions described above, two overarching phenomena led to the development of two parallel core strategies for survival and coping: (a) keeping from being overwhelmed by threatening or dangerous feelings and (b) managing helplessness, powerlessness, and lack of control. Because so few resources were available for help, most of the strategies described by participants were internally oriented and emotion focused. The strategies within each core category are illustrated in Figure 2.

Keeping from being overwhelmed by threatening or dangerous feelings. Being sexually abused produced confusing and intense emotions in the child victims. Lacking the cognitive skills to process overwhelming feelings of grief, pain, and rage, these children developed strategies to keep from being overwhelmed. These strategies were (a) reducing the intensity of troubling feelings, (b) avoiding or escaping feelings, (c) exchanging the overwhelming feelings for other, less threatening ones, (d) discharging or releasing feelings, (e) not knowing or remembering experiences that generated threatening feelings, and (f) dividing overwhelming feelings into manageable parts.

The first strategy used by participants in this research was reducing the intensity of the feelings. Participants used various methods to reframe their abuse so that their resultant feelings were less intense; to dull, numb, or not experience negative feelings that emerged or threatened to emerge; or to comfort themselves. By mentally or verbally reframing their abuse, victims found ways to excuse their perpetrators or to minimize the importance of the trauma. Lisa reported, "I never, never blamed him. . . . He was just a boy. . . . He didn't know any better." To modify the intense feelings that arose, participants dulled and numbed those feelings with substances such as alcohol, drugs, cigarettes, and food and by sleeping or becoming depressed. Liz became depressed to tone down the rage she did not allow herself to feel. Participants kept feelings from emerging in a number of ways. Paula commented, "The feelings are in the words"; thus, one strategy for not feeling was not to talk. Meghan analyzed her experiences instead: "I lived in my head." As these emotions emerged, participants

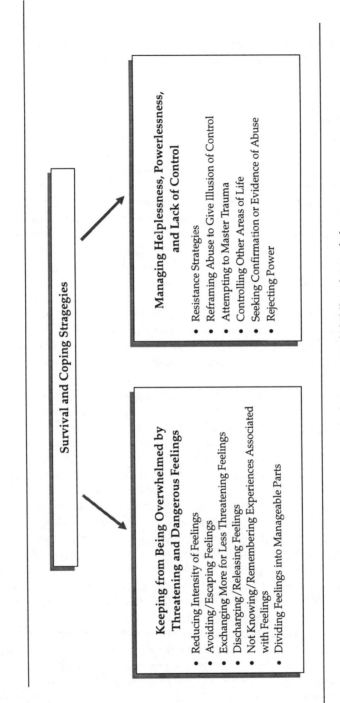

Survival and Coping Stragegies

Keeping from Being Overwhelmed by Threatening and Dangerous Feelings

- Reducing Intensity of Feelings
- Avoiding/Escaping Feelings
- Exchanging More for Less Threatening Feelings
- Discharging/Releasing Feelings
- Not Knowing/Remembering Experiences Associated with Feelings
- Dividing Feelings into Manageable Parts

Managing Helplessness, Powerlessness, and Lack of Control

- Resistance Strategies
- Reframing Abuse to Give Illusion of Control
- Attempting to Master Trauma
- Controlling Other Areas of Life
- Seeking Confirmation or Evidence of Abuse
- Rejecting Power

Figure 2. Survival and coping strategies of women who have survived childhood sexual abuse.

"stuffed" or consciously repressed them. Liz said, "I didn't mind how much it bothered me, I learned to repress the emotions," while Lisa swallowed her feelings with cinnamon rolls. Participants used a variety of ways to find comfort. Amaya found comfort outside herself: "The grandmother, she was a very spiritual woman. . . . She used to rock and sing to us." Others, unable to find comfort from outside, nurtured themselves with animals or dolls: "I used to play with paper dolls. . . . They were my friends. They could never hurt me." Participants used a variety of means to meet unmet emotional needs: "I used sex for validation 'cause that makes me pretty and that means you love me." Meghan became "mother hen" from the time she was little, receiving approval, attention, and appreciation from her family. Participants coped spiritually in a number of ways, some finding spiritual solace or relief by praying to or raging against God, while others rejected religious systems that they saw as being supportive of their abuse. Some sought alternative spiritual paths. Kitty believed that God would not give her any more than she could handle.

The second strategy for keeping from being overwhelmed was avoiding or escaping the threatening or dangerous feelings. In many instances, similar substrategies (e.g., drugs or alcohol) facilitated different processes. In a previous example, alcohol was used to dull and numb feelings as one way to reduce the intensity of those feelings. In some of the examples that follow, alcohol was used to escape. Strategies for escaping and leaving took both problem- and emotion-focused directions (Folkman & Lazarus, 1980, 1985) and included attempts to physically avoid or escape abuse, ignore the abuse, escape its reality, or leave mentally or emotionally. In their attempts to physically escape abuse, participants went to their rooms, ran away, moved out, married young, or separated themselves from others: "I isolated forever." When physical escape seemed impossible, some victims thought of dying or actually attempted suicide when they were children or adolescents in an effort to escape their abuse. To prevent either sexual abuse or related physical abuse, participants attempted to distract their perpetrators, tried talking them out of abusing them, or told them to stop. Velvia remembered, "I kept wanting it to be like it was and I kept asking him, 'Let's just read.' . . ." They also reported having developed heightened intuition about danger or having lied to others about their abuse to avoid being punished or further abused. Participants attempted to escape their abuse by hiding, both literally and figuratively. Ananda found refuge in a canyon, while Meghan strove for invisibility by being very, very good. Danu's conflict revealed itself in her poetry: "I didn't want to be/ 'miss smarty pants.'/ I tried to be quieter/ more secret and private./ I knew it would be safer/ if no one noticed me." Lauren and Kitty hid their bodies with oversized clothes. To ignore or escape the reality of their abuse, participants wished, fantasized, denied, avoided, and minimized: "I avoid things . . . the other side of denial. I won't look at it." Lauren "left the story behind," and the abuse gradually became less and less real in her mind until it was forgotten. Sometimes victims simply left mentally or emotionally. Kitty said, "Mind, take me outa there!" and it did. Some experienced tunnel vision, floating, "spacing out," or separating from their bodies or other people. Ananda described "a kind of spiritual leaving this planet."

Another way that the research participants avoided being over-whelmed was to exchange threatening or dangerous feelings for other, less distressing ones. Overwhelming feelings could be exchanged by overriding the feelings with other, more intense feelings; replacing them with less threatening, substitute feelings; or distracting them-selves with activities that produced innocuous feelings. Participants overrode dirty feelings by physically scrubbing them away. Some used self-induced physical pain, such as self-mutilation, to override emotional pain. Kitty commented, "Physical pain keeps me from feeling my feelings. That's where my anorexia came from. . . . The physical pain of not eating. I can't feel things when I'm in pain." The women who experienced feelings of pain and grief as dangerous developed an ability to switch immediately to anger or rage, substi-tuting the latter emotions for the pain that threatened to overwhelm them. Others bypassed the more threatening feelings of anger or rape, switching to tears: "I have [anger] for about two seconds, then I cry; it turns into sadness." Participants also distracted themselves from their feelings by turning to activities that produced innocuous or pleasant feelings: "The crunching kind of distracts me from the pain inside"; "I looked at other things."

The fourth strategy for keeping from being overwhelmed was discharging or releasing feelings. Verbal activities included writing in journals or talking to "get the feelings out." The use of humor was especially effective. Mimicking her usual 12-step meeting greeting ("My name is Paula, and I'm an alcoholic"), one participant declared, "Hello, I'm Paula, and I'm sorry!" They also shouted or screamed to release tension. Paula, a highly competitive athlete, used physical strategies that ranged from athletics to self-harm. She cut crosses in her skin and vomited to release her feelings: "I'll go purge and, uh, I'll feel elated, and better, and I also got rid of some of the feelings as a way of letting go." Artistic endeavors also facilitated release: "To this day, if I get those feelings, I can draw, and not necessarily feel better, but less pressure."

Not knowing or remembering experiences associated with threatening or dangerous feelings was the fifth strategy—a complex category involving head memories, head knowledge, clues or evidence, bodily sensations, intuition, and feelings or emotions. Head memories were one of the most haunting and difficult aspects of having been sexually abused. Virtually every participant had experienced some degree of memory loss surrounding her abuse, as illustrated by Velvia's comments: "There are some things that I remember, but only up to a certain point, and I don't know what happened next. . . . [T]he place where it stops sticks in my head. . . ." Some participants depended on head knowledge to know that they had been sexually abused. Audre disclosed, "The only reason I know about [the abuse] is because my abuser called me about a year ago to tell me." Detective work was rampant in survivors' searches for outside evidence or clues of their abuse. Some sought verification from siblings or nonoffending parents. Others depended on feelings about places or photographs to cue them about when their abuse had occurred: "We moved to a big huge house when I was 11. And that's when I think that it started, 'cause I don't remember anything in the old house." Survivors experienced "body memories," or physical sensations, frequently in the absence of head memories or knowledge. Kitty suffered intense pelvic pain whenever she talked about abuse: "Somebody'd be talking about being attacked, and I would experience all this pain in my stomach and in my female part of me." Others experienced nausea, trembling, and abreactions as a result of talking about sexual abuse. Intuition also contributed to a survivor's knowledge that she had been abused. Participants reported that intuition—in the form of a sudden awareness or hunch—was a powerful source of knowing at the moment of insight but that it could quickly fade to disbelief. Feelings or emotions were experienced as the least trustworthy of all evidence, particularly if unaccompanied by other forms of knowing. Despite the intensity of feelings of terror, deep sadness, and shame, women in the study were far more likely to believe they were "crazy" than to trust their feelings or emotions as evidence of sexual abuse: "I'm having all these feelings and all these symptoms . . . but maybe it has to with my mother dropped me on my head or she dressed me funny. . . ."

Dividing overwhelming feelings into manageable parts was a complex process of partitioning emotions into different compartments or separating them from cognitions, sensations, behaviors, or intuitions. Dividing was one of the ways in which memories were lost and knowing was jeopardized. Participants exercised three forms of dividing: "disassociating," dividing up overwhelming emotions, and dividing up cognitive functions. Participants typically used the lay term *disassociate* rather than *dissociate* to explain the process of altering consciousness. Although disassociation was used to escape feelings, it also provided the gateway for dividing. Dividing up overwhelming emotions took place as overwhelming or disparate emotional states were compartmentalized in order to make them more manageable. On one end of a continuum were facades or masks that hid the more vulnerable aspects of self. Participants had also developed different parts of themselves. The more rigid divisions were characterized by some degree of amnesia or distortion of behavior, motor coordination, self-perception, or time characteristic of dissociative disorders (Braun, 1986):

> I'm not sure that I really thought that I did survive . . . going away and seeing myself laying there on the bed—I can see my face, I can see the little girl laying there with her head kind of turned, her eyes closed, sweat or something, you know. She's—her head's wet—me—I guess it must be me.

In addition to dividing emotional states, participants separated cognitive functions such as actions, emotions, thoughts, bodily sensations, and intuitions, congruent with Braun's (1988) BASK (behavior, affect, sensation, knowledge) model of dissociation. Kitty learned to crawl out of her body: "I could see me screaming, but I couldn't hear." She "was actually frozen and could do nothing. . . . I wondered at the time why couldn't I do something? Why couldn't I move?"

Managing helplessness, powerlessness, and lack of control. In addition to developing strategies to keep from being overwhelmed by emotions, participants had developed strategies for managing powerlessness in the face of their abuse. Six categories of survival and coping strategies were used to manage helplessness, powerlessness, and lack of control: (a) creating resistance strategies, (b) reframing abuse to create an illusion of control or power, (c) attempting to master the trauma, (d) attempting to control other areas of life besides the abuse, (e) seeking confirmation or evidence from others, and (f) rejecting power.

One way in which participants managed their lack of power was to resist or rebel. Meghan refused to eat. Kitty spoke of her resistance: "Those fuckers aren't gonna get me. I'm not gonna kill myself. . . . [T]hat's when they win." Some reframed the abuse to create an illusion of control or power. Meghan believed that she could control her abuse: "If somehow I could be good enough and do things right enough, she wouldn't be like that anymore." Survivors attempted to master the trauma, at times recapitulating their abuse: "If I can create pain that I can feel, and I'm in control, it's different. It's totally different." Others turned to helping abused people. Participants frequently tried to control other areas of life besides the abuse. Barbara became " . . . a savior. I ride a white horse, rescue." Meghan stated, "I couldn't manage the abuse, but I could manage the household." All of the participants sought confirmation or evidence from others in order to control their own perceived reality. Only Liz rejected power: "I don't want to be like her. . . . She was very powerful. . . . I'm afraid of power in myself, even."

Consequences of Strategies for Survival and Coping

The strategies used by participants were not without consequences. In every case, those strategies succeeded in keeping them from being overwhelmed by feelings or aided them in managing helplessness, powerlessness, and lack of control. However, while their strategies for survival and coping were successful, that success was also costly.

Two women saw the creation of alter personalities—their primary survival and coping strategy—as a sane alternative to psychosis, or "going crazy." However, they both paid the price of living fragmented lives.

When asked what being overwhelmed by feelings meant to her, Meghan responded, "Screaming metal . . . pain and anguish that goes on and on and on and never stops." She has continued to spiral back through depression, pain, and anguish that, at times, feel as if they will never end. Paradoxically, her strategies worked to keep over-whelming feelings at bay until she actively began the therapy process. As she has faced the emotions she buried, she has been overwhelmed many times.

Participants had fears, wishes, or dreams of dying, yet all are alive today. But while all still live, they did not feel they survived intact; as Barbara disclosed, "I'm not sure I survived," and as Liz said, "Part of me died."

Another paradox arose during the examination of the conse-quences of the strategy to manage helplessness, powerlessness, and lack of control. Often, the very strategies adopted by participants to exercise power or control backfired, ultimately taking control of the survivors. One woman, whose childhood refusal to eat resulted in her doctor prescribing crackers and cream cheese for breakfast (the only food she would eat), found in adulthood that she turned repeatedly—and sometimes compulsively—to these same foods.

Many times, participants commented that they were barely surviving—that they were in pain, exhausted, or overwhelmed. However, surviving and coping [were] what participants did best. Liz declared, "My will to survive is strong, stronger than I realized." In a conversation among the participant-coresearchers, Meghan said angrily, "I don't want to be surviving. I want to be living. I want to have some fun. I want to be happy. And that's what's not happening right now." Liz responded, "First you have to survive. You have to survive it. And that's where I'm getting to, is the realization that I'm surviving this stuff again."

Each of the survivors echoed Meghan's feelings. Four had become drug- and alcohol-free in their efforts to move beyond mere survival to healing, wholeness, and empowerment. Paula disclosed, "I'm just startin' to realize that this is worth it. [My drawings are] more elaborate, they're bigger, I'm using more mediums, they're more detailed." Velvia used the word "empowerment" to describe a process that went beyond survival. Amaya wrote,

> Today I got in touch with *mi otro yo* [my other me]. . . .
> She is so powerful, so sure of herself, so strong, so real, so alive.
> I did not die like I thought I would when I felt her.
> Instead, I got in touch with the missing part of my inner power and
> wholeness.

The pain, grief, and terror that the survivors had experienced and continued to wrestle with are very real, and the healing process is long and arduous. However, throughout the research, participants expressed hope. Despite her terror and pain, Kitty reflected, "I have hope in my life. . . . There's just a little bit of sunlight coming in. There's a little bit of heaven up there that comes inside of my soul and heals."

Discussion

Although the counseling literature is rich with descriptions of specific outcomes of childhood sexual abuse, this study is distinctive in its systematic examination of the survival and coping strategies from the perspectives of women who were sexually abused as children. A theoretical model of the survival and coping strategies of 11 participants was constructed through qualitative data analysis, which included engaging participants in the analytic process in order to ensure that the model reflected their personal constructs. This model establishes, from a multitude of strategies and symptoms, a coherent, construct-focused framework for understanding the often-confusing constellation of behavior patterns of the survivors of abuse.

Cultural norms set the stage for sexual abuse. As Banyard and Graham-Bermann (1993) emphasized, it is important for researchers and practitioners to examine the social milieu in which particular stressors are experienced. In relation to childhood sexual abuse, an examination of social forces helps to shift the focus of coping from a purely individual analysis to an individual-in-context analysis, thereby normalizing the victim's experience and reducing self-blame.

The powerlessness of girls, which can be attributed to the societal positioning of women and children, to their physical size, and to undependable resources for intervention available to abuse victims, explains the overwhelming predominance of emotion-focused over problem-focused coping strategies used by the participants in this study. In addition, the context of denial and secrecy surrounding sexual abuse in the lives of girls and women may further exacerbate a preference for emotion-focused coping.

The present analysis is congruent with Long and Jackson's (1993) findings that victims of childhood sexual abuse attempted to have an impact on the actual abuse situation by using problem-focused strategies, while they managed their distress through emotion-focused coping. The two core strategies—keeping from being overwhelmed by threatening and dangerous feelings and managing helplessness, powerlessness, and lack of control—parallel Long and Jackson's emotion-focused and problem-focused strategies. Long and Jackson found that few victims attempted problem-focused strategies and speculated that resources may not have been available, either in fact or in the cognitive appraisals of victims. The present research demonstrated that options for problem-focused coping were, in fact, not readily available. In addition, specific cultural and family norms served to convince children of the limited efficacy of problem-focused solutions.

Researchers and practitioners may need to think beyond the categories of emotion- and problem-focused coping strategies (Banyard & Graham-Bermann, 1993). L. Benishek proposed that certain so-called emotion-focused strategies, such as dissociation, may, in fact, be problem focused (personal communication, December 1, 1993). Indeed, according to Banyard and Graham-Bermann (1993), "There are times when emotion-focused strategies may be used as problem-

focused solutions to a stressful dilemma" (p. 132). Additional qualitative research in this area may prove fruitful.

Mahoney (1991) described core ordering processes as deep-struc-
ture processes that "lie at the core of every person's lifelong efforts to
organize and reorganize their experience" (p. 179). Of his four proposed core ordering processes (valence, reality, identity, and power),
the present analysis yielded two: valence, which encompasses processes of motivation and emotion, and power, which is characterized
by processes of control and ability. These two processes correspond,
respectively, to the core strategies found in this research related to
participants' keeping from being overwhelmed with feelings and
managing helplessness, powerlessness, and lack of control. Because
this research was pursued inductively without imposing preexisting
categories on the data, the core ordering processes of identity and
reality did not emerge. However, it would be appropriate to reanalyze
the data with these categories in mind. The process of identity, for
example, can be seen in Liz's statement about seeing herself lying on
the bed during her abuse: "She . . . I guess it must be me." Although
the present research did not address identity or reality, it provided a
more detailed understanding of the processes of valence and power,
particularly as they were experienced by the survivors of sexual abuse
in this investigation.

The emergent theoretical model of survival and coping was, in
effect, Morrow's interpretation of 11 participants' constructions of
their survival and coping. As is frequently the case in qualitative
research, the results of this analysis are unique to the particular
investigator, participants, and context of this study. The transferability
of this theoretical model for survival and coping takes place as the
reader examines these results in the context of specific circumstances
of interest.

Feminist researchers have expressed concern about the potential
for the exploitation of women and other marginalized groups in
academic research and have urged investigators to examine closely
what participants receive in exchange for their contributions (Landrine, Klonoff, & Brown-Collins, 1992). Their recommendations have
influenced the present investigation in two ways. First, the categories
that emerged from this research made sense to and were useful, in a
practical sense, to the participants themselves. When the developing
model for survival and coping was presented to the participant-
coresearchers, one woman took the information home to her husband,
with whom she had experienced painful and confusing dynamics
surrounding her abuse. Her response endorsed the applicability of
this model in practice, not only for spouses or partners, but for families

and the therapeutic relationship as well: ". . . [I]t felt like months and months . . . of stuff that just felt so hard . . . trudging through this sludge—it was like the clarity! It was just unbelievable . . . the closeness between us." It appears that presenting this model to clients and significant others has potential, as a psychoeducational tool, to ease the difficult and perilous journey that individuals must travel as they work through abuse trauma and its consequences.

In addition, the collaborative research process itself has implications for research with the survivors of sexual abuse. Participant-coresearchers described their experiences of collaborative meaning-making as "important" and "empowered." Coparticipatory data analysis therefore holds promise as an empowering model for researchers and participants alike.

Finally, from a standpoint of the "psychology of human effectiveness" (Gelso & Fassinger, 1992, p. 293), the resilience and resourcefulness of the participants in this investigation cannot be overstated. What appears at first glance to be a profusion of dysfunctional symptoms becomes, upon closer examination, rational and reasonable coping strategies given the extremity of the stressors to which these women, as children, were subjected. For example, dividing various aspects of the self into alter personalities enabled victims to disperse trauma among various parts of the self, thereby decreasing the potential for being overwhelmed. In addition, multiplicity provided for self-nurturing and furnished a cognitive structure in which valuable functions and personality characteristics were preserved until they could be safely reintegrated. This investigation focused on the strengths of the survivors of sexual abuse and encourages practitioners to view clients who have been sexually abused in light of those strengths, rather than from a perspective that emphasizes pathology (Adams & Betz, 1993; Hill, 1993; Howard, 1992). Given the prevalence of sexual abuse, adaptation to childhood trauma must be considered a part of the process of normal development for a large number of individuals. The present findings may facilitate a reevaluation of that adaptation and offer clients and their therapists a conceptual framework to facilitate healing.

References

Adams, E. M., & Betz, N. E. (1993). Gender differences in counselors' attitudes toward and attributions about incest. *Journal of Counseling Psychology, 40,* 210-216.

Adler, P. A., & Adler, P. (1987). *Membership roles in field research.* Newbury Park, CA: Sage.

Banyard, V. L., & Graham-Bermann, S. A. (1993). Can women cope? A gender analysis of theories of coping with stress. *Psychology of Women Quarterly, 17*, 303-318.

Braun, B. G. (1986). Issues in the psychotherapy of multiple personality disorder. In B. G. Braun (Ed.), *Treatment of multiple personality disorder* (pp. 3-28). Washington, DC: American Psychiatric Press.

Braun, B. G. (1988). The BASK (behavior, affect, sensation, knowledge) model of dissociation. *Dissociation, 1*, 4-23.

Briere, J. (1989). *Therapy for adults molested as children: Beyond survival.* New York: Springer.

Courtois, C. A. (1988). *Healing the incest wound: Adult survivors in therapy.* New York: Norton.

Erickson, F. (1986). Qualitative methods in research on teaching. In M. C. Wittrock (Ed.), *Handbook of research on teaching* (3rd ed., pp. 119-161). New York: Macmillan.

Fine, M. (1992). *Disruptive voices: The possibilities of feminist research.* Ann Arbor: University of Michigan Press.

Folkman, S., & Lazarus, R. S. (1980). An analysis of coping in a middle-aged community sample. *Journal of Health and Social Behavior, 21*, 219-239.

Folkman, S., & Lazarus, R. S. (1985). If it changes it must be a process: Study of emotion and coping during three stages of a college examination. *Journal of Personality and Social Psychology, 48*, 150-170.

Geffner, R. (1992). Current issues and future directions in child sexual abuse. *Journal of Child Sexual Abuse, 1*(1), 1-13.

Gelso, C. J., & Fassinger, R. E. (1992). Personality, development, and counseling psychology: Depth, ambivalence, and actualization. *Journal of Counseling Psychology, 39*, 275-298.

Glaser, B. G. (1978). *Theoretical sensitivity.* Mill Valley, CA: Sociology Press.

Glaser, B. G., & Strauss, A. L. (1967). *The discovery of grounded theory: Strategies for qualitative research.* Hawthorne, NY: Aldine.

Herman, J. L. (1992). *Trauma and recovery: The aftermath of violence: From domestic abuse to political terror.* New York: Basic Books.

Hill, C. E. (1993). Editorial. *Journal of Counseling Psychology, 40*, 252-256.

Horowitz, M. (1979). Psychological response to serious life events. In V. Hamilton & D. M. Warburton (Eds.), *Human stress and cognition: An information processing approach* (pp. 237-265). Chichester, England: Wiley.

Hoshmand, L.L.S. (1989). Alternate research paradigms: A review and teaching proposal. *The Counseling Psychologist, 17*, 3-79.

Howard, G. S. (1992). Behold our creation! What counseling psychology has become and might yet become. *Journal of Counseling Psychology, 39*, 419-442.

Johnson, B. K., & Kenkel, M. B. (1991). Stress, coping, and adjustment in female adolescent incest victims. *Child Abuse & Neglect, 15*, 293-305.

Kluft, R. P. (Ed.). (1985). *Childhood antecedents of multiple personality.* Washington, DC: American Psychiatric Press.

Landrine, H., Klonoff, E. A., & Brown-Collins, A. (1992). Cultural diversity and methodology in feminist psychology. *Psychology of Women Quarterly, 16*, 145-163.

Lazarus, R. S., & Folkman, S. (1984). *Stress, appraisal, and coping.* New York: Springer.

LeCompte, M. D., & Goetz, J. P. (1982). Problems of reliability and validity in ethnographic research. *Review of Educational Research, 52*, 31-60.

Lincoln, Y. S., & Guba, E. G. (1985). *Naturalistic inquiry.* Beverly Hills, CA: Sage.

Loftus, E. F. (1993). The reality of repressed memories. *American Psychologist, 48,* 518-537.

Long, P. J., & Jackson, J. L. (1993). Childhood coping strategies and the adult adjustment of female sexual abuse victims. *Journal of Child Sexual Abuse, 2*(2), 23-39.

Lundberg-Love, P. K., Marmion, S., Ford, K., Geffner, R., & Peacock, L. (1992). The long-term consequences of childhood incestuous victimization upon adult women's psychological symptomatology. *Journal of Child Sexual Abuse, 1*(1), 81-102.

Mahoney, M. J. (1991). *Human change processes: The scientific foundations of psychotherapy.* New York: Basic Books.

Miles, M. B., & Huberman, A. M. (1984). *Qualitative data analysis: A sourcebook of new methods.* Beverly Hills, CA: Sage.

Morgan, D. L. (1988). *Focus groups as qualitative research.* Newbury Park, CA: Sage.

Neimeyer, G. J., & Neimeyer, R. A. (1993). Defining the boundaries of constructivist assessment. In G. J. Neimeyer (Ed.), *Constructivist assessment: A casebook* (pp. 1-30). Newbury Park, CA: Sage.

Peshkin, A. (1988). In search of subjectivity: One's own. *Educational Researcher, 17,* 17-21.

Polkinghorne, D. E. (1991). Two conflicting calls for methodological reform. *The Counseling Psychologist, 19,* 13-114.

Roth, S., & Cohen, L. J. (1986). Approach, avoidance, and coping with stress. *American Psychologist, 41,* 813-819.

Russell, D. E. H. (1986). *The secret trauma: Incest in the lives of girls and women.* New York: Basic Books.

Stinson, M. H., & Hendrick, S. S. (1992). Reported childhood sexual abuse in university counseling center clients. *Journal of Counseling Psychology, 39,* 370-371.

Strauss, A. L. (1987). *Qualitative analysis for social scientists.* Cambridge, England: Cambridge University Press.

Strauss, A., & Corbin, J. (1990). *Basics of qualitative research: Grounded theory procedures and techniques.* Newbury Park, CA: Sage.

Strickland, B. R. (1978). Internal-external expectancies and health-related behaviors. *Journal of Consulting and Clinical Psychology, 46,* 1192-1211.

Wyatt, G. E., & Newcomb, M. (1990). Internal and external mediators of women's sexual abuse in childhood. *Journal of Consulting and Clinical Psychology, 58,* 758-767.

APPENDIX E

▼

An Ethnography

THE ELEMENTARY SCHOOL PRINCIPAL
Notes From a Field Study
Harry F. Wolcott

"Harry, you ought to watch the company you keep," quipped a colleague from the university when he encountered me at lunch one day with a group of five elementary school principals. "He does!" came the immediate retort from the principal sitting next to me.

The principals had just completed an all-morning meeting at the school district central office, where they had been appointed to serve as a Principal Selection Committee for the school district. As such, they were to interview and recommend candidates to fill new positions as elementary school principals for the following school year. I had been present at their morning session in the role of an ethnographer inquiring into the life and work of the elementary school principal from an anthropological perspective.

This chapter draws on a larger study designed to provide an ethnographic-type account of the elementary school principalship by

SOURCE: This selection first appeared in *Education and Cultural Process: Toward an Anthropology of Education*, edited by George Spindler, pp. 176-204, published by Holt, Rinehart and Winston in 1974. It was reprinted by Waveland Press in 1987, under the title *Education and Cultural Process: Anthropological Approaches*, and by Sage Publications in 1994, in *Transforming Qualitative Data: Description, Analysis, and Interpretation*, by Harry F. Wolcott (pp. 115-148). It is used here by permission of the author.

means of an extensive case study of one principal (Wolcott 1973). In the present chapter, I have selected from the field notes an episode in which attention is drawn to the behavior of a small group of principals rather than to the behavior of an individual. The context of this episode is the proceedings of the Principal Selection Committee. A major portion of the chapter is devoted to a descriptive account of the proceedings of this committee and a discussion and comment based on the data presented. The chapter begins with an overview of the perspective and methods basic to the entire field study.[1]

The Ethnographic Approach

The apparent neglect of attention to the *actual* behavior of school administrators in the literature on educational administration led to the proposal for conducting this research. That literature could well be augmented by a series of detailed ethnographic-type accounts of the actual behavior of people occupying roles in professional education, contextualized not only in terms of the formally organized institution in which they work but also in terms of their lives as human beings interacting within the context of a broader cultural milieu. This study was designed specifically to provide such data about the elementary school principalship.

The ethnographer's task is the recording of human behavior in cultural terms. The standard ethnography provides an account of some cultural process, such as law or divorce, or the way of life of some particular group of people, such as the Tikopia or the Children of Sanchez. This study is ethnographic to the extent that the principal who provides the focus for it is seen as an interacting member of a cultural system. Because the study is social and cultural rather than psychological in orientation, its scope includes not only the behavior of the principal himself but also the behavior of those with whom a principal interacts in the course of his professional life. This includes to some degree his spouse, his family, and his friends and to a greater degree teachers, other administrators, parents, and pupils. These roles, and the interaction of the people filling them, are the human elements of a cultural system, the school system of one community. To the extent that the cultural system involved in this study is similar to other cultural systems serving the same purpose, this ethnography of a single principal should produce knowledge relevant to the understanding of such roles and cultural systems in general.

There are other ways one might proceed in studying a school administrator, one of which would be for the ethnographer to obtain such a position. In prior fieldwork, however, I had become acutely aware of the limitations on one's ability to objectively observe processes in which he is deeply involved as a participant (Wolcott 1967).

The literature dealing with school administration might have been expected to serve as a source of information about administrative behavior, but that body of writings is susceptible to several of the limitations that characterize the literature of professional education more generally. One such limitation is that much of the literature is hortatory or normative in content. It tells principals (or teachers or superintendents) how they *ought* to act. It is prescriptive rather than descriptive. Literature of this type can provide a source for inquiring into the *ideal* world of formal education (Lee 1963), but it fails to provide an account of what actually goes on or how the ideals are translated into real behavior. The literature that *is* empirically based, on the other hand, provides factual data that tend to tell too little about too much. Such data prove valuable as a source of census information; for example, we can readily obtain a description of the "average" American elementary school principal (Department of Elementary School Principals [DESP] 1968):

a male
married
between the ages of 35 and 49
has had 10 to 19 years total experience in schools
was an elementary classroom teacher just prior to assuming
    his administrative post.

This description fits the case study principal perfectly. Yet the data provide little insight into how one becomes a principal, how a principal acts, or what he finds satisfying and perplexing about his role.

The barrage of questionnaires that confront public school personnel to inventory their training, habits, and preferences might also be expected to provide data about the principalship. However, the people who compose these questionnaires have frequently failed to do careful preliminary fieldwork. The information obtained in answer to questions such as "Should a principal attend church regularly?" may reveal little more than the tendency of school administrators to give "expected" responses. Such studies seem to ignore the consequence that if the questions one asks are not crucial, then differences in responses are not crucial either.

The nearest approximation we usually get to the actual behavior of administrators is from data based on self-reporting techniques. These techniques have frequently been employed in studies of school principals. Although self-reporting is somewhat comparable to one of the standard methods by which ethnographic accounts have been obtained—intensive interviews with a single or a few selected informants—it is far more subject to problems of informant reliability than is the method of intensive interviewing employed as one of a number of data-gathering techniques in the ethnographer's multi-instrument approach.

The ethnographic approach taken in this study has not been widely employed in conducting research in school settings. To my amazement, I have occasionally been asked, "Did the principal know you were making the study?" I spent weeks searching for a suitable and willing subject, and I did not request formal permission from the school district to conduct the study until I had the personal permission and commitment of the selected individual. His family, his faculty and staff, his fellow principals, and many visitors to the school knew something about the research project. The faculty assigned me the nickname "The Shadow" as a way to jokingly acknowledge my presence and purpose at their school, and the name was learned by some of the pupils, too.

In order to learn how it is to be a principal, every aspect of the principal's life had some potential relevance for the study. I was once asked (somewhat facetiously, I suppose) whether I planned to take the principal's temperature each day. I replied, not at all facetiously, that I would have recorded that information if it were readily available, just as it might be interesting to know what the principal and his family ate at each Sunday dinner, but I would obviously need priorities in my data gathering. My attention has been drawn primarily to such aspects of the principal's life as the who, what, where, and when of his personal encounters, the cultural themes manifested in his behavior and in his attempts to influence the behavior of those about him, and the problems and paradoxes inherent in the role of the principal. Although the behavior of one principal served as the focus of the study, the fieldwork provided extensive opportunities for observing many principals, ranging from the rather frequent and often informal contacts of the case study principal with administrators at nearby schools to his participation in the official sessions and formal meetings of his school district and his memberships in county, regional, and state organizations of elementary school principals.

Methods in Fieldwork

An "ethnographic approach" implies commitment to a perspective in both the methods of field research and the handling of data in subsequent writing, but it does not explicate the methods for doing either. Whenever it has been expedient to describe my research methodology by a brief label, I have leaned toward the term "field study." Zelditch (1962) has stated a case for the merits of the participant observer approach in the field study without going to the extreme of insisting that participant observation entails only participating and observing. He argues, "A field study is not a single method gathering a single kind of information" (p. 567); rather, the participant observer employs three different modes in his research: "enumeration to document frequency data; participant observation to describe incidents; and informant interviewing to learn institutionalized norms and statuses" (p. 566). I shall use these three categories—enumeration, participant observation, and interviewing—to describe the specific techniques employed during my fieldwork.

Enumeration and Census Data

1. Collecting copies of official notices sent to and from school to pupils, parents, or faculty (greatly facilitated by having a faculty mailbox in the office and by a school secretary who did not mind making an extra carbon of routine reports and correspondence).
2. Collecting copies of records (or, at the end of the year, the records themselves) of enrollments, reports, the principal's personal log of events, and daily notices written in a faculty notebook.
3. Collecting "time and motion" data by noting, at 60-second intervals over a carefully sampled period of two weeks at school, what the principal was doing, where he was, with whom he was interacting, and who was talking.
4. Mapping and photographing the school and neighborhood.[2]

Participant Observation

The primary methodology used at the beginning of the study was that of participant observation. Customarily, the principal introduced me by saying, "This is Harry Wolcott. He is from the university and doing some research in which I'm involved." This brief introduction seemed to serve as a sufficient explanation of my presence to all but the most curious, but anyone who asked was welcome to a fuller description. The principal and staff were remarkable in their capacity for allowing me to observe and record without insisting that I become an active participant in their conversations and activities. Although simply "keeping up" with a busy principal precluded the possibility of my ever being a totally passive observer, my active participation at school was limited primarily to engaging in the social banter of the faculty room during lunch or at coffee breaks.

I made it a practice to carry my notebook with me and to make entries in it almost continuously. My intent was to create a precedent for constant note taking so that the people would feel it was natural for me to be writing regardless of the topics or events at hand. Notes were taken in longhand in complete and readable form whenever possible. When I could not make complete notes and still remain present as an observer, I jotted brief notes in the margins of my notebook and completed the full account later, often before leaving the school building. I never returned to the school until a complete account from a previous period of observation was finished. Nothing was gained by my mere presence as an observer; until the notes from one visit were a matter of record, there was no point in returning to school and reducing the impact of one set of observations by imposing a more recent one. Ultimately, the longhand entries were transcribed onto 5 by 8 papers, each entry describing a single event, whether a lengthy transcription such as that containing my notes of the three meetings of the Principal Selection Committee or brief entries such as

> The principal said that when he called his wife to tell her he would be home by 5:30 this evening she replied, "So early! Why—what's wrong?"

> As the principal is trying various keys in the lock [he had just received some duplicates from the central office but did not know which doors they fit], a little second-grade girl comes up quietly behind him, pokes him gently in the ribs, and says, "Boo." "Oh, my," he says. The little girl continues happily down the hall.

One of the objectives of this research was to see the principal in as many different settings appropriate to an ethnographic study as possible. It was easier, of course, to intrude on his professional life in connection with his work as a school administrator than to intrude into his personal life. At the school I was excluded, by prior arrangement, from only a few "touchy" parent conferences. Although more symbolic than functional, a table and chair were moved into the principal's office for my use. My observation extended to such settings as school or school district activities or meetings; meetings of local, regional, or state educational organizations; formal or informal staff gatherings; in-service programs; and traveling to meetings with groups of principals.

In reviewing plans for the fieldwork with colleagues, I had been cautioned against becoming "overidentified" with the principal, particularly since he was the formally appointed status leader of the school. I visited often with teachers and staff members, including visits at school on days when I knew the principal was away. "Oh, checking up on us, eh?" someone would inevitably joke, leading me to feel that the caution against being overidentified with "the boss" had been well given.

My apprehension about being overidentified with the principal did not extend to those settings where he was away from his school. However, there are few guidelines for a researcher in accompanying a subject to see about a new battery for his automobile or to attend a service club luncheon. I was able to include within the scope of my observations such settings as the principal's home and family, business meetings at his church and the Sunday school class he teaches, trips to local businesses for school and personal reasons, Kiwanis luncheons, a family wedding and reception, and brief meetings with friends and neighbors.

Informant Interviewing

These interviews were of several types. First were taped interviews of approximately one hour duration, structured but open-ended, which provided excellent data concerning the principal's family life (interviews with his wife and mother) and the perceptions of him as a school administrator (interviews with thirteen faculty and two staff members). The interviews took time to arrange and conduct, and they seemed to take an eternity to transcribe, but they proved extremely valuable for uncovering the range of perceptions and the extent of the affective content expressed by the teachers regarding their work and the people with whom they associated professionally. The fact that I requested each interview as a personal favor and that no interviewing was done until I had spent over half a year at the school undoubtedly contributed to the extensive and useful data gathered via this method.

Another approach was to ask all the pupils in each fifth- and sixth-grade classroom to write briefly (and anonymously) what they thought they would remember about the principal. The phrases I suggested to them to start their writing were "What kind of a principal is he?," "Pleasant memories are . . . ," and "One time I won't forget . . ." The comments I received ran the gamut of opinion, from the succinct response from a boy who wrote that his principal is "a Dam stopit one," to the reflection by a sixth-grade girl that "he is the kind of a principal who helps you figure it out." One boy wrote, "I won't fore get the time when my freind and I were blamed fore bilding a fire in the bath room."

The principal himself served as a primary informant, as he was not only the focus of the research but was to some extent a co-worker as well. I was never too explicit about what data I was gathering, nor did I often share my hunches or tentative analyses with him, but he correctly assumed that a brief recounting of what had occurred at school since my last visit would be helpful to the study. He enjoyed talking and visiting (I found that he did the talking one-third of the total school day during the "time and motion" study), so this self-appointed task came easily to him. At times he reflected on his personal feelings and philosophy, and these statements provided valuable insights into his "ideal world." The juxtaposition of actual behavior and ideal behavior provides an excellent means for describing and analyzing a cultural system, and I was fortunate in having an informant who talked easily about aspects of his ideal world.

On a few occasions, I emphasized the informant role and asked the principal to relate specific accounts. Plans were always discussed in advance when these sessions were to be taped. Important tapes included a session in which the principal summarized the opening of school and gave a forecast of the coming year, a session in which I asked him to review the wedding list and chat about the people who had been invited to his daughter's marriage and reception, and a session recorded in my automobile as we drove through the school attendance area while the principal described the neighborhood to three new teachers who accompanied us.

A ten-page questionnaire designed for the study was distributed to all the faculty and staff at the end of the fieldwork. The questionnaire was particularly valuable in enabling me to obtain systematic data about the staff, as I could see no point in holding a long taped interview with each of the twenty-nine members of the regular and part-time staff. This questionnaire provided standard census data and information concerning each teacher's perceptions of the school, community, and classroom. It also provided an opportunity for all staff members to state their feelings about an "ideal" principal.

The use of the questionnaire provided me with a chance to thank the staff for their patience and help during the study. I felt that the questionnaire might also give me an opportunity to elicit staff reaction to the research project, and the last statement of the questionnaire was, "Some things the researcher may never have understood about this school are . . ." The question did not evoke much response, but it was flattering to read "I think you probably understand more than we may think." I delighted in the humor of one teacher who assumed (correctly) that I did not know "there is no Kotex dispenser in the [women's] restroom."

My presence in the school district throughout the study was, I suppose, viewed as a mixed blessing. The mild but constant surveillance produced little overt strain that could not be alleviated by joking, but I provided so little feedback that there was no "payoff" for the many people who shared their perceptions and feelings with me. Still, a sympathetic and nonevaluative listener can provide an unusual opportunity for emotional catharsis, and I was amazed at how often teachers and principals seemed to appreciate an opportunity to "speak their minds." In this regard, I feel that my position as observer and information getter was considerably enhanced by the fact that, like the teachers and administrators who were the subjects of the study, I spoke the "language" of educators and had been "on the firing line" as a classroom teacher. I believe the case study principal also found some comfort in having a part-time cohort with whom he could share something of the nature, complexity, and extent of problems that confronted him in the course of his daily work.

From the Field Notes: Proceedings of the Principal Selection Committee

Any number of episodes recorded during the course of the fieldwork could have been drawn on here to illustrate aspects of a principal's professional life. Many would call attention to the routine of a typical day and to the incessant questions, problems, and meetings that seem to make constant demands on a principal's time and resources. I have chosen instead to draw on a rather unique set of events, the proceedings of the Principal Selection Committee. This committee met three times during one month in the spring of 1967. These meetings provided a special setting in which the principals appointed to an ad hoc screening committee found themselves compelled to review and define—for the purpose of evaluating candidates—the critical attributes and qualifications of their role. This charge to interview and endorse certain candidates to join their ranks, although directed only to the principals appointed to the committee, served as an annual renewal ceremony for all the elementary school principals of the district. The fact of their appointment and task, and the results of their interviews and deliberations, served to reaffirm publicly the standards and responsibilities of their office. The necessity for adding new members to their ranks occasioned a time when, like the elders among North American Indian tribes, the principals were obliged to "review, analyze, dramatize, and defend their cultural heritage" (Pettitt 1946).

The circumstances underlying the committee's existence—who appointed it, the task it was given, how binding its recommendations would be—provide clues about the formal context in which it worked. As the committee convened, for example, no one explained or questioned why it had five principals (among the twenty-seven elementary school principals in the district), how or why the four new members had been selected by the director of elementary education and why one member had been retained from the prior year (especially after the director commented, "I tried to eliminate people who had ideas from the past"), how many vacancies or at which schools they would occur ("We will need two people, maybe three. We should pick our best people, not for [specific] positions but for ability, because we don't know where they will go"), or how binding the committee's actions would be on the ultimate recommendation that the superintendent would make to the school board. It was customary in this school district for the director of elementary education to appoint committees of varying sizes and varying purposes, and it was part of her job to "know" when she had sufficient authority to make appointments on her own or when she, in turn, needed the approval of the assistant superintendent or superintendent. The principals seemed to assume that she would be present during their meetings, and she slipped easily into the role of informal chairperson of the group.

For the principals appointed to the committee, to select "two, maybe three" candidates apparently provided sufficient parameters for their task since in their ultimate decision they ranked the most "controversial" of the acceptable candidates as number four. No one pressed to learn why the number of vacancies was ambiguous. Two new schools were to be opened in the fall. If "maybe three" vacancies were to occur, there was more than mere conjecture about which principals might be in disfavor among the powers in the central office. (The third vacancy proved later to be due to an as yet unannounced plan for administrative reorganization that required the full time services of one elementary school principal in the central office.)

Although the recommendation of the committee could be ignored by the superintendent, it did not necessarily mean it would be. The new members checked with the principal who had already served on the committee to reassure themselves that recommendations made the previous year had been honored. The confidence expressed in the superintendent was formal and reciprocal. The committee showed no inclination to test the extent of its power or to threaten the power of the superintendent by making radical or unexpected recommendations. Attention was addressed specifically to assessing each candidate's standing "in the eyes of the superintendent" during discussions prior and subsequent to the interviews. In turn, official recognition was accorded to the committee through brief appearances before and during its sessions by the director of personnel, the assistant superintendent, and the superintendent.

During the total twelve hours of interview and discussion through which members of the Principal Selection Committee sat, fourteen possible candidates were reviewed. A brief profile of the candidates as a group showed them to include male and female applicants from within and outside the district, all holding master's degrees and all experienced elementary school teachers. In age, they ranged from thirty-one to sixty-one years. Their total experience in professional education varied from eight to thirty-nine years.

The extent of significant variation among the candidates is less than this description implies. One applicant who was not seriously considered and who was not invited for an interview accounted for most of the variation. She was the only female applicant and had served in an administrative capacity for only one year some fourteen years previously. In age and teaching experience, she had thirteen more years than the next most senior applicant. The committee shared the feelings of one principal who summarized, "I think she's a wonderful gal and a fine teacher, but I question anyone going into this at 61." Although age provided the immediate basis for a decision not to consider her further, it is likely that sex would have been the critical issue had she been younger. Three of the district's twenty-seven elementary schools were administered by women. As one male principal had candidly remarked on a prior occasion, "It's going to be a long time before we put in another woman." Some candidates were dropped after only a brief comment as the committee sought ways to reduce the number of people who were to be accorded interviews and serious consideration. Regarding a relatively young newcomer in the district who had asked to be considered, for example, no one added any further comment after one principal expressed the opinion, "I see too many people ahead of him." Someone added, "The same with so-and-so." A third principal immediately suggested dropping both their names. Consideration of another applicant, an administrator from outside the district, was summarily ended when the personnel director, during a brief preview of the slate of candidates, recalled that this applicant had "already been hired [i.e., offered a contract] once in this district" and certainly should not have the opportunity to turn them down again. The committee members agreed that there was no point in retaining names of people who were not going to be considered among the top eligible candidates, and they expressed concern over the problem of "getting the hopes up" among candidates called in for interviews. Yet any time a candidate's name was about to be dropped permanently, there was some hedging about giving everyone a chance. The frequent statement, "Let's just leave his name on for now" revealed a reluctance to take decisive and final action (eliminating a candidate) when less decisive action (ranking eight "top" candidates for three positions) accomplished the same purpose without requiring the ultimatum.

As the preliminary discussion of the candidates continued, based on the perusal of each candidate's folder of letters and recommendations, two procedural questions were discussed. The first was whether candidates would be selected only from within the district. The assistant superintendent observed that no outsider had been appointed to an elementary school principalship for many years. "We shouldn't overlook good people from outside, but in the past when things have been equal we have given preference for 'in-district.' " The tradition of selecting applicants from within the district was reaffirmed in the final recommendation made by the committee, although two out-of-district candidates were called for interviews. The rationale for interviewing "outsiders" was that the district did not wish to foster the impression that promotions to administrative positions were made only from within the ranks. To reaffirm among committee members that good candidates were always being sought, one principal recounted how an outstanding principal from California had "almost" been hired in a previous year. Another principal reminded the committee that any candidate "might come teach with us first" and work up into a principalship through promotion within the system.

The other procedural question dealt with the manner of conducting the interviews. The alternatives considered were to hold informal interviews, to ask candidates a set of prearranged questions (e.g., "What do you see as the role of the principal?," "How can the principal make the best use of teacher competencies?"), or to guide the interview by using either an "in-basket"[3] or a problem approach. The pros and cons of each approach were discussed briefly. When the director of elementary education recalled that in a prior year one of the present applicants had been interviewed by using a structured interview technique, interest in that approach quickly subsided. Although never formally resolved, the actual procedure followed in the interviews was unstructured and was oriented primarily to getting a candidate to talk freely about his experiences, his beliefs about teaching, and his thoughts about the role of the school and the role of the principal.

Excerpts from the interviews and discussions are presented in the following. I have rearranged the actual order of interviews and have presented the candidates here according to the final rank order decided on by the committee. The name of each candidate's ordinal position in the final ranking is used as a pseudonym.

Mr. Seventh

Mr. Seventh, age forty-eight, was an out-of-district candidate. Off and on, he had been working toward a doctorate in education at the local university. He had served in administrative capacities, first as a principal and more recently as an assistant superintendent, for twenty-two of his twenty-five years in education. At the beginning of his brief interview, he was asked whether he would plan to stay in the district if he completed his doctorate. He said that even with a doctorate, he felt he might be able to advance sufficiently in a district of this size (over 20,000 students) to keep him there. He added that he might not finish his doctorate anyway. One principal joked with him about wanting to "go beyond" the principalship: "Isn't the principal about the best thing you can be?"

One of the interviewing principals had served years before as a teacher in a school where the candidate was principal, and he later said of him, "I think he'd be a pretty good candidate—he's pretty strong." At age forty-eight, however, the committee seemed reluctant to endorse him. Their reservations were reinforced by their suspicion that he wanted to get into their school district only because of its proximity to the university so that he could complete his graduate work. When it finally came time to draw the line on candidates, Mr. Seventh's presumed lack of commitment to the principal role and his potential mobility, especially were he to complete his graduate studies, served as the basis for a low ranking. As one principal summarized, "I would have ranked Seventh higher, but I think of the elementary principalship as a career. He's a stronger candidate than some of the others, but I just don't think he's going to stay. He'll stay about four or five years and use us as a stepping stone."

Mr. Fifth

Mr. Fifth, age thirty-nine and also from outside the district, had been principal of a large elementary school in a growing but still rural community for the previous five of his twelve years in public school work. In spite of his long tenure, his experience, which was confined primarily to rural schools, was regarded as a serious handicap. "Coming from those rural communities, he will be facing a real change if he comes here to be an elementary school principal," noted one committee member. "Would he be willing to come here as a *teacher?*" asked another. At the time they decided to invite him for an interview, members of the committee also tacitly assumed that his age and experience had probably narrowed the range of positions he would accept to that of a principalship. They found themselves in agreement that his rural-conservative school experience had probably failed to provide him with a sufficiently "exciting" background from which he might make a contribution to their own schools (thus rather subtly reinforcing the explicit preference for candidates who have worked in their own district, one they perceive as a school system in which the program *is* exciting).

Committee members were cordial in their greetings and introductions when Mr. Fifth appeared for his interview. He was directed to choose one of the (few) comfortable chairs in the meeting room, prompting the personnel director to joke, "It won't be this comfortable again." After a folksy prelude, the director of elementary education asked, "What things have you been doing and how have you been involved?"

Mr. Fifth: Ma'am?

Director of Elementary Education: Well, if you were a principal, what kinds of changes would you want to make?

Mr. Fifth: It would depend on what I found. If I found some needs, I would move in and meet those needs.

Interviewing Principal: How do you see the role of the counselor in relation to the principal?

Mr. Fifth: I see the principal as a sort of mediator—right in the middle, if there is a middle.

He described a two-stage role for the principal, first in getting the cooperation of the staff and then in a "selling" role to convince the parents. To illustrate, he elaborated on an experimental "group counseling situation" recently set up at his school, a topic of immediate interest to the interviewing principals because of districtwide efforts to develop a counseling program at each elementary school.

Interviewing Principal: How were the children selected for your group counseling?

Mr. Fifth: Well, being in the school for four years, I pretty well knew which children needed help. Our goals were to help Bill Jones get some subjects so he could do his doctorate. But, of course, if I was setting up a [real] program, I would identify which kids needed certain things.

Interviewing Principal: How have you gotten teacher involvement in curriculum development in your district?

Mr. Fifth: We gave them their choice: "Do you want math or do you want social studies?" You see, they had a choice of what they would do. [There was some laughter at this. One interviewer asked, "No third choice?" Another joked, "Oh, there's a third choice, all right."]

Interviewing Principal: Is everyone on one of the two committees?

Mr. Fifth: Yes.

Interviewing Principal: Why do you say you like autonomy?

Mr. Fifth: I like to be an individual, just like you do.

Interviewing Principal: Do you like your teachers to be individuals, too?

Mr. Fifth: Yes. As a matter of fact, I encourage it.

Interviewing Principal: What do you feel is the role of the departmentalized program in the elementary school?

Mr. Fifth: We have "self-contained,"[4] yet I guess there are more exceptions than the rule. [He described his reading program, a one-hour uninterrupted period during which the children are regrouped.] It's a sort of modified Joplin plan. . . . We have Bible class, but we don't let it interfere with reading.

His discussion of the reading program prompted him to comment about the extensive "help" received at his school from a nearby teachers' college:

Mr. Fifth: So much help can be a problem. For example, in our building we have fourteen teachers, two aides, nine high school cadet helpers, twenty-eight teacher trainees (ranging from part-time observers to student teachers), plus our own music and special education people, plus five more coming in doing research from the college. After describing how many people are in and out of the building, you could see why I would want to leave.

Interviewing Principal: It's not so rare here, either. This morning I had thirteen visitors, four teacher trainees, seven students observing from the university, and three policemen, plus the regular faculty.

The question of salary was introduced as a point of information by one of the interviewing principals, who explained that in the district an administrator's salary is dependent not on school size but on tenure. The personnel director explained the administrative salary schedule in some detail: "Roughly, a principal gets one-fifth above the teaching schedule. So in your case, the teaching salary of $8,000 for a teacher with a master's degree and ten years of experience [the maximum years of nondistrict experience acceptable in the school district for purposes of salary evaluation] plus one-fifth is about $11,000 for ten months. A total of 205 days; $11,000." Mr. Fifth said that at present he was on an eleven-month contract. "You gain a month there" was the reply. He was informed that many school personnel work for the school district in the summer, writing curriculum or teaching summer school, "but not on the administrative [salary] schedule, of course."

Following the interview, committee members chatted as they watched Mr. Fifth walk out onto the parking lot, get into his pickup truck, and drive away. "My wife once applied for a teaching position in that district," commented one principal. "It was *very* conservative!!"

In the review of the candidates at the conclusion of all the interviews, the following comment of one interviewing principal seemed to summarize the reaction to Mr. Fifth: "We're doing *so much* here for boys and girls. We've gone about as far as we can. These fellows from outside have a real disadvantage because they're still talking about getting kids in and out of rooms, holding ball games, and so on. I think he'd come along pretty well in a couple of years. He'd know our lingo and he'd be doing a good job. It might just take him a little longer."

A second principal concluded the discussion: "The more he talked, the farther I got from him."

Mr. Fifth, Mr. Seventh, and, in all, the names of ten applicants were excluded from the list of candidates recommended to the superintendent. Slight as the variation was among the original panel of fourteen candidates, the variation among the final four candidates chosen was even less. The four were married males between the ages of thirty-one and thirty-four. They all had been in professional education from eight to twelve years, had taught in the upper elementary grades, and held degrees received five to ten years earlier at the master's level. All the candidates had been with the district from five to ten years. Although they held somewhat different positions at the moment (administrative intern, teacher on leave to pursue a doctoral program, resource teacher, junior high vice-principal), each candidate had managed to alter his status from that of the full-time elementary classroom teacher he had once been; none now had direct teaching responsibilities. With the exception of the resource teacher (an extra teacher assigned full-time to a school to provide instructional assistance to the staff), all had held positions specifically entailing administrative duties. All four were considered eminently qualified to assume a principalship. Each candidate had achieved his present visibility *within* the district. With the exception of Mr. Fourth, each had achieved this visibility without stepping on the wrong toes.

Mr. Fourth's problem, at least in part, was that he had run head-on into a not-unknown obstacle in the path of a young man heading for the elementary principalship—the female administrator. A brief comment here concerning the different roles played by men and by women in the hierarchy of the elementary school, particularly in the professional relationship of the administration-bound male vis-à-vis the authority-holding female, may help put Mr. Fourth's problems as a candidate into perspective.

At the teaching level, the world of the elementary school is a world of women. At the administrative level, the ratio of men to women is almost exactly reversed: 85 percent of the elementary school teachers are females (NEA Research Report 1967:14), and 78 percent of the elementary school principals are males (DESP 1968:11). The administration-bound male must obviously be able to survive in a predominantly female setting among his teacher colleagues. In addition, he must be able to survive in such relationships as that of student teacher-master teacher or teacher-supervisor, where his immediate superior is most frequently a woman. And finally, there is a considerable likelihood that among the principals under whom he serves as a teacher, he will be assigned to a "woman principal"[5] at least once—an assignment that probably exceeds random chance because female administrators seem particularly sensitive about securing teachers with whom their male pupils can "identify." Thus, although women administrators do not exert a majority influence in the formal organization of their peers (indeed, in that era just prior to the women's liberation movement, I believe I detected a tendency among male principals to keep their few female colleagues "in their place" in their professional organizations by relegating to them such assignments as taking charge of table decorations, sending out invitations and thank you letters, and performing minor bookkeeping tasks), the women exert a powerful influence as gatekeepers to the principalship.

Among the fourteen candidates reviewed by the Principal Selection Committee, the only two whose current dossiers contained overtly negative statements were two candidates working with female principals. Both had already achieved nonteaching assignments at their schools as resource teachers, and both maintained high involvement in the activities of the local teacher association. It was their active participation in the teacher association that provided the basis for some of the criticism that each candidate received in his evaluation. One principal noted two complaints in her written evaluation: one, that the candidate was "traditional" in his approach to teaching (an implied criticism and a somewhat irrelevant one since he was neither serving as a classroom teacher nor being considered for a teaching position); and two, that he conducted too much of the business of the teacher association at school, thus detracting from his responsibility as a resource teacher to assist the teaching faculty. "First things should be first," the principal had admonished in summary.

"In other words," the personnel director commented after the evaluation was read aloud to the committee, "the teachers aren't getting the help they need."

"That's the only man left on her staff," observed one principal. "As I recall, she wasn't satisfied with the only other guy on her staff last year, either."

Mr. Fourth

Mr. Fourth had been highly regarded as a candidate the previous year. His candidacy was critically reviewed because members of the committee expressed some hesitation about his present status, particularly concerning a prevalent rumor that Mr. Fourth and his principal were not getting along very well. Differences between Mr. Fourth and his woman principal were more than hinted at; they were openly aired by committee members. The candidate himself commented on their relationship during his interview: "She's not too good for a man's ego—especially if you're a little inefficient like I am."

Unlike the procedure followed with any other candidate, Mr. Fourth's principal was invited to meet with the committee to share her views about his candidacy. Her discussion began with these comments:

I think his one big problem is relating to people, because he tends to want to move too fast. . . . One thing he feels inadequate about is making small talk that makes people feel comfortable when they come to school. . . . I think he is better with men than women. I've talked to him about how as an administrator he will be working mostly with women, and he'll have to observe certain amenities.

To the direct question, "Do you think he should be an administrator —say, for example, in a smaller school or some special setting?" she replied, "If I had my druthers, I'd like to have him in a situation where he could get some help—especially in human relations. I think we need to realize he's been in a very difficult position this year, working with a woman. . . . He has told me, 'It hasn't been any morale boost to work *with you*.' "

Immediately after the conference with Mr. Fourth's principal, one principal said, "Well, she hasn't changed my ideas any. We talked last year about his impulsiveness and these other problems." Another principal said, "There's no question of his ability. But I do feel some reservations about him." Another added, "A member of my staff said he walked right by her the other day without speaking. She felt badly about it. Of course, that doesn't pertain here."

Mr. Fourth's position as a former favorite was altered only slightly, but it was sufficient to put him out of the running. One committee member noted that no doubt the outcome would have been different had Mr. Fourth still been assigned to his former school, working with a male principal who had helped both to groom and to sponsor him for the step into administration.

Mr. Third

Mr. Third was less well known among committee members than any other in-district candidate. He had the briefest tenure in the district (five years), and this was his second consecutive year on leave in order to pursue graduate study toward a doctoral degree at the university. He helped reestablish his longevity by remarking to the committee as he entered for his interview, "I sat *here* last year," but the committee had already been reminded by the holdover member that Mr. Third had been "high on our list" the year before.

The search for topics to discuss was more difficult with a candidate who had not been active in the district for the past year and a half. As Mr. Third noted, "I've sort of lost track of some of these different programs." The discussion soon turned to the candidate's observations on the doctoral program at the university. The committee was receptive to his criticism that the "whole question of curriculum and administration at the university is all geared to secondary school." He told them that the set of qualifying examinations he had just written were all of the order, "Imagine yourself the principal of a *secondary school*. What would you do if . . ."

One interviewing principal asked how Mr. Third's previous school district compared with this one.

Mr. Third: The principals in this school district have a little more autonomy in the selection of staff.

Interviewing Principal: Is this autonomy a good thing?

Mr. Third: I think this situation is good.

Interviewing Principal: Why do you?

Mr. Third: So a staff can develop its abilities to the maximum. For example, maybe one staff can do more with "flexibility" than another.

Several times during the interview, Mr. Third reaffirmed his belief in the importance of the elementary school principalship. In his concluding remarks, he summarized, "I think the elementary principalship is a great challenge and quite different from other areas. You are working closely with individuals and different programs. . . . I've been an assistant principal, and now I'd like to try another notch up the ladder."

Mr. Third seemed to have made a good impression on the members of the committee. Their favorable reaction created some dilemmas that they discussed following his interview. One problem was his brief tenure: "He's the least experienced." Although his experience prior to coming to the district included two years as a teaching vice-principal, it was noted that he had held no position other than classroom teacher in his three active years in the district. An earlier bias expressed in the case of Mr. Seventh, who had been suspected of planning to come to the district in order to pursue a doctoral program at the university and then "moving on," was reinterpreted to differentiate between in-district candidates and out-of-district ones. "It's different in using the district if you've come up through the ranks or from outside it," suggested one principal. Mr. Third "might just be willing to stick around," posited another.

Mr. Third's recent efforts as a conscientious and effective supervisor of student teachers, fulfilling a part-time position on the university staff along with his program of studies, were duly noted by principals who had seen him in action: "Often these guys on a degree program don't have time to spend in supervising, but that's not the case here." Another principal added, "We've had some supervisors from the university who have missed a whole term."

Someone questioned, "We don't have anything on the salary schedule for a Ph.D. Couldn't he do better somewhere else?"

"He's told us he likes this district and wants to stay here," assured the assistant superintendent. "He doesn't want to be a professor."

I am quite sure I was the only person at the meeting who did not realize that the candidate was the superintendent's son-in-law.

Mr. Second

Enthusiastic support of Mr. Second's candidacy was expressed before, during, and after his formal interview. His excellent performance as a teacher and resource teacher, that he "dealt with difficult situations very well" as an active member of the local teacher organization, his "energy and interest," his active role in church work, even that his father had been a principal—all were duly reviewed before the interview began. If there was any reservation expressed at all, it was only to suggest that a promotion to the principalship might be a bit premature at present. Although comments like "he was highly considered last year" and "I think he has matured greatly" tended to dispel such reservations among committee members, one principal reminded the committee, "He'll be around another year."

Mr. Second's interview began with the suggestion that he describe his "present situation," his experience, and the new programs he was working on. He launched easily into a fifteen-minute description of the educational program in the school where he was presently assigned. The following discussion was precipitated by his account of that program.

Interviewing Principal: I think we've heard a lot about the program at your school, and it's been a real good education. Now let's hear about how you think of *yourself* in a program—what do *you* want in a program?

Another Interviewing Principal: Yes, what do you think is the unique role of the elementary school?

Mr. Second: I think it is to take each child where he is and take him as far as he can go. But that isn't unique to the elementary school. It's also junior high, isn't it? Yet I'm not qualified for the junior high.

Another Interviewing Principal: Who has the responsibility for making improvements in a school's program?

Mr. Second: That's the principal's job—along with the whole faculty, of course. As an administrator, you should be the last one to take the glory.

To signal the start of the closing ritual during the interviews, each candidate was asked if he had questions to address to the members of the committee. No candidate seemed to have a crucial question he wanted to ask, but none forfeited the implicit challenge to be able to ask *something*. The out-of-district candidates wondered which position they were being interviewed for. The in-district candidates already knew that this information was not yet available and that the decision about the annual "administrator shuffle" had not been announced and probably had not been made. Their questions concerned the dates when appointments were to be announced or the types of appointments to be made. The top two candidates expressed their concern about appointments to smaller schools since the word was out that one of the new appointments might be for a "two-role" person (e.g., principal of two smaller schools, or principal plus some other assignment in one school). Mr. Second's query set off the following series of remarks in this regard.

Mr. Second: I've been curious as to just how the joint principalships between two schools work out?

Interviewing Principal One: I've worked with it, and it leaves a lot to be desired.

Interviewing Principal Two: I think we took a step backward when we went to it.

Interviewing Principal One: I think it is better to combine a half-time principal and a half-time resource teacher in *one* school.

Interviewing Principal Three: That looks good on paper, but it never seems to work out.

Interviewing Principal Two: Of course, you know which one will give—just like when we principals have a conflict between supervision and administration.

Interviewing Principal One: There are no half-time jobs.

Interviewing Principal Four: How about combining the role of principal and the role of counselor?

Interviewing Principal One: With the role we're trying to create for the counselor, those two roles are not always compatible. When the axe has to fall, I'm the one who has to do it.

Mr. First

Presently serving in his second year as a full-time junior high school vice-principal, Mr. First had already established himself in an administrative niche. His request to get "back" into the elementary schools was met with a pose of suspicion by members of the committee that masked (but just barely) the significance they attributed to his application as a reaffirmation of the importance of the role of the elementary school.

The discussion prior to Mr. First's interview included the following comments:

Assistant Superintendent (reviewing his record): He's been a junior high vice-principal two years, but it only took one year to make him want to come back.

Interviewing Principal One: He's been so nice to work with over there that for selfish reasons I'd like to see him stay at the junior high level. How did he happen to get put into junior high?

Director of Elementary Education: They talked him into it one summer when I was away. They desperately needed a junior high vice-principal. He didn't know what his chances were for an elementary school position, so he took it.

Interviewing Principal One: Should he stay at junior high? Can he do any good there? Can he move up?

Interviewing Principal Two: I think we should interview him and find out his feelings about junior high, whether he wants to get back into elementary, and if so, why.

Interviewing Principal Three: How often do we ask people to do things in the district because it will be good for the district rather than for them? I'm not sure we're even doing these guys a favor.

Assistant Superintendent: Do you think that First's role on the Teacher-School Board Salary Committee has made a difference in how the board might regard him? When we bring names to the board, they react.

Interviewing Principal One: It might, but it shouldn't.

Mr. First's interview got off to a late but jovial beginning; he had thought his appointment was 11:40 a.m. instead of 10:40 a.m. and had to be telephoned at his school. His arrival precipitated the exchange of a few moments of raillery among those present. He knew everyone on the committee.

Interviewing Principal: What makes you think you want to be in a gang like this?

Mr. First: Are you serious? Do you want me to answer?

Interviewing Principal: Yes. That's really why we are all here.

Mr. First: Well, this is where I belong. This is where my training and my interest is.

Mr. First described programs and problems at his junior high school. He explained how he had tried to break down the resistance of those parents who "have the attitude that the school only calls once a year and that's when the kid is in trouble." He cited several aspects of secondary school administration that he disliked: "I don't like the sports emphasis in high school, the problems with buses and scheduling, the court cases. Last year I spent one day out of every two weeks in court. I'd rather be working with kids earlier in their lives, not in the kind of conference I sat in recently with a parent when a doctor told the mother her alternatives are either to give the daughter 'The Pill' or lock her up in a cage."

Another question gave him an opportunity to remind the committee of both his prior experience as a school administrator ("When I was an elementary principal in the Midwest," he began, "we had this problem . . .") and of an early encounter he had had with administrative rigidity. He described the attendance area of that school, a predominantly black slum area in a large city, as a "third-generation ADC neighborhood."[6] He discussed the program he had tried to initiate at the school: "It was a very peculiar nongraded program for a very peculiar neighborhood, a program for which the teachers and I were ready but the administration was not. I felt like I'd been kicked real hard when they turned down the program. That was about the time the director of elementary education came through recruiting teachers for this district. That's how I happened to come here."

Interviewing Principal: When you went back to the classroom after being an administrator, what were some of the problems?

Mr. First: Unwinding!! Not worrying so much about 50-minute programs. . . . One of my goals once was to go into teacher education. I used to think you could do the most good there, but I think now that's too far removed. You can do more good in the public schools—you're closer there. But it has some distasteful parts, too, like worrying over school budget elections or hassling with the school board over a $100 raise.

Final Deliberation

Members of the Principal Selection Committee deliberated for almost an hour after interviewing the last of the candidates before reaching a decision on their recommendation to the superintendent. One principal suggested a straw vote to rank all candidates and "see how near we are to one mind." The director of elementary education proposed that they identify and rank the top five candidates. Selecting a panel of five candidates for a maximum of three positions followed the earlier recommendation of the personnel director, who had suggested they rank more candidates than needed because "someone might not take it." When the straw ballot was taken, four "favorite" in-district candidates topped the list. That number was informally adopted as the number of candidates the committee would recommend. Another straw vote was taken that reaffirmed the original ranking of the top candidates but revealed that one committee member was disrupting what was an otherwise highly agreed on rank order.

Interviewing Principal One: There's someone who is ranking a top candidate low. I wonder if there is something we should have talked about.

Interviewing Principal Two: I'm the one voting him low. Not because I have anything against him, but I still feel we have an obligation to another candidate. So I'm voting higher for him than I really feel about him. Yet I don't know if that's right, either.

Discussion, without further voting, revealed that all the members were satisfied with the composite results of the ranking and with the specific recommendation of the top candidates, as agreed on from

Mr. First to Mr. Fourth. The director of elementary education summarized: "I'll give these results, and our first vote, to the assistant superintendent. I'll tell him that before we would recommend anyone besides these top four, we would want to discuss it."

The meeting, and the Principal Selection Committee itself, disbanded. "I'd much rather interview teachers," commented the case study principal. "So would I," added the director of elementary education.

Discussion and Comments

The proceedings of the Principal Selection Committee were presented here because that event, although well removed from the daily routine of any principal, brought into bold relief several aspects central to the professional life of the case study principal and to the principals with whom he worked. The present discussion is limited to three interrelated dimensions of the principalship that seem to pervade the life and work of a principal and that are substantially reflected in the data presented. These dimensions are (1) the lack of professional knowledge associated with the role, (2) an esteem for personal feelings, and (3) a proclivity toward variety-reducing behavior.

Lack of Professional Knowledge
Associated With the Role

Throughout my fieldwork, I was struck with the number of occasions in which principals communicated to each other uncertainties about what they "should" be doing and what their "real" role is. To any outsider, whether teacher, pupil, parent, or even researcher, the principals I met were always ready to describe and defend the importance of the elementary school and their contribution to its mission. In their own gatherings, however, free from their usual audiences and oblivious to the observer, they probed constantly for guidelines to answer one common and basic question: "What is the role of the principal?"

The role uncertainty of the principalship seems due in part to the problem of the lack of any professional (i.e., private and/or technical) knowledge or skill that clearly distinguishes the administrator from those administered. This problem is referred to broadly in the field of educational administration as that of working from a "limited knowledge base." Evidence of the limited knowledge base is illustrated in two ways in the proceedings of the Principal Selection Committee. First, in examining dialogue recorded during the committee's proceedings, one becomes aware of the absence of an esoteric technical vocabulary that might have been expected in other settings in the deliberations of such a "board of examiners." Except for Mr. Fifth's use of the terms "self-contained" and "a sort of modified Joplin plan," the vocabulary evident throughout the proceedings reflects the ambiguous and general terms that characterized the professional language of administrators observed throughout the study: "real challenge," "meeting needs," "good situation," "involvement . . . more autonomy," "unique program," "doing so much for boys and girls," and so forth. Indeed, to the extent that there is an esoteric language shared among professional educators (a language sometimes referred to jokingly within their circles as "pedagese"), principals express concern with their own ability to keep up with the latest changes in techniques or terminology. One principal observed, "You hire one or two new teachers and listen to them and you don't even know what they're talking about."

A second example of the problem of a limited knowledge base is suggested by the lack of systematic procedures by which the principals made evaluations necessary for ranking candidates. Having to make judgments that result in identifying one person as superior to another or that distinguish qualified from unqualified personnel can be a difficult and, for some people, a distasteful business. Nonetheless, the work of the schools is inexorably bound up with evaluating the performance of both staff and pupils. One of the crucial aspects of the principal's job in this school district, as it is elsewhere, is the annual process of preparing evaluative recommendations regarding personnel, particularly for those on probationary status. The lack of special skill or knowledge available to principals in performing this evaluative function was reflected collectively by the Principal Selection Committee in the haphazard approach its members took in interviewing and assessing candidates for the principalship. Whatever specific criteria each member of the committee used as a basis for judgment seemed to be assiduously avoided as a topic for mutual discussion and concern. One senses that each principal felt that regardless of the criteria he or his cohorts used, ultimately the group would reach substantially the same decisions regarding the selection and ranking of the candidates at hand. It should be pointed out in this regard that the final decision of the committee did reflect just such a consensus.

An Esteem for Personal Feelings

The case study principal and his colleagues seemed to share a distaste for formal evaluative tasks. Their reluctance was particularly apparent in the comments and jokes they made throughout the year about preparing their formal "teacher evaluations" and by the collective anxiety they exhibited as the deadline neared for submitting those reports to the central office. The same distaste was apparent throughout the meetings of the Principal Selection Committee as they spoke of "getting this over with." But their lack of regard for the formality of evaluation *procedures* should not be confused with their regard for the personal feelings of those whom they were evaluating. Their esteem for the feelings of the candidates, for the feelings of each other, and for their own feelings and intuitions as part of the assessment task is repeatedly revealed in the dialogue. If the role of the principal can be characterized by a lack of professional knowledge, as suggested in the preceding, a compensating behavior of those who serve in it may be to give the affective domain considerably more importance than one generally associates with the processes of administration.

All candidates were interviewed graciously under circumstances in which the formalities inherent in the setting, such as meeting by a tight schedule of appointments at the central office or holding most interviews seated around a large conference table in the formally designated boardroom, were consciously underplayed. The interviewers attempted to engage candidates in light social banter as they arrived for interviews. They asked open-ended questions, starting always with a question intended to put each candidate at ease and let him "tell something about himself." No question addressed to or response of a candidate was treated with the air of a grueling interrogation. Concern was expressed about interviewing any candidate for whom an invitation to appear for an interview might serve inappropriately to arouse his hopes. At the same time, the names of persons whom the committee never intended to consider as serious candidates were gently retained rather than summarily dropped. The only candidate really "rejected," and this primarily at the suggestion of the personnel director, was an out-of-district candidate who had once accepted and then rejected a contract offered him by the school district.

The personal feelings of the interviewing principals also made their way into the discussion of literally every candidate. Some of the statements regarding personal feelings were quite explicit: "I think I know him less well than some of the others, but I have a better feeling about him" or "I feel some reservations about how he relates to kids, but there's no question of his ability."

Not only were feelings of the interviewers introduced into the discussions, so too were feelings imputed to the candidates themselves. Most often, such descriptions put the candidate in a favorable light or showed concern for his own feelings: "He has as good a feeling about children as anyone I know" or "I think it would be a terrible blow to him if he didn't get a principalship."

Under conditions in which most comments are favorable, however, even the least hint of negativism served as a signal of caution: "He may be a bit bitter about education. He's talked to me about changing jobs and about being an administrator." (This comment brought a retort from another principal: "If he's somewhat bitter now, this would be the worst possible thing for him.")

A Proclivity Toward "Variety-Reducing" Behavior

The proceedings of the Principal Selection Committee reveal a tendency among the principals to engage in what might be described as "variety-reducing" behavior.[7] This terminology comes from the field of general cybernetic systems. In the present case, it draws attention to the fact that when the principals had to express preferences or exercise choices that might be expected either to generate or to reduce the variation in certain aspects of the schools, their behavior reveals an inclination to reduce and to constrain. Their attention was directed toward keeping things "manageable" by drawing on and reinforcing the existing system rather than by nurturing or even permitting the introduction of variation. This behavior is exemplified most clearly in the results of the major task confronting them: identifying candidates to receive official sanction. In that gentle but effective culling, a panel of fourteen applicants was reduced to a final trio in which the successful members appeared so similar as to be virtually interchangeable. Whatever potential for variation extant among that original panel in terms of age, sex, background, recent experience, type and amount of formal education, marital status—in this instance even height, weight, and manner of speech and dress—was successfully narrowed in the final selection. And while this process was going on, the principals also lent whatever support they could to reducing the potency of other variety-generating agents with whom their work brings them into continual contact, such as local colleges and universities or central office administrators ready to saddle the principalship with a double role.

That the behavior of the principals in the episode gives such overt evidence of variety-reducing behavior is, in one sense, hardly surprising. The task to which they were assigned was by definition a variety-reducing task; there were almost five times as many aspirants as positions to be filled. Furthermore, the very terms that the concept of "variety-reducing" calls to mind are terms that are descriptive of management processes: organize, systematize, categorize, constrain, control. What may be unusual is the extent to which variation was so thoroughly and systematically reduced, albeit this seemed to be neither an immediate nor a conscious concern of any of the principals on the committee.

Conclusion

I would like to conclude with a note of reflection relating the role of the principal to the emphasis placed on "change" in the public schools. This observation relates particularly to the preceding discussion on the phenomenon of variety-reducing behavior observed during the proceedings of the Principal Selection Committee.

The public schools have a seeming penchant for change. School people write, read, and talk constantly of new programs, new "hardware," new approaches. One can gather the impression from educators that anything "old" is suspect and that "changed" is automatically assumed to be "improved." In the last decade, a whole vocabulary of change, including terms particularly familiar to students of cultural dynamics such as "change agent," "acculturation," "innovation," and "diffusion," became the vogue in educational circles.

The school principal, charged directly with the role of being the instructional leader of his school, is often described as both instrumental and essential in the continuing process of introducing change into the school. The case study principal and his colleagues recognized this charge and responsibility. They acknowledged not only their formal obligation but also their personal commitment to fostering change in the interests of a better education for children.

In looking at the totality of a typical "live" elementary school as the person charged with administering it might do rather than at what is going on in any particular setting within it, one can appreciate that a school is a very dynamic institution. An elementary school is in a constant state of change without anyone having to do anything to induce or encourage the process. More than 500 people moved constantly into, out of, and within the school in this case study each day. New pupils, parents, teachers, substitutes, specialists, solicitors, salesmen, servicemen, and visitors arrived constantly to replace former ones or to swell the ranks of those already present. New problems, programs, and personnel are introduced constantly in schools as pupils graduate or move away, teachers "turn over," or interest groups demand and governmental agencies offer to subsidize new curricula and services.

Regardless of what he *says* about the desirability of creating a climate for change, the principal already lives with incessant change as a way of life. If an occasional principal demonstrates such a tolerance of or personal need for change that he actually becomes an innovator who induces significant change into his own school, really creating something new or introducing new degrees of freedom into the setting (rather than simply manipulating or restructuring what was already present), I would think he would be a rare principal indeed. I do not believe I encountered such people among the career administrators with whom I came in contact during my fieldwork. The life of innovative programs or schools, and the tenure of innovative administrators, is frequently short-lived (see Fleming 1967; Miles 1964; Redefer 1950; Rogers 1962; Smith and Keith 1971).

Faced as he is with the inevitability of change as an inherent and major aspect of his task, even though he may not recognize it as such, the school principal is successful in his work as he is able to contain and constrain the ever-changing group that he is assigned to administer. If his survival in that role necessitates his constant effort at variety reduction, we may have an important clue in helping to explain why certain dimensions of public school education remain so relatively unchanged in spite of the constant attempts to change them both from within and from without, for it may be that the only way one can hope to maintain any control in a system that is inherently so volatile and constantly changing in some dimensions—in this case, its personnel—is to exert all the influence one can in reducing the potential variety that might enter the system via routes more amenable to restraint. Although it presents a curious paradox between their ideal and actual roles as "agents of change," if principals actually serve to constrain rather than facilitate the dynamic aspects of formal education, that is exactly the paradox that I am suggesting here.

The paradox may be explained by reanalyzing the extent to which managing change is already an inherent and significant part of the principal's role. Change comes in the form of a constantly changing population, both in the local community of parents and children and, perhaps even more, in the day-to-day composition of the adult cadre present at school. How long does it take to orient a new substitute teacher so that her day at school will not be a fiasco? What amenities are required for meeting a parent new to the community or orienting a relief custodian or secretary new to the school? How much more variation might a principal be expected to seek out per day after spending a not-so-unusual two hours orienting "thirteen visitors, four teacher trainees, seven students observing from the university, and three policemen" plus handling the new problems generated by over 500 pupils and staff members already part of the daily complement?

Programmatically, the public schools may still warrant the assertion made by Willard Waller years ago that they are "museums of virtue" (Waller 1932:34), but although the air of virtue about them may have remained, the characteristic of "museum-ness" has not. Most urban elementary schools today are large, bustling institutions. The people who manage them live their professional lives among a constantly changing and volatile group of children and adults in which everyone, including themselves, has only relatively temporary status. The irony for the elementary school principal is that the extent of change with which he lives is neither acknowledged by those about him nor even necessarily recognized by himself. Indeed, he listens to the cries for change and often joins ritually with those who attempt to bring it about. Yet ultimately his own actions, in a constant press to keep the institution manageable at all, may tend to reduce the variation with all the ploys and powers characteristic of administrators in general and an elementary school principal in specific: "We'll have to see about that," "Mrs. X has some good qualities as a teacher, but she and I just aren't seeing eye to eye. I'm going to have to suggest that she either transfer or resign," "It's a grand idea, but there's no money in the budget for it," or "These fellows from outside have a real disadvantage. . . . I think he'd come along pretty well in a couple of years. He'd know our lingo and be doing a good job."

Could it be that those people who seek to become and are able to survive as principals, through a perhaps inadvertent but apparently critical and essential proclivity toward variety-reducing behavior, have their greatest impact on education not as agents of change but rather as advocates of constraint? If so, we may be better able to account for the remarkable stability and uniformity that has characterized American elementary schools in spite of the forces for change swirling constantly about them.

Notes

Grateful acknowledgment is expressed to Max Abbott, Norman Delue, Joanne M. Kitchel, and George D. Spindler for critical comment and editorial assistance in the preparation of this material. At the time of this writing, the author was a professor of education and anthropology and a research associate at the Center for the Advanced Study of Educational Administration (CASEA) at the University of Oregon. The author wishes to acknowledge the support of CASEA during a portion of his time devoted to the preparation of this chapter.

1. A discussion of the methodology employed here has also appeared in *Human Organization* (Wolcott 1970). A more thorough discussion appears as Chapter 1, "A Principal Investigator in Search of a Principal," in the completed monograph (Wolcott 1973).

2. This part of the research was conducted by my research assistant, an experienced geographer, who developed a socioeconomic map of the school attendance area (Olson 1969). Although I carried out the balance of the field research, it was invaluable to have assistance in the analysis of enumeration and interview data by someone less closely connected with the school setting and thus presumably more able to restrict his analysis to the data at hand.

3. The in-basket approach (see Hemphill et al. 1962) presents a series of hypothetical problems typical of those that require the attention of an administrator, presented in the form in which they might come across his desk in notes, memoranda, notices, or letters. A whole set of simulated materials has been developed for use in graduate courses in elementary school administration (University Council for Educational Administration 1967, 1971).

4. "Self-contained" refers to the organizational program of a school in which one teacher remains with the same group of pupils throughout the day.

5. In this regard, note how the term "principal" is often qualified with the adjective "woman" if the role occupant is female, just as the term "teacher" is usually qualified with the term "man" when the role occupant is male, particularly in referring to teachers at the elementary school level.

6. An ADC, or Aid to Dependent Children, neighborhood (i.e., a neighborhood with many families on welfare).

7. I am indebted to anthropologist Alfred G. Smith for suggesting to me the concept of variety-reducing versus variety-generating behavior as a means of analyzing administrative strategies.

References and Further Reading

Department of Elementary School Principals, NEA, 1968, *The Elementary School Principalship in 1968*. Washington, D.C.; Department of Elementary School Principals, National Education Association.

Fleming, Emett E., 1967, "Innovation Related to the Tenure, Succession and Orientation of the Elementary Principal," Northwestern University, unpublished doctoral dissertation.

Fuchs, Estelle, 1966, *Pickets at the Gates*. New York: Free Press.

———, 1969, *Teachers Talk: Views from Inside City Schools*. New York: Anchor Books and Doubleday.

Griffiths, Daniel E., Samuel Goldman, and Wayne J. McFarland, 1965, "Teacher Mobility in New York City," *Educational Administration Quarterly* 1:15-31.

Hemphill, John K., Daniel E. Griffiths, and Norman Frederiksen, 1962, *Administrative Performance and Personality*. New York: Bureau of Publications, Teachers College, Columbia University.

Lee, Dorothy, 1963, "Discrepancies in the Teaching of American Culture." In George D. Spindler, ed., *Education and Culture: Anthropological Approaches*. New York: Holt, Rinehart & Winston.

Miles, Matthew B., ed., 1964, *Innovation in Education*. New York: Bureau of Publications, Teachers College, Columbia University.

National Education Association Research Report, 1967, "Estimates of School Statistics 1967-1968," *Research Report 1967 R-19*. Washington, D.C.: National Education Association.

Olson, John A., 1969, "Mapping: A Method for Organizing Data About Your School Attendance Area," *Oregon School Study Council Bulletin*, vol. 12, no. 7.

Pettitt, George A., 1946, *Primitive Education in North America*. Berkeley: University of California Publications in Archaeology and Ethnology 48. (Excerpted in Walter Goldschmidt, ed., *Exploring the Ways of Mankind*. New York: Holt, Rinehart & Winston, 1960)

Redefer, Frederick L., 1950, "The Eight Year Study . . . After Eight Years," *Progressive Education* 18:33-36.

Rogers, Everett M., 1962, *Diffusion of Innovations*. New York: Free Press.

Sarason, Seymour B., 1971, *The Culture of the School and the Problem of Change*. Boston: Allyn & Bacon.

Smith, Louis M., and Pat M. Keith, 1971, *Anatomy of Educational Innovation: An Organizational Analysis of an Elementary School*. New York: John Wiley.

Spindler, George D., 1963, "The Role of the School Administrator," in George D. Spindler, ed., *Education and Culture: Anthropological Approaches*. New York: Holt, Rinehart & Winston.

University Council for Educational Administration, 1967, *The Madison Simulation Materials: Edison Elementary Principalship*. Columbus, Ohio: University Council for Educational Administration.

———, 1971, *The Monroe City Simulations: Abraham Lincoln Elementary School*. Columbus, Ohio: University Council for Educational Administration.

Waller, Willard W., 1932, *The Sociology of Teaching*. New York: John Wiley. (Science Edition, 1965)

Wolcott, Harry F., 1967, *A Kwakiutl Village and School*. New York: Holt, Rinehart & Winston.

———, 1970, "An Ethnographic Approach to the Study of School Administrators," *Human Organization* 29:115-122.

———, 1973, *The Man in the Principal's Office: An Ethnography*. New York: Holt, Rinehart & Winston.

Zelditch, Morris, Jr., 1962, "Some Methodological Problems of Field Studies," *American Journal of Sociology* 67:566-576.

APPENDIX F

A Case Study

CAMPUS RESPONSE TO A STUDENT GUNMAN

Kelly J. Asmussen
John W. Creswell

With increasingly frequent incidents of campus violence, a small, growing scholarly literature about the subject is emerging. For instance, authors have reported on racial [12], courtship and sexually coercive [3, 7, 8], and hazing violence [24]. For the American College Personnel Association, Roark [24] and Roark and Roark [25] reviewed the forms of physical, sexual, and psychological violence on college campuses and suggested guidelines for prevention strategies. Roark [23] has also suggested criteria that high-school students might use to assess the level of violence on college campuses they seek to attend. At the national level, President Bush, in November 1989, signed into law the "Student Right-to-Know and Campus Security Act" (P.L. 101-542), which requires colleges and

SOURCE: The material in this appendix is reprinted from the *Journal of Higher Education, 66,* 575-591. Copyright 1995, the Ohio State University Press. Used by permission.

universities to make available to students, employees, and applicants an annual report on security policies and campus crime statistics [13].

One form of escalating campus violence that has received little attention is student gun violence. Recent campus reports indicate that violent crimes from thefts and burglaries to assaults and homicides are on the rise at colleges and universities [13]. College campuses have been shocked by killings such as those at The University of Iowa [16], The University of Florida [13], Concordia University in Montreal, and the University of Montreal–Ecole Polytechnique [22]. Incidents such as these raise critical concerns, such as psychological trauma, campus safety, and disruption of campus life. Aside from an occasional newspaper report, the postsecondary literature is silent on campus reactions to these tragedies; to understand them one must turn to studies about gun violence in the public school literature. This literature addresses strategies for school intervention [21, 23], provides case studies of incidents in individual schools [6, 14, 15], and discusses the problem of students who carry weapons to school [1] and the psychological trauma that results from homicides [32].

A need exists to study campus reactions to violence in order to build conceptual models for future study as well as to identify campus strategies and protocols for reaction. We need to understand better the psychological dimensions and organizational issues of constituents involved in and affected by these incidents. An in-depth qualitative case study exploring the context of an incident can illuminate such conceptual and pragmatic understandings. The study presented in this article is a qualitative case analysis [31] that describes and interprets a campus response to a gun incident. We asked the following exploratory research questions: What happened? Who was involved in response to the incident? What themes of response emerged during the eight-month period that followed this incident? What theoretical constructs helped us understand the campus response, and what constructs were unique to this case?

The Incident and Response

The incident occurred on the campus of a large public university in a Midwestern city. A decade ago, this city had been designated an "all-American city," but more recently, its normally tranquil environment has been disturbed by an increasing number of assaults and homicides. Some of these violent incidents have involved students at the university.

The incident that provoked this study occurred on a Monday in October. A forty-three-year-old graduate student, enrolled in a senior-level actuarial science class, arrived a few minutes before class, armed with a vintage Korean War military semiautomatic rifle loaded with a thirty-round clip of thirty caliber ammunition. He carried another thirty-round clip in his pocket. Twenty of the thirty-four students in the class had already gathered for class, and most of them were quietly reading the student newspaper. The instructor was en route to class.

The gunman pointed the rifle at the students, swept it across the room, and pulled the trigger. The gun jammed. Trying to unlock the rifle, he hit the butt of it on the instructor's desk and quickly tried firing it again. Again it did not fire. By this time, most students realized what was happening and dropped to the floor, overturned their desks, and tried to hide behind them. After about twenty seconds, one of the students shoved a desk into the gunman, and students ran past him out into the hall and out of the building. The gunman hastily departed the room and went out of the building to his parked car, which he had left running. He was captured by police within the hour in a nearby small town, where he lived. Although he remains incarcerated at this time, awaiting trial, the motivations for his actions are unknown.

Campus police and campus administrators were the first to react to the incident. Campus police arrived within three minutes after they had received a telephone call for help. They spent several anxious minutes outside the building interviewing students to obtain an accurate description of the gunman. Campus administrators responded by calling a news conference for 4:00 P.M. the same day, approximately four hours after the incident. The police chief as well as the vice-chancellor of Student Affairs and two students described the incident at the news conference. That same afternoon, the Student Affairs office contacted Student Health and Employee Assistance Program (EAP) counselors and instructed them to be available for any students or staff requesting assistance. The Student Affairs office also arranged for a new location, where this class could meet for the rest of the semester. The Office of Judicial Affairs suspended the gunman from the university. The next day, the incident was discussed by campus administrators at a regularly scheduled campuswide cabinet meeting. Throughout the week, Student Affairs received several calls from students and from a faculty member about "disturbed" students or unsettling student relations. A counselor of the Employee Assistance Program consulted a psychologist with a specialty in dealing with trauma and responding to educational crises. Only one student immediately set up an appointment with the student health counselors. The campus and local newspapers continued to carry stories about the incident.

When the actuarial science class met for regularly scheduled classes two and four days later, the students and the instructor were visited by two county attorneys, the police chief, and two student mental health counselors who conducted "debriefing" sessions. These sessions focused on keeping students fully informed about the judicial process and having the students and the instructor, one by one, talk about their experiences and explore their feelings about the incident. By one week after the incident, the students in the class had returned to their standard class format. During this time, a few students, women who were concerned about violence in general, saw Student Health Center counselors. These counselors also fielded questions from several dozen parents who inquired about the counseling services and the level of safety on campus. Some parents also called the campus administration to ask about safety procedures.

In the weeks following the incident, the faculty and staff campus newsletter carried articles about post-trauma fears and psychological trauma. The campus administration wrote a letter that provided facts about the incident to the board of the university. The administration also mailed campus staff and students information about crime prevention. At least one college dean sent out a memo to staff about "aberrant student behavior," and one academic department chair requested and held an educational group session with counselors and staff on identifying and dealing with "aberrant behavior" of students.

Three distinctly different staff groups sought counseling services at the Employee Assistance Program, a program for faculty and staff, during the next several weeks. The first group had had some direct involvement with the assailant, either by seeing him the day of the gun incident or because they had known him personally. This group was concerned about securing professional help, either for the students or for those in the group who were personally experiencing effects of the trauma. The second group consisted of the "silent connection," individuals who were indirectly involved and yet emotionally traumatized. This group recognized that their fears were a result of the gunman incident, and they wanted to deal with these fears before they escalated. The third group consisted of staff who had previously experienced a trauma, and this incident had retriggered their fears. Several employees were seen by the EAP throughout the next month, but no new groups or delayed stress cases were reported. The EAP counselors stated that each group's reactions were normal responses. Within a month, although public discussion of the incident had subsided, the EAP and Student Health counselors began expressing the need for a coordinated campus plan to deal with the current as well as any future violent incidents.

The Research Study

We began our study two days after the incident. Our first step was to draft a research protocol for approval by the university administration and the Institutional Review Board. We made explicit that we would not become involved in the investigation of the gunman or in the therapy to students or staff who had sought assistance from counselors. We also limited our study to the reactions of groups on campus rather than expand it to include off-campus groups (for example, television and newspaper coverage). This bounding of the study was consistent with an exploratory qualitative case study design [31], which was chosen because models and variables were not available for assessing a campus reaction to a gun incident in higher education. In the constructionist tradition, this study incorporated the paradigm assumptions of an emerging design, a context-dependent inquiry, and an inductive data analysis [10]. We also bounded the study by time (eight months) and by a single case (the campus community). Consistent with case study design [17, 31], we identified campus administrators and student newspaper reporters as multiple sources of information for initial interviews. Later we expanded interviews to include a wide array of campus informants, using a semi-structured interview protocol that consisted of five questions: What has been your role in the incident? What has happened since the event that you have been involved in? What has been the impact of this incident on the university community? What larger ramifications, if any, exist from the incident? To whom should we talk to find out more about the campus reaction to the incident? We also gathered observational data, documents, and visual materials (see table 1 for types of information and sources).

The narrative structure was a "realist" tale [28], describing details, incorporating edited quotes from informants and stating our interpretations of events, especially an interpretation within the framework of organizational and psychological issues. We verified the description and interpretation by taking a preliminary draft of the case to select informants for feedback and later incorporating their comments into the final study [17, 18]. We gathered this feedback in a group interview where we asked: Is our description of the incident and the reaction accurate? Are the themes and constructs we have identified

TABLE 1   Data Collection Matrix: Type of Information by
Source

Information/ Information Source	Interviews	Observations	Documents	Audio-Visual Materials
Students involved	Yes		Yes	
Students at large	Yes			
Central administration	Yes		Yes	
Campus police	Yes	Yes		
Faculty	Yes	Yes	Yes	
Staff	Yes			
Physical plant		Yes	Yes	
News reporters/papers/television	Yes		Yes	Yes
Student health counselors	Yes			
Employee Assistance Program counselors	Yes			
Trauma expert	Yes		Yes	Yes
Campus businesses			Yes	
Board members			Yes	

consistent with your experiences? Are there some themes and constructs we have missed? Is a campus plan needed? If so, what form should it take?

Themes

Denial

Several weeks later we returned to the classroom where the incident occurred. Instead of finding the desks overturned, we found them to be neatly in order; the room was ready for a lecture or discussion class. The hallway outside the room was narrow, and we visualized how students, on that Monday in October, had quickly left the building, unaware that the gunman, too, was exiting through this same passageway. Many of the students in the hallway during the incident had seemed unaware of what was going on until they saw or heard that there was a gunman in the building. Ironically though, the students had seemed to ignore or deny their dangerous situation. After exiting the building, instead of seeking a hiding place that would be safe, they had huddled together just outside the building. None of the students had barricaded themselves in classrooms or offices or had exited at a safe distance from the scene in anticipation that the gunman might return. "People wanted to stand their ground and stick around," claimed a campus police officer. Failing to respond to the potential danger, the class members had huddled together outside the building; talking nervously. A few had been openly emotional and crying. When asked about their mood, one of the students had said, "Most of us were kidding about it." Their conversations had led one to believe that they were dismissing the incident as though it were trivial and as though no one had actually been in danger. An investigating campus police officer was not surprised by the students' behavior:

> It is not unusual to see people standing around after one of these types of incidents. The American people want to see excitement and have a morbid curiosity. That is why you see spectators hanging around bad accidents. They do not seem to understand the potential danger they are in and do not want to leave until they are injured.

This description corroborates the response reported by mental health counselors: an initial surrealistic first reaction. In the debriefing by counselors, one female student had commented, "I thought the gunman would shoot out a little flag that would say 'bang'." For her, the event had been like a dream. In this atmosphere no one from the targeted class had called the campus mental health center in the first twenty-four hours following the incident, although they knew that services were available. Instead, students described how they had visited with friends or had gone to bars; the severity of the situation had dawned on them later. One student commented that he had felt fearful and angry only after he had seen the television newscast with pictures of the classroom the evening of the incident.

Though some parents had expressed concern by phoning counselors, the students' denial may have been reinforced by parent comments. One student reported that his parents had made comments like, "I am not surprised you were involved in this. You are always getting yourself into things like this!" or "You did not get hurt. What is the big deal? Just let it drop!" One student expressed how much more traumatized he had been as a result of his mother's dismissal of the event. He had wanted to have someone whom he trusted willing to sit down and listen to him.

Fear

Our visit to the classroom suggested a second theme: the response of fear. Still posted on the door several weeks after the incident, we saw the sign announcing that the class was being moved to another undisclosed building and that students were to check with a secretary in an adjoining room about the new location. It was in this undisclosed classroom, two days after the incident, that two student mental health counselors, the campus police chief, and two county attorneys had met with students in the class to discuss fears, reactions, and thoughts. Reactions of fear had begun to surface in this first "debriefing" session and continued to emerge in a second session.

The immediate fear for most students centered around the thought that the alleged assailant would be able to make bail. Students felt that the assailant might have harbored resentment toward certain students and that he would seek retribution if he made bail. "I think I am going to be afraid when I go back to class. They can change the rooms, but there is nothing stopping him from finding out where we are!" said one student. At the first debriefing session the campus police chief was able to dispel some of this fear by announcing that during the initial hearing the judge had denied bail. This announcement helped to reassure some students about their safety. The campus police chief thought it necessary to keep the students informed of the gunman's status, because several students had called his office to say that they feared for their safety if the gunman were released.

During the second debriefing session, another fear surfaced: the possibility that a different assailant could attack the class. One student reacted so severely to this potential threat that, according to one counselor, since the October incident, "he had caught himself walking into class and sitting at a desk with a clear shot to the door. He was beginning to see each classroom as a 'battlefield'." In this second session students had sounded angry, they expressed feeling violated, and finally [they] began to admit that they felt unsafe. Yet only one female student immediately accessed the available mental health services, even though an announcement had been made that any student could obtain free counseling.

The fear students expressed during the "debriefing" sessions mirrored a more general concern on campus about increasingly frequent violent acts in the metropolitan area. Prior to this gun incident, three young females and a male had been kidnapped and had later been found dead in a nearby city. A university football player who experienced a psychotic episode had severely beaten a woman. He had later suffered a relapse and was shot by police in a scuffle. Just three weeks prior to the October gun incident, a female university student had been abducted and brutally murdered, and several other homicides had occurred in the city. As a student news reporter commented, "This whole semester has been a violent one."

Safety

The violence in the city that involved university students and the subsequent gun incident that occurred in a campus classroom shocked the typically tranquil campus. A counselor aptly summed up the feelings of many: "When the students walked out of that classroom, their world had become very chaotic; it had become very random, something had happened that robbed them of their sense of safety." Concern for safety became a central reaction for many informants.

When the chief student affairs officer described the administration's reaction to the incident, he listed the safety of students in the classroom as his primary goal, followed by the needs of the news media for details about the case, helping all students with psychological stress, and providing public information on safety. As he talked about the safety issue and the presence of guns on campus, he mentioned that a policy was under consideration for the storage of guns used by students for hunting. Within four hours after the incident, a press conference was called during which the press was briefed not only on the details of the incident, but also on the need to ensure the safety of the campus. Soon thereafter the university administration initiated an informational campaign on campus safety. A letter, describing the incident, was sent to the university board members. (One board member asked, "How could such an incident happen at this university?") The Student Affairs Office sent a letter to all students in which it advised them of the various dimensions of the campus security office and of the types of services it provided. The Counseling and Psychological Services of the Student Health Center promoted their services in a colorful brochure, which was mailed to students in the following week. It emphasized that services were "confidential, accessible, and professional." The Student Judiciary Office advised academic departments on various methods of dealing with students who exhibited abnormal behavior in class. The weekly faculty newsletter stressed that staff needed to respond quickly to any post-trauma fears associated with this incident. The campus newspaper quoted a professor as saying, "I'm totally shocked that in this environment, something like this would happen." Responding to the concerns about disruptive students or employees, the campus police department sent plainclothes officers to sit outside offices whenever faculty and staff indicated concerns.

An emergency phone system, Code Blue, was installed on campus only ten days after the incident. These thirty-six ten-foot-tall emergency phones, with bright blue flashing lights, had previously been approved, and specific spots had already been identified from an earlier study. "The phones will be quite an attention getter," the director of the Telecommunications Center commented. "We hope they will also be a big detractor [to crime]." Soon afterwards, in response to calls from concerned students, trees and shrubbery in poorly lit areas of campus were trimmed.

Students and parents also responded to these safety concerns. At least twenty-five parents called the Student Health Center, the university police, and the Student Affairs Office during the first week after the incident to inquire what kind of services were available for their students. Many parents had been traumatized by the news of the event and immediately demanded answers from the university. They wanted assurances that this type of incident would not happen again and that their child[ren were] safe on the campus. Undoubtedly, many parents also called their children during the weeks immediately following the incident. The students on campus responded to these safety concerns by forming groups of volunteers who would escort anyone on campus, male or female, during the evening hours.

Local businesses profited by exploiting the commercial aspects of the safety needs created by this incident. Various advertisements for self-defense classes and protection devices inundated the newspapers for several weeks. Campus and local clubs [that] offered self-defense classes filled quickly, and new classes were formed in response to numerous additional requests. The campus bookstore's supply of pocket mace and whistles was quickly depleted. The campus police received several inquiries by students who wanted to purchase handguns to carry for protection. None [was] approved, but one wonders whether some guns were not purchased by students anyway. The purchase of cellular telephones from local vendors increased sharply. Most of these purchases were made by females; however, some males also sought out these items for their safety and protection. Not unexpectedly, the price of some products was raised as much as 40 percent to capitalize on the newly created demand. Student conversations centered around the purchase of these safety products: how much they cost, how to use them correctly, how accessible they would be if students should need to use them, and whether they were really necessary.

Retriggering

In our original protocol, which we designed to seek approval from the campus administration and the Institutional Review Board, we had outlined a study that would last only three months—a reasonable time, we thought, for this incident to run its course. But during early interviews with counselors, we were referred to a psychologist who specialized in dealing with "trauma" in educational settings. It was this psychologist who mentioned the theme of "retriggering." Now, eight months later, we begin to understand how, through "retriggering," that October incident could have a long-term effect on this campus.

This psychologist explained retriggering as a process by which new incidents of violence would cause individuals to relive the feelings of fear, denial, and threats to personal safety that they had experienced in connection with the original event. The counseling staffs and violence expert also stated that one should expect to see such feelings retriggered at a later point in time, for example, on the anniversary date of the attack or whenever newspapers or television broadcasts mentioned the incident again. They added that a drawn-out judicial process, during which a case were "kept alive" through legal maneuvering, could cause a long period of retriggering and thereby greatly thwart the healing process. The fairness of the judgment of the court as seen by each victim, we were told, would also influence the amount of healing and resolution of feelings that could occur.

As of this writing, it is difficult to detect specific evidence of retriggering from the October incident, but we discovered the potential consequences of this process firsthand by observing the effects of a nearly identical violent gun incident that had happened some eighteen years earlier. A graduate student carrying a rifle had entered a campus building with the intention of shooting the department chairman. The student was seeking revenge, because several years earlier he had flunked a course taught by this professor. This attempted attack followed several years of legal maneuvers to arrest, prosecute, and incarcerate this student, who, on more than one occasion, had tried to carry out his plan but each time had been thwarted by quick-thinking staff members who would not reveal the professor's whereabouts. Fortunately, no shots were ever fired, and the student was finally apprehended and arrested.

The professor who was the target of these threats on his life was seriously traumatized not only during the period of these repeated incidents, but his trauma continued even after the attacker's arrest. The complex processes of the criminal justice system, which, he believed, did not work as it should have, resulted in his feeling further victimized. To this day, the feelings aroused by the original trauma are retriggered each time a gun incident is reported in the news. He was not offered professional help from the university at any time; the counseling services he did receive were secured through his own initiative. Eighteen years later his entire department is still affected in that unwritten rules for dealing with disgruntled students and for protecting this particular professor's schedule have been established.

Campus Planning

The question of campus preparedness surfaced during discussions with the psychologist about the process of "debriefing" individuals who had been involved in the October incident [19]. Considering how many diverse groups and individuals had been affected by this incident, a final theme that emerged from our data was the need for a campuswide plan. A counselor remarked, "We would have been inundated had there been twenty-five to thirty deaths. We need a mobilized plan of communication. It would be a wonderful addition to the campus considering the nature of today's violent world." It became apparent during our interviews that better communication could have occurred among the constituents who responded to this incident. Of course, one campus police officer noted, "We can't have an officer in every building all day long!" But the theme of being prepared across the whole campus was mentioned by several individuals.

The lack of a formal plan to deal with such gun incidents was surprising, given the existence of formal written plans on campus that addressed various other emergencies: bomb threats, chemical spills, fires, earthquakes, explosions, electrical storms, radiation accidents, tornadoes, hazardous material spills, snowstorms, and numerous medical emergencies. Moreover, we found that specific campus units had their own protocols that had actually been used during the October gun incident. For example, the police had a procedure and used that procedure for dealing with the gunman and the students at the scene; the EAP counselors debriefed staff and faculty; the Student Health counselors used a "debriefing" process when they visited the students twice in the classroom following the incident. The question that concerned us was, what would a campuswide plan consist of, and how would it be developed and evaluated?

As shown in table 2, using evidence gathered in our case, we assembled the basic questions to be addressed in a plan and cross-referenced these questions to the literature about post-trauma stress, campus violence, and the disaster literature (for a similar list drawn from the public school literature, see Poland and Pitcher [21]). Basic

TABLE 2   Evidence From the Case, Questions for a Campus
Plan, and References

Evidence From the Case	Question for the Plan	References Useful
Need expressed by counselors	Why should a plan be developed?	Walker (1990); Bird et al. (1991)
Multiple constituents reacting to incident	Who should be involved in developing the plan?	Roark & Roark (1987); Walker (1990)
Leadership found in units with their own protocols	Should the leadership for coordinating be identified within one office?	Roark & Roark (1987)
Several unit protocols being used in incident	Should campus units be allowed their own protocols?	Roark & Roark (1987)
Questions raised by students reacting to case	What types of violence should be covered in the plan?	Roark (1987); Jones (1990)
Groups/individuals surfaced during our interviews	How are those likely to be affected by the incident to be identified?	Walker (1990); Bromet (1990)
Comments from campus police, central administration	What provisions are made for the immediate safety of those in the incident?	
Campus environment changed after incident	How should the physical environment be made safer?	Roark & Roark (1987)
Comments from central administration	How will the external publics (e.g., press, businesses) be appraised of the incident?	Poland & Pitcher (1990)
Issue raised by counselors and trauma specialist	What are the likely sequelae of psychological events for victims?	Bromet (1990); Mitchell (1983)
Issue raised by trauma specialist	What long-term impact will the incident have on victims?	Zelikoff (1987)
Procedure used by Student Health Center counselors	How will the victims be debriefed?	Mitchell (1983); Walker (1990)

elements of a campus plan to enhance communication across units should include determining what the rationale for the plan is; who should be involved in its development; how it should be coordinated; how it should be staffed; and what specific procedures should be followed. These procedures might include responding to an immediate crisis, making the campus safe, dealing with external groups, and providing for the psychological welfare of victims.

Discussion

The themes of denial, fear, safety, retriggering, and developing a campuswide plan might further be grouped into two categories, an organizational and a psychological or social-psychological response of the campus community to the gunman incident. Organizationally, the campus units responding to the crisis exhibited both a loose coupling [30] and an interdependent communication. Issues such as leadership, communication, and authority emerged during the case analysis. Also, an environmental response developed, because the campus was transformed into a safer place for students and staff. The need for centralized planning, while allowing for autonomous operation of units in response to a crisis, called for organizational change that would require cooperation and coordination among units.

Sherrill [27] provides models of response to campus violence that reinforce as well as depart from the evidence in our case. As mentioned by Sherrill, the disciplinary action taken against a perpetrator, the group counseling of victims, and the use of safety education for the campus community were all factors apparent in our case. However, Sherrill raises issues about responses that were not discussed by our informants, such as developing procedures for individuals who are first to arrive on the scene, dealing with non-students who might be perpetrators or victims, keeping records and documents about incidents, varying responses based on the size and nature of the institution, and relating incidents to substance abuse such as drugs and alcohol.

Also, some of the issues that we had expected after reading the literature about organizational response did not emerge. Aside from occasional newspaper reports (focused mainly on the gunman), there was little campus administrative response to the incident, which was contrary to what we had expected from Roark and Roark [25], for example. No mention was made of establishing a campus unit to manage future incidents—for example, a campus violence resource center—reporting of violent incidents [25], or conducting annual safety audits [20]. Aside from the campus police mentioning that the State Health Department would have been prepared to send a team of trained trauma experts to help emergency personnel cope with the tragedy, no discussion was reported about formal linkages with community agencies that might assist in the event of a tragedy [3]. We also did not hear directly about establishing a "command center" [14] or a crisis coordinator [21], two actions recommended by specialists on crisis situations.

On a psychological and social-psychological level, the campus response was to react to the psychological needs of the students who had been directly involved in the incident as well as to students and staff who had been indirectly affected by the incident. Not only did signs of psychological issues, such as denial, fear, and retriggering, emerge, as expected [15], gender and cultural group issues were also mentioned, though they were not discussed enough to be considered basic themes in our analysis. Contrary to assertions in the literature that violent behavior is often accepted in our culture, we found informants in our study to voice concern and fear about escalating violence on campus and in the community.

Faculty on campus were conspicuously silent on the incident, including the faculty senate, though we had expected this governing body to take up the issue of aberrant student or faculty behavior in their classrooms [25]. Some informants speculated that the faculty might have been passive about this issue because they were unconcerned, but another explanation might be that they were passive because they were unsure of what to do or whom to ask for assistance. From the students we failed to hear that they responded to their post-traumatic stress with "coping" strategies, such as relaxation, physical activity, and the establishment of normal routines [29]. Although the issues of gender and race surfaced in early conversations with informants, we did not find a direct discussion of these issues. As Bromet [5] comments, the sociocultural needs of populations with different mores must be considered when individuals assess reactions to trauma. In regard to the issue of gender, we did hear that females were the first students to seek out counseling at the Student Health Center. Perhaps our "near-miss" case was unique. We do not know what the reaction of the campus might have been had a death (or multiple deaths) occurred, although, according to the trauma psychologist, "the trauma of no deaths is as great as if deaths had occurred." Moreover, as with any exploratory case analysis, this case has limited generalizability [17], although thematic generalizability is certainly a possibility. The fact that our information was self-reported and that we were unable to interview all students who had been directly affected by the incident so as to not intervene in student therapy or the investigation also poses a problem.

Despite these limitations, our research provides a detailed account of a campus reaction to a violent incident with the potential for making a contribution to the literature. Events emerged during the process of reaction that could be "critical incidents" in future studies, such as the victim response, media reporting, the debriefing process, campus changes, and the evolution of a campus plan. With the scarcity of literature on campus violence related to gun incidents, this study breaks new ground by identifying themes and conceptual frameworks that could be examined in future cases. On a practical level, it can benefit campus administrators who are looking for a plan to respond to campus violence, and it focuses attention on questions that need to be addressed in such a plan. The large number of different groups of people who were affected by this particular gunman incident shows the complexity of responding to a campus crisis and should alert college personnel to the need for preparedness.

Epilogue

As we conducted this study, we asked ourselves whether we would have had access to informants if someone had been killed. This "near-miss" incident provided a unique research opportunity, which could, however, only approximate an event in which a fatality had actually occurred. Our involvement in this study was serendipitous, for one of us had been employed by a correctional facility and therefore had direct experience with gunmen such as the individual in our case; the other was a University of Iowa graduate and thus familiar with the setting and circumstances surrounding another violent incident there in 1992. These experiences obviously affected our assessment of this case by drawing our attention to the campus response in the first plan and to psychological reactions like fear and denial. At the time of this writing, campus discussions have been held about adapting the in-place campus emergency preparedness plan to a critical incident management team concept. Counselors have met to discuss coordinating the activities of different units in the event of another incident, and the police are working with faculty members and department staff to help identify potentially violence-prone students. We have the impression that, as a result of this case study, campus personnel see the interrelatedness and the large number of units that may be involved in a single incident. The anniversary date passed without incident or acknowledgment in the campus newspaper. As for the gunman, he is still incarcerated awaiting trial, and we wonder, as do some of the students he threatened, if he will seek retribution against us for writing up this case if he is released. The campus response to the October incident continues.

References

1. Asmussen, K. J. "Weapon Possession in Public High Schools." *School Safety* (Fall 1992), 28-30.

2. Bird, G. W., S. M. Stith, and J. Schladale. "Psychological Resources, Coping Strategies, and Negotiation Styles as Discriminators of Violence in Dating Relationships." *Family Relations*, 40 (1991), 45-50.

3. Bogal-Allbritten, R., and W. Allbritten. "Courtship Violence on Campus: A Nationwide Survey of Student Affairs Professionals." *NASPA Journal*, 28 (1991), 312-18.

4. Boothe, J. W., T. M. Flick, S. P. Kirk, L. H. Bradley, and K. E. Keough. "The Violence at Your Door." *Executive Educator* (February 1993), 16-22.

5. Bromet, E. J. "Methodological Issues in the Assessment of Traumatic Events." *Journal of Applied Psychology*, 20 (1990), 1719-24.

6. Bushweller, K. "Guards with Guns." *American School Board Journal* (January 1993), 34-36.

7. Copenhaver, S., and E. Grauerholz. "Sexual Victimization among Sorority Women." *Sex Roles: A Journal of Research*, 24 (1991), 31-41.

8. Follingstad, D., S. Wright, S. Lloyd, and J. Sebastian. "Sex Differences in Motivations and Effects in Dating Violence." *Family Relations*, 40 (1991), 51-57.

9. Gordon, M. T., and S. Riger. *The Female Fear*. Urbana: University of Illinois Press, 1991.

10. Guba, E., and Y. Lincoln. "Do Inquiry Paradigms Imply Inquiry Methodologies?" In *Qualitative Approaches to Evaluation in Education*, edited by D. M. Fetterman. New York: Praeger, 1988.

11. Johnson, K. "The Tip of the Iceberg." *School Safety* (Fall 1992), 24-26.

12. Jones, D. J. "The College Campus as a Microcosm of U.S. Society: The Issue of Racially Motivated Violence." *Urban League Review*, 13 (1990), 129-39.

13. Legislative Update. "Campuses Must Tell Crime Rates." *School Safety* (Winter 1991), 31.

14. Long, N. J. "Managing a Shooting Incident." *Journal of Emotional and Behavioral Problems*, 1 (1992), 23-26.

15. Lowe, J. A. "What We Learned: Some Generalizations in Dealing with a Traumatic Event at Cokeville." Paper presented at the Annual Meeting of the National School Boards Association, San Francisco, 4-7 April 1987.

16. Mann, J. *Los Angeles Times Magazine*, 2 June 1992, pp. 26-27, 32, 46-47.

17. Merriam, S. B. *Case Study Research in Education: A Qualitative Approach*. San Francisco: Jossey-Bass, 1988.

18. Miles, M. B., and A. M. Huberman. *Qualitative Data Analysis: A Sourcebook of New Methods*. Beverly Hills, Calif.: Sage, 1984.

19. Mitchell, J. "When Disaster Strikes." *Journal of Emergency Medical Services* (January 1983), 36-39.

20. NSSC Report on School Safety. "Preparing Schools for Terroristic Attacks." *School Safety* (Winter 1991), 18-19.

21. Poland, S., and G. Pitcher. *Crisis Intervention in the Schools*. New York: Guilford, 1992.

22. Quimet, M. "The Polytechnique Incident and Imitative Violence against Women." *SSR*, 76 (1992), 45-47.

23. Roark, M. L. "Helping High School Students Assess Campus Safety." *The School Counselor*, 39 (1992), 251-56.

24. ———. "Preventing Violence on College Campuses." *Journal of Counseling and Development*, 65 (1987), 367-70.

25. Roark, M. L., and E. W. Roark. "Administrative Responses to Campus Violence." Paper presented at the annual meeting of the American College Personnel Association/National Association of Student Personnel Administrators, Chicago, 15-18 March 1987.

26. "School Crisis: Under Control," 1991 [video]. National School Safety Center, a partnership of Pepperdine University and the United States Departments of Justice and Education.

27. Sherill, J. M., and D. G. Seigel (eds.). *Responding to Violence on Campus*. New Directions for Student Services, No. 47. San Francisco: Jossey-Bass, 1989.

28. Van Maanen, J. *Tales of the Field*. Chicago: University of Chicago Press, 1988.

29. Walker, G. "Crisis-Care in Critical Incident Debriefing." *Death Studies*, 14 (1990), 121-33.

30. Weick, K. E. "Educational Organizations as Loosely Coupled Systems." *Administrative Science Quarterly*, 21 (1976), 1-19.

31. Yin, R. K. *Case Study Research, Design and Methods*. Newbury Park, Calif.: Sage, 1989.

32. Zelikoff, W. I., and I. A. Hyman. "Psychological Trauma in the Schools: A Retrospective Study." Paper presented at the annual meeting of the National Association of School Psychologists, New Orleans, La., 4-8 March 1987.

References

Aanstoos, C. M. (1985). The structure of thinking in chess. In A. Giorgi (Ed.), *Phenomenology and psychological research* (pp. 86-117). Pittsburgh, PA: Duquesne University Press.

Agar, M. H. (1980). *The professional stranger: An informal introduction to ethnography*. San Diego: Academic Press.

Agar, M. H. (1986). *Speaking of ethnography*. Beverly Hills, CA: Sage.

Agger, B. (1991). Critical theory, poststructuralism, postmodernism: Their sociological relevance. In W. R. Scott & J. Blake (Eds.), *Annual review of sociology* (Vol. 17, pp. 105-131). Palo Alto, CA: Annual Reviews.

Allport, G. W. (1942). *The uses of personal documents in psychological science*. New York: Social Science Research Council.

Angrosino, M. V. (1989a). *Documents of interaction: Biography, autobiography, and life history in social science perspective*. Gainesville: University of Florida Press.

Angrosino, M. V. (1989b). Freddie: The personal narrative of a recovering alcoholic—Autobiography as case history. In M. V. Angrosino, *Documents of interaction: Biography, autobiography, and life history in social science perspective* (pp. 29-41). Gainesville: University of Florida Press.

Angrosino, M. V. (1994). On the bus with Vonnie Lee. *Journal of Contemporary Ethnography, 23*, 14-28.

Asmussen, K. J., & Creswell, J. W. (1995). Campus response to a student gunman. *Journal of Higher Education, 66,* 575-591.

Atkinson, P., & Hammersley, M. (1994). Ethnography and participant observation. In N. K. Denzin & Y. S. Lincoln (Eds.), *Handbook of qualitative research* (pp. 248-261). Thousand Oaks, CA: Sage.

Bailey, K. D. (1978). *Methods of social research.* New York: Free Press.

Barritt, L. (1986). Human sciences and the human image. *Phenomenology and Pedagogy, 4*(3), 14-22.

Barzun, J., & Graff, H. (1992). *The modern researcher* (5th ed.). New York: Harcourt Brace Jovanovich.

Bernard, H. R. (1994). *Research methods in anthropology: Qualitative and quantitative approaches* (2nd ed.). Thousand Oaks, CA: Sage.

Bertaux, D. (1981). *Biography and society: The life history approach in the social sciences.* Beverly Hills, CA: Sage.

Bertaux, D., & Bertaux-Wiame, I. (1981). Life stories in the bakers' trade. In D. Bertaux (Ed.), *Biography and society: The life history approach in the social sciences* (pp. 169-190). Beverly Hills, CA: Sage.

Bloland, H. G. (1995). Postmodernism and higher education. *Journal of Higher Education, 66,* 521-559.

Bogdan, R. C., & Biklen, S. K. (1992). *Qualitative research for education: An introduction to theory and methods.* Boston: Allyn & Bacon.

Bogdan, R., & Taylor, S. (1975). *Introduction to qualitative research methods.* New York: John Wiley.

Bogdewic, S. P. (1992). Participant observation. In B. F. Crabtree & W. L. Miller (Eds.), *Doing qualitative research* (pp. 45-69). Newbury Park, CA: Sage.

Borgatta, E. F., & Borgatta, M. L. (Eds.). (1992). *Encyclopedia of sociology* (Vol. 4). New York: Macmillan.

Bowen, C. D. (1969). *Biography: The craft and the calling.* Boston: Little, Brown.

Boyle, J., & McKay, J. (1995). "You leave your troubles at the gate": A case study of the exploitation of older women's labor and "leisure" in sport. *Gender & Society, 9,* 556-575.

Brickhous, N., & Bodner, G. M. (1992). The beginning science teacher: Classroom narratives of convictions and constraints. *Journal of Research in Science Teaching, 29,* 471-485.

Bruckerhoff, C. E. (1991) *Between classes: Faculty life at Truman High.* New York: Columbia University, Teachers College Press.

Buber, M. (1958). *I and thou* (2nd ed.; R. G. Smith, Ed. and Trans.). New York: Scribner.

Burrell, G., & Morgan, G. (1979). *Sociological paradigms and organizational analysis.* London: Heinemann.

Carspecken, P. F., & Apple, M. (1992). Critical qualitative research: Theory, methodology, and practice. In M. L. LeCompte, W. L. Millroy, & J. Preissle (Eds.), *The handbook of qualitative research in education* (pp. 507-553). San Diego: Academic Press.

Chapin, F. S. (1920). *Field work and social research.* New York: Century.

Charmaz, K. (1983). The grounded theory method: An explication and interpretation. In R. Emerson (Ed.), *Contemporary field research* (pp. 109-126). Boston: Little, Brown.

Chenitz, W. C., & Swanson, J. M. (1986). *From practice to grounded theory: Qualitative research in nursing.* Menlo Park, CA: Addison-Wesley.

Clifford, J. L. (1970). *From puzzles to portraits: Problems of a literary biographer.* Chapel Hill: University of North Carolina Press.

Clifford, J., & Marcus, G. E. (Eds.). (1986). *Writing culture: The poetics and politics of ethnography.* Berkeley: University of California Press.

Colaizzi, P. F. (1978). Psychological research as the phenomenologist views it. In R. Vaile & M. King (Eds.), *Existential phenomenological alternatives for psychology* (pp. 48-71). New York: Oxford University Press.

Cole, A. (1994, April). *Doing life history research in theory and in practice.* Paper prepared for the annual meeting of the American Educational Research Association, New Orleans, LA.

Conrad, C. F. (1978). A grounded theory of academic change. *Sociology of Education, 51,* 101-112.

Corbin, J., & Strauss, A. (1990). Grounded theory research: Procedures, canons, and evaluative criteria. *Qualitative Sociology, 13*(1), 3-21.

Cottle, T. J. (1991). A family prepares for college. *Journal of Higher Education, 62,* 79-86.

Crabtree, B. F., & Miller, W. L. (1992). *Doing qualitative research.* Newbury Park, CA: Sage.

Creswell, J. W. (1994). *Research design: Qualitative and quantitative approaches.* Thousand Oaks, CA: Sage.

Creswell, J. W., & Brown, M. L. (1992). How chairpersons enhance faculty research: A grounded theory study. *Review of Higher Education, 16*(1), 41-62.

Creswell, J. W., & Miller, D. L. (1997). *Validity (verification) in qualitative research: Perspectives, terms, procedures, and methodologies.* Unpublished manuscript, Department of Educational Psychology, University of Nebraska–Lincoln.

Creswell, J. W., & Urbom, J. (1997). *A theory of balance between personal and professional lives for academic chairpersons.* Unpublished manuscript, Department of Educational Psychology, University of Nebraska–Lincoln.

Cunningham, J. W., & Fitzgerald, J. (1996). Epistemology and reading. *Reading Research Quarterly, 31*(1), 36-60.

Davidson, F. (1996). *Principles of statistical data handling.* Thousand Oaks, CA: Sage.

Denzin, N. K. (1970). *The research act: A theoretical introduction to sociological methods.* Chicago: Aldine.

Denzin, N. K. (1989a). *Interpretive biography.* Newbury Park, CA: Sage.

Denzin, N. K. (1989b). *Interpretive interactionism.* Newbury Park, CA: Sage.

Denzin, N. K., & Lincoln, Y. S. (1994). *Handbook of qualitative research.* Thousand Oaks, CA: Sage.

Derrida, J. (1981). *Positions.* Chicago: University of Chicago Press.

Dey, I. (1993). *Qualitative data analysis: A user-friendly guide for social scientists.* London: Routledge.

Dey, I. (1995). Reducing fragmentation in qualitative research. In U. Keele (Ed.), *Computer-aided qualitative data analysis* (pp. 69-79). Thousand Oaks, CA: Sage.

Dollard, J. (1935). *Criteria for the life history: With an analysis of six notable documents.* New Haven, CT: Yale University Press.

Drew, N. (1986). Exclusion and confirmation: A phenomenology of patients' experiences with caregivers. *Image: Journal of Nursing Scholarship, 18*(2), 39-43.

Dukes, S. (1984). Phenomenological methodology in the human sciences. *Journal of Religion and Health, 23*(3), 197-203.

Edel, L. (1984). *Writing lives: Principia biographica.* New York: Norton.

Eisner, E. W. (1991). *The enlightened eye: Qualitative inquiry and the enhancement of educational practice.* New York: Macmillan.

Ely, M., Anzul, M., Friedman, T., Garner, D., & Steinmetz, A. C. (1991). *Doing qualitative research: Circles within circles.* New York: Falmer.

Emerson, R. M., Fretz, R. I., & Shaw, L. L. (1995). *Writing ethnographic fieldnotes.* Chicago: University of Chicago Press.

Erlandson, D. A., Harris, E. L., Skipper, B. L., & Allen, S. D. (1993). *Doing naturalistic inquiry: A guide to methods.* Newbury Park, CA: Sage.

Fay, B. (1987). *Critical social science.* Ithaca, NY: Cornell University Press.

Ferguson, M., & Wicke, J. (1994). *Feminism and postmodernism.* Durham, NC: Duke University Press.

Fetterman, D. M. (1987, April). *Qualitative approaches to evaluation research.* Paper presented at the annual conference of the American Educational Research Association, Washington, DC.

Fetterman, D. M. (1989). *Ethnography: Step by step.* Newbury Park, CA: Sage.

Field, P. A., & Morse, J. M. (1985). *Nursing research: The application of qualitative approaches.* Rockville, MD: Aspen Systems.

Fischer, C. T., & Wertz, F. J. (1979). An empirical phenomenology study of being criminally victimized. In A. Giorgi, R. Knowles, & D. Smith (Eds.), *Duquesne studies in phenomenological psychology* (Vol. 3, pp. 135-158). Pittsburgh, PA: Duquesne University Press.

Flinders, D. J., & Mills, G. E. (1993). *Theory and concepts in qualitative research.* New York: Columbia University, Teachers College Press.

Fox-Keller, E. (1985). *Reflections on gender and science.* New Haven, CT: Yale University Press.

Frontman, K. C., & Kunkel, M. A. (1994). A grounded theory of counselors' construal of success in the initial session. *Journal of Counseling Psychology, 41,* 492-499.

Geertz, C. (1973). Deep play: Notes on the Balinese cockfight. In C. Geertz (Ed.), *The interpretation of cultures: Selected essays* (pp. 412-435). New York: Basic Books.

Geertz, C. (1995). *After the fact: Two countries, four decades, one anthropologist.* Cambridge, MA: Harvard University Press.

Geiger, S. N. G. (1986). Women's life histories: Method and content. *Signs: Journal of Women in Culture and Society, 11,* 334-351.

Gilchrist, V. J. (1992). Key informant interviews. In B. F. Crabtree & W. L. Miller (Eds.), *Doing qualitative research* (pp. 70-89). Newbury Park, CA: Sage.

Gioia, D. A., & Pitre, E. (1990). Multiparadigm perspectives on theory building. *Management Review, 15,* 584-602.

Giorgi, A. (1975). An application of phenomenological method in psychology. In A. Giorgi, C. T. Fischer, & E. L. Murray (Eds.), *Duquesne studies in phenomenological psychology* (Vol. 2, pp. 82-103). Pittsburgh, PA: Duquesne University Press.

Giorgi, A. (Ed.). (1985). *Phenomenology and psychological research.* Pittsburgh, PA: Duquesne University Press.

Giorgi, A. (1994). A phenomenological perspective on certain qualitative research methods. *Journal of Phenomenological Psychology, 25,* 190-220.

Glaser, B. G. (1978). *Theoretical sensitivity.* Mill Valley, CA: Sociology Press.

Glaser, B. G. (1992). *Basics of grounded theory analysis*. Mill Valley, CA: Sociology Press.

Glaser, B., & Strauss, A. (1965). *Awareness of dying*. Chicago: Aldine.

Glaser, B., & Strauss, A. (1967). *The discovery of grounded theory*. Chicago: Aldine.

Glaser, B., & Strauss, A. (1968). *Time for dying*. Chicago: Aldine.

Glesne, C., & Peshkin, A. (1992). *Becoming qualitative researchers: An introduction*. White Plains, NY: Longman.

Goetz, J. P., & LeCompte, M. D. (1984). *Ethnography and qualitative design in educational research*. Orlando, FL: Academic Press.

Goffman, E. (1989). On fieldwork. *Journal of Contemporary Ethnography, 18*, 123-132.

Grigsby, K. A., & Megel, M. E. (1995). Caring experiences of nurse educators. *Journal of Nursing Research, 34*, 411-418.

Gritz, J. I. (1995). *Voices from the classroom: Understanding teacher professionalism*. Unpublished manuscript, Administration, Curriculum, and Instruction, University of Nebraska–Lincoln.

Guba, E., & Lincoln, Y. S. (1988). Do inquiry paradigms imply inquiry methodologies? In D. M. Fetterman (Ed.), *Qualitative approaches to evaluation in education* (pp. 89-115). New York: Praeger.

Guba, E. G., & Lincoln, Y. S. (1989). *Fourth generation evaluation*. Newbury Park, CA: Sage.

Guba, E. G., & Lincoln, Y. S. (1994). Competing paradigms in qualitative research. In N. K. Denzin & Y. S. Lincoln (Eds.), *Handbook of qualitative research* (pp. 105-117). Thousand Oaks, CA: Sage.

Hamel, J. (1993). *Case study methods*. Newbury Park, CA: Sage.

Hammersley, M., & Atkinson, P. (1995). *Ethnography: Principles in practice* (2nd ed.). New York: Routledge.

Harding, S. (1987). *Feminism and methodology*. Bloomington: Indiana University Press.

Harper, W. (1981). The experience of leisure. *Leisure Sciences, 4*, 113-126.

Harris, M. (1968). *The rise of anthropological theory: A history of theories of culture*. New York: T. Y. Crowell.

Heilbrun, C. G. (1988). *Writing a woman's life*. New York: Ballantine.

Heinrich, K. T. (1995). Doctoral advisement relationships between women. *Journal of Higher Education, 66*, 447-469.

Helling, I. K. (1988). The life history method: A survey and discussion with Norman K. Denzin. *Studies in Symbolic Interaction, 9*, 211-243.

Hill, B., Vaughn, C., & Harrison, S. B. (1995, September/October). Living and working in two worlds: Case studies of five American Indian women teachers. *The Clearinghouse, 69*(1), pp. 42-48.

Hoshmand, L. L. S. T. (1989). Alternative research paradigms: A review and teaching proposal. *The Counseling Psychologist, 17*(1), 3-79.

Howe, K., & Eisenhardt, M. (1990). Standards for qualitative (and quantitative) research: A prolegomenon. *Educational Researcher, 19*(4), 2-9.

Huberman, A. M., & Miles, M. B. (1994). Data management and analysis methods. In N. K. Denzin & Y. S. Lincoln (Eds.), *Handbook of qualitative research* (pp. 428-444). Thousand Oaks, CA: Sage.

Humphrey, E. (1991). *Searching for life's meaning: A phenomenological and heuristic exploration of the experience of searching for meaning in life.* Doctoral dissertation, Union Institute.

Husserl, E. (1931). *Ideas: General introduction to pure phenomenology* (D. Carr, Trans.). Evanston, IL: Northwestern University Press.

Husserl, E. (1970). *The crisis of European sciences and transcendental phenomenology* (D. Carr, Trans.). Evanston, IL: Northwestern University Press.

Hutchison, S. A. (1986). Creating meaning: A grounded theory of NICU nurses. In W. C. Chenitz & J. M. Swanson (Eds.), *From practice to grounded theory* (pp. 191-204). Menlo Park, CA: Addison-Wesley.

Jacob, E. (1987). Qualitative research traditions: A review. *Review of Educational Research, 57*, 1-50.

Johnson, J. M., & Ferraro, K. J. (1984). The victimized self: The case of battered women. In J. A. Kotarba & A. Fontane (Eds.), *The existential self in society* (pp. 119-130). Chicago: University of Chicago Press.

Johnson, J., Holcombe, M., Simms, G., & Wilson, D. (1992). Writing in the classroom: Case studies of three home economics teachers. *Journal of Vocational Home Economics Education, 10*(1), 46-58.

Jorgensen, D. L. (1989). *Participant observation: A methodology for human studies.* Newbury Park, CA: Sage.

Karen, C. S. (1990, April). *Personal development and the pursuit of higher education: An exploration of interrelationships in the growth of self-identity in returning women students—Summary of research in progress.* Paper presented at the annual meeting of the American Educational Research Association, Boston.

Kearney, M. H., Murphy, S., & Rosenbaum, M. (1994). Mothering on crack cocaine: A grounded theory analysis. *Social Science Medicine, 38*(2), 351-361.

Kelle, E. (Ed.). (1995). *Computer-aided qualitative data analysis*. Thousand Oaks, CA: Sage.

Kerlinger, F. N. (1964). *Foundations of behavioral research: Educational and psychological inquiry*. New York: Holt, Rinehart & Winston.

Kerlinger, F. N. (1979). *Behavioral research: A conceptual approach*. New York: Holt, Rinehart & Winston.

Kidder, L. (1982). Face validity from multiple perspectives. In D. Brinberg & L. Kidder (Eds.), *New directions for methodology of social and behavioral science: Forms of validity in research* (pp. 41-57). San Francisco: Jossey-Bass.

Kincheloe, J. L. (1991). *Teachers as researchers: Qualitative inquiry as a path of empowerment*. London: Falmer.

Krueger, R. A. (1994). *Focus groups: A practical guide for applied research* (2nd ed.). Thousand Oaks, CA: Sage.

Kus, R. J. (1986). From grounded theory to clinical practice: Cases from gay studies research. In W. C. Chenitz & J. M. Swanson (Eds.), *From practice to grounded theory* (pp. 227-240). Menlo Park, CA: Addison-Wesley.

Kvale, S. (1996). *InterViews: An introduction to qualitative research interviewing*. Thousand Oaks, CA: Sage.

Lancy, D. F. (1993). *Qualitative research in education: An introduction to the major traditions*. New York: Longman.

Landis, M. M. (1993). *A theory of interaction in the satellite learning classroom*. Unpublished doctoral dissertation, University of Nebraska–Lincoln.

Langness, L. L. (1965). *The life history in anthropological science*. New York: Holt, Rinehart & Winston.

Lather, P. (1991). *Getting smart: Feminist research and pedagogy with/in the postmodern*. New York: Routledge.

Lather, P. (1993). Fertile obsession: Validity after poststructuralism. *Sociological Quarterly, 34*, 673-693.

Lauterbach, S. S. (1993). In another world: A phenomenological perspective and discovery of meaning in mothers' experience with death of a wished-for baby: Doing phenomenology. In P. L. Munhall & C. O. Boyd (Eds.), *Nursing research: A qualitative perspective* (pp. 133-179). New York: National League for Nursing Press.

LeCompte, M. D., & Goetz, J. P. (1982). Problems of reliability and validity in ethnographic research. *Review of Educational Research, 51*, 31-60.

LeCompte, M. D., Millroy, W. L., & Preissle, J. (1992). *The handbook of qualitative research in education*. San Diego: Academic Press.

Lincoln, Y. S. (1995). Emerging criteria for quality in qualitative and interpretive research. *Qualitative Inquiry, 1*, 275-289.

Lincoln, Y. S., & Guba, E. G. (1985). *Naturalistic inquiry*. Beverly Hills, CA: Sage.

Lofland, J. (1974). Styles of reporting qualitative field research. *American Sociologist, 9*, 101-111.

Lofland, J., & Lofland, L. H. (1995). *Analyzing social settings: A guide to qualitative observation and analysis* (3rd ed.). Belmont, CA: Wadsworth.

Lomask, M. (1986). *The biographer's craft*. New York: Harper & Row.

Lonkila, M. (1995). Grounded theory as an emerging paradigm for computer-assisted qualitative data analysis. In U. Kelle (Ed.), *Computer-aided qualitative data analysis: Theory, methods and practice* (pp. 41-51). Thousand Oaks, CA: Sage.

Marcel, G. (1971). *The philosophy of existence* (R. F. Grabow, Ed. and Trans.). Philadelphia: University of Pennsylvania Press.

Marshall, C., & Rossman, G. B. (1995). *Designing qualitative research* (2nd ed.). Thousand Oaks, CA: Sage.

Martens, M. L. (1992). Inhibitors to implementing a problem-solving approach to teaching elementary science: Case study of a teacher in change. *Social Science and Mathematics, 93*, 150-156.

Mastera, G. (1995). *The process of revising general education curricula in three private baccalaureate colleges*. Unpublished manuscript, Administration, Curriculum, and Instruction, University of Nebraska–Lincoln.

Maxwell, J. (1996). *Qualitative research design: An interactive approach*. Thousand Oaks, CA: Sage.

May, K. A. (1986). Writing and evaluating the grounded theory research report. In W. C. Chenitz & J. M. Swanson (Eds.), *From practice to grounded theory* (pp. 146-154). Menlo Park, CA: Addison-Wesley.

McCormick, S. (1994). A nonreader becomes a reader: A case study of literacy acquisition by a severely disabled reader. *Reading Research Quarterly, 29*(2), 157-176.

McCracken, G. (1988). *The long interview*. Newbury Park, CA: Sage.

Medoff, P., & Sklar, H. (1994). *Streets of hope: The fall and rise of an urban neighborhood*. Boston: South End.

Meloy, J. M. (1994). *Writing the qualitative dissertation: Understanding by doing*. Hillsdale, NJ: Lawrence Erlbaum.

Merleau-Ponty, M. (1962). *Phenomenology of perception* (C. Smith, Trans.). London: Routledge and Kegan Paul.

Merriam, S. (1988). *Case study research in education: A qualitative approach*. San Francisco: Jossey-Bass.

Miles, M. B., & Huberman, A. M. (1994). *Qualitative data analysis: A sourcebook of new methods* (2nd ed.). Thousand Oaks, CA: Sage.

Miller, W. L., & Crabtree, B. F. (1992). Primary care research: A multimethod typology and qualitative road map. In B. F. Crabtree & W. L. Miller (Eds.), *Doing qualitative research* (pp. 3-28). Newbury Park, CA: Sage.

Morgan, D. L. (1988). *Focus groups as qualitative research*. Newbury Park, CA: Sage.

Morrow, R. A., & Brown, D. D. (1994). *Critical theory and methodology*. Thousand Oaks, CA: Sage.

Morrow, S. L., & Smith, M. L. (1995). Constructions of survival and coping by women who have survived childhood sexual abuse. *Journal of Counseling Psychology, 42,* 24-33.

Morse, J. M. (1994). Designing funded qualitative research. In N. K. Denzin & Y. S. Lincoln (Eds.), *Handbook of qualitative research* (pp. 220-235). Thousand Oaks, CA: Sage.

Moustakas, C. (1994). *Phenomenological research methods*. Thousand Oaks, CA: Sage.

Munhall, P. L., & Oiler, C. J. (Eds.). (1986). *Nursing research: A qualitative perspective*. Norwalk, CT: Appleton-Century-Crofts.

Natanson, M. (Ed.). (1973). *Phenomenology and the social sciences*. Evanston, IL: Northwestern University Press.

Nelson, L. W. (1990). Code-switching in the oral life narratives of African-American women: Challenges to linguistic hegemony. *Journal of Education, 172,* 142-155.

Nielsen, J. M. (Ed.). (1990). *Feminist research methods: Exemplary readings in the social sciences*. Boulder, CO: Westview.

Nieswiadomy, R. M. (1993). *Foundations of nursing research* (2nd ed.). Norwalk, CT: Appleton & Lange.

Oiler, C. J. (1986). Phenomenology: The method. In P. L. Munhall & C. J. Oiler (Eds.), *Nursing research: A qualitative perspective* (pp. 69-82). Norwalk, CT: Appleton-Century-Crofts.

Olesen, V. (1994). Feminisms and models of qualitative research. In N. K. Denzin & Y. S. Lincoln (Eds.), *Handbook of qualitative research* (pp. 158-174). Thousand Oaks, CA: Sage.

Patton, M. Q. (1980). *Qualitative evaluation methods*. Beverly Hills, CA: Sage.

Patton, M. Q. (1990). *Qualitative evaluation and research methods*. Newbury Park, CA: Sage.

Peshkin, A. (1993). The goodness of qualitative research. *Educational Researcher, 22*(2), 24-30.

Plummer, K. (1983). *Documents of life: An introduction to the problems and literature of a humanistic method*. London: George Allen and Unwin.

Polkinghorne, D. E. (1989). Phenomenological research methods. In R. S. Valle & S. Halling (Eds.), *Existential-phenomenological perspectives in psychology* (pp. 41-60). New York: Plenum.

Polkinghorne, D. E. (1994). Reaction to special section on qualitative research in counseling process and outcome. *Journal of Counseling Psychology, 41,* 510-512.

Ragin, C. C. (1987). *The comparative method: Moving beyond qualitative and quantitative strategies*. Berkeley: University of California Press.

Redfield, R. (1963). *The little community: Viewpoints for the study of a human whole*. Chicago: University of Chicago Press.

Reinharz, S. (1992). *Feminist methods in social research*. New York: Oxford University Press.

Rhoads, R. A. (1995). Whales tales, dog piles, and beer goggles: An ethnographic case study of fraternity life. *Anthropology and Education Quarterly, 26,* 306-323.

Richards, T. J., & Richards, L. (1994). Using computers in qualitative research. In N. K. Denzin & Y. S. Lincoln (Eds.), *Handbook of qualitative research* (pp. 445-462). Thousand Oaks, CA: Sage.

Richardson, L. (1990). *Writing strategies: Reaching diverse audiences*. Newbury Park, CA: Sage.

Richardson, L. (1994). Writing: A method of inquiry. In N. K. Denzin & Y. S. Lincoln (Eds.), *Handbook of qualitative research* (pp. 516-529). Thousand Oaks, CA: Sage.

Riemen, D. J. (1986). The essential structure of a caring interaction: Doing phenomenology. In P. M. Munhall & C. J. Oiler (Eds.), *Nursing research: A qualitative perspective* (pp. 85-105). Norwalk, CT: Appleton-Century-Crofts.

Roman, L. G. (1992). The political significance of other ways of narrating ethnography: A feminist materialist approach. In M. L. LeCompte, W. L. Millroy, & J. Preissle (Eds.), *The handbook of qualitative research in education* (pp. 555-594). San Diego: Academic Press.

Rosenau, P. M. (1992). *Post-modernism and the social sciences: Insights, inroads, and intrusions*. Princeton, NJ: Princeton University Press.

Rubin, H. J., & Rubin, I. S. (1995). *Qualitative interviewing*. Thousand Oaks, CA: Sage.

Sanjek, R. (1990). *Fieldnotes: The makings of anthropology*. Ithaca, NY: Cornell University Press.

Schwandt, T. A. (1993). Theory for the moral sciences: Crisis of identity and purpose. In D. J. Flinders & G. E. Mills (Eds.), *Theory and concepts in qualitative research: Perspectives from the field* (pp. 5-23). New York: Columbia University, Teachers College Press.

Seidman, I. E. (1991). *Interviewing as qualitative research.* New York: Columbia University, Teachers College Press.

Sells, S. P., Smith, T. E., Coe, J. J., Yoshioka, M., & Robbins, J. (1994). An ethnography of couple and therapist experiences in reflecting team practice. *Journal of Marital and Family Therapy, 20,* 247-266.

Slife, B. D., & Williams, R. N. (1995). *What's behind the research? Discovering hidden assumptions in the behavioral sciences.* Thousand Oaks, CA: Sage.

Smith, L. M. (1987). The voyage of the Beagle: Field work lessons from Charles Darwin. *Educational Administration Quarterly, 23*(3), 5-30.

Smith, L. M. (1994). Biographical method. In N. K. Denzin & Y. S. Lincoln (Eds.), *Handbook of qualitative research* (pp. 286-305). Thousand Oaks, CA: Sage.

Sparkes, A. C. (1992). The paradigms debate: An extended review and celebration of differences. In A. C. Sparkes (Ed.), *Research in physical education and sport: Exploring alternative visions* (pp. 9-60). London: Falmer.

Spiegelberg, H. (1982). *The phenomenological movement* (3rd ed.). The Hague, Netherlands: Martinus Nijhoff.

Spindler, G. D., & Spindler, L. (1970). *Being an anthropologist: Fieldwork in eleven cultures.* New York: Holt, Rinehart & Winston.

Spindler, G., & Spindler, L. (1987). Teaching and learning how to do the ethnography of education. In G. Spindler & L. Spindler (Eds.), *Interpretive ethnography of education: At home and abroad* (pp. 17-33). Hillsdale, NJ: Lawrence Erlbaum.

Spradley, J. P. (1979). *The ethnographic interview.* New York: Holt, Rinehart & Winston.

Spradley, J. P. (1980). *Participant observation.* New York: Holt, Rinehart & Winston.

Stake, R. (1994). Case studies. In N. K. Denzin & Y. S. Lincoln (Eds.), *Handbook of qualitative research* (pp. 236-247). Thousand Oaks, CA: Sage.

Stake, R. (1995). *The art of case study research.* Thousand Oaks, CA: Sage.

Stewart, A. J. (1994). Toward a feminist strategy for studying women's lives. In C. E. Franz & A. J. Stewart (Eds.), *Women creating lives: Identities, resilience and resistance* (pp. 11-35). Boulder, CO: Westview.

Stewart, D., & Mickunas, A. (1990). *Exploring phenomenology: A guide to the field and its literature* (2nd ed.). Athens: Ohio University Press.

Stewart, D. W., & Shamdasani, P. N. (1990). *Focus groups: Theory and practice.* Newbury Park, CA: Sage.

Strauss, A. (1987). *Qualitative analysis for social scientists.* New York: Cambridge University Press.

Strauss, A., & Corbin, J. (1990). *Basics of qualitative research: Grounded theory procedures and techniques.* Newbury Park, CA: Sage.

Strauss, A., & Corbin, J. (1994). Grounded theory methodology: An overview. In N. Denzin & Y. Lincoln (Eds.), *Handbook of qualitative research* (pp. 273-285). Thousand Oaks, CA: Sage.

Stringer, E. T. (1993). Socially responsive educational research: Linking theory and practice. In D. J. Flinders & G. E. Mills (Eds.), *Theory and concepts in qualitative research: Perspectives from the field* (pp. 141-162). New York: Columbia University, Teachers College Press.

Sudnow, D. (1978). *Ways of the hand.* New York: Knopf.

Swingewood, A. (1991). *A short history of sociological thought.* New York: St. Martin's.

Tesch, R. (1988). *The contribution of a qualitative method: Phenomenological research.* Unpublished manuscript, Qualitative Research Management, Santa Barbara, CA.

Tesch, R. (1990). *Qualitative research: Analysis types and software tools.* Bristol, PA: Falmer.

Thomas, J. (1993). *Doing critical ethnography.* Newbury Park, CA: Sage.

Thomas, W. I., & Znaniecki, F. (1958). *The Polish peasant in Europe and America.* New York: Dover. (Originally published 1918-1920)

Tierney, W. G. (1995). (Re)presentation and voice. *Qualitative Inquiry, 1,* 379-390.

Trujillo, N. (1992). Interpreting (the work and the talk of) baseball. *Western Journal of Communication, 56,* 350-371.

Valerio, M. (1995). *The lived experience of teenagers who are pregnant: A grounded theory study.* Unpublished manuscript, Administration, Curriculum, and Instruction, University of Nebraska–Lincoln.

Van Kaam, A. (1966). *Existential foundations of psychology.* Pittsburgh, PA: Duquesne University Press.

Van Maanen, J. (1988). *Tales of the field: On writing ethnography.* Chicago: University of Chicago Press.

Wallace, A. F. C. (1970). *Culture and personality* (2nd ed.). New York: Random House.

Weiss, R. S. (1992). *Learning from strangers: The art and method of qualitative interview studies.* New York: Free Press.

Weitzman, E. A., & Miles, M. B. (1995). *Computer programs for qualitative data analysis.* Thousand Oaks, CA: Sage.

Willis, P. (1977). *Learning to labour: How working class kids get working class jobs.* Westmead, UK: Saxon House.

Winthrop, R. H. (1991). *Dictionary of concepts in cultural anthropology.* Westport, CT: Greenwood.

Wolcott, H. F. (1983). Adequate schools and inadequate education: The life history of a sneaky kid. *Anthropology and Education Quarterly, 14*(1), 2-32.

Wolcott, H. F. (1987). On ethnographic intent. In G. Spindler & L. Spindler, *Interpretive ethnography of education: At home and abroad* (pp. 37-57). Hillsdale, NJ: Lawrence Erlbaum.

Wolcott, H. F. (1990a). On seeking—and rejecting—validity in qualitative research. In E. W. Eisner & A. Peshkin (Eds.), *Qualitative inquiry in education: The continuing debate* (pp. 121-152). New York: Columbia University, Teachers College Press.

Wolcott, H. F. (1990b). *Writing up qualitative research.* Newbury Park, CA: Sage.

Wolcott, H. F. (1992). Posturing in qualitative research. In M. D. LeCompte, W. L. Millroy, & J. Preissle (Eds.), *The handbook of qualitative research in education* (pp. 3-52). San Diego: Academic Press.

Wolcott, H. F. (1994a). The elementary school principal: Notes from a field study. In H. F. Wolcott, *Transforming qualitative data: Description, analysis, and interpretation* (pp. 115-148). Thousand Oaks, CA: Sage.

Wolcott, H. F. (1994b). *Transforming qualitative data: Description, analysis, and interpretation.* Thousand Oaks, CA: Sage.

Yin, R. K. (1989). *Case study research: Design and method.* Newbury Park, CA: Sage.

Young, P. V. (1939). *Scientific social surveys and research.* Englewood Cliffs, NJ: Prentice Hall.

Ziller, R. C. (1990). *Photographing the self: Methods for observing personal orientation.* Newbury Park, CA: Sage.

Author Index

Subject Index

About the Author

John W. Creswell is Professor of Educational Psychology at Teachers College, University of Nebraska–Lincoln. He is affiliated with a graduate program in educational psychology specializing in quantitative and qualitative methods in education. In this program, he specializes in qualitative and quantitative research designs and methods, multimethod research, and faculty and academic leadership issues in colleges and universities. He has authored six books—two on faculty research performance, three on the academic leadership of department chairpersons, and one on research methods. His latest research methods book, *Research Design: Qualitative and Quantitative Approaches* (Sage, 1994), compares and contrasts qualitative and quantitative research in several phases of the research design process. He lives in Lincoln, Nebraska, with his wife and two teenage children and continues to write.